Acclaim for Jack Miles's

CHRIST

Jack Miles

CHRIST

Jack Miles is a writer whose work has appeared in numerous national publications, including *The Atlantic Monthly*, *The New York Times*, *The Boston Globe*, *The Washington Post*, and *The Los Angeles Times*, where he served for ten years as literary editor and as a member of the newspaper's editorial board. The recipient of a Ph.D. in Near Eastern languages from Harvard University and a former Jesuit, he has been a Regents Lecturer at the University of California, director of the Humanities Center at Claremont Graduate University, and visiting professor of humanities at the California Institute of Technology. His first book, *God: A Biography*, won a Pulitzer Prize and has been translated into fifteen languages. Currently senior advisor to the president of the J. Paul Getty Trust, a foundation supporting art and scholarship, Dr. Miles lives with his wife and daughter in Southern California.

CHRIST

A CRISIS IN THE LIFE OF GOD

CHRIST

A CRISIS IN THE LIFE OF GOD

Jack Miles

Vintage Books

A DIVISION OF RANDOM HOUSE, INC.

NEW YORK

FIRST VINTAGE BOOKS EDITION, NOVEMBER 2002

Copyright © 2001 by Jack Miles

All rights reserved under International and Pan-American
Copyright Conventions. Published in the United States by Vintage Books,
a division of Random House, Inc., New York, and simultaneously in Canada
by Random House of Canada Limited, Toronto. Originally published in hardcover
in the United States by Alfred A. Knopf, a division of Random House, Inc.,
New York, in 2001.

Vintage and colophon are registered trademarks of Random House, Inc.

Owing to limitations of space, all acknowledgments of permission
to reprint previously published material will be found following the index.

The Library of Congress has cataloged the Knopf edition as follows:
Miles, Jack.
Christ: a crisis in the life of God / Jack Miles.—1st ed.
p. cm
Includes bibliographical references and index.
ISBN 0-375-40014-1 (alk. paper)
1. Incarnation—Biblical teaching. 2. Jesus Christ—Person and offices—
Biblical teaching. 3. Bible. N.T.—Criticism, interpretation, etc.
4. Bible as literature. I. Title.
BT220.M55 2001
232—dc21   2001033808

Vintage ISBN: 0-679-78160-9

Author photograph © Marilyn Sanders

www.vintagebooks.com

Printed in the United States of America
10 9 8 7 6 5 4 3 2 1

For
Mary Anne, Terrence,
Catherine, Michael,
and Mary

Contents

O the hope of Israel,
    the saviour thereof in time of trouble. . . .
Why shouldest thou be as a man astonied,
    as a mighty man that cannot save?
                                —Jeremiah 14:8–9

Then said the Jews, Will he kill himself?
because he saith, Whither I go, ye cannot come.
                                —John 8:22

And therefore as himselfe sayd No man can take
away my soule *And* I haue power to lay it downe
So without doubt, no man did, nor was there any
other than his owne Will, the cause of his dying
at that tyme.

                                —John Donne, *Biathanatos*

CHRIST

A CRISIS IN THE LIFE OF GOD

Crucifixion and the Conscience of the West

All mankind is forgiven, but the Lord must die. This is the revolutionary import of the epilogue that, two thousand years ago, a group of radical Jewish writers appended to the sacred scripture of their religion. Because they did so, millions in the West today worship before the image of a deity executed as a criminal, and—no less important—other millions who never worship at all carry within their cultural DNA a religiously derived suspicion that somehow, someday, "the last will be first, and the first last" (Matt. 20:16).

The Crucifixion, the primal scene of Western religion and Western art, has lost much of its power to shock. At this late date, perhaps only a non-Western eye can truly see it. A Japanese artist now living in Los Angeles once recalled the horror most Japanese feel at seeing a corpse displayed as a religious icon, and of their further revulsion when the icon is explained to them. They ask, she said: "If he was so good, why did he die like that?" In Japanese culture, "good people end their lives with a good death, even a beautiful death, like the Buddha. Someone dying in such a hideous way—for us, he could only be a criminal."

Her perception is correct. The crucifix is a violently obscene icon. To recover its visceral power, children of the twenty-first century must imagine a lynching, the body of the victim swollen and distorted, his head hanging askew above a broken neck, while the bystanders smile their twisted smiles. Then they must imagine that grisly spectacle reproduced at the holiest spot in whatever edifice they call holy. And yet to go even this far is still to miss the meaning of the image, for this victim is not just innocent: He is God Incarnate, the Lord himself in human form.

Winners usually look like winners, and losers like losers. But thanks to this paradoxical feature of the Christian myth, there remains lodged deep in the political consciousness of the West a readiness to believe that the apparent loser may be the real winner unrecognized. In Christianity's epilogue to the God-story that it inherited from Judaism, the Lord God becomes human without ceasing to be the Lord and, unrecognized by all but a few, experiences the human condition at its worst before winning in the end a glorious victory. By losing to Caesar, he wins a duel with the Devil and defeats death itself. The Bible ends as the greatest comedies so often end: with a solemn and festive wedding. The creator of a new heaven and a new earth in which every tear is wiped away becomes the spouse of the entire human race. By losing everything, God wins everything, for everybody, and the last word he speaks, with his bride at his side, is "Come!"

One of many implications of this epilogue to God's life story has been that in the West no regime can declare itself above review. All power is conditional; and when the powerless rise, God may be with them. The motif of divinity in disguise is not unique to Christianity; but the Christian motif of unrecognized divinity judicially tried, officially condemned, tortured by his captors, executed in public, buried, and only *then* rising from the dead and ascending into heaven is, if not literally unique, then at least unique in the breadth of its political influence. Every verse in "Sweet Little Jesus Boy," a black gospel tune sung at Christmas, ends with the wistful line "And they didn't know who he was." As his executioners nail him to the cross, Jesus prays: "Father, forgive them, for they know not what they do" (Luke 23:34). Wherever lines like these or the ideas behind them have spread, human authority has begun to lose its grip on unimpeachable legitimacy. In the West, any criminal may be Christ, and therefore any prosecutor Pilate. As the abolitionist poet James Russell Lowell put it:

Truth forever on the scaffold, Wrong forever on the throne—
Yet that scaffold sways the future, and, behind the dim unknown,
Standeth God within the shadow, keeping watch above his own.

The great Western myth is designed to raise a second, more profound and more disturbing question, however: If God had to suffer and die, then God had to inflict suffering and death upon himself. But why would God do this?

Tout comprendre, c'est tout pardonner, the French say: To understand everything is to forgive everything. Every perpetrator was first a victim. Behind every crime stretches a millennial history of earlier crimes, each in its way an extenuating circumstance. But to whom does this infinite regression lead in the end if not to God? The guilt of God is certainly not a Christian dogma, and yet it is an emotionally inescapable implication of the Christian myth, visible and audible in countless works of Christian art. The pathos of those artistic enactments—those masses and oratorios, passion plays and memorial liturgies, and above all those paintings and sculptures in which the unspeakable is left unspoken—is inseparable from the premise that God is inflicting this pain upon himself for a reason. "The real reason," as Albert Camus wrote in his haunting novel *The Fall,* "is that he himself knew he was not altogether innocent."

A rural American folk hymn from the early nineteenth century captures this pathos in words of striking simplicity:

> What wondrous love is this, O my soul, O my soul?
> What wondrous love is this, O my soul?
> What wondrous love is this that caused the Lord of Bliss
> To bear the awful curse for my soul, for my soul,
> To bear the awful curse for my soul?
>
> To God and to the Lamb I will sing, I will sing,
> To God and to the Lamb I will sing.
> To God and to the Lamb who is the great I AM,
> While millions join the theme, I will sing, I will sing,
> While millions join the theme, I will sing.

"The great I AM" is, of course, God himself. The Lamb who is the great I AM is that same God turned into a sacrificial animal. The emotion the hymn is intended to evoke is rather like what many feel on visiting a battlefield where grave markers stretch to the far horizon. So many subjected to capital punishment, and so few, surely, guilty of anything approaching capital crime. Why had they to die? And did they die for me? *What wondrous love was this?*

Yet what brings tears to the eyes of some brings vomit to the mouths of others. For some, a military cemetery is a monument only to vanity and hypocrisy. For some, the Crucifixion will ever be what it was for Friedrich Nietzsche in *The Anti-Christ:*

> *God on the cross*—are the horrible secret thoughts behind this symbol not understood yet? All that suffers, all that is nailed to the cross, is *divine.* All of us are nailed to the cross, consequently *we* are divine. We alone are divine. Christianity was a victory, a nobler outlook perished of it—Christianity has been the greatest misfortune of mankind so far.

If Apollo and Dionysus are divine, then the brilliant and passionate are godlike. If the crucified Christ is divine, then the suffering are godlike. He is their ideal, and they pursue it through their own suffering. ("All of us are nailed to the cross, consequently *we* are divine.") Nietzsche found this dignification of suffering perverse, a wanton inversion of the natural order. Spiritually speaking, he said, the early Christians stank in his nostrils like Polish Jews.

Nietzsche's visceral reaction, like his visceral anti-Semitism, commonly prompts a visceral counterreaction, but by this visceral intensity on both sides we may measure the power of what he was reacting against in the first place. His reaction was not gratuitous. He had seen, and seen correctly, something utterly shocking at the heart of the Christian myth, a "frightening hidden premise" to which the genteel Christianity of the late nineteenth century had grown numb. And he was prepared to offer a shocking anti-myth in order to make the original horror visible again. In *The Anti-Christ,* written in the last months before he lost his mind, Nietzsche asked:

> What is good? Everything that heightens the feeling of power in man, the will to power, power itself.
> What is bad? Everything that is born of weakness.
> What is happiness? The feeling that power is *growing,* that resistance is overcome.
> Not contentedness but more power; not peace but war; not virtue but fitness (Renaissance virtue, *virtù,* virtue unadulterated by morality).
> The weak and the failures shall perish: first principle of *our* love of man. And they shall even be given every possible assistance.
> What is more harmful than any vice? Active pity for all the failures and all the weak: Christianity.

As we look back on a century of genocide, the sarcasm of "And they shall even be given every possible assistance" is ghastly, even as rhetoric.

And yet the larger point is powerfully made. The divinization of the victim is the wellspring of revolution, even as the demonization of the victim is the wellspring of repression.

To Christianity's "the last shall be first," somnolently intoned from countless German pulpits, Nietzsche reacts—like a madman in the back pew—with outraged astonishment. The last first! Why should the *first* not be first? Do they not deserve it? What have the last done that they should displace the first? *Leave the losers at the bottom where they belong!* The madman's outburst disrupts the church service, but the opening outrage, in truth, was that verse droned from the pulpit. The madman's offense was to take it seriously, as a statement that, if it could not be accepted, would have to be forcefully rejected. And the ushers who struggle to subdue the madman must struggle as well, if they are sincere Christians, with their human, all too human, tendency to agree with him.

Can there be such a thing as innocent, fully human suffering? Do not all adults have a little something on their consciences? Paradoxically, perhaps, humans believe more spontaneously in the innocence of animals than they do in their own. On a visit to Turin some months after writing *The Anti-Christ,* Nietzsche, long on the brink of insanity, was driven over the brink by the spectacle of a horse being flogged savagely by a coachman. The distraught philosopher flung himself on the fallen beast, wrapping his arms around its neck, seeking in vain to defend it. From the asylum where he was taken, he wrote his last semicoherent letter, signing it "The Crucified," and then sank irretrievably into the madness that would last until his death a decade later.

That helpless horse has everything to do with Nietzsche's obsession with the Crucifixion and no little to do with the tenacity of the Christian myth in minds less susceptible to it than his. Ancient Israel felt toward the lamb the sensitivity that modern Europeans typically feel toward the horse. Hyperdomesticated, like the human animal itself, and therefore poignantly vulnerable to abuse, the lamb invited metaphorical use in myth and ritual. Thus, in the Book of Exodus, the blood of the Passover lamb saved the Israelites from the Angel of Death whom God had sent against Egypt. Smeared on the lintels of the Israelites, this blood warned the angel that these were the houses he must "pass over" on his awful errand. In the Book of Isaiah, several centuries later, reference was made to a mysterious servant who, like a lamb, suffered without protest. In the Acts of the Apostles, this lamb is identified as the divine Christ, who has shed (and shared) his blood to save all mankind not from any passing threat but from mortality itself:

An Ethiopian had been on a pilgrimage to Jerusalem. He was a eunuch, an officer at the court of the *kandake,* or queen, of Ethiopia, her chief treasurer. On his way home, he sat in his chariot reading the prophet Isaiah. The Spirit said to Philip, "Catch up with that chariot." When Philip ran up, he heard him reading Isaiah the prophet aloud and asked, "Do you understand what you are reading?" He replied, "How can I, with no one to explain it to me?" But he urged Philip to get in and take the seat next to him. Now the passage of scripture he was reading was this:

> *Like a lamb led to the slaughterhouse,*
> *Like a sheep dumb before its shearers,*
> *He never opens his mouth.*
> *In his humiliation fair judgment is denied him,*
> *His descendants—who will ever speak of them,*
> *Since his life on earth has been cut short?*

The eunuch turned to Philip and said, "Tell me, is the prophet referring to himself or someone else?" Starting, therefore, with this text of scripture, Philip proceeded to explain the good news of Jesus to him.

Farther down the road they came to a body of water, and the eunuch said, "Look, here is some water; is there anything to prevent my being baptized?" He ordered the chariot to stop; then Philip and the eunuch both went down into the water, and he baptized him. (Acts 8:27–38; passage in italics from Isa. 53:7–8)

The atrocity of castration burns behind the lines that the eunuch is reading. Was he shorn of his testicles when he was just a lamb? Did he open his mouth before the shearers? In his humiliation was fair judgment denied him? And who will ever speak of his descendants? When he asks (in what tone of voice?) "Is the prophet referring to himself or someone else?" whom does he have in mind?

We do not know, but how can we refrain from guessing? It was a subtle but powerful literary move on Luke's part to make Christianity's first convert outside Palestine a black eunuch and to give him just these verses to read. The enslaved eunuch is, if you will, just the kind of convert Nietzsche would have predicted, believing as he did that Christianity is a religion for slaves and other emasculate losers, a cult of resentment deriving all its malignant energy from their bad luck. And yet, so far as we can tell, Philip says nothing to the eunuch about the eunuch's own suffering, only directing his attention to the sufferings of the prophesied Lamb of God. What this kindles in the man, however, is a desire to undergo the death-and-resurrection rite of baptism, uniting his humiliation with God's own and trusting that it will lead to exaltation in just the way that so appalled Nietzsche.

Castration is an atrocity within an atrocity. Perhaps someone in Ethiopia could have been hunted down and punished for castrating Philip's convert, but who can be punished for perpetrating the human condition itself? To use the language of the myth, who is to be blamed for our expulsion from Eden? It is the Lord himself who cursed what he created. "Dust you are, and to dust you shall return," he swore (Gen. 3:19), bringing death into a world that, until that moment, had known only life. That was the curse, but can we make him bear it? Our offense was so mild, his punishment so ferocious. Can we avenge ourselves upon him?

No, we cannot; we cannot make him "bear the awful curse" that he has inflicted on his creatures. But he can make himself bear it. And when he does, all lesser offenses can be caught up in one primal offense, his own, for which, though not without a wrenching change in his character, he can wreak the ultimate vengeance upon himself and deliver the ultimate gift—eternal life—as atonement. In the words of Paul (2 Cor. 5:19), he can "reconcile the world to himself" and himself to the world. As God, the Lord cannot cease to exist; but as Christ, he can taste death. Betrayed and abandoned, he can breathe his last breath in pain. The myth that he once did so has within it, as the greatest literature always does, the power to still that rage against the universe which any individual history can engender.

It doesn't take castration, after all, to raise the question. It doesn't take genocide. Far, far smaller misfortunes easily suffice. Cesare Pavese, a brilliant poet dead by his own hand at the age of forty-two, wrote, famously: "No one ever lacks a good reason for suicide." He did not mean to trivialize the act, only to suggest that we refrain from it, more than we realize, by selective inattention to sorrows that, dwelt upon, would undercut our will to live. The myth and, especially, the ritual of the crucified God are ways to bring those sorrows, those horrors, to mind without succumbing to them. What they take away is not guilt, divine or human, but anger, not the sin of the past but the still uncommitted sin of the future.

In Louis Begley's novel *Mistler's Exit,* a wealthy American advertising executive impulsively flies to Venice to see again some of his favorite Titians. A young woman whom he meets in his hotel accompanies him

on his visit to the great painter's *Martyrdom of Saint Lawrence,* but he surprises her—and perhaps himself—with his sarcasm about it. "I haven't
noticed," he says,

> that it's a part of religious iconography to have the Father or the Son
> attend torture sessions of the martyrs. In fact, right now I can't think
> of any painting of the crucifixion or the deposition where the Father
> or the Holy Ghost looks on. . . . One wonders why. Celestial squea-
> mishness? Or is it respect for the logic of the faithful? Fear that belief
> might be strained beyond the breaking point if the Father actually
> observed such things being done to the Son and did nothing to stop
> them?

Mistler is not the connoisseur he thinks he is. Medieval and Renaissance art frequently portrayed the Father, garbed as a priest, holding the
transverse beam of the cross in his own hands, as if displaying the suffering Son to the viewer, while the Spirit, in the form of a dove, hovers
near. All these paintings illustrate the perfect identity of the Father and
the Son at the climax of the Son's agony. A celebrated example is Masaccio's *The Holy Trinity with the Virgin and Saint John,* in which the Father
elevates the body of the Son above an altar just as, in the Mass, the priest
elevates the consecrated bread, the sacramental body of Christ, above an
altar. "This is my body" is, in effect, the silent caption of the painting,
but the words are the Father's, not the Son's, for it is he, not the Son,
who looks outward at the viewer. The suffering of the Son and the suffering of the Father are one as the Father and the Son are one with the
Spirit in—recalling the title of the painting—the Trinity.

In Begley's novel, Mistler's young companion does not know that he
is dying of cancer. The martyred saint and the crucified savior are psychological surrogates. The death Mistler wants God to notice is his own,
and his deepest grievance, to quote the psychologist Allen Wheelis, is his
"awareness that, before we die, nothing is going to happen. That big
vague thing, that redemptive fulfillment, is an illusion, a beckoning bribe
to keep us loyal. A symphony has a climax, a poem builds to a burst of
meaning, but we are unfinished business. No coming together of strands.
The game is called because of darkness." Mistler does not believe in God,
but his rage that the big vague thing is not going to happen is so huge
and so personally felt that he craves the vindication of repudiating the
God in whom he does not believe. Moreover, were it only possible, he
would willingly take a step beyond repudiation and punish God.

But what if he were looking at a painting in which, if he chose to see it so, he could see God being punished for Mistler's death? What sort of difference would that make? Subliminally, paintings by artists like Masaccio, El Greco, and Titian have stilled the rage in many Mistlers, but what finds its way to the painters' canvases can be found as well in an artistically alert reading of the scriptures that inspired them. Such is the reading—a reading of the New Testament as a work of imaginative literature—that this book will attempt.

Paradise Lost, Paradise Regained: The English language may never surpass John Milton's four-word summary of the Bible. But there is another way to "justify the ways of God to man," as Milton aspired to do, than by granting God blanket immunity and then bowdlerizing his testimony lest he incriminate himself. An interpretation of the Bible in which God is allowed to be more hero than saint and in which it is taken for granted that no hero is without his flaw, not even the hero of a divine comedy, is the kind that, if a new Milton ever arose, could yield a new biblical epic.

Diós escribe derecho con líneas torcidas: God writes straight with crooked lines. The first, spoken pathos of the crucifix as an icon—that the crucified is both innocent and divine—yields to a second, unspoken pathos: that he is both divine and guilty. He is guilty less of sin than of ignorance. At the start, he was ignorant of his own power: He had to discover it by using it and by misusing it. Later, he was blind to his own weakness: That, too, he had to discover by succumbing to it. At length, he chose to undergo a human death in order both to prove to himself and to reveal to the world the full, mixed truth about himself, the truth that the horrified Nietzsche could only denounce.

Jesus bore, ironically, the name of the greatest warrior of his people. That we call him Jesus is an accident of Latin translation. *Iēsous* in the original Greek of the Gospels translates Hebrew *yehoshua'* or *yeshua'*, alternate forms of the name Joshua, a name compounded of Hebrew words meaning "The Lord is salvation." But how can this Joshua save others if he cannot save himself?

As the time for his execution draws near, God gives his answer to that question in a poem that includes the lines

> Unless a grain of wheat falls into the earth and dies,
> it remains but a single grain.
> Yet if it dies, it yields a rich harvest.

(John 12:24)

The grain that must fall into the earth and die is the divine identity itself, which must be violently revised: "This is the very reason why I have come to this hour." As he hangs in agony, they say of him, "He saved others, himself he cannot save" (Mark 15:31). The irony is not in their mouths. They speak, as they imagine, the simple truth. The irony is in our ears, and in his.

The world is a great crime, and someone must be made to pay for it. Mythologically read, the New Testament is the story of how someone, the right someone, does pay for it. The ultimately responsible party accepts his responsibility. And once he has paid the price, who else need be blamed, who else need be punished? The same act that exposes all authority as provisional renders all revenge superfluous. And because the death of God does this, it functions within the myth as not just another death but a redemptive death, one that saves us from the violence that we might otherwise feel justified in inflicting on one another. God must die, yes, but he will rise, and at his empty tomb, where none is king, all may be forgiven and may submit to one another. Thus does his kingdom come. Thus does the Lamb of God take away the sin of the world.

A Note to the Reader

In what follows, the text of the New Testament will be considered rather as if it were a stained-glass window. That is, it will be looked *at* and appreciated as a work of art, rather than seen *through* in an attempt to discern the historical events that lie behind it. Most recent books about the New Testament have had historical reconstruction rather than literary art as their animating concern, and most, accordingly, have sought to see through the text. Readers particularly interested in the difference between those books and this one—the difference between seeing through and looking at—may wish to skip to the epilogue, "On Writing the Lives of God," or to the second appendix, "The Bible as Rose Window." Readers more interested in the story as a story than in ancient history or in critical methodology may proceed directly to Part One and to the opening words of the Gospel According to John: "In the beginning was the Word."

PART ONE

The Messiah, Ironically

In the beginning was the Word,
And the Word was with God,
And the Word was God.

—John 1:1

B efore God spoke his first words, "Let there be light," the words
that began the making of the world, what was he thinking?
What was he thinking during the eternity of silence when "the
earth was formless and void, darkness was upon the face of the
deep, and God's Spirit breathed over the waters" (Gen. 1:1)? In its opening words, the Gospel According to John consciously echoes the opening words of the Book of Genesis—"In the beginning, when God
created the heavens and the earth"—but establishes its own beginning at
a time *before* that famous beginning. Back then, it says, is when *this* story
really began.

HIS LIFE BEFORE HE WAS BORN

What was God thinking? The thought that he entertained in silence
before he thought or spoke any other reality into existence, John says in
his oracular way, was the all-encompassing thought of himself. This is
the Word that was with God and *was* God at the beginning before the
beginning. All God's subsequent self-revelations, everything that he has
said or done, made happen or allowed to happen, the whole of history

and reality since then—all of these later words, John suggests, derive from the great Word of primeval divine self-consciousness. And as all of them in their different ways have enlightened mankind about what God is like, all have been life that gave light:

> Through him all things were made,
> And without him nothing was made that has been made.
> What came to be through him was life,
> And the life was the light of mankind.
>
> (John 1:3–4)*

Now comes the premise of the Gospel itself. At a certain point in time, this unspoken divine self-consciousness itself came to expression. The all-encompassing Word itself "became flesh and dwelt among us" (John 1:14). God spoke himself aloud in the form of a human being who lived a human life among other human beings.

Why did God do this? Because the human race, to whom God had given dominion over the world, was estranged from him: "The world did not know him" (John 1:10). God had chosen a special people to be his own, but even many of them rejected him: "His own received him not" (John 1:11). At length, in a final effort to achieve reconciliation with them and with the human race as a whole (collectively, his own self-image and therefore intimately connected with his own identity), God became one of them. This time, too, he was rejected, yet through that very rejection he accomplished something glorious. He began his own life anew; and because he did, his human creatures are now able to begin their lives anew as well, living them not as human beings ordinarily do but rather with a portion of the all-encompassing "fullness" (John 1:16) that was his before the beginning and will remain his after the end. The Gospel is the story of how this new, all-transforming relationship was inaugurated, and John gives his own credentials by confessing, in a tone of awe, "And we have seen his glory":

> For the Word became flesh
> And dwelt among us.

---

*Translations of biblical citations are my own except when otherwise indicated: KJV = King James Version; RSV = Revised Standard Version; NJB = New Jerusalem Bible; JPS = Jewish Publication Society Tanakh; REB = Revised English Bible. There is nothing corresponding to italic type in the original Hebrew, Aramaic, and Greek. In this book the use of italics in translations serves various purposes, which will be explained as the occasion arises. On the use of the designation "Old Testament," see Appendix I, especially pp. 259–60.

And we have seen his glory,
Glory as of the Father with his only Son,
Full of gracious truth.

(1:14)

The prologue to the Gospel According to John says not a word about crucifixion or resurrection, and never so much as mentions the name of Jesus. In the way of all such mythic proems or "prologues in heaven," it delivers, in poetry, the quintessence of a story that it assumes we all know. It sets the tone and, above all, makes the true identity of the protagonist known to the reader in a way that it will not be known to most of those to whom the protagonist will say what he has to say through the action that now begins.

"THE WINNOWING-FORK IS IN HIS HAND"

The act of divine self-expression by which the Word became flesh might not seem to require either birth or death. If God neither begins nor ends, then these two definitive features of human existence might seem exactly wrong for any divine self-revelation. Far more in character for God, at least for God as a reader of the Old Testament may recall him, would be an appearance, without warning, in the form of a grown man. In the Book of Joshua, for example, the Lord appears just before the battle of Jericho in the form of a warrior with sword drawn:

> Now when Joshua was near Jericho, he looked up and saw a man standing in front of him, grasping a naked sword. Joshua walked up to him and said, "Are you with us or with our enemies?" He replied, "Neither one. I am here as the commander of the Lord's host." Joshua fell flat on the ground, worshipping him and saying, "What does my Lord command his servant?" The commander of the Lord's host answered Joshua, "Take the sandals off your feet, for the place where you stand is holy." And Joshua did so. (Josh. 5:13–15)

Joshua's reaction makes it clear that this "commander of the Lord's host" is the Lord himself, the divine warrior in person. The Lord confirms this impression by giving Joshua the same order that he gave Moses when he appeared to him as a burning bush: "Take the sandals off your feet, for the place where you stand is holy." It is no more beyond God to appear in the form of a man than it is beyond him to appear in the form of a bush. To be sure, it is one thing for God to make an isolated appearance

in the form of a bush and another for him to plant a seed, water it, culti-
vate it, and have it grow up to be God-made-bush. And it is yet another
thing for him to conceive a human being with a fully human (and, not
incidentally, Jewish) genealogy, gestation, birth, and childhood, and have
it grow up to be God-made-man. But this last step, incomprehensible as
it first seems, is a step in a known direction.

The question of why God the Father saw fit to proceed in this way,
choosing to experience human birth and death as God the Son, is best
dealt with later. Suffice it to say, for now, that it is the adult Jesus who was
first recognized as Messiah and as God Incarnate. All four of the Gospels
initially began with Jesus, as a grown man, being baptized in the Jordan
River by John the Baptist. All four recognized the descent of the Spirit of
God upon him at that moment as the inauguration of his career if not
of the Incarnation itself. This, they all agree, is the moment when the
Gospel story begins in earnest. Postponing genealogies and Christmas
legends to a later, retrospective moment, we may enter the Gospel story
at the dramatic moment when God Incarnate appears full-grown and as
if from nowhere like the Lord Commander of Joshua 5, but this time
without a sword.

> In the fifteenth year of Tiberius Caesar's reign, when Pontius Pilate
> was governor of Judea, Herod tetrarch of Galilee, his brother Philip
> tetrarch of the territories of Ituraea and Trachonitis, Lysanias tetrarch
> of Abilene, during a term when the high-priesthood was held by
> Annas and Caiaphas, the word of God came to John the son of Zech-
> ariah, in the desert. He went through the whole Jordan Valley pro-
> claiming a baptism of repentance for the forgiveness of sins, as it is
> written in the book of the sayings of Isaiah the prophet:
>
> > *The voice of one crying in the wilderness:*
> > *Clear a way for the Lord!*
> > *Make straight his paths.*
> > *Let every valley be raised,*
> > *Every mountain and hill lowered,*
> > *The crooked made straight*
> > *And the rough smooth*
> > *So that all flesh will see the salvation of God.*
>
> > (Luke 3:1–6; passage in italics
> > from Isa. 40:3–5)

The action of the New Testament begins with the memory of a broken promise. Isaiah's language is wonderful, but he describes a triumphal

march that never occurred. Mountains were going to be leveled and valleys filled to create a parade route for the Israelite exiles marching home from Babylon to Jerusalem—but the parade was canceled. The exiles to whom the Lord spoke through Isaiah did not return home in glory. Many of them never returned at all, and those who did merely exchanged one imperial ruler for another. The Persians defeated the Babylonians, but Israel was just one part of the spoils of war. Yes, a new temple of sorts was built by imperial order in the tiny, Persian-governed province of Yahud, but no Psalms were ever written in its praise. For those old enough to remember, the sight of the Second Temple was a cause more of grief than of joy: "Many of the priests and Levites and the chiefs of the clans, the old men who had seen the first House [Temple], wept loudly at the sight of the founding of this House. Many others raised their voices in a shout of joy. The people could not tell the shouts of joy from the sound of weeping" (Ezra 3:12-13). The Lord himself had to apologize for the paltriness of the Second Temple:

> Who is there left among you who saw this House in its former splendor? How does it look to you now? It must seem like nothing to you. But be strong, O Zerubbabel, be strong, O high priest, Joshua son of Jehozadak; be strong, all you people of the land, and act! For I am with you. . . . The glory of this latter House shall be greater than that of the former one. (JPS; Hag. 2:3-4, 9)

But the glory of the Second Temple never did become greater than—in fact, it never approached—the glory of the First. The Zerubbabel whom the Lord exhorted through Haggai was a son of David, an *anointed* son of David—that is, a messiah—but he was a failed messiah, and his name was half-expunged from the record.

As the Baptist speaks, five hundred years have passed, and a spectacular Third Temple is nearing completion in Jerusalem, but this Third Temple, King Herod's Temple, whose remains can still be seen in Jerusalem, is the work of a Roman puppet, an Idumaean married into a collaborationist Jewish clan. Is this Temple the fulfillment of the Lord's ancient promise? Many in the Baptist's day are impressed by it. Indeed, the entire ancient world is impressed by it. But dissident Jewish groups—notably the Pharisees (forerunners of the Judaism of today) and the Essenes (who wrote the Dead Sea Scrolls)—keep their distance. John does the same, preaching in the desert rather than on the steps of Herod's monument to himself. The memory of the past and the reality of the present—the great and holy temple that never was and the great and unholy temple that is—conspire against elation of the sort heard in Isaiah. That promised triumph did not happen the first time. Will it happen this time?

What the Lord says through the Baptist, moreover, is disturbing in another way:

> He said . . . to the crowds who came to be baptized by him, "Brood of vipers, who warned you to flee from the wrath to come? Bear the fruit that accords with repentance, and do not start telling yourselves, 'We have Abraham as our father,' because, I tell you, God can raise up children to Abraham from these stones. Yes, even now the axe is laid to the root of the trees. Any tree that fails to bear good fruit will be cut down and thrown into the fire." (Luke 3:7–9)

It is not that the rhetorical question "Brood of vipers, who warned you to flee from the wrath to come?" is particularly disturbing. This is the usual prophetic idiom for a call to repentance. The Lord is accustomed to saving his friends by destroying their enemies. What disturbs is the fact that the Lord seems audibly irritated with Israel for making so much of its national identity—which is to say, of course, for insisting so much on being *his* people: "I tell you, God can raise up children to Abraham from these stones."

The Baptist is identified elsewhere in the Gospel of Luke as the Old Testament prophet Elijah come down to earth in fulfillment of a prophecy made in the very last verse of the Old Testament:

> Behold, I shall send you Elijah the prophet,
> Before the great and awesome Day of the Lord.
> He will reconcile parents to their children,
> And children to their parents,
> Lest I put the country under a curse of total destruction.
>
> (Mal. 4:5–6; some editions, 3:23–24)

When the Baptist speaks—prophetically, in the name of the Lord, just as Elijah did—what he says is not altogether unlike things that the Lord has said before. The Lord has shown himself capable of mocking his chosen people for ethnic pride on more than one previous occasion. Speaking through Ezekiel, he said with blistering contempt for mere pedigree:

> Your father was an Amorite and your mother a Hittite. At birth, on the day you were born, there was no one to cut your umbilical cord or

wash you in water to clean you, or rub you with salt, or wrap you in swaddling clothes. No one looked at you with kindness enough to do any of these things out of pity for you. You were dumped in the open fields in your own filth on the day of your birth. I spotted you kicking on the ground in your blood as I passed by, and I said to you, lying there in your blood: "Live!" And I made you grow like the grass of the fields. (Ezek. 16:3–6)

Ezekiel is a fairly ferocious precedent for what the Baptist says, yet the Baptist's tone is still jarring when directed at an oppressed people living in an occupied land. The passage from Isaiah that Luke uses as keynote for this episode is, after all, an oracle of consolation, not mockery. It says, to quote the King James translation familiar from Handel's *Messiah,* that God is done punishing Israel:

> Comfort ye, comfort ye, my people,
> saith your God.
> Speak ye comfortably to Jerusalem,
> and cry unto her
> that her warfare is accomplished,
> that her iniquity is pardoned.
>
> (KJV; Isa. 40:1–2)

The Baptist, however, seems intent less on building confidence that God will eventually save his people than on undermining it.

Finally, there is the surprise that the Baptist's message is preached to the oppressor as well as to the oppressed:

There were tax collectors [Romans or Jews in Roman employ], too, who came for baptism, and they said to him, "Teacher, what must we do?" He said to them, "Exact no more than the appointed rate." Some soldiers [Jewish mercenaries under Roman command and perhaps a Roman officer or two] questioned him as well: "What about us? What should we do?" He told them, "No intimidation! No extortion! Be satisfied with your pay." (Luke 3:12–14)

When the Lord spoke to Isaiah of Israel's redemption, did he confine himself to predicting that the mercenaries of Nebuchadnezzar, the Caesar of the day, would be content with their pay and merely abstain from intimidation and extortion? Did he proclaim the glorious day when Jews collecting taxes for Babylon would collect no more than the going rate?

Far from it: The Lord gloated savagely over the prospect of reducing such minions of the oppressor to bloody cannibalism.

> The warrior's captive will be taken back,
>   and the tyrant's prey set free.
> I myself will fight those who fight you,
>   and I myself will save your children.
> I will make your oppressors eat their own flesh;
>   they will be as drunk on their own blood as on new wine.
> And all flesh will know
>   that I am the Lord, your Savior,
>   your Redeemer, the Mighty One of Jacob.
>
> (Isa. 49:25–26)

Drinking one another's blood: Israel's vision of ultimate, unspeakable horror. This rather than anything gentler or more benign is what was to be understood in the divine promise that Luke quotes: "All flesh will see the salvation of God." Israel was not to be amiably reconciled with the Lord's enemies, but spectacularly and crushingly victorious over them and gloriously rewarded at their expense.

> You shall suck the milk of nations,
> You shall suck the breasts of kings.
>
> (Isa. 60:16)

Yet, to repeat, nothing like that happened. God's promise of victory was broken. Now, as the oppressors in the crowd are noticeably not warned that theirs is the root to which the divine axe is most especially to be laid, how can the suspicion not arise that the promise will be broken again? And yet John clearly expects the Lord to arrive in power.

If the Lord is about to intervene massively in human affairs, if the "Day of the Lord" is at hand, who will be the agent of his intervention, and what will the agent be like?

A feeling of expectancy had arisen. People were beginning to wonder whether John might be the Messiah. But John told them all: "I baptize you with water, but one more powerful than I is coming, and I am not fit to loosen the strap of his sandal. He will baptize you with the Holy Spirit and fire. The winnowing-fork is in his hand, to clear his threshing-floor and to gather the grain into his barn. The chaff, however, he will burn in an eternal fire." (Luke 3:15–17)

The threshing floor, where the kernel is violently separated from the husk of the harvested grain, is frequently a biblical metaphor for the battlefield. In this metaphor, the Lord is the miller; his enemy is the husk or chaff; the grain is ultimately his cherished prize, the spoils of his war, though it may suffer in the process. By employing this imagery to speak of the soon-to-arrive "one more powerful than I," John transfers to that still unidentified one both the large hopes and the inescapable doubts that attach to the ancient image of God the Avenging Warrior, the Mighty One of Jacob. Hope contends with memory. How wonderful it would be if the divine warrior should again come righteously to Israel's rescue! But will he?

JOHN HAILS HIM, STRANGELY, AS "THE LAMB OF GOD"

This question becomes acute when the "one more powerful than I" appears in person and is acclaimed as the very antithesis of a warrior:

> The next day, [John] saw Jesus coming toward him and said, "Behold, the Lamb of God, who takes away the sin of the world. It was of him that I said, 'After me comes one greater than I,' because he existed before me. I did not know him myself, and yet my purpose in coming to baptize with water was that he might be revealed to Israel." (John 1:29–31)

❧ *The Lamb of God?* A lion would be more to the purpose, a rapacious and terrifying cat of the sort that still prowled the Jordan Valley when God, speaking through Jeremiah, promised to maul the Edomites "as when a lion comes up from the jungle of the Jordan to the perennial pasture. Thus, in an instant, will I drive them from her [Israel]; and over her I will appoint whom I choose. For who is like me? Who will challenge me? What shepherd can stand before me?" (Jer. 49:19).

The Lamb of God? What is the meaning of this strange phrase? Occurring where it does in the Gospel, it is at once novel, familiar, and ominous. The phrase is novel in the ears of the Baptist's audience simply because, in just this formulation, it has never been used before. It is vaguely familiar because the sacrifice of lambs in the Jerusalem temple is a well-known practice, based on passages in Torah that require such sacrifice for the expiation of certain kinds of sin. In some sense, these lambs could be described as "lambs of God," but Jesus is a man, not an animal.

Addressing him as an animal, what does the Baptist imply about him? Something unspeakable has suddenly been half-spoken.

Most of the countless millions who have read or heard the acclamation "Behold, the Lamb of God" since the Gospel According to John was written have heard a reference to Christ sacrificing himself on the cross, but the scene derives much of its power from the fact that the onstage participants cannot begin to dream of such a thing. By vicariously sharing their ignorance, the reader can experience, as in Greek tragedy, mingled terror and pity at the inexorable approach of an atrocity. The Gospel story intends, ultimately, to go well beyond the catharsis of tragedy, but innocent incomprehension in the Gospel narrative has much in common, at any given moment, with its counterpart in Greek tragedy.

Expiation by animal sacrifice is a notion whose background, in the Bible, goes all the way back to the first chapters of the Book of Genesis. During the brief, happy period before it occurred to God to forbid anything, the first human couple were given only two commands, both so positive that they were, in effect, two blessings: The pair were to be fruitful and multiply, and they were to have dominion over the earth. Later, after the Lord issued a prohibition and they violated it, he turned his double blessing into a double curse. The blessing of dominion over the earth became the curse of endless labor—in effect, slavery to rather than dominion over the earth. The blessing of fertility became the curse of involuntary reproduction—in effect, a slavery to lust and its consequences. The first curse was spoken against the man, the second against the woman, but obviously both were cursed each time. Having cursed his creatures with these two great sorrows, the Lord added the curse of death: "Dust you are, and to dust you shall return" (Gen. 3:19).

What these old curses have to do with the acclamation of Jesus as the "Lamb of God, who takes away the sin of the world" is that they and their consequences are the "sin of the world" that will finally be taken away.

In Israelite and Jewish ritual, what the sacrifice of a lamb took away was indeed more curse than sin. Little in the Book of Leviticus strikes the modern reader as more alien than the notion that there is something not just unclean but morally offensive about a variety of natural conditions, including those of a woman during or after menstruation, a man and woman after the transmission of semen, anyone experiencing incontinence or any other involuntary discharge (including the involuntary emission of semen), or anyone afflicted with a skin disease. According to

Leviticus, anyone in one of these conditions was required to make
amends to God by sacrificing a lamb. Yet, however alien this requirement
may seem to the modern mind, it was not irrational in its original context. It represented ancient Israel's acknowledgment that the Lord had
not yet reversed—if he ever would—the curse that he had spoken against
all his human creatures shortly after making them. All human misfortune
originated, ultimately, in the disobedience that provoked God so drastically and impulsively to undo his own work. Thus, in Leviticus 14, when
a poor leper was required to sacrifice an expiatory lamb (a rich leper
had to sacrifice two lambs and a ewe), the ceremony functioned as expiation not really for any sin of the leper himself but effectively for the
sin that brought the primeval curse. The sacrifice is, in the end, an acknowledgment of the human condition as an experience of continuing
punishment.

Illness does feel, whether one would wish it so or not, like punishment for a crime one has not committed. "Why is this happening to
me?" one asks involuntarily. "What did I ever do to deserve this?" Dismissing the question does not mean escaping it, for there is no escaping
it. The ritual of Leviticus gives external expression to the experience of
entrapment in an involuntary condition. As for sexual "pollution," the
same ritual externalizes the universal experience of passion as passivity, as
an impulse running so far out of control that it feels less like anything
that a couple does than like something done to them or through them.
The involuntary emission of semen and the involuntary discharge of
blood (sometimes even now called "the curse" in an unrecognized allusion to Genesis) are perfect natural symbols for this condition.

This human vulnerability to mortal illness and this human helplessness before an uncontrollable impulse are ritually acknowledged by, first,
slaying an animal—that is, inflicting gratuitous, terminal punishment
upon its innocent vulnerability—and, second, linking the slain animal
ritually to the particular human beings whose analogous helplessness and
vulnerability are to be acknowledged. This linkage is enacted in Leviticus 14, when blood from the sacrificed animal is smeared on the ear,
thumb, and big toe of the leper for whom the lamb has been slain. In
Exodus 24, the vulnerability of the entire nation of Israel, captive in its
involuntary covenant with the Lord, is acknowledged when Moses fills
basins with the blood of slain oxen and then flings the blood over the
heads of the assembled people. These ritual actions are almost unimaginably wild and primitive, yet the driven and desperate human condition

that they so vividly acknowledge remains essentially unchanged. Therein lies their intuitive brilliance, and "Behold, the Lamb of God" builds directly upon it.

Later, when a helpless paralytic is laid before him, Jesus will say, surprisingly, "Friend, your sins are forgiven" (Luke 5:20). The man's paralysis, like the leprosy of Leviticus 14, is not a punishment for any sin of his own but for the original sin that led God to curse his world with afflictions like leprosy and paralysis. When Jesus cures the paralysis, God demonstrates that he intends to revoke his ancient curse. Consistent with this vision, Jesus demands of those whom he heals not prior repentance but faith—faith that God has both the will and the power to take away this "sin" and remake his world.

Having gone this far, however, one must immediately add a qualification. According to the same ancient texts to which the Baptist alludes, the sacrifice of a lamb cannot effect expiation for the kind of deliberate and avoidable sin that we most typically think of as sin—the kind that the Baptist speaks of: exploitation, extortion, intimidation. Sins of this sort can be made good only by repentance and, where harm has been done, by commensurate atonement. Thus, in a deservedly famous passage:

> When men fight and one of them hurts a pregnant woman and she suffers a miscarriage but no further harm results, the man responsible will pay compensation as determined by the woman's husband, paying as much as the judges allow. If further harm is done, however, you will demand life for life, eye for eye, tooth for tooth, hand for hand, foot for foot, burn for burn, wound for wound, stroke for stroke. (Exod. 21:22–25)

Though this passage is no exhortation to mercy, neither is it a license for revenge. It is a warning that atonement should be no more than commensurate: an eye for an eye, not an eye for a tooth nor a life for an eye. More to the point, when the sin is of this nature, the sinner is not readmitted to the community merely by offering a lamb to the Lord.

Can the Lamb of God that will "take away the sin of the world" take away this kind of sin as well—true sin and not just the curse of the human condition—and do so, indeed, for the whole world? If the world has sinned, should the world not make reparation? Conversely, if someone else is making reparation, then is that someone else not the guilty party and the world innocent?

Even as these questions are rushing in, John baptizes this Lamb of God and exclaims immediately afterward: "I saw the Spirit descend upon him from heaven like a dove and rest on him. I myself did not know him, but he who sent me to baptize with water had said to me, 'The man on whom you see the Spirit descend and rest is the one who is to baptize with the Holy Spirit.' I have seen it, and I bear witness: He is God's Chosen One" (John 1:32–34). And then there comes a voice from heaven saying: "You are my Son; this day have I begotten you" (Luke 3:22).

The voice from heaven quotes an Old Testament text (see italicized words below) in which God is heard speaking to the King of Israel:

> He said to me:
> "*You are my Son;*
>   *this day have I begotten you.*
> Ask of me, and I will make the nations your inheritance,
>   and the ends of the earth your possession.
> You shall break them with a rod of iron,
> and smash them to bits like a potter's pot."
>
> (Ps. 2:7–9)

The improbable and appalling conjunction of expiatory lamb and messianic warlord receives its first statement here, and the disturbing power of Jesus as a character has everything to do with such combinations. No set of foreign ideas could surpass, in its ability either to attract or to offend a Jewish audience, these native Jewish ideas made daring and new by unforeseen combination.

❦ The notion that a human being could ever be sacrificed in expiation—treated, that is, as an animal rather than as a human being—was repugnant in a Jewish culture that had rationalized animal sacrifice quite explicitly as a substitute for human sacrifice. That the hoped-for son of David should play the role of sacrificial animal is an even more repugnant notion. That the "Son of God," who, as John pointedly says, "existed before me," though the two are of the same age, should play this role begins to seem not just outrageous but blasphemous. ●

Please note that at this moment Jesus himself has yet to speak his first word. We are at the very beginning, and no one yet has any idea what these hints will add up to. Baptism with water—ritual immersion as a symbol of repentance, a cleansing before reform—has a kind of natural logic to it. But what are John's listeners to understand by baptism "with the Holy Spirit *and fire*" (Luke 3:16)? Is baptism by fire to be understood as judgment by a stern Jesus with "the winnowing-fork in his hand," determined to gather the grain and burn the chaff? Perhaps, but if the avenger is simultaneously the "Lamb of God," how stern an avenger can he be?

•And whatever may be guessed about the baptism that Jesus will administer, there remains the still more remarkable fact that God Incarnate has begun his redemptive work with an act of public repentance. Everything that will follow, the entire public life of God-made-man, will be performed under the sign of this repentance. The fact bears repeating: *God has repented!* But of what? What has he done wrong? As these disturbing questions swirl in the air, God's great enemy, the Devil, suddenly takes notice. •

THE DEVIL TRIES TO TAKE HIS MEASURE

Filled with the Holy Spirit, Jesus turned back from the Jordan and was led by the Spirit into the desert, where for forty days he was put to the test by the Devil. During that time he ate nothing, and by the end of it he was hungry. Then the Devil said to him, "If you are the Son of God, command this stone to become a loaf." But Jesus replied, "Scripture says, 'Man does not live by bread alone.'"

Then, leading him to a height, the Devil showed him in a moment of time all the kingdoms of the world and said to him, "To you will I give all this power and their glory, for it has been handed over to me, for me to give to whom I choose. Worship me, and it shall all be yours." But Jesus answered him, "Scripture says, 'You must worship the Lord your God; him alone must you serve.'"

Then he led him to Jerusalem and set him on the highest parapet of the Temple. "If you are the Son of God," he said to him, "cast yourself down from here, for scripture says, 'He has commanded his angels to guard you,' and again, 'They will bear you in their arms lest you strike your foot against a stone.'"

But Jesus answered him, "Scripture says, 'Do not put the Lord your God to the test.'"

Having run through every way of tempting him, the Devil left him, until the opportune moment. (Luke 4:1–13)

In this episode, which gave rise to the proverb "Even the Devil can quote scripture," Jesus and the Devil confront each other as dueling Jewish intellectuals. Jesus wins the verbal duel, but the Devil exercises an ominous physical control over his opponent, and physical control is far from beside the point. It bears on the question that the Devil wants answered, namely: How much power does Jesus really have at his disposal? The arena in which this question is posed is not the Judean desert but the entire sweep of Israelite history.

When the Devil suggests that Jesus turn a stone into a loaf of bread, he is talking about more than mere hunger. Behind that suggestion stands the memory of an earlier moment in the desert when the Lord fed all Israel with miraculous food. Of this experience, Moses would say, forty years later: "[The Lord your God] humbled you and starved you, then fed you with manna, which you had not known, nor had your fathers known it, that he might teach you that *man does not live by bread alone,* but by all that proceeds from the mouth of the Lord" (Deut. 8:3). What the Devil is really saying to Jesus is "Are you God, the god who, back then, performed a food miracle in the desert? If so, prove it by performing another." Jesus proves that he hears the allusion in the question by including the same allusion in his answer, but the answer evades the real question. Jesus could lack the divine power at issue and still give the same clever answer. The Devil has learned nothing. •

A question with higher stakes lies buried in the second exchange. The Devil says, "To you will I give all this power . . . for it has been handed over to me." Handed over to him by whom? By whom, if not by the Lord himself? The Devil alludes provocatively to the Lord's disturbing earlier decision to deliver the world into Babylonian hands.

On the eve of Babylonia's victory, the Lord told Jeremiah to make yokes, symbols of servitude, and deliver them to the Jerusalem representatives of Israel's immediate neighbors, Moab, Edom, Ammon, Tyre, and Sidon. The cover letter with this "gift" was the following (note the italicized phrase):

> You must tell your masters this: I by my great power and outstretched arm made the earth and the people and animals that are on the earth, and I give them to whom I please. Now *I have handed all these countries over* to Nebuchadnezzar, king of Babylon, my servant; I have even put the animals of the wild at his service. . . . Any nation or kingdom that will not serve Nebuchadnezzar, king of Babylon, and will not bow its neck to the yoke of the king of Babylon, I will punish with sword, famine, and plague. . . . The nation, however, that will submit its neck to the yoke of the king of Babylon and serve him, I will leave in peace on its own land . . . to farm it and live on it. (Jer. 27:4–6, 8, 11)

As for Israel's neighbors, so also for Israel. True, Babylonia's ascendancy proved brief, but its fall was followed by the rise of another foreign power. Would it not then be reasonable to infer that the Lord has transferred his power successively to the empires that have succeeded the Babylonian: the Persian, the Greek, and now the hated Roman? And if scripture itself, in the Book of Daniel, equates the gods of those empires with devils in the service of the great Devil, then may the commanding Devil not challenge Jesus in the name of the God who has "handed over" such power to him?

The myth that God had handed Israel over to Babylonia when the Israelites sinned evolved, historically, into the more comprehensive myth that God had handed the world over to the Devil when Adam and Eve sinned. In a parallel way, the promised victory over Babylonia that would restore Israel's glory evolved into the promise of a more comprehensive victory that would reverse the "fallen" human condition itself. After the rise of Christianity, the developed form of this myth became a capacious and durable framework within which false gods and evil kings of all sorts could be "demonized"—that is, identified as demons or tools of the Devil—while the just awaited God's definitive intervention. It is in this sense that everything which is "of this world" or "worldly" is presumptively sinful: Until God's final victory, it is all to some extent under the Devil's control.

This vision of a world under provisional but real demonic control frames even a work as late as John Milton's *Paradise Regained*. In that poem, the demonic legions, anxious at the appearance in the world of a man who may be God Incarnate, turn to their commander,

> To him their great dictator, whose attempt
> At first against mankind so well had thrived
> In Adam's overthrow, and led their march
> From Hell's deep-vaulted den to dwell in light,
> Regents and potentates and kings, yea gods
> Of many a pleasant realm and province wide.
>
> (First Book, lines 115–118)

The demons are afraid that Jesus will drive them back into "Hell's deep-vaulted den" from the pleasant realms and wide provinces where since "Adam's overthrow" they have held sway as regents, potentates, kings, and even gods. In the Gospel, Milton's source, the Devil, still uncertain about Jesus and trying to take his measure, tempts him to reclaim the handed-over power immediately.

In his reply, Jesus does not reclaim the power, but he hints that he could. He reminds his opponent that ultimate power remains with the Lord. "You must worship the Lord your God; him alone must you serve," he says, quoting Moses for the second time. But he does not deny the claim per se. He leaves hanging the question of whether and when the Lord will reclaim the power that is ultimately his. Jesus neither con-firms nor denies that—for now—the Devil has the power that he claims has been handed over to him.

In the third temptation, the Devil does not just allude to scripture but quotes it brazenly and with a hint of menace. Taking insolent liberties, he transports Jesus bodily to a parapet of the Temple in Jerusalem. There, while taunting Jesus to throw himself over the parapet and be rescued by his angels, the Devil implicitly threatens that he himself will throw his captive over the parapet so as to observe with his own eyes whether any angels arrive to break his fall.

The Devil does not deny that ultimate power rests with the Lord, yet he hints: "What good will that do you if he will not use his power on your behalf?" This is, of course, just the question that Israel has been asking for half a millennium. The Devil quotes a Psalm that includes, just before the verses he quotes, an expression of confidence in the Lord's military power:

> A thousand may fall at your side,
>> ten thousand at your right hand,
>> but it [death] will not come near you.
> You need only open your eyes
>> to see the recompense of the wicked. . . .
> No disaster can overtake you,
>> no plague come near your tent.
> *He has commanded his angels*
>> *to guard you* wherever you go.
> They will bear you in their arms
>> *lest you strike your foot against a stone.*

> (Ps. 91:7–12)

What Jew could read this Psalm without flinching? "It will not come near you," the Psalm says. Oh, won't it? Have the Romans, one of the empires that the Devil claims to control, not been "near" Israel for dec-ades? Have they not been "recompensed for their wickedness" all too handsomely? If the Lord did not rescue Israel from the gods of Rome, will he rescue Jesus from their commander? And granting that this is the Lord himself who is being taunted, will he protect even himself? *Why is he so restrained?*

Herod's Temple is built on a gigantic scale, towering on its eastern side over a deep gorge. We must imagine Jesus gazing into that gorge as the Devil's taunts ring in his ears. How much confidence does Jesus have in himself? We cannot know how fully he accepts his own identity as proclaimed by the prophet John or at what point he first fully understands it. He speaks not a single word to the Devil in his own name or on his own authority but foils him only by quoting Moses against him. The three quotations are all to the point, and yet they completely fail to humble the diabolical opponent. Is Jesus holding himself grandly above the fray? Or is his caution the caution of the kidnapped?

Even as God Incarnate fully conscious of his identity, Jesus might well be ultra-circumspect in this encounter, recalling that the Devil has bested him not just once but twice before. The first time came in the Garden of Eden when by manipulating Eve into eating the forbidden fruit, the Devil trapped the Lord into wrecking his own creation. In *Paradise Regained,* the Devil pauses, before leaving for his encounter in the desert with the admittedly mysterious and potentially menacing Jesus, to look back on that early victory and draw encouragement from it. Speaking to his minions, he says:

> I, when no other durst, sole undertook
> The dismal expedition to find out
> And ruin Adam, and the exploit performed
> Successfully; a calmer voyage now
> Will waft me; and the way found prosperous once
> Induces best to hope of like success.

> (First Book, lines 100–104)

But the strategy the Devil actually follows in his desert encounter with Jesus recalls the one he followed on the second occasion when he bested the Lord. This second victory came when, appealing to the Lord's sense of his own greatness, Satan lured him into torturing the innocent Job.

On both those occasions, the Lord recovered and then set about repairing the damage that he had done respectively to Adam and Eve and to Job, thereby sharply limiting the extent of Satan's victories. And yet, on both occasions the Lord was clearly wounded. No less important, Satan was far from vanquished. On this third occasion, recognizing the approach of the endgame, the Devil chooses to retreat rather than attack, but the retreat is merely tactical: He leaves only "until the opportune moment." When that moment arrives, he will ignore Jesus' mind and go straight for his body.

DISCIPLES, UNSOUGHT, FOLLOW AFTER HIM

Returning to the Jordan River, Jesus is again acclaimed by John:

> As John stood there again with two of his disciples, Jesus walked by, and John looked toward him and said, "Behold, the Lamb of God." And the two disciples heard what he said and followed Jesus. Jesus turned and saw them following him and said, "What do you want?" They said, "Rabbi [which means "teacher"], where do you live?" He replied, "Come and see," so they went and saw where he lived. It was about the tenth hour [late afternoon]. (John 1:35–39)

Jesus' first followers, Galileans like himself, leave John to follow the one whom John has acclaimed. Jesus does not recruit them. He merely accepts them.

"The next day," the passage continues:

> after Jesus had decided to leave for Galilee, he met Philip [another Galilean] and said, "Follow me." . . . Philip found Nathanael and said to him, "We have found the one that Moses, in the Law, and the prophets as well, wrote about, Jesus son of Joseph, from Nazareth." Nathanael said to him, "Can any good come from Nazareth?" Philip replied, "Come and see." When Jesus saw Nathanael coming, he said to him, "Now here, surely, is an Israelite without guile." Nathanael asked, "How do you know me?" Jesus replied, "Before Philip called you, I saw you under the fig tree." Nathanael answered, "Rabbi, you are the Son of God, you are the King of Israel." Jesus replied, "You believe this just because I said: 'I saw you under the fig tree.' You are going to see greater things than that." And then he added, "Truly I tell you, you will see heaven open and the angels of God ascending and descending over the Son of Man." (John 1:43, 45–51)

Jesus commands assent as effortlessly as God does in Genesis when he commands Abram to leave his kinfolk in Haran and go to Canaan, and the resemblance is fully intended. Indeed, Jesus is more peremptory with Philip than the Lord is with Abram, for in Genesis 12, the Lord offers material incentives to Abram ("I will make you a great nation"), while Jesus offers none to Philip or Nathanael or the others. Is Jesus grateful for their acclamation and allegiance? To judge from his arch manner with Nathanael, it does not seem so.

Classical Hebrew and Aramaic, the Semitic languages in which the

Old Testament is written, are relatively poor in adjectives and often ex-press by a noun phrase what an Indo-European language would express by a noun with an adjective. Thus, Jesus refers to two of his disciples as "sons of storm," meaning that they are stormy men. A "son of man," then, is in the first instance simply a human being, and it is striking that while others in the Gospels sometimes refer to Jesus as "Son of God," he himself often stresses his humanity—especially when defining his own identity or mission—by referring to himself as "Son of Man." As it hap-pens, however, "Son of Man" had begun to function at the turn of the Common Era as a mysterious title. If we hear it as a title rather than merely as an idiom, then the scene that echoes in Jesus' words to Nathanael is Daniel 7:13–14:

> In a dream I saw the clouds of heaven,
>   and there he was, one like a son of man,
> And he came to the Ancient of Days,
>   and was presented before him.
> To him was given dominion and glory and sovereignty,
>   that all races, nations, and languages should serve him.
> His is an everlasting dominion that shall not pass away,
>   and his kingdom shall not be destroyed.

Here, as often in the Gospels, Jesus is provoked to use the title "Son of Man" by someone else's applying to him a title like the one Nathanael has just used: "King of Israel." But when he declines some such accolade, Jesus invariably implies not simply "I am less than what you think I am" but "I am both less and more."

To awestruck fellow human beings like Nathanael, Jesus may be most naturally acclaimed as "the Son of God": It is his holiness that is most remarkable about him. To God himself, however, what is remarkable about God Incarnate is that he is God *Incarnate*. Households transformed by the arrival of a newborn typically speak of "*the* baby" as if there were only one baby in the world. In the life of God, God Incarnate is, in a similar sense, "*the* man." What Jesus says to Nathanael, playing on the ambiguity of the phrase, is, equivalently: "You call me a divine being merely because I know your mind and can read your past. I tell you, I am a human being, but you will see the sky split open and the angels throng about the head of this 'human being.'"

So, then, if Jesus is not the King of Israel, it is because he is more: He is the Emperor of All Peoples. Yet his first followers were drawn to him because the Baptist had identified him as "the Lamb of God." How can an emperor be a lamb, or a lamb an emperor?

HE PERFORMS HIS FIRST MIRACLE, BUT RELUCTANTLY

Were Jesus' first disciples troubled by his cool reception of them? If we imagine that they were, the episode that now follows may seem like the completion of their recruitment, though Jesus' manner remains abrupt and unaccommodating throughout. Back home in Galilee, he attends a wedding in the village of Cana.

> The mother of Jesus was there, and Jesus and his disciples had also been invited. And they ran out of wine, since the wine provided for the feast had all been used, and the mother of Jesus said to him, "They have no wine." Jesus replied, "Woman, what is that to you and me? My hour has not yet come." His mother said to the servants, "Do whatever he tells you." There were six stone water jars standing there, meant for the ablutions that are customary among the Jews; each could hold twenty or thirty gallons. Jesus said to the servants, "Fill the jars with water," and they filled them to the brim. Then he said to them, "Draw some out now and take it to the head waiter." They did this; the head waiter tasted the water, and it had turned into wine. Having no idea where it came from—though the servants who had drawn the water knew—the head waiter called the bridegroom and said, "Everyone serves good wine first and the poorer wine when the guests are half drunk; but you have kept the best wine till now."
>
> This was the first of Jesus' signs. . . . He revealed his glory, and his disciples believed in him. After this, he went down to Capernaum with his mother, his brothers, and his disciples, but they stayed there only a few days. (NJB; John 2:1–12 with modifications)

The Devil asked Jesus to turn stones into bread. Jesus' mother stops just short of asking him to perform a nearly duplicate miracle and turn water into wine. True, she merely notes the fact that the wine has run out, but he rightly hears a challenge. Though we need hear no disrespect in his addressing his mother as "Woman," his words "what is that to you and me? My hour has not yet come" seem clearly to resist her. In the Gospel of John, whenever Jesus refers to "my hour," he is referring to his death, and he speaks as if expecting her to understand the reference. In the end, he relents, but what has his death to do with wine at the wedding? What point is he making to her?

When she declines to reply to him and addresses herself instead to the attendants, she suggests—as the Devil does in his confrontation with Jesus—that she knows something about him that others do not but has, at the same time, a question about him. What would that question be?

The answer may lie in the point of the miracle, which seems to involve Jesus' disciples more than it does the embarrassed wedding hosts. The episode concludes, "He revealed his glory, and his disciples believed in him," recalling words from the prologue (1:14) "And we have seen his glory." If she has prevailed upon him to reveal his glory to them before he intended to do so, she may be attempting to bind them to him for his own good; and he may be cooperating with her by changing the water not just into a fresh supply of the existing wine but into new and better wine. All Jesus' miracles are, for John, "signs," and no detail in them is without meaning.

Just a few days later, when Jesus goes to Jerusalem, his disciples go with him, but his brothers notably do not. His mother may have known that they would not, and have wanted him not to be alone when, at the Jerusalem Temple, he performed a reckless and violent act that would have one meaning, as she half-guessed, for those who had already glimpsed his "glory" and quite another meaning for those who had not.

HE STAGES AN ATTACK ON
THE TEMPLE, THEN RETREATS

Since the time of the Jewish Passover was approaching, Jesus went up to Jerusalem. In the Temple compound, he found people selling cattle, sheep and doves, and the money changers sitting there. Making a whip out of cords, he drove them all out of the Temple, sheep and cattle as well. He scattered the money changers' coins, knocked their tables over, and said to the dove sellers, "Get these things out of here, and stop turning my Father's house into a market." Then his disciples remembered the words of scripture, "I am eaten up with zeal for your house." The Jews spoke up saying, "By what right do you do these things? Show us a sign." Jesus answered, "Destroy this Temple, and in three days I will raise it up." The Jews replied, "It has taken forty-six years to build this Temple! Are you going to raise it up again in three days?" But he spoke of the temple of his body. When Jesus rose from the dead, his disciples remembered what he had said, and they

believed in the scripture and the words that he had spoken. (John /
2:14–22)

Jesus' violent attack on the Temple is the first public action of his career,
and it is a career-defining action. Herod's Temple was not just the central
shrine of the Jewish religious establishment; it was also the seat of such
political power as the nation retained. How do his disciples react to his
audacity?

When they recall "I am eaten up with zeal for your house," a line
from Psalm 69, they seek to define him as a zealous and righteous
prophet, like so many before him, including John the Baptist. But he is
rather more than that: No prophet went so far as to attack the Temple
physically. Jesus' fierce conduct evokes, if anything, a cleansing visitation
of the Lord himself as imagined by the prophet Malachi:

> The Lord whom you seek will suddenly come to his temple. . . .
> But who can endure the day of his coming,
>   and who can stand when he appears?
> For he is like a refiner's fire,
>   or like the cleaner's lye.
>
> (Mal. 3:1–2)

Jesus assumes the authority predicated of him by the Baptist's words "the
winnowing-fork is in his hand." But authority like this cannot be assumed with impunity. Jesus' provocation of the Jerusalem authorities is
potentially a capital offense. In the Synoptic Gospels, it is in fact the most
prominent of the charges brought against him at his later trial. But the
boldness of his conduct is exceeded by the boldness of his language in
explaining it. When "the Jews" demand a "sign," some proof that Jesus
has the right to usurp the Temple authorities as he has done, the destruction of the Temple is the very last thing on their minds. Why is it the first
thing on his mind in his audacious answer to them?

The destruction of the Temple weighs on the mind of God Incarnate
for at least three reasons: first, because it was God himself who destroyed
the First Temple, the first "House"; second, because he knows that a
new destruction is coming; and, third, because he knows that he will not
stop it.

The destruction of the First Temple, God made abundantly clear at
the time, was not Babylonia's doing but his. Speaking through Jeremiah
shortly before Nebuchadnezzar arrived from the north, he said:

> I have forsaken my House.
>   I have abandoned my inheritance.
> I have given my soul's beloved
>   into the hands of her foes. . . .
> She has raised her voice against me;
>   therefore I hate her.

> (Jer. 12:7–8)

Though it is a convention of classical Hebrew poetry to present victory and defeat as the jubilation or lamentation of women, it is also true that, then as now, military defeat has a special and horrible meaning for women. In a later passage never read in church, the Lord gave more details about just what he had in mind for her whom he had come to hate:

> Do you ask yourself,
>   "Why is all this happening to me?"
> It is because your guilt is great,
>   that your skirts have been pulled up
>   and you have been raped. . . .
> Because you have forgotten me,
>   and put your trust in falsehood,
> I have pulled your skirts up over your face
>   to let your shame be seen.
> Ugh! Your adulteries, your squeals of pleasure,
>   your vile prostitution!
> On the hills, in the dales,
>   I have seen your depravity.
> Jerusalem, woe is coming upon you!

> (13:22, 25–27)

"I have pulled your skirts up over your face. . . ." We may assume that when disaster came for Jerusalem in the sixth century B.C.E., such scenes were actually enacted. Has war not always been so? But now the Lord revisits the scene of the rape, and his mood is defensive and arrogant. His words "Destroy this Temple, and in three days I will raise it up" are like those of an arsonist who visits, unrecognized, a church that he once torched. "Burn this place down," he says, apropos of nothing, "and I can rebuild it for you in nothing flat."

The reference to reconstruction in three days echoes at least as loudly as the reference to destruction. In three days he will raise it up? *Five hundred years* have gone by and he has not raised it up. The Second Temple, as we have seen, was an embarrassment. The very name of Zerubbabel, the kinglet who built it, was ludicrous, meaning "Born-in-Babylon"—a name perhaps sarcastically substituted for his real one after he was discredited and deposed by the Persians, who were the real power in "restored" Israel. As for the Temple that Jesus now visits, though Jewish taxes have paid for it, is it the Lord's Temple or Herod's? Observing its commercialization, Jesus feels anger as a Jew but, as the Lord Incarnate, he also feels shame. If the chosen people have to conduct their very worship as junior partners in a foreign-owned enterprise, the blame is not theirs. He had promised it would not be so, and he has not kept his promise.

The worst, however, is that the Lord, now incarnate as Jesus, knows that this Temple, too, will soon be destroyed, with consequences worse than anything he prophesied through Jeremiah, and that he will not intervene to stop it. He knows that when that time comes, the Romans will need so many crosses to crucify Jews after putting down their desperate rebellion that the hills around Jerusalem will literally be deforested (a ghastly detail mentioned by the first-century historian Josephus). Because the subject is so much on the Lord's mind, it is provocatively close to his lips.

But then what? Much of the uncanniness of the character of Jesus derives from the way he makes familiar objects and images strange by combination. The expiatory lamb is familiar; a *human* lamb is strange. The Temple is equally familiar; a *human* temple ("He spoke of the temple of his body") is strange again. A human temple marked for destruction, a temple that will be sacrificed like a lamb, is strangeness squared. And note well that Jesus does not say, "If you destroy this Temple. . . ." What he says is, defiantly, "*Destroy* this Temple." He dares the authorities to kill him. A lamb who taunts the butcher? His followers do not hear the defiance. "The Jews" do not hear it either. No one yet makes the bizarre double or triple equation that Jesus makes. But all have seen the defiance in his destructive action, which speaks more clearly and no less loudly than these words; and all know that unless he either quits Jerusalem or provides something unprecedented by way of an explanatory, legitimizing "sign," he has put himself in mortal danger.

In the end, Jesus chooses to leave Jerusalem when the Passover feast is over, strongly suggesting that, whatever his full intentions are, they do not center on reforming Temple practice, much less on seizing power. He has come to his Temple suddenly, as the prophet Malachi predicted, only to announce a profound change in his relationship to it. His attack, the one and only violent action reported of him, is a mere staged attack, a demonstration, and the demonstration is the whole of the agenda. His equation of the Temple and his own body goes beyond Louis XIV's *"L'état c'est moi."* No "real" messiah could ignore the seat of Jewish political power and commercial life. But Jesus is an ironic, "unreal" messiah, a yes-and-no messiah who has no such agenda. The horrendous attacks that the Lord unleashed against the Temple in the past are definitively in the past. When such attacks occur in the future, and they will not be long in coming, he will not claim that they are his attacks, nor will he defend against them. The Lord of Hosts, the hero of Jewish song and story, will be a noncombatant.

The Gospels report recurring questionings of Jesus' sanity, and one can easily see why. It would have been easy for the Temple authorities to contain his little raid, intellectually, in the capacious category of crazy visitors to the great national shrine. If he had been serious, then he would have had to go on from this raid to others; he would have had to exhort his followers to conduct their own raids. But he does nothing of the sort. He leaves Jerusalem because, now that he has substituted himself for the Temple, he has nothing to do there but die and rise, and the hour of his death and resurrection has not yet come.

INTERLUDE: THE BURDEN OF HIS OMNISCIENCE

While he was in Jerusalem for the feast of the Passover, many believed in his name when they saw the signs that he performed. Jesus, however, knew all people and did not entrust himself to them, for he never needed evidence about anyone: He could tell what they had within. (John 2:23–25)

God Incarnate's ability to "tell what they had within" is a power that God did not have at the start of his creative activity but acquired only gradually, even as his physical power seemed to ebb away. Just after creating the world, when his strength was at its apex, the Lord still had to ask Adam and Eve, "Who told you that you were naked?" (Gen. 3:11). By the end of his career, he is physically quiescent, but his mental powers have grown apace. The Book of Daniel features both divine clairvoyance and divine prescience—that is, both the ability to "tell what someone had in him" and the ability to read the future. But then thousands of years lie between the moment when the Lord creates the first man in Genesis and the moment when he appears, in Daniel, as "the Ancient of Days," a

white-haired sage seated on a throne, burdened with his own knowledge
and emotionally detached.

Jesus too seems burdened with his own knowledge and emotionally
detached as a result. Though he is only about thirty (Luke 3:23), he seems
much older, knowing in the way of an older man, weary in the same
way. But if Jesus seems to have been born old, it is only because he *was*
born old. As the son of Joseph, he may have only three decades behind
him, but as God Incarnate he has a curriculum vitae three millennia
long. Recalling this, we need not be surprised that he rarely displays conventional curiosity about or interest in other people. He asks his interlocutors many questions for their sake but never one for his own sake.
Jesus never needs to ask: He knows.

Related to this is the fact that Jesus' schedule seems to have only one
appointment on it. His "hour," the time predestined for his execution in
Jerusalem, is fixed and obligatory. Everything else seems random and
optional. He seems to choose as his disciples the first men who come
along. He works his miracles for those sufferers who happen to cross his
path. It is as if, because his intentions comprehend all mankind, he may
begin anywhere, with anybody. There is never anyone whom Jesus simply must meet. No human encounter is forbidden. None is required.

The private life of Jesus differs from the private life of the Lord God
inasmuch as Jesus does seem to have a private life, while the Lord
God does not. True, God does talk to himself during the creation and
again just before the great flood. From the call of Abraham onward,
however, every word he says is specifically addressed. He never muses,
never thinks aloud, never says anything as an aside to himself. Unless he
has something to say *to someone,* he has nothing to say.

God Incarnate, in sharpest contrast, seems to have a private life that
has swallowed his public life whole. The Gospel of John reads at times
like a book-length soliloquy with occasional digressions into conversation. Jesus' interlocutors often seem to be mere occasions for thought,
like the students of a meditative teacher given to speaking his medita-
tions aloud. Yet the difference is not so great as it seems. Even when Jesus
talks over the heads of his auditors or keeps on talking when a given interlocutor has departed or fallen wholly silent, the meaning of his speech
always requires completion by the identity of the hearer. The difference
is that, unlike God, Jesus invariably seems to understand his interlocutors' desires better than they do themselves.

Jesus, like God, never engages in small talk. Small talk serves the needs
of people who need time to get to know one another. Jesus needs no

VERY INTERESTING THOUGHT -

such time. He already knows all that he needs to know. And his speeches are carried in a narrative that reflects his own stringent priorities. The New Testament, like the Old Testament, is morally serious to the virtual exclusion of charm and, often enough, even of information. It is not that there is no humor in the Bible, but its humor, like everything else in it, is always a means to a moral end. Nothing in the Bible is ever said merely to inform or amuse; neither knowledge nor beauty nor any other human good is ever pursued for its own sake. As a result, the Bible provides only some of the aesthetic pleasure that we have learned to expect of imaginative writing, while the distinct aesthetic effect that it does produce is one of concentrated and commanding moral urgency. The speeches of Jesus, like the speeches of God, have that about them which says, in effect, "This is neither a school exercise, reader, nor an idle entertainment, nor even a beautiful work of art. This is reality. This is serious. *Pay attention!*"

The rule of thumb for the interpretation of texts written to this ascetic recipe might be stated as follows: *Since everything insignificant has been left out, assume that everything kept in is significant.* Reading a text in this way might also, more loosely, be described as reading it as if it were written by God. The kind of close scrutiny, the magnification of detail, that such interpretation entails is exhausting to undertake and, at first, bewildering even to behold. But the Bible did receive such attention, for centuries, and the habits of biblical exegesis, as they have been crystallized and secularized, have led in the West to a relative scripturalization of all imaginative literature—indeed all imaginative production. Poems, plays, and novels would not now be subjected to such close and earnest examination, in other words, nor would their authors be revered as the source of otherwise unavailable truth, if biblical exegesis had not first set the pattern: a text understood to contain more than first meets the eye and a central character—understood to be the ultimate author of the text—who never, for even the most fleeting instant, consents to be taken casually. In the oracular gravity of a filmmaker (architect, novelist, mezzo soprano) who clearly believes that what has been brought forth is no mere movie (building, novel, aria), we may see the secularized continuation of the biblical antigenre of pure moral consequence. The interviewing journalist who would withhold homage before this gravity is like a prophet who would decline the word of the Lord. At issue is something far deeper or altogether other than mere pomposity. With consummate art, the Bible insists that it is not art at all, and by that very insistence it has had its deepest impact on the Western artistic ideal.

HE SPEAKS OF A NEW CREATION, BUT PRIVATELY

The classic biblical combination of intense moral seriousness and extreme narrative economy appears at full strength in an episode that begins not long after Jesus' raid on the Temple, when

> one of the Pharisees called Nicodemus, a leader of the Jews . . . came
> to Jesus by night and said, "Rabbi, we know that you have come from
> God as a teacher. No one could perform the signs that you do unless
> God was with him." Jesus answered:
>
>> Truly I tell you,
>> no one can see the Kingdom of God
>> without being born anew.
>
>> (John 3:1–3)

Where is Jesus lodging when Nicodemus comes to see him? What do his quarters look like? As the two of them speak, are they seated, standing, or pacing about? What are they wearing? Is Nicodemus an elder statesman among the Pharisees or a young searcher of the same age as the man he has come to visit? As usual in the Bible, none of this information is provided; and as usual in the Bible, its absence forces the attention of the reader to the information that the writer does provide.

Thus, in the three verses just quoted, it matters that Nicodemus is a Pharisee and therefore a believer in resurrection; it matters that he is coming to Jesus not on his own account but as "a leader of the Jews"; it matters that, by the same token, Nicodemus and his circle have been favorably impressed by Jesus' public "signs," of which the only one so far mentioned is his violent action in the Temple; and finally it matters that Nicodemus arrives under cover of darkness.

It matters as well, of course, that Jesus can read minds.

Jesus chooses to decline Nicodemus' conventional homage ("Rabbi, we know that you have come from God as a teacher"), saying, in effect, that a man like Nicodemus cannot (or, at least, does not yet) know enough to tell whether Jesus comes from God or not. To acquire that ability, he will have to be "born anew." But in raising this strange topic, Jesus responds not to what Nicodemus has said but to what Jesus knows he is thinking. It is unlikely, after all, that Nicodemus has come by night merely to compliment a visitor from Galilee. Jesus continues:

Truly I tell you,
no one can enter the kingdom of God
without being born of water and Spirit.
What is born of human nature is human;
what is born of the Spirit is spirit.
Do not be surprised when I say:
You must be born anew.
The breath of the wind blows where it pleases.
You can hear its sound,
but you cannot tell where it comes from or where it goes.
So it is with everyone who is born of the Spirit.

(3:5–8)

When Nicodemus asks, mildly, "How is that possible?" Jesus rebukes
him again:

You are a teacher of Israel, yet you do not understand this? Truly I tell
you, we speak only of what we know and testify only to what we have
seen, yet you people reject our testimony. If you do not believe me
when I speak to you of the things of earth, how will you believe
me when I speak to you of the things of heaven? (3:9–12)

If the Gospel of John were printed as drama, there would be a stage
direction at around this point: "Exit Nicodemus," or perhaps "Exit Nicodemus, muttering," or "Exit Nicodemus, agitated." Nicodemus never
speaks again in this scene. "How is that possible?" are his last words. If
Jesus' goal was to confound this inquirer, he would seem to have succeeded. Yet Nicodemus happens to be the man who will bury Jesus after
his crucifixion, so somehow Jesus did reach him. What is there about
Jesus' speech that a "teacher of Israel"—someone who knows the tradition out of which Jesus is speaking—might use to turn himself into a
disciple?

With reference to "being born of water and Spirit," Nicodemus
might think of Genesis 1:1 and the time when "darkness was upon the
face of the deep, and God's Spirit breathed over the face of the waters."
It is an undernoticed fact that in Genesis God does not create darkness
but only contains it. After creating light, "God *separated* the light from
the darkness. God called the light Day, and the darkness he called Night.
And there was evening, and there was morning, the first day" (Gen. 1:4–5,
italics added). Day, which God has created, is a space cleared within darkness, which he did not create. Time begins when light begins, occupying

the same cleared space in the primeval darkness, which itself is timeless. "And God said: 'Let there be lights in the firmament of the heavens to separate the day from the night; *and let them be for signs and for seasons and for days and years*'" (RSV; Gen. 1:14, italics added). As light is a space cleared within darkness, so time is a space cleared within eternity by God's chronometers, the sun, the moon, and the stars. As for the waters, once again God does not create them but only contains or restrains them, opening the dry land as an ordered space within the chaos of the waters: "Let the waters under the heavens be gathered together into one place, and let the dry land appear" (1:9). Night and ocean as mankind knows them are the remains of the uncreated chaos of darkness and water that God dammed up to make the world. •

When Nicodemus, who comes to God Incarnate out of the night, is told that he must be "born anew," as I have translated the phrase, following the Revised Standard Version, he is being pushed to guess that the new birth being spoken of will occur as part of, or in anticipation of, a descent into chaos, followed by a new creation of the cosmos itself from darkness, water, and Spirit—in brief, a new birthday for the whole world.

Only God can perform such a cosmic feat, but will he? Will he start over? Jesus seems to hint at nothing less, but how strange that such a vast possibility should be spoken of at night, in private if not in secret, with just one interlocutor. And if a new creation is called for, does it not follow that there is some crippling defect, some mistake or disgrace, in the old creation? Nicodemus' question "How is that possible?" leads inevitably to the question And why is it necessary? And Jesus' answer is: "The breath of the wind blows where it pleases." In brief, God has his reasons.

Greek, like Hebrew, uses a single word for breath, wind, and spirit, and the three have a powerful experiential linkage. The experience of even the smallest child includes two kinds of blowing: the blowing of the wind and the blowing of the child's own breath. Since breathing stops at death, it is an easy step to associate breath with life and then to make the further inference that the wind, which seems to breathe, must also be alive. Ancient Israel went yet one more step and asserted that the living spirit that blows sometimes fiercely in the storm and sometimes sweetly from the mouth of a babe is the breath of the living God. In the Bible, the breath/wind/spirit that moves in each man, woman, or child moved first as God's own breath/wind/Spirit. He breathed it into the first man, and thereafter all human life and breath belongs to him. He can breathe a corpse to life as surely as he did a mud statue in Genesis 2. His Spirit—in the wind, in the lungs, and in the mind—is this vivifying power in person.

In the Old Testament, the most frequently cited encounter of water and Spirit—more frequently cited than the Genesis encounter—is the encounter in Exodus of a wind from God with the waters of the Red Sea. God's breath, blown from his nostrils, dried up the sea so that the Israelites might flee to safety from the pursuing Egyptian army, which drowned when the wind stopped and the waters rushed back. On the far shore, the Israelites sang a song of victory over their drowned enemy:

> A blast from your nostrils and the waters piled high;
> the waves stood firm as a dyke;
> the bed of the sea became firm ground. . . .
> [Then] you exhaled, and the sea closed over them;
> they sank like lead beneath the mighty waters.
>
> (NJB Exod. 15:8, 10 with modifications)

The Jordan River, where the Spirit descended upon Jesus at his baptism, would part at another blast from God's nostrils when the Israelites crossed from the desert into Canaan.

The most vivid, memorable, and explicit of all biblical equations of breath, wind, and life-giving Spirit comes, however, in Ezekiel:

[The Lord God] said, "Prophesy over these bones. Say, 'Dry bones, hear the word of the Lord. The Lord God says this to these bones: I am now going to make breath enter you, and you will live. I will put sinews on you, I will make flesh grow on you, I will cover you with skin and give you breath, and you will live; and you will know that I am the Lord.'" I prophesied as I had been ordered. While I was prophesying, there was a noise, a rattling sound; it was the bones coming together. And as I looked, they were covered with sinews; flesh was growing on them and skin was covering them, yet there was no breath in them. He said to me, "Prophesy to the Spirit; prophesy, son of man. Say to the Spirit, 'The Lord God says this: Come from the four winds, Spirit; blow on these dead, so that they come to life!'" I prophesied as he had ordered me, and the wind entered them; they came to life and stood up on their feet, a great, a mighty host. Then he said, "Son of man, these bones are the whole House of Israel. They keep saying, 'Our bones are dry, our hope has gone; we are doomed.' So prophesy and say to them, 'The Lord God says this: I am now going to open your graves; I will raise you up from your graves, my people, and lead

you back to the soil of Israel. And you will know that I am the Lord.'"
(37:4–14)

Does Jesus intend Nicodemus to remember Ezekiel? The passage is so well known and so striking that it is difficult to imagine Nicodemus' *not* making the association, particularly after being challenged to ask himself what he should be expected to recall as a "teacher of Israel." It matters, as noted earlier, that Nicodemus is a Pharisee, practicing a form of Judaism one of whose innovations was a belief in the resurrection of the dead.

In the intellectual tradition that began in ancient Israel, revolutions did not come by deletion or replacement but by transformative expansion or, in the broader sense of the word, by midrash. Transformative expansion is what occurs when the "son of man" of Daniel 7 is made to refer not just to the period following Alexander the Great but also to an actual human being, Jesus of Nazareth, who was born during that period. Transformative expansion is what occurs when Ezekiel's vision (in which "son of man" does mean simply "man") is made to refer not just to national rebirth but also, simultaneously, to personal resurrection. And, as we shall see later, transformative, midrashic expansion is what happens most dramatically when the lamb whose blood saved the Israelites from God's Angel of Death at the first Passover becomes the divine lamb or Lamb of God whose blood at the second Passover saves all mankind from God's ancient curse. In sum, instead of "Exit Nicodemus, agitated," perhaps we may understand, after all, "Exit Nicodemus, inspired."

HE TALKS, BUT TO HIMSELF,
OF GOD AS ILLNESS AND AS REMEDY

Chastened or inspired, the Jewish leader makes his way back into the night. Left alone, God Incarnate, like Hamlet in the "To be or not to be" soliloquy, ponders the scarcely comprehensible death that awaits him. Having put his human life in mortal peril by his action in the Temple, he now says shocking things of and to himself that he is not yet ready to say to Nicodemus—or to anyone:

> No one has gone up to heaven
> except the one who came down from heaven,
> the Son of Man.
> As Moses lifted up the snake in the desert,

so must the Son of Man be lifted up
so that everyone who believes in him may have eternal life.

(John 3:13–15)

In the Old Testament, the Lord is oblivious of himself. In the New, the Lord Incarnate is obsessed with himself. The Lord says so little about himself in the Old Testament that who he is must be inferred from what he does. In Exodus (JPS; 3:13–17), when pushed by Moses, the Lord actually makes this very point about himself, if somewhat gropingly. Moses asks, "When I come to the Israelites and say to them 'The God of your fathers has sent me to you,' and they ask me, 'What is his name?,' what shall I say to them?" God's answer comes in four stages, and he seems to be making it up as he goes along. First, he says, "I am who I am" or perhaps "I am what I do," which is an answer but not a name. It is an explanation for why he has no name and needs none. Second, shortening his first answer into a kind of makeshift name, the Lord says, "Tell them, 'I AM sent me to you.'" I AM is his raw or naked name, a name that is not just conventionally but inherently unspeakable. How can you speak it— how, at least, can you speak it routinely—without encountering all kinds of syntactic confusion? Third, conceding a bit more to Moses' need for credentials, he says, "Thus shall you speak to the Israelites: 'Yahweh [a name with an audible link to "I am what I do" but in the third person], the God of your fathers, the God of Abraham, the God of Isaac, and the God of Jacob, has sent me to you.'" Fourth and last, with unexpected solemnity, he ratifies what he has just done, saying:

Let this be my name forever.
Thus will I be called for all eternity.

To repeat, the impression conveyed is that the Lord is naming himself on the spot, discovering the need for a name and coining the name in the same moment. And why should we be surprised? Until asked to provide a name for himself by a human being, why would the Lord need one? He lives among no other gods. It matters not how he is addressed, because no one addresses him. He is the only one of his kind. No one exists with whom he might be confused. And at this point in his story, he has not yet required human beings to address him in prayer. When he thinks of himself, what else can he think but "I am"?

How very different it is for Jesus. Though he is God, he is also a man.

There is the whole male population with whom he might be confused. Knowing this, he resorts to extreme language to distinguish himself from them. But the Incarnation, which occasions this need, is itself a radical response to a still deeper need: The Lord, at long last, has become a question to himself. Very simple identities do not happen into crisis; complex identities do. The Lord's behavior from the beginning was certainly contradictory enough to have been problematic for him no less than for his creatures, but his absolute confidence and blissful oblivion of self long kept him from regarding himself as a problem. Now, as God Incarnate, while very far from shedding the manner of unquestioning invincibility, he says things that are so strange and so utterly unprecedented that, whatever his manner, they betray radical conflict.

Among these self-characterizations, the most startling comes in a soliloquy derived from the Book of Numbers. Thinking back to his origin in heaven and forward to his human death, Yahweh Incarnate recalls, of all unexpected moments, the time when he sent a plague of poisonous snakes—"fiery serpents"—upon the Israelites. Wandering in the desert, they had complained of hunger and thirst. The snakes were his reaction to their complaint. After many had died of snakebite, the survivors turned to Moses desperate for relief, more than ready to repent of their crime of complaint. Moses then prayed to the Lord, who instructed him to break one of the Sinai commandments and make a graven image of a serpent. "Set it on a pole," he told Moses, "and everyone who is bitten, when he sees it, shall live" (21:4–9). Moses obeyed, the plague was lifted, and the people moved on.

Now, alone in the night, more than a millennium later, having committed a capital offense against the religiopolitical establishment in Jerusalem, Jesus imagines himself "lifted up" on the gallows of his day and compares himself, in that condition, to the serpent that Moses "lifted up" on that pole in the desert. The serpent was lifted up so that the dying Israelites could be cured of fatal snakebite. Yahweh Incarnate will be lifted up "so that everyone who believes in him may have eternal life." This is the equation, but it is a deeply shocking equation, for what did the Israelites see when they looked at the bronze serpent? Antiquarians may say what they will about sympathetic magic or apotropaic medicine. In the story as we now have it, what the Israelites saw was a reminder that the Lord had been prepared to kill them in large numbers for no greater offense than complaining of hunger and thirst. When they looked at the bronze serpent, even though it cured them, they saw a reminder of why they had so greatly to fear him. The snakes, after all, were not the cause of their dying. The Lord himself was the cause.

What, then, does Jesus suggest that all mankind will see when they look upon him lifted up on the cross or, later, look upon an image of him in that condition? How can we avoid saying that they will look upon the cause as well as the cure of their distress? To the objection that this comparison is far-fetched, I would reply that it is Jesus himself who has fetched the comparison from afar. The bronze serpent is a detail from an obscure episode in Israelite history. The comparison is so arcane, so recherché, that it can only be fully, provocatively intended.

Anyone who sets out to comment on the character of Jesus quickly finds himself in competition with his subject. Jesus is more provocative in characterizing himself than most commentators begin to guess. I include not just learned commentators but naughty screenwriters, satirical novelists, nihilist philosophers, everybody. The latter all intend to blaspheme, and they all succeed (blasphemy is an easy target to hit). Jesus, however, blasphemes with a resourcefulness that exceeds theirs, because he knows so much better than they do whereof he speaks. Was there no other image available to him than that of the killer snake? Could he not have compared himself, for example, to the pillar of cloud by day and the pillar of fire by night that led the Israelites through the desert? Why dredge up this brutal incident and this grotesque symbol? Why, if not because in this incident human crime and divine punishment are so excruciatingly ill-matched? The death penalty for a complaint about bad food? How can divine innocence not be called into question? Why conjure up the memory of the bronze serpent if not to suggest that those who will see Jesus upon the cross will look upon not just the remedy for the human condition but also its cause?

Though Jesus' gnomic line in the Temple alluded to his destruction, the means of destruction was not then named. Here it is. In this soliloquy, Jesus alludes for the first time to his crucifixion, and the allusion is, of course, highly oblique, audible only by people who already know the rest of the story. And then, at this of all moments, Jesus speaks perhaps the most quoted single line in the New Testament:

For thus has God loved the world:
he has given his only Son
so that everyone who believes in him may not perish
but may have eternal life.

(John 3:16)

Jesus makes the astonishing statement that God is giving his son, his incarnate self, to the world as, through Moses, he gave the serpent to the Israelites—namely, as an icon against and a remedy for his own past ruthlessness. How hauntingly the next lines resound, against the now awakened memory of God's murderous revenge, as God protests that *this* time he has not come to judge:

> For God sent his Son into the world
> *not to judge the world,*
> but so that through him the world might be saved.
>
> (NJB 3:17, italics added)

As the stage goes dark, vast promises and dark confessions hang in the air together, their meaning scarcely decipherable. The world is somehow a lost world, a world that must be saved. Its salvation somehow requires a new creation. This much he has revealed to Nicodemus. But the new creation somehow requires in turn the death of the creator. This is the shocking prospect that the incarnate God has so far dared confide to no one but himself.

INTERLUDE: THE ASEXUALITY OF THE FATHER AND THE SEXUALITY OF THE SON

The celibacy—more exactly, the asexuality—of the Lord God might well seem to make him a refutation in person of the notion that gods are made in the image of men and women. Who, one might ask, modeling a deity on humanity as we know it, could possibly leave sex out? The immortals of both the Greek and the Indian pantheon are sexual, even though they are spared not just ordinary death but also, to a large extent, ordinary birth—birth preceded by laborious pregnancy and ending in painful parturition. If they are thus made in the image, at least the dream-image, of mankind, why could it not be so for the Lord as well?

Faith answers that if the Lord were simply an extrapolation of or a dreamy improvement upon mankind, then he would indeed be a sexual being. The fact that he is not such is a proof of his authenticity, a proof that we know him only because he has revealed himself to us, a proof that we have *not* created him in our image. There are, however, at least two other ways to take up this question.

The first begins with the fact that, as even a naive and prescientific observation of nature will reveal, everything sexual dies, while contrariwise everything that does not die is not sexual. It might then have been (and may still be) intuitive rather than counterintuitive to imagine that a deity who did not die could not be sexual, and then to associate divine immortality—as ancient Israel clearly did—with things like the wind, which neither mate nor perish. From such an intuition it would follow that sexual experience, however intense, could not be, as often in the history of religion it has seemed to be, a brief, ecstatic participation in divinity. On the contrary, sexuality would be understood to point not upward to divinity but forward to reproduction and then downward to death.

Speculation along these lines may seem to read a modern vision of sexuality back into Israelite antiquity, but this coincidence is interesting in its own right. Twentieth-century molecular biology has taught us to see the individual animal, including whatever counts as the animal's sexual experience, as just a machine by which one gene makes another gene. Only the simplest animals reproduce by asexual cloning, passing on the whole of their genetic endowment to their descendants. More complex, sexual animals transmit only half of their genetic identity in any one act of reproduction—and later die, even when their genes live on. Evolutionary biology and the new evolutionary psychology have taught us to see experientially enhancing features of human sexuality, such as concealed ovulation and year-round estrus in the female, as just so many means to the end of reproductive maximization—always, of course, in the interest of the gene.

As evolutionary science, with this impersonal and objective view of sexual experience, increasingly becomes the new common sense, the highly personal, intensely subject-centered sexual philosophy of a Sigmund Freud comes to seem the intellectual oddity of a bygone era. A century ago, "personal matters" were preeminently sexual matters, and intensely private. In our own era, sexual matters are decreasingly private, increasingly impersonal, and decreasingly consequential as a result. When everyone's sex life is just part of a large, collective, impersonal, well-understood, but ultimately meaningless process, it can seem to matter little whether God—or anyone—has a sex life or not.

There is, however, another, very different way to explain the asexuality of the Lord—namely, by seeing it as the projection of an impulse, as natural and even healthy as sex itself, to repress sex. This impulse may find its starkest mythological expression in a relatively little-noticed episode in the Book of Genesis in which a Semitic version of "the sensuous immortals"—to borrow Pratapaditya Pal's genial characterization of the gods of India—is stamped out by the direct intervention of the Lord:

> When men began to multiply on the face of the earth, and daughters were born to them, the sons of God saw that the daughters of men were fair; and they took to wife those of them that they chose. Then the Lord said, "My spirit shall not abide in man forever, for he is flesh. Let his days be a hundred and twenty years." The Nephilim [demigods] were on the earth in those days, and later as well, after the sons of God had gone in to the daughters of men, who bore them children. These were the supermen of yore, the men of legend. (Gen. 6:1–4)

The "sons of God" in this episode seem, as it opens, to have no female counterparts, no "daughters of God," with whom they might have sexual relations. They seem to discover sex only when they encounter the daughters of men. In any case, the offspring of these divine-human couplings, unless the Lord steps in, will inherit immortality from their divine fathers and sexuality from their human mothers. By this double inheritance, they will be, then, very like the lucky gods of Greece, Rome, and India. But the Lord refuses to tolerate this new class of sensuous immortals. He seems to assign to them, as already to everyone of purely human descent, a finite, if lengthy, lifespan.

A similar intervention has come a bit earlier, when the Lord God intervenes to ensure that Adam, newly aware of his nudity and newly sentenced to death, does not escape his punishment and become a sensuous immortal:

> Then the Lord God said, "Behold, the man has become like one of us, knowing good and evil. But wait! What if he should put forth his hand and take of the tree of life as well, and should eat and live forever. . . ." Therefore, the Lord God expelled him from the Garden of Eden to till the ground whence he was taken. He drove the man out; and east of the garden of Eden he placed the cherubim and a flaming sword, which turned every way, to guard the way to the tree of life. (3:22–24)

The Lord can countenance sexuality, as from the very beginning in Adam and Eve; he can countenance immortality, as in the sons of God. What he cannot allow is the conjunction of the two, as in the Nephilim, who all die in the great flood that immediately follows.

The appeal of the combination of sexuality and immortality as personified in innumerable sexually active immortals is clearly universal. In the biblical tradition, however, it faces, in God, a repressive counter-force—a second, equally compelling, personified idea that considers the first idea and opposes it. If the sensuous immortals are the apotheosis of sexual indulgence, the Lord is—at least in such episodes as the two just considered—the apotheosis of sexual restraint. And though it is perhaps easier to recognize human projection in sexually active gods than in this strictly celibate god, it is possible to recognize projection—the human personality in a recognizable guise—in him as well.

Does sexual repression result from him, or did it create him in the first place? The answer should be evident. Even if we grant that many have repressed themselves sexually by introjecting a repressive deity who began as someone else's projection, many others, clearly, have managed repression without this particular aid. What one must concede if one believes that gods are human projections is that there exists a cultural antisex instinct nearly as deep in the human species as the biological sex instinct itself. If the Lord did not exist in his anomalous asexuality as the personification of this counterinstinct, the counterinstinct would find some other mythic way to express itself. In other words, the statement with which this interlude began—that an asexual deity cannot be made in the image of his worshipers—is mistaken. Such a deity may indeed be a projection, but if so, a useful and necessary projection, because in every regard, not just as regards sex, human existence requires both indulgence and repression, and myths are written to make what is required seem both inevitable and wondrous.

The sensuous immortals have their ways of being, if not quite sexually repressive, then at least socially conservative. The Lord has his ways of being, if not quite sexually indulgent, then at least selectively accommodating. As for Jesus, what is most remarkable about his sexuality is that, though he remains celibate for all that the Gospels ever tell us of him, his sexual tolerance is exceptional to the point of being a public scandal to his contemporaries. This being the case, the possibility of pre- or extramarital sexual experience can no more be ruled out of his character, on the ground that it is never spoken of, than can the possibility that, had he lived longer, he might have married.

What is called for is not, in the manner of a modern novelist like Nikos Kazantzakis, to supply Jesus with a love life that the Gospels do not supply. What is called for is only to refrain from explicitly foreclosing possibilities that the Gospels leave implicitly open. The confession about himself that God has become human to make has far more to do with power and weakness than it does with indulgence and repression. For that confession, it matters rather more that the Lord should have become some woman's helpless baby than that he should have become any woman's hungry lover. And yet Jesus, speaking to Nicodemus or (more revealingly) to himself, says that it is love that has sent him into the world. And once God has become God Incarnate, he cannot speak the word *love* and leave out all reference to his own body. His is now an embodied love.

Moreover, when the disciples of John the Baptist express concern about the size of the crowds that Jesus and his disciples are attracting, John characterizes Jesus as a bridegroom in his response to them:

> It is the bridegroom who has the bride;
> and yet the bridegroom's friend,   \
> who stands by and listens,
> is filled with joy at the bridegroom's voice.
> This is the perfect joy that I feel.
> He must increase,
> I must decrease.

(John 3:29–30)

If John answers a question about himself, he raises one about Jesus. If Jesus is the bridegroom, who is the bride?

In the Old Testament, the Lord describes his relationship to Israel as that of a man to, variously, an infant daughter, a female foundling, a nubile young woman, a prostitute, a bride, a wife, the mother of his children, an unfaithful wife abandoned to rape and sexual humiliation, and a divorced, elderly wife whom he has remarried and taken back into his home. There is never the shadow of a doubt, however, that these relationships are metaphorical. The Lord has no divine spouse, and he has no sexual relations with any human being. He is celibate because he is the only one of his kind. This being the case, what does John mean to suggest when he calls God Incarnate a bridegroom?

Since there is no ordinary human bride on the scene, John may mean to suggest that Jesus, like God, is a metaphorical bridegroom. "The Father loves the Son," Jesus says, "and has entrusted everything to his hands" (3:35)—everything, including Israel, his metaphorical bride. Yet because Jesus is a male human being, the use of the word *bridegroom* cannot fail to direct attention to his sexual potency and to raise the question of whether now might not be the moment when, through Jesus, God's celibacy might end. God is a species unto himself. God Incarnate belongs as well to the human species. He has undergone an ordinary human birth. Will he now enter an ordinary human marriage?

The celibacy of the Lord God initially had less to do with his relationship to women than with his relationship, as sovereign and sole creator, with time and with history. As noted earlier, God asserted his ascendancy over recurring time by creating the sun and moon by which days, months, and years are measured. He asserted his ascendancy over nonrecurring time—one unrepeatable event following another in a sequence of indefinite length—by creating that by which such time is measured: namely, human generation. Both kinds of time are God's creation of order out of atemporal chaos.

The Old Testament measures nonrecurring, historical time genealogically. The nearest equivalent in classical Hebrew to the modern word *history*—and it is by no means a close equivalent—is *toledot,* "generations." Just as the God who created the sun and the moon is not himself implicated in any solar system, so also the God who created humankind male and female is not himself implicated in any process of sexual generation. Men and women reproduce; God creates.

Having neither progenitors nor offspring, God has, accordingly, no *toledot,* no generative history, except by vicarious participation in the generative history of his creatures or by metaphorical representation of his real relationship to them. He may be metaphorically their father. He may also be metaphorically their husband (he may even, though very rarely, be their wife). In reality, however, God is his own species, or his own genus, and it is a genus that does not reproduce.

But, to repeat, now that God has become man, now that he himself belongs to the species that he has created, does his relationship to *toledot* not change? Matthew and Luke go so far as to give his genealogy in detail. Though John provides no genealogy, his revision of God's relationship to *toledot* is more radical in another way, for he seems to assume that Jesus, though divine, has received his human nature in the ordinary way from a human father as well as a human mother. If God is now irretrievably involved in the life process of the human species by his human birth, why may he not allow himself the further involvement of a human marriage?

From the very earliest moments, Christian theology praised God for subjecting himself to ordinary human birth. If he had gone on from there to consummate an ordinary human marriage, would Christian theology have withheld its praise? Surely it would not have been difficult for such an action to be accommodated in, for example, the early Christian hymn celebrating

> Christ Jesus,
> who, being in the form of God,
> did not count equality with God
> a thing to be clung to,
> but emptied himself,
> taking the form of a slave,
> being born as men are born.
> And being in every way like a man,
> he humbled himself further and was obedient unto death,
> even death on a cross.

> (Phil. 2:5–8)

If God's surrender of his godlikeness and his descent into the welter of human generation could be celebrated at one point, why not at all points? Would the experience of sex be any less proper to the condition of being "in every way like a man" than the experience of birth?

That such a step was logically possible raises the question of whether and why it was psychologically impossible. Historically, it might be noted, the Gospels were written at a time when celibacy was thought the proper condition for any philosopher. Sexual arousal was to be eschewed as a disturbance of that *ataraxia,* or inner serenity, which was the pinnacle of wisdom. Historically, then, the Gospel writers, writing in Greek for Greek-speakers, may have portrayed Jesus as celibate simply because this is how sages in Hellenistic culture were conventionally portrayed.

As a matter of literary characterization, however, what the Old Testament shows God thinking about sexual arousal matters more than what Hellenistic culture thought about it. Indirectly, God characterized himself when, for example, in a passage quoted earlier, the Lord said that he was sending Babylon to rape Jerusalem because of her infidelity to him. Yes, the marriage was metaphorical, and so the rape is metaphorical as well, just a lurid evocation of military defeat. Moreover, because the Lord's relationship with Israel is essentially a relationship with the men of the nation, Israel's infidelity to him is essentially a male sin. When the Lord cries out, "Ugh! Your adulteries, your squeals of pleasure, / Your vile prostitution!" (Jer. 13:27), he means, in the first instance, to demean the men of the nation by comparing them to a sexually aroused woman. All the same, the comparison would not be demeaning if such arousal were not thought repugnant in itself.

Speaking through Ezekiel, the Lord made the same demeaning comparison even more explicitly:

> At the entry to every lane you made yourself cubicles, defiling your beauty and spreading your legs to all and sundry in countless acts of prostitution. You have fornicated even with your neighbors, the Egyptians with their huge erections, provoking my anger with further acts of harlotry. . . . So then, whore, hear the word of the Lord. . . . For all this, I will assemble all the lovers whom you pleasured, whether you loved them or not. Yes, I shall assemble them around you and strip you bare in front of them, and let them ogle your bare body from head to toe. I will pass on you the sentence that adulterers and murderers receive; I shall hand you over to their jealous fury; . . . they will rip off your finery, take away your jewelry and leave you stark naked. Then they will call a public assembly to deal with you—to stone you to death and hack you to pieces with their swords, to burn down your cubicles and wreak justice upon you, while many other women look on. (Ezek. 16:25–26, 35–41)

In ancient Israel, adultery was a capital offense (Deut. 22:22). Scenes like this did occur. What merits attention here, however, is the Lord's apparent repugnance toward sexual desire and sexual activity themselves—toward the obscene spreading of the female legs and the obscene size of the male member. God spoke this way again at Ezekiel 23 when he compared Jerusalem to a whore named Oholibah:

> She began whoring worse than ever, remembering her youth, when she had played around in Egypt. She had been in love with those lechers, back then, with their donkey erections, ejaculating as violently as horses. "You craved the debauchery of your youth, when they used to pinch your nipples in Egypt and fondle your young breasts. And so, Oholibah, Lord Yahweh says this: 'I shall set all your lovers against you. You recoil from them now, but I shall bring them to assail you from all directions: men from Babylon, men from Chaldea, men from Pekod and Shoa and Koa, and all those men from Assyria.'" (19–23)

Once again male apostasy is compared to female debauchery, and once again Israel's enemies are compared to men gathered to punish an adulteress, but along the way the act of copulation itself is made to seem bestial and revolting.

Yet such scenes do not exhaust the full range of God's feelings, and perhaps the best clue to the rest of the repertory lies in a book of the Bible in which God himself does not appear. The Song of Songs—read for centuries as an allegory of the relationship between God and, variously, Israel, the church, or the individual soul—is now recognized to be secular love poetry, one of the oldest surviving examples of the genre. Yet the Song of Songs, though secular in itself, is nonetheless relevant to any consideration of the Lord's attitude toward sexual arousal, because it provides a kind of extended footnote on the marital metaphor. It shows us what should be understood when the Lord uses words like *bride, bridegroom, husband,* and *wife.*

This is particularly the case as regards the place of female desire in any sexual relationship. The speakers in the Song of Songs are a young, unmarried couple. Both are passionate, but her ardor may well exceed his:

> On my bed at night I seek my heart's desire.
> I seek him, but I cannot find him!
>> Let me arise then and go about the city.
>> In the streets, on the corners I will seek my heart's desire.
> I seek him, but I do not find him!
> The watchmen come upon me
>> as they make their nightly rounds.
>> "Have you seen my heart's desire?"
> Just as I leave them
>> I find my heart's desire.
> I embrace him and will not let him go,
>> till I bring him to my mother's home
>> into the very room where she conceived me!
>
> (3:1–4)

The image of an amorous young woman, alone on the streets of a dark city, avidly seeking her lover is deliberately audacious. Though her lover is evidently a man of whom her parents approve, she cannot take to the streets without awakening, for the reader, echoes of Ezekiel's language about another kind of woman in the streets. The point, of course, is that what was made repugnant there is made beautiful here.

When this young woman's lover speaks, he says things like:

> I have come into my garden,
>> O my sister, O my bride,
> I have gathered my myrrh, I have plucked my fragrant herbs,
>> Let me eat my honey and my honeycomb,
>> Let me drink my wine and my milk.
>
> (5:1)

The Song of Songs presents sexual pleasure as the supreme luxury, the luxury of luxuries. Luxury, rather than the fruitfulness of procreation, is the mood the poet creates by turning the pleasure the couple have in each other's company into the centerpiece of an arrangement including many other sensuous and delicious pleasures—of food and drink, fabric and fragrance—all in a setting of perfectly protected languor.

> I charge you, O daughters of Jerusalem,
>   by the gazelles, by the wild deer,
> Do not rouse, do not wake my love,
>   before it please.
>
> (2:7)

The Genesis command to be fruitful and multiply is forgotten in the Song of Songs. The lovers do not promise each other offspring as numerous as the stars of the sky. Children are never mentioned in this poem, yet the mood is one of bounty and joy. If all this bounteous goodness is summoned up when John addresses Jesus as bridegroom, just as it is whenever God uses the same word of himself, is there any reason why Jesus may not become a bridegroom in the physical as well as the spiritual sense of the word?

Jesus may seem to suggest a reason for celibacy when he answers a question that links sexuality and mortality in a deliberately provocative way:

> Sadducees [aristocratic priests] approached him, maintaining as they do that there is no resurrection, and they challenged him as follows: "Teacher, Moses wrote that if a man dies childless, the man's brother must marry the widow and raise up heirs for his dead brother. But what of seven brothers? The first died childless, and the second married the widow. Then he died childless, and the third married the widow, and so on until all seven had died, and then the woman herself died. After the resurrection, whose wife will she be? All seven of them were married to her!"
>
> Jesus said to them, "The children of this world marry and are given in marriage, but those who merit resurrection from the dead in the world to come will neither marry nor be given in marriage, for they will be immortal. As children of the resurrection, they will be children of God and equal to the angels. (Luke 20:27–36)

Belief in the immortality of the soul and, for the just, an eventual resurrection of the body was common among the Pharisees, whose views

Jesus shares. By contrast, the Sadducees—members of the priestly clan of Zadok, who administer the Temple and exercise, in addition, as much civil authority as the Romans allow the Jews—believe in neither. The conundrum that the Sadducees pose to Jesus appears to be a standard argument of theirs against the Pharisees. Rather than answer the question, Jesus questions the question and finds it irrelevant to the condition of those who will have risen from the dead. The risen, he says, will neither marry (if they are men) nor be given in marriage (if they are women). Jesus knows, as his questioners do not, that the resurrection of the just will begin with him. He is to be, in Paul's later phrase (1 Col. 1:18), "the firstborn from the dead." This being the case, his celibacy might serve as a sign that this cosmic transformation is at hand.

But then again, it need not. There is a difference, after all, between transformation and simple abolition. If sexuality were to be simply abolished, why resurrect the body at all? Why not simply allow the soul, already understood to be immortal, to live on incorporeally? The issue may be put more bluntly as the question, If there is no marriage after the resurrection, is there sex? But this question may be usefully joined to another question: Were Adam and Eve married? In some sense, obviously, they were; their union could not have been more legitimate than it was. Yet in another sense their union was like the union of the unmarried lovers of the Song of Songs. The silence of that poem about procreation is suggestively like the silence of Genesis 2, where the Lord creates the first woman not to bear children but rather because "It is not good for the man to be alone" (2:18). In that vision of the creation of the human species, procreation begins only "after the fall," when immortality has been lost; paradise, though it clearly includes sexual union, seems not to involve reproduction. The recovery of immortality could entail, then, a return to just this condition, which, whatever it might be called, would not be marriage as the Sadducees imagine it.

As for the angels, the statement that resurrected men and women are "equal to the angels" refers rather to angelic immortality than to supposed angelic asexuality. Angels were imagined by both Jesus and his hearers to be physically male rather than sexlessly neuter. According to a Jewish legend preserved in the Book of Jubilees, the holiness of the angels is signaled by the fact that they are all born circumcised. True, their only available sexual partners (angelic homosexuality aside) are human; and as we saw when discussing the Nephilim, God has forbidden such miscegenation or hybridization. But it seems at the very least gratuitous to suppose that God will forbid sexual congress *within* the human species simply because the just have become "equal to the angels" in their immortality.

At John 12:24, Jesus uses an arresting image for death and resurrection:

> Unless a grain of wheat falls into the earth and dies,
> it remains but a single grain.
> Yet if it dies, it yields a rich harvest.

In 1 Corinthians 15:35–56, Paul seizes Jesus' image and plays variations on it like a jazz saxophonist. Think of plants in all their spectacular shape, size, and variety—everything from the orchid to the redwood. Compared to them, their seeds are nothing: so small, so drab, and, by comparison, so uniform. Just as we cannot predict the delicacy of the orchid or the grandeur of the redwood by looking at their seeds, so, Paul says (in his own language, of course), we cannot predict what our risen bodies will be like by looking at the "seed" bodies we now inhabit.

And as for bodily life in general, so also, it would seem to follow, for sexual life. Rather than abolished, sexuality will be transformed in ways that are beyond predicting or imagining. If in its broadest outlines, the story of the Bible is the story of how God first turned his blessings of fertility and dominion into curses and then turned his curses back into blessings, then there would seem to be little reason why God Incarnate, as the "firstborn from the dead," may not marry. Although God clearly abhors adultery, especially female adultery, and although his abhorrence verges, in his very angriest moments, on disgust with female sexual desire and even with the sexual act itself, his otherwise positive use of marriage as a metaphor for his relationship with Israel strongly suggests that he must now think of real marriage in a similarly positive way for himself. And when we say the word *marriage,* we must not imagine anything less ardent or less abandoned than the feelings given utterance in the Song of Songs.

All this being the case, there is, to repeat, every reason to assume that if Jesus had not died early, he would have married. In the Gospels, all of his key followers are married men, and none of them seems to have thought that imitating Jesus entailed celibacy. When we meet some of them later in the New Testament, well after his death and resurrection, they are all still married. Deeper understanding of and commitment to him have not changed their minds on this point. In the absence of any evidence to the contrary, we should assume that God Incarnate, precisely because he is God *Incarnate,* is capable of marriage and even, at some point, likely to marry. Certainly, this is what others of either sex would assume of him, not knowing his divine second identity. But even if they did know it, they could coherently make the same assumption.

Their making it adds only another element of suspense to this complex character's self-revelation. The end of virginity is a major border-crossing event in a man's life. For God Incarnate, a first sexual experience would be at the same time a new and distinct crossing from the divine to the human condition analogous to if less significant than the one he made at birth. Jesus apparently never makes that crossing, but it matters much to the character of his interactions with women that he could have made it. He is not a eunuch. He has taken no vow of celibacy. Hailed by God's prophet as the divine bridegroom, he may someday be a human bridegroom as well.

And yet is this divine bridegroom, whether humanly married or humanly single, to be slaughtered as a sacrificial beast? Only some days or weeks earlier, John was greeting him as "the Lamb of God." What strange marriage awaits a bridegroom who is also a lamb? These disturbing questions arise just as God Incarnate is about to have the longest conversation that the Bible records between God and a woman.

HE ADMITS, BUT TO A HERETIC, THAT HE IS THE MESSIAH

The Bible's narrative parsimony, to repeat a point made earlier, requires that every detail provided carry a great deal of weight. The New Testament's most frequent way of meeting this requirement is via the kind of allusion to the Old Testament that can make an otherwise mute detail eloquent simply by association. An Old Testament place-name rich with association becomes a remarkably telling detail in the episode that begins when Jesus, traveling from Judea through Samaria to Galilee, stops, tired and thirsty, at Jacob's Well,

> near the land that Jacob gave to his son Joseph. . . . Jesus, tired from the journey, sat down by the well. It was about noon. When a Samaritan woman came to draw water, Jesus said to her, "Give me a drink." His disciples had left for town to buy food. The Samaritan woman said

to him, "You are a Jew. How can it be that you ask me, a Samaritan, for a drink?" (Jews do not mix with Samaritans.) (John 4:5–9)

Jacob, who was given the name Israel, had twelve sons, whose descendants are collectively called the "children of Israel," or Israelites. Judah, Jacob's fourth son by his first wife, Leah, is the ancestor of the Jews, the dominant group in the land as the scene opens. Joseph, Jacob's first son by his second (but favored) wife, Rachel, is the ancestor of the Samaritans, the Jews' principal local rival. (The name Samaritan comes from the Greek pronunciation of the name of a long-destroyed city in their territory.)

Galilee, Jesus' home region, is linked to Samaria both ethnically and historically. The Galileans, like the Samaritans, trace their ancestry to other sons of Jacob than Judah (a Nazarene like Jesus could have been counted a descendant of Jacob's son Zebulon). Galilee, like Samaria, was conquered, occupied, and settled by Assyria in the eighth century B.C.E., while Judea withstood Assyria, falling to Babylonia only in the sixth century B.C.E.

The Galileans have come to be counted as virtual Jews because they take the Jewish side on the largest religious point at issue between the Jews and the Samaritans—namely, the proper place for the ritual sacrifice of animals. For the Jews, the rebuilt Jerusalem Temple is the only legitimate place for such sacrifice. The Samaritans, for centuries, have had a rival temple in Shechem, the very "land that Jacob gave to his son Joseph." By acknowledging Jerusalem as the shrine city of all Israel, the Galileans have cast their lot with the Jews and against the Samaritans and are allowed into the Jewish Temple as equals.

Depending on the circumstances, however, the Galileans seem to be in something of a mixed category. To the Samaritans of Shechem, Jesus seems a Jew, but twice in the Gospel of John Jews from Judea take him to be a Samaritan. Galilee, like Samaria, had been spurned as heterodox and illegitimate by the Judean exiles when they returned from Babylon in the late sixth century B.C.E. The key problem was that the Samaritans and Galileans alike had intermarried with settlers brought in by Assyria and (or so it was feared and alleged) had introduced alien practices into the ancestral religion. The dispute that divided the Jews from the Samaritans at that time thus initially divided the Jews from the Galileans as well. However, during an interlude of independence from foreign rule (164–64 B.C.E.), a Hellenized Jewish dynasty ruling from Jerusalem successfully imposed its Jerusalem-centered religious establishment on a number of non-Jewish or irregularly Israelite groups within the territory that it controlled. Galilee was one of these territories. As Jesus begins his career this conquest is recent, Galilee is heavily settled by Greek immigrants, and both the orthodoxy and the loyalty of the Galileans remain somewhat suspect in Jerusalem—as if to say, "Scratch a Galilean, and find a Samaritan."

Jesus himself, though at home in Galilee, is Jewish rather than Galilean by birth, according to the two Gospels, Matthew and Luke, that give his genealogy. In both, Joseph, Jesus' father, though resident in Nazareth of Galilee, is in fact an ethnic Jew tracing his lineage back to King David. (Joseph's ancestral town is David's own ancestral city, Bethlehem of Judah.) Many, if not most, historians suspect that this Jewish/Messianic genealogy was created after the fact; but for literary purposes, Jesus—who clearly regards Jerusalem as the center of the world—must be regarded as both religiously and genealogically Jewish. Even for literary purposes, however, to say that he is a Jew without giving any weight at all to his Galilean derivation is to miss something that at several points adds a crucial complexity to his identity.

All this is an unavoidably laborious way of showing how very much the Gospel can suggest simply by noting that Jesus has stopped "near the land that Jacob gave to his son Joseph." The New Testament is like a skin on every square inch of which the Old Testament is tattooed. The Gospel writers, in particular, cannot move a muscle without bringing some portion of the Hebrew scriptures into view. Recall that Jesus has just been acclaimed by the Baptist as the bridegroom of Israel and that what the divine bridegroom proverbially faced in his marriage to Israel was his wife's promiscuity: her incorrigible habit of "whoring" after false gods. In the eyes of the Jews—and on this point, Jesus stands with them—Samaria represents schism if not heresy: religious "whoring," self-righteously institutionalized and defiantly defended. This is the context in which Jesus finds himself unexpectedly deep in conversation with a woman who is both a Samaritan and living with a man who is not her husband. She is, in short, both a figurative and a literal adulterer.

Jesus replied to her:

> "If you only knew what God is offering
> and who it is who says to you,
> 'Give me a drink,'
> you would be the one to ask,
> and he would give you living water."

"You have no bucket, sir," she replied, "and the well is deep. How do you get this living water? Are you greater than our father, Jacob, who gave us this well and drank from it himself, along with his sons and his cattle?"

Jesus replied:

> "Whoever drinks this water
> will thirst again;
> but no one who drinks the water that I shall give
> will ever thirst again:
> The water that I shall give
> will become a spring of water, welling up for eternal life."

"Sir," the woman said, "give me some of that water, so that I may never thirst again nor ever again come here to draw water." (4:10–15)

In a culture in which drawing and hauling water was women's work, the well was a place where women, ordinarily kept secluded, could be seen in public and even addressed. At Genesis 29:11, the insouciant Jacob actually risks kissing a strange young woman at a well. If flirtation and gallantry always proceed by delicate double entendres, then the well is a place where anything said might have a second, concealed meaning.

As we have seen in his conversation with Nicodemus, Jesus is given to speaking in theological double entendre. But what happens when he speaks his solemn variety of double meaning in a place where another kind is commonly heard? As a Jew, he has taken a socially unexpected liberty by speaking to the woman at all. When his plain opening line, "Give me something to drink," takes poetic flight, what is she to think? What does he, who reads minds, expect her to think?

Jesus asks the woman for water, but before she can give him any (Does she ever? How like the Bible not to bother telling us), he says that she should be asking him for "living water." Although "living water" is a Greek expression for spurting water, water that bubbles out of a spring as if alive, does the woman really think that the spurting water Jesus says he can give her is spring water? Might she not find that interpretation, in the culturally permissive environs of a well, all too innocent a reading of what the Jewish stranger is hinting at? She tries once, flat-footedly, for a clarification, and then responds more cleverly, in a way that will do her no harm if the stranger is not flirting but can keep the ball in play if he is: "Sir, give me some of that water, so that I may never thirst again nor ever again come here to draw water."

Rather than continue speaking of water, living or otherwise, Jesus abruptly changes the subject: "Go, call your husband, and come back here" (John 4:16). Why is her husband's presence required? To hear Jesus expound further on the subject of living water? It is as if Jesus, having heard the woman's ambiguously flirtatious response to his ambiguously flirtatious overture, has read her mind and decided to shame her.

> The woman answered, "I have no husband." Jesus said to her, "You are right to say, 'I have no husband,' for you have had five, and the one you have now is not your husband. You have spoken the truth." "I see that you are a prophet, sir," said the woman. "Our fathers worshipped on this mountain, though you people say that Jerusalem is the place where one must worship." (4:17–20)

Jesus makes a pointed comment about her personal life. Rather than either confirm or deny the charge, she makes a reference to the religious differences of the Jews and the Samaritans. Is she answering one change of subject with another?

No, she is simply anticipating his next step. The fact that Jesus has read her mind alerts her to his being more than the average thirsty traveler. But if he is a Jewish prophet, then after upbraiding her for her marital infidelity, she expects that he will upbraid her nation for its religious promiscuity. In fact, she may detect that he has done so already. In Aramaic, the language that Jesus and the woman would be speaking, the word for husband, *ba'al,* "lord," is also a word that may be used to refer to a foreign god. Whence the elaborate pun: "You, Milady, have had five milords" is the same as "You Samaritans have had five gods."

Once the Samaritan woman knows what game is being played, she proves herself very nearly Jesus' equal in playing it. She sees his religious allusion and trumps it. Her remark "Our fathers worshipped on this mountain, though you people say that Jerusalem is the place where one must worship" has an elegant edge, for *Our* in that sentence does not include the Samaritans alone but also the Jews and therefore also Jesus. Once upon a time, all Israel—the forefathers of the Jews as well as the forefathers of the Samaritans—worshipped here at Shechem, she correctly notes. Shechem is the place where Abraham, then still called Abram, built his first crude stone altar after being called to Canaan; it is the land that Jacob, Abraham's grandson, gave Joseph, Abraham's great-grandson; it is the town where Joseph is buried, his bones having been carried lovingly through the desert by Moses and Joshua. Perhaps most important of all, Shechem is the mountain where Joshua built the first national shrine in the promised land. On that occasion, after conquering Canaan, all Israel gathered for celebration and rededication, and Israel's ardor and enthusiasm for God reached a peak that would never be attained again. "Our" Shechem, the Samaritan woman demurely hints, is the home of the old-time religion of Israel. It is "you" Jews who insist on transferring everything to upstart Jerusalem.

Jesus responds both as a loyal Jew refusing to back down before the standard Samaritan claim and as God Incarnate on the eve of the moment when he will trump the claims of both Shechem and Jerusalem with a new covenant "in spirit and truth":

> "Believe me, woman, the hour is coming
> when you will worship the Father
> neither on this mountain nor in Jerusalem.
> You [Samaritans] worship what you do not know;
> we [Jews] worship what we know;
> for salvation comes from the Jews.
> But the hour is coming—indeed, is already here—when true
>   worshippers will worship the Father in spirit and truth.
> Such is the worshipper whom the Father seeks.
> God is Spirit, and those who worship him
> must worship in spirit and truth."

The woman said to him, "I know that the Messiah . . . is coming; and when he comes, he will explain everything." Jesus said, "I am, who is speaking to you." (4:21–26)

The Samaritans regard only Torah as sacred scripture, and the Messiah whom they await to this day is not a second David, an anointed king, but a second Moses, an anointed prophet. Moses foretold the coming of this prophet in Deuteronomy 18, a passage that the Samaritan woman quotes when she says "he will explain everything":

> From among yourselves, from among your own brethren, the Lord your God will raise up a prophet like me. You must listen to him. This is just what you asked the Lord your God to do at Horeb [Mount Sinai] on the day of the Assembly, when you said, "Let me never hear the voice of the Lord my God or see this great fire again, or I shall die." Then the Lord said to me, "What they have said is right. From

their own brethren I will raise up a prophet like yourself. I will put my words into his mouth, and he shall tell them everything I command him." (18:15–18)

By his reply to the woman, Jesus assumes the identity of a second Moses or prophetic messiah more explicitly than he did when Philip characterized him (John 1:45) as "him of whom Moses . . . wrote." But he goes a step further—the reader is allowed to notice, whether the Samaritan woman does so or not—when he replies to her in a strange sentence using the original name of God (Exod. 3:14). Translated above as "I am, who is speaking to you," the sentence could just as well be translated "He who is speaking to you is I AM."

The woman believes Jesus' claim for just the reason that Nathanael did: Jesus has read her mind and her past. Returning from Jacob's Well (just outside town), she asks the townspeople, "Could this be the Messiah?" (John 4:29). They hurry out to see Jesus, he speaks to them, and many are persuaded that indeed he is: "They said to the woman, 'Now we believe no longer because of what you told us; we have heard him ourselves, and we know that he is indeed the Savior of the World'" (4:42).

Savior of the World, again, and not just, as Nathanael too narrowly called him, King of Israel. The Samaritans may consider themselves Israel, but they are well aware that the Jews consider them "the World"—that is, not Israelites but Gentiles. The struggle over "Who is an Israelite?" was the first century's version of the fierce twentieth-century struggle over "Who is a Jew?" Salvation, Jesus has unapologetically told the woman, "comes from the Jews," but in his view it evidently does not end with them. By making his first non-Jewish convert (Israelite yes, Jewish no), Jesus himself has taken a first, crucial step toward the creation of the universal jurisdiction that he sees prophesied for the Son of Man in the Book of Daniel.

❧ While Jesus speaks to the woman at the well, his disciples are in town buying food. When they return, they offer him some of it. His reply is a reflection on the paradoxical step he has taken by bringing his message to these schismatic Israelites before he has brought it with any clarity to the Jews. If the Samaritans are as good (that is, as bad) as Gentiles, then the divine bridegroom of Israel has made a preliminary overture to the human race, and the human race would seem to have accepted it. What lies ahead is daunting, but the time is ripe, Jesus says, and in any event, it is in this ironic way that God has decided to complete—and redeem—the labor that he began so long ago:

> My food is to do the will of him who sent me,
> and to complete his work.
> Do you not say,
> "Four months, then comes the harvest?"
> Well, look around you, I say, look at the fields.
> Already they are white, ripe for the harvesting.
>
> (John 4:34–35)

Having stopped at Shechem just for food and drink, Jesus ends up staying on for an extra two days. He surprised the Samaritan woman by telling her to go and call the husband he knew she did not have. She may have surprised him when she went and called the entire town. His disciples, surprised in their turn to see him speaking to her alone, can only be the more surprised as he lengthens his stay and turns what could have been merely a momentary indiscretion into a potential scandal.

The conversation between Jesus and the Samaritan woman is, as already noted, the longest conversation that God has with any woman in all of scripture. That she is not a Jew, that they are alone together, that they are meeting at a well, that she is a woman of whose checkered marital career he is fully aware, that he speaks to her in deliberate double meanings, that she responds to him intelligently and almost playfully, that he is known to approve of marriage, and that John has just acclaimed him as a bridegroom—all these factors taken together make this scene as suggestive in its way as John's earlier proclamation of Jesus as the Lamb of God. Jesus is a bridegroom without a bride. The Samaritan is a woman without a husband. If we apply to those facts alone the rule *Since everything insignificant has been left out, assume that everything kept in is significant,* what results?

What results is the distinct suggestion of promiscuity on his part. Israel's "whoring" was a metaphor for its interest in other gods. The corresponding "whoring" for God would be interest in other peoples. *Promiscuity* is just the right word for what Jesus' disciples see in his behavior in Shechem. Whatever role they expect him to play, they expect him to play it *for them*—faithfully for them rather than promiscuously for them and for others as well. If the scene at the well gains in dramatic interest from the potential sexual promiscuity flickering within it, it is

God Incarnate's religious promiscuity that, by the end of the scene, has become the real scandal—not hers but his.

WHO DO HIS DISCIPLES THINK HE IS?

As Jesus leaves Samaria for Galilee with his disciples, who do they think he is? To judge only from the little that they themselves have said about him, they think he is the Messiah; but they have heard first the Baptist, then Jesus himself, and then the Samaritans assign him other roles, for a total of seven, in the following order of appearance:

1. Judge
2. Lamb of God
3. Messiah (Son of David and adopted Son of God)
4. Son of Man
5. Temple
6. Bridegroom
7. Prophet and Lawgiver (a second Moses)

1. and 2. Judge, Lamb of God. The Baptist has proclaimed Jesus in the contradictory first two of these seven roles. He has acclaimed him as the divine miller with his winnowing-fork in his hand, who will separate the wheat from the chaff, saving the wheat and burning the chaff. Then, he has hailed him as the Lamb of God, who will "take away" rather than punish the sin of the world, the image evoking a reconciliation of mankind with God but one that comes, disturbingly, by way of human sacrifice.

3. Messiah (Son of David and adopted Son of God). Jesus' early followers do not resolve the contradiction between judge and lamb, with its hint of tension between God's relationship to Israel and his relationship to the world, but instead embrace Jesus in his third role: Messiah. At his baptism, a voice from heaven quoted Psalm 2:7, in which God adopts David, the King of Israel, as his son:

> You are my son;
> this day have I begotten you.

Andrew, who left the Baptist to follow Jesus, tells his brother, Peter: "We have found the Messiah" (John 1:41). Philip tells his friend Nathanael:

"We have found him of whom Moses, in the Law, and also the prophets wrote" (1:45). Nathanael acclaims Jesus as "King of Israel" (1:49).

4. *Son of Man*. Jesus, though willing to be acclaimed as Messiah, introduces a fourth, evidently more comprehensive role: Son of Man. The phrase itself means simply "human being," but Jesus enlarges its meaning by predicting: "You will see heaven open and the angels of God ascending and descending over the Son of Man" (1:51), alluding to a passage in the Book of Daniel (7:13–14) in which God gives "one like a Son of Man" jurisdiction over the whole world.

Readers of the Gospel know from John's prologue, as the disciples do not, that Jesus is God Incarnate. Readers of the Gospel also know, however, as the disciples again do not, that the Devil exercises a degree of physical control over Jesus that bears comparison with the physical control that Rome exercises over Israel. Ultimate power may rest with God, but in many external matters the Devil seems to be allowed to have his way. Though deftly quoting Moses to the Devil and easily overcoming all the Devil's temptations, Jesus nonetheless does not humiliate or unambiguously defeat him. Just why he does not—whether because he lacks the power or the will or because he has a plan that somehow includes tactical self-restraint—even the audience cannot guess.

5. *Temple*. Returned from the desert and the Devil, Jesus seems determined almost immediately to act out his first role, that of divine judge. He enters the Jerusalem Temple as if to cleanse his ancestral "House" with refiner's fire and cleaner's lye. But then, asked to prove his authority over the Temple, Jesus speaks, unexpectedly, of its destruction. None of his hearers quite understands him when he says, "Destroy this Temple, and in three days I will raise it up" (John 2:19), but the line lodges in their minds. Breathtakingly, Jesus has substituted his own body for the central, physical object of the Jewish religion—and then predicted its immolation.

When Nicodemus visits Jesus in another scene not witnessed by the disciples, what he hears is exhilarating in its vision of a new creation in water and the Spirit, a new creation in which the curses of the first creation may become blessings again. After Nicodemus disappears into the night, however, the audience hears Jesus draw a disturbing comparison between himself lifted up on the cross and the bronze serpent lifted up on a pole in the desert (John 3:14). What disturbs is the suggestion that though by his death he may be the cure of the world's affliction, he is also its cause.

6. *Bridegroom.* Having left or perhaps fled Jerusalem, Jesus and his disciples meet John the Baptist in the Judean countryside. John compares Jesus to a bridegroom and himself to the friend of the bridegroom. This image serves to cast the Baptist in a subordinate role, but its connotations go much further. In the Old Testament, God, as the bridegroom of Israel, is a betrayed bridegroom. Israel, his spouse, is unfaithful to him, though he insists that, even after punishing her, he will always be faithful to her. If the lamb is a bridegroom, then is the expiatory suffering of the lamb the suffering of a betrayed husband who, rather than punish his wife, will now passively endure her rejection? But then if that is how these two images might be combined, how do they, in combination, yield a meaning compatible with the role of messianic redeemer? The disciples, who believe that Jesus is the Messiah, have heard the prophet John acclaim him as both lamb and bridegroom. Nicodemus, possibly, and the reader, certainly, have heard Jesus say that it is love that has sent him into the world. The disciples have heard less about love, yet the inescapable prominence of love in the bridegroom metaphor must have begun to affect their understanding of what kind of messiah Jesus will be.

7. *Prophet and Lawgiver (a second Moses).* When the Samaritans accept Jesus as Messiah, they see him as a new Moses rather than a new David. He is the prophet who Moses promised would eventually come; but like Moses himself, he is a prophet who does not just predict the action of God but also imparts teaching, or *torah,* a prophet who "will explain everything." According to a widely held popular belief, Elijah had been the promised second Moses, and therefore any further appearance of a Moses redux would have to be Elijah redux. It was Elijah who, proverbially, would resolve all disputes and answer all questions. When John the Baptist says of Jesus that "he must increase, and I must decrease," he surrenders this role to Jesus, who recapitulates the functions of all God's past intermediaries in himself. That the Samaritans, for whom Elijah, who lived and worked in their part of Israel, was a towering figure, accept Jesus, a Jew rather than a Samaritan, in this role means, for them, that the role is incipiently international. If this Jew, this non-Samaritan, can be accepted as their savior, then it can only be because he is "the Savior of the World." That he agrees to be accepted in this way means that he too acknowledges that he is a Moses whose *torah* is intended for all mankind.

PART TWO

A Prophet Against
the Promise

After the two days [in Samaria] had passed, Jesus went on to Galilee. Although he had said that a prophet is without honor in his own
country, the Galileans welcomed him on his arrival, having seen all
that he had done at Jerusalem during the feast, which they too had
attended.

He went back to Cana in Galilee, where he had changed the water
into wine. Now at Capernaum, there was a royal official whose son lay
ill. When he heard that Jesus had arrived in Galilee from Judea, he
went and urged him to come and cure his son, who was on the point
of death. Jesus said to him, "Unless you people see signs and portents,
you will not believe!"

—John 4:43–48

Believe what? Jesus does not say, for he clearly seeks more than
assent to some limited set of propositions about himself. What
he wants is commitment of a far more global and personal sort,
an open-ended and undefined commitment that can only be
compared with belief in God. Yet when Jesus asks this kind of faith, he
goes beyond what even God has previously asked. As already noted,
when the Lord calls Abram to venture into a strange land, the venture is

linked to a great reward: Abram is to be made "a great nation." The implication is that, absent some good reason to venture abroad, the Lord himself would have expected Abram to stay home. Similarly, after bringing Israel out of Egypt "with mighty hand and outstretched arm" (Deut. 4:34), the Lord had no hesitation in adducing this miracle as a credential and a proof that he was a deity to be reckoned with. The Lord Incarnate, however, indignantly refuses to offer such credentials or traffic in such demonstrations. Why the indignation? He was willing enough to prove himself to Abram and Moses. Why is he unwilling to do so now when, if ever, a demonstration seems called for? Or is he unable rather than unwilling?

HIS INAUSPICIOUS FIRST CURE: A ROMAN CHILD

Jesus takes offense when a royal official asks that his son be cured of a fatal illness, rebuking the man as he rebuked the Devil in the desert, his mother during the wedding feast, and the Jews at the Temple. When the man insists, Jesus yields, but he has placed a novel frame around his own action, saying (but why, exactly?), "I am doing you this favor, but you should not have asked it":

> "Sir," said the official, "come down before my child dies."
> "Go home," said Jesus, "your son will live."
> The man believed what Jesus had said and headed for home; and while he was still en route, his servants met him with the news that his boy was going to live. He asked them when the boy had begun to recover. They answered, "The fever left him yesterday at one in the afternoon." The father realized that this was just when Jesus had said, "Your son will live." And so he believed, and all his household as well. (4:49–53)

Jesus seems either to be of two minds about the use of his divine power or else to be concealing something with regard to just how much power he has. Clearly, he has exceptional power of some sort at his disposal. Just as clearly, he is on guard against allowing the case for himself as an exceptional being to rest on that power.

A further ambivalence may result from the character of the man who requests the cure. As a "royal official," this man is either a Roman or, more likely, a Galilean Jew in the employ of the local puppet king, Herod Antipas. If it was a large step to preach to the Samaritans, it is a larger one to work a miracle for this instrument of Roman oppression. This is Jesus' first significant action since returning to Galilee from Jerusalem. Do the Galileans, who may have seen other charismatics defect to the Romans, look askance at his making his power so readily available to a Roman collaborator? There can be little doubt that Jesus notices whatever they notice. Is he also troubled by it? Is he peremptory with this official because of it?

A DEMON CRIES OUT, "I KNOW WHO YOU ARE"

From Cana in "upper" or hill-country Galilee, Jesus goes down to Capernaum on the shore of the Lake of Galilee, where, on the Sabbath, he preaches in the synagogue.

> In the synagogue there was a man possessed by the spirit of an unclean devil, and he shouted in a loud voice, "Hah! What do you want with us, Jesus of Nazareth? Have you come to destroy us? I know who you are—the Holy One of God!" But Jesus rebuked him, saying, "Be still! Come out of him!" And the devil, throwing the man down among them, went out of him without otherwise harming him at all. Amazement seized them, and they said to one another, "What is it about his speech? He gives orders to unclean spirits with authority and power, and they come out." And the news of him spread all through the surrounding countryside. (Luke 4:33–37)

Few scenes are so electrifying as that of a madman in a house of worship shrieking out what no one dares say: obscenities, blasphemies, unspeakable truths. When the voice of the possessed is also the voice of a devil, one of the treacherous company of devils, the blue flame only crackles brighter. This devil, trapped but defiant, taunts Jesus as if to strip off his disguise: "I know who you are—the Holy One of God!" But the devil is also frightened: "Have you come to destroy us?"

The title "the Holy One" is never used in the Old Testament of anyone but God himself—sometimes alone, more often in the phrase "the Holy One of Israel." And the devil is right to associate the designation with destruction; for when God had destruction in mind, "Holy One" is often how he chose to refer to himself. So it was when he chose to humiliate Assyria, the nation that had once been "the club of [his] anger, the cudgel of [his] rage" (Isa. 10:5). When the Assyrians had dared to boast of their victories, this was, for God, "as if a club should wield him who holds it!" (10:15). It was time to incinerate the offender:

> The light of Israel will become a fire, *and his Holy One a flame;*
>   and it will burn and devour his thorns and thistles in a single day.
> The glory of his forest and of his fruitful land
>   the Lord will destroy, both soul and body,
>   and it will be as when a sick man wastes away.
> The remnant of the trees of his woods will be so few
>   that a child will be able to list them.
>
> (10:17–19, italics added)

Alas, as with the promised humiliation of Babylonia after the destruction of Jerusalem, this promised humiliation of Assyria after the conquest of Galilee never came about—not, at any rate, in a way that brought vindication to the Lord's chosen people. Babylonia defeated Assyria, Persia defeated Babylonia, Greece defeated Persia, and Rome Greece, but each time Israel simply changed hands as part of the spoils of war. Taking the gods of those nations to be, as in the Book of Daniel, demons with national assignments, we may see their presence in oppressed Israel as simply part and parcel of the oppression. This particular demon's desire to know whether the Holy One has become incarnate "to destroy us" is the mythic equivalent of Rome's question as to whether it will face an unstoppable Jewish rebellion.

That the Holy One regrets his failure to vindicate the children of Israel may be measured by the inner turmoil he reveals at the prospect of punishing them in the first place. His rage was uncontrollable, yet he could not deny the pain he felt at yielding to it, for

> When Israel was a child, I loved him,
>   and out of Egypt I called my son.
> The more I called them,
>   the more they went from me;
> They kept sacrificing to the Baals,
>   and burning incense to idols.

Because of this, he had resolved to

> Let the sword rage against their cities,
>   consume their limbs
>   and devour their bones.

And yet, and yet:

> How can I give you up, O Ephraim!
>> How can I hand you over, O Israel!
> My heart recoils within me,
>> my pity stirs.
> I will not let loose my fierce anger,
>> I will not again destroy Ephraim;
> For I am God and not man,
>> *the Holy One in your midst,*
> and I will not come in wrath.
>
> (Hos. 11:1–2, 5–6, 8–9, italics added)

The Holy One in their midst was torn in two back then, but, as usual, his rage bested his mercy, and he thrashed Ephraim with Assyria, the club of his anger. Centuries have passed since then, but does God ever forget? The demon in the synagogue has reason to fear that God is belatedly about to complete the agenda he then announced. Even the human observers note that Jesus gives orders "with authority and power." But Jesus himself, though willing enough to claim authority, has seemed reluctant to exercise power, particularly against the political establishment. God was once, with his child Israel, "like someone lifting an infant to his cheek" (NJB Hos. 11:4). But will he now use his power on behalf of his child or not? It seems not, and yet it seems equally remote from his agenda to punish his child any further. As God Incarnate, God seems to have lost his appetite for punishment. He no longer delivers furious oracles against his people, warning that because of the corruption of some—above all, of the king—all must and will suffer the most violent and humiliating of punishments. But if he has ceased to be a threat to his own people, has he ceased as well to be a threat to their enemies? And if so, then on what does he base his continuing covenant relationship with them?

THE MEN OF NAZARETH, INSULTED, TRY TO KILL HIM

From Capernaum, after performing several other healings and exorcisms, Jesus goes to Nazareth,

> where he had been brought up, and [he] went into the synagogue on the Sabbath day as he usually did. He stood up to read, and they

handed him the scroll of the prophet Isaiah. Opening the scroll, he found the passage where it is written:

> *The spirit of the Lord is upon me,*
> *for he has anointed me*
> *to bring good news to the afflicted.*
> *He has sent me to proclaim liberty to captives,*
> *sight to the blind,*
> *to let the oppressed go free,*
> *to proclaim a year of favor from the Lord.*

He then rolled up the scroll, gave it back to the assistant, and sat down. And all eyes in the synagogue were fixed upon him. Then he began to speak to them: "Today this scripture is fulfilled even as you listen." He won the approval of all. They were astonished by the gracious words that came from his lips. (Luke 4:16–22; passage in italics from Isa. 61:1–2)

By quoting Isaiah, Jesus claims that he is both an anointed prophet, a messianic prophet of the sort that Samaria awaited, and a messianic king of the sort that Judea awaited, one capable of setting in motion the wondrous events that Isaiah foretold. Have centuries passed? Are the cities still ruined? No matter: The moment may nonetheless be at hand, for later in the same prophecy that Jesus reads in the synagogue, Isaiah said:

> They shall build up the ancient ruins,
>   they shall raise up the wreckage that was.
> They shall repair the sacked cities,
>   the devastations *of many generations.*
>
>   (61:4, italics added)

Can it ever be too late for God? The question cannot be more real or more current for Jesus' hearers than it is. Christian commentary over the centuries has faulted the Jewish contemporaries of Jesus for failing to grasp that he was preaching spiritual, not material, redemption, but the Lord himself had conditioned his people for centuries to expect material redemption. The Lord made this point not just once but repeatedly, insistently, and aggressively. In the same oracle that Jesus quotes, for example, the Lord promised:

> Aliens shall guard and feed your flocks,
>   foreigners shall be your plowboys and vineyard workers;
> But you, you shall be called the priests of the Lord,
>   men shall speak of you as the ministers of our God;

You shall partake of the wealth of the nations,
   and in their riches you shall glory.
In place of your disgrace you shall have a double portion,
   in place of dishonor you shall have joy.

(61:5–7)

If such a thing is now to come about (and what else would the men in the Capernaum synagogue infer from "Today this scripture is fulfilled even as you listen"?), it will not come about by mere exorcisms and healings. Much more will be required if Israel is to "partake of the wealth of the nations and in their riches . . . glory." God Incarnate has demonstrated his divine power, but can he be a miracle worker on this scale? Can he make political history again as he did when he crushed Pharaoh?

Jesus' neighbors, the people among whom he grew up, are impressed, to a point, but they are skeptical as well: "They said, 'Is this not Joseph's son?' But he answered, 'No doubt you will quote me the proverb "Physician, heal yourself," and tell me, "We have heard about all that happened in Capernaum. Do the same in your own country!"' And he went on, 'Truly I tell you, no prophet is ever welcomed in his own country'" (Luke 4:22–24). Jesus rebukes his neighbors preemptively. He faults them for wanting him to cure diseases and cast out demons before they have made any such request of him. If he had gone no further with his rebuke, he would have dealt with them more or less as we have seen him dealing with others who wanted to predicate their acceptance of him on his exercise of divine power. However, he goes on as if to defend himself against the complaint, which no one has voiced, that his most impressive miracle to date has been performed on behalf of a Roman collaborator.

"There were many widows in Israel, I can assure you," he says,

in Elijah's day, when heaven remained shut [rain did not fall] for three years and six months while a great famine raged throughout the land. Yet Elijah was not sent to any of them but to a widow at Zarephath, a town in the vicinity of Sidon. And in the prophet Elisha's time, there were many lepers in Israel, but none of them was cured—only Naaman the Syrian. (4:25–27)

Jesus' words are targeted, like a boxer's punch, to land where they will hurt most, and they succeed in their intent. Zarephath, the first of the two places Jesus mentions, is in Phoenicia (modern Lebanon), which borders Galilee on the north; Syria, the second place mentioned, borders Galilee on the east. These are, in other words, Galilee's nearest neighbors, the foreigners who might come first to mind. Mentioning them, Jesus reaches back nine hundred years, to the time when God sent the prophet Elijah to a widow in Phoenicia. What he does not say—but does not need to say to a synagogue audience—is that on that occasion Elijah performed a miracle very like the one Jesus has just performed for the royal official: Elijah brought a widow's dying son back to life and health. As for Naaman the Syrian, whom the prophet Elisha cured of leprosy, he was not just a foreigner but, like the royal official in Capernaum, an officer working for a foreign king. Does Jesus mean, outrageously, to suggest that the prophecy that is being "fulfilled even as you listen" will be fulfilled on behalf of Israel's neighbors and enemies rather than on behalf of Israel? The idea is offensive in itself, the more so because it is offered so defiantly right in the Nazareth synagogue: "When they heard this, everyone in the synagogue was furious. They sprang to their feet and dragged him out of town. Taking him up to the brow of the hill their town was built on, they sought to throw him off the cliff, but he passed right through the crowd and walked away" (4:28–30).

"The Lamb of God," John called him. "Destroy this Temple," he himself had dared the authorities in Jerusalem, just after causing the disruption that has made him a marked man. Now, days after his return to Galilee, he has provoked an attempt on his life. Attempts were made on Elijah's life as well, but in the end Elijah did not die but was taken alive to heaven in a fiery chariot. According to some interpreters, as already noted, Elijah was the very messianic prophet whose coming Moses had foretold, the second Moses who had come and gone but would come again when "the Day of the Lord," God's definitive and final intervention in human history, was about to begin. When Jesus claims that the fulfillment of Isaiah's great prophecy is finally at hand, he may well be claiming that he himself is, among other things, Elijah redux, having taken this role over from John the Baptist.

As God Incarnate, Jesus can and does assume and combine the functions of every human intermediary that God has ever used. But to suggest that Elijah, on his return, would deploy his powers on behalf of other nations rather than Israel or even of other nations no less than Israel is to speak a combination of blasphemy and treason. Jesus cannot be surprised that the hearts of his hearers are filled with a mixture of terror and rage.

Clearly, Jesus does not believe that his "good news" for "the afflicted" will be bad news for Israel, but how then will it be good news? The Lord, who sent the prophets and spoke his grand promises through them, may reserve the right to determine what those promises meant and what they mean. But if they no longer mean what they once seemed to mean, then what they do they mean? If "liberty to captives" is about something other than releasing Israel from the prison of foreign rule, then what is it about? God Incarnate would seem to have some explaining to do.

He does his explaining in a long outdoor sermon preached to a crowd too large for any synagogue to hold, expounding a moral vision that has the same paradoxical relationship to Torah that his proclamation of redemption has to prophecy. Before hearing that sermon, however, we must answer the question the men of the synagogue ask: Is this not Joseph's son?

INTERLUDE: THE STORY OF HIS BIRTH

Is Jesus Joseph's son? The answer is yes and must be yes, even though it is not by Joseph's seed that Jesus was conceived in his mother's womb:

> And in the sixth month the angel Gabriel was sent from God
>   unto a city of Galilee, named Nazareth,
> To a virgin espoused to a man whose name was Joseph,
>   of the house of David; and the virgin's name was Mary.
> And the angel came in unto her, and said, Hail,
>   thou that art highly favoured, the Lord is with thee:
>   blessed art thou among women.
> And when she saw him, she was troubled at his saying,
>   and cast in her mind what manner of salutation this should be.
> And the angel said unto her, Fear not, Mary: for thou hast
>   found favour with God.
> And, behold, thou shalt conceive in thy womb,
>   and bring forth a son, and shalt call his name JESUS.
> He shall be great, and shall be called the Son of the
>   Highest: and the Lord God shall give unto him the
>   throne of his father David:
> And he shall reign over the house of Jacob for ever;
>   and of his kingdom there shall be no end.
> Then said Mary unto the angel, How shall this be,
>   seeing I know not a man?
> And the angel answered and said unto her, The Holy Ghost
>   shall come upon thee, and the power of the Highest shall
>   overshadow thee: therefore also that holy thing which
>   shall be born of thee shall be called the Son of God.

(KJV; Luke 1:26–35)

The "virgin birth," as Christian tradition has called it, does not prove that Jesus is God Incarnate but only that he has a divine vocation. There is famous precedent in the Old Testament for divine collaboration in the human conception of those for whom God has special plans. The post-menopausal Sarah—"It had ceased to be with Sarah after the manner of women" (Gen. 18:11)—conceived Isaac with the help of the Lord. Hannah, who was unable to conceive because "the Lord had shut up her womb" (1 Sam. 1:5), conceived Samuel when she prayed to the Lord and "the Lord remembered her" (1:19). Mary's virginal conception of Jesus is merely an intensified variation on an old Israelite theme—in this case, the theme of divine participation in the birth of great leaders of the people. To put this negatively, God could easily have induced conception in a virgin without bringing it about that when she gave birth, he himself should be her baby.

It is the identity of the baby, not the manner of the birth, that is unprecedented, but this Gabriel reveals only in part. The titles that he applies to Mary's unborn son—"Son of the Highest" and "Son of God"—signify divine election, but not necessarily divinity itself. In the repertory of the titles used of Jesus, "the Holy One" as used by the demon in Capernaum is far more august, and even "the Son of Man," used with all the weight that Jesus gives it when calling Nathanael to be his disciple, is more mysterious and far-reaching. Mary is told only that her son is to be the Messiah, the descendant of King David who, ruling as David ruled, will restore Israel to greatness: "He shall reign over the House of Jacob for ever; and of his kingdom there shall be no end."

Here is where Joseph comes in, for it is he, not Mary, who is descended from David (Mary's descent is not mentioned), and therefore it is as Joseph's son that Jesus is of the royal line. Unless Joseph is legitimate in the role of Jesus' father, even though he is not the biological father, then Jesus is illegitimate in the role of messianic Son of David.

So then, yes, the answer to the question, Is this not Joseph's son?, is legitimately affirmative. Because it is, we may say that on Christmas Day in the year One, God became a Jew. When Luke gives Jesus' formal, human genealogy, which he does just after Jesus' baptism, he does so through the paternal, not the maternal, line, describing Jesus as "about thirty years old, being the son (as was supposed) of Joseph, son of Heli, son of Matthat, son of Levi," and so forth. As the genealogy continues, we learn that Jesus' lineage extends back to "son of Nathan, son of

David, son of Jesse," and further back to "son of Perez, son of Judah, son of Jacob." At the end of the line, Jesus is "son of Seth, son of Adam, son of God" (Luke 3:23–38).

No special claim is made for Adam by calling him "son of God." Adam was the child of God in the sense that all human beings may be called children of God. But a solemnity is conveyed nonetheless. In the Old Testament, genealogies tend to be given at times of either transition or inauguration, and the baptism of Jesus—the point in the narrative where Luke inserts this genealogy—is both. Luke's point in giving him a genealogy that stretches back to the very beginning is to enhance the importance of the moment when Jesus begins his career, but there is a secondary and equally important point—namely, that Jesus, besides being a son of David, is also a son of Judah and a son of Adam, which is to say: a Jew before he is the Messiah, and a man before he is a Jew.

As we noted earlier, God could have become human without beginning his human existence in a woman's womb. After his resurrection, he will ascend into heaven, floating upward before the eyes of his followers until "a cloud [hides] him from view" (Acts 1:9). Why could he not simply have floated downward at the start of his career? Would anything be different? The power that "the Christmas story," a story built around an ordinary human birth, seems still to exert after so many tellings is answer enough.

And it came to pass in those days, that there went out a decree from Caesar Augustus, that all the world should be taxed. (And this taxing was first made when Cyrenius was governor of Syria.) And all went to be taxed, every one into his own city. And Joseph also went up from Galilee, out of the city of Nazareth, into Judaea, unto the city of David, which is called Bethlehem; (because he was of the house and lineage of David:) To be taxed with Mary his espoused wife, being great with child.

And so it was, that, while they were there, the days were accomplished that she should be delivered. And she brought forth her first-born son, and wrapped him in swaddling clothes, and laid him in a manger; because there was no room for them in the inn.

And there were in the same country shepherds abiding in the field, keeping watch over their flock by night. And, lo, the angel of the Lord came upon them, and the glory of the Lord shone round about them: and they were sore afraid. And the angel said unto them, Fear not: for, behold, I bring you good tidings of great joy, which shall be to all people. For unto you is born this day in the city of David a Saviour, which is Christ the Lord. And this shall be a sign unto you; Ye shall find the babe wrapped in swaddling clothes, lying in a manger.

And suddenly there was with the angel a multitude of the heavenly host praising God, and saying, Glory to God in the highest, and on earth peace, good will toward men.

And it came to pass, as the angels were gone away from them into heaven, the shepherds said one to another, Let us now go even unto Bethlehem, and see this thing which is come to pass, which the Lord hath made known unto us. And they came with haste, and found Mary, and Joseph, and the babe lying in a manger. And when they had seen it, they made known abroad the saying which was told them concerning this child. And all they that heard it wondered at those things which were told them by the shepherds.

But Mary kept all these things, and pondered them in her heart. And the shepherds returned, glorifying and praising God for all the things that they had heard and seen, as it was told unto them. (KJV; Luke 2:1–20)

The fact that God should have become a man acquires most of its literary interest from the unexpected *kind* of man that God becomes; and it is the character of the adult Jesus that contrasts most strikingly with the character of God as previously revealed. However, that God should have begun his human life as an infant is compelling in a different and opposite way because although men are all different, babies are all alike. Full participation in the human condition requires a beginning in the leveling anonymity of infancy. The adult Jesus of Nazareth, as we have begun to see, has a highly developed, distinctive, and by no means always appealing personality. He provokes reactions that are as contradictory as he is. The infant Jesus of Bethlehem, by contrast, releases emotions that are as simple and uncomplicated as, at this early point, he himself still is. Had God begun his human career, miraculously, as an adult, he would have forfeited all this.

Part of the pathos and the appeal of an infant is the infant's ignorance of the circumstances of his or her birth. Though all babies are alike, all birth scenes are different. Is the baby the daughter of a refugee, or the son of a great athlete? Is the father a wealthy merchant, or a drug-addicted pickpocket? Has the mother died in childbirth? Is the world around the child at war? The circumstances surrounding the birth of Jesus are well calculated to enhance his pathos and his appeal, for noble as his Jewish lineage is, his birth coincides with a humiliating event in the life of the Jews—namely, a census conducted by a foreign power.

In ancient Israel, it was a grievous sin even for the country's own king to conduct a census, perhaps because the practice of people-counting was understood to be a foreign usage connected always and only with taxation and forced labor. In 2 Samuel 24, David conducts a census over the strenuous objections of Joab, the commander of his army; and God, enraged, reacts by sending a pestilence upon Israel that kills seventy thousand on the first day. When God makes Mary and Joseph ciphers in the census of Caesar Augustus, he emphasizes their helplessness—and the helplessness of his own infant self—before foreign power at its most onerous. Whether or not the Messiah will end this kind of humiliation, he will at least have shared it first.

That the census that brings Joseph to Bethlehem is a census of the whole world and not just of Judea makes clear that it is the human condition and not just the Jewish condition that God is taking on—the condition of Judea oppressed by Rome, in the first place, but thereafter that of all oppressed people at the mercy of officious power. What mitigates such vulnerability, as all the world knows, is money, but Joseph and Mary appear to have little in their purse. If they could buy their way into the inn, one assumes that they would do so, but apparently they cannot. They must lay their newborn in a feeding trough, a manger. Where do they themselves sleep? In a classically biblical way, Luke leaves it to us to imagine where they sleep. Tradition has placed the three in a stable, but not all mangers are found in stables. For all the text tells us, they could be sleeping in the open, the adults lying on the ground near the animal feeder that they have turned into a makeshift crib.

An adult of either sex feels an involuntary, instinctual impulse to protect the newborn—the human being in a condition of maximum vulnerability. In the Gospel of Luke, the impulse to protect is both reined in and spurred on by the fact that this newborn is not just a messiah (a christ), but "Christ *the Lord*." The angels call him by the name or title *ho kurios,* which was commonly used in the Greek Old Testament to refer to God himself. As *ho kurios* reduced to the condition of a helpless newborn, baby Jesus has become an icon for infant vulnerability scarcely equaled in all of literature. As W. B. Yeats put it in "A Prayer for My Son,"

> Though You can fashion everything
> From nothing every day, and teach
> The morning stars to sing,
> You have lacked articulate speech

> To tell Your simplest want, and known,
> Wailing upon a woman's knee,
> All of that worst ignominy
> Of flesh and bone.

The infant Jesus is the more intensely an icon of vulnerability because even on the night when the angels are singing "Peace, good will toward men," no one hearing the story of his birth quite forgets the story of his death. Every victim of judicial murder was once a newborn. Jesus' involuntary defenselessness at the beginning of his life mirrors and anticipates his voluntary defenselessness at its end.

> And, behold, there was a man in Jerusalem, whose name was Simeon; and the same man was just and devout, waiting for the consolation of Israel: and the Holy Ghost was upon him. And it was revealed unto him by the Holy Ghost, that he should not see death, before he had seen the Lord's Christ. And he came by the Spirit into the temple: and when the parents brought in the child Jesus, to do for him after the custom of the law, then took he him up in his arms, and blessed God, and said,
>
>> Lord, now lettest thou thy servant depart in peace,
>>   according to thy word:
>> For mine eyes have seen thy salvation,
>> Which thou hast prepared before the face of all people;
>> A light to lighten the Gentiles, and the glory of thy people
>>   Israel.
>
> And Joseph and his mother marvelled at those things which were spoken of him. And Simeon blessed them, and said unto Mary his mother, Behold, this child is set for the fall and rising again of many in Israel; and for a sign which shall be spoken against; (Yea, a sword shall pierce through thy own soul also,) that the thoughts of many hearts may be revealed. (KJV; Luke 2:25–35)

Simeon, inspired by God, not only knows that the infant in his arms is the Messiah; he also divines, as the child's parents do not, what this will mean in practice both for Israel and for the boy himself. Simeon's words are a patchwork of famous phrases from Isaiah, but his rearrangement of them has a point. Though it promises "the glory of thy people Israel," it lays rather more stress on what God will do through Israel for the rest of the world, muting nationalistic or militaristic promises made even in the very passages that he so selectively quotes. The phrase "a light to lighten the Gentiles," for example, occurs at Isaiah 42:6–7 (KJV):

[I will] give thee for a covenant of the people,
　for a light of the Gentiles;
To open the blind eyes, to bring out the prisoners from the prison,
　and them that sit in darkness out of the prison house.

An inspiring vision, but the same passage contains verses in which God announces that, after a long and anguished delay, he is about to unleash his fierce power against Israel's oppressors:

> For long I have kept quiet, held myself at bay,
> 　moaning like a woman in labor,
> 　panting and gasping for air.
> But now I will ravage hill and mount,
> 　will blight all their growth;
> I will turn the torrents into firm ground
> 　and dry up the bogs.
> I will lead the blind by a path they do not know,
> 　by paths they know not will I conduct them.

(Isa. 42:14–16)

Simeon, who is inspired by God, hints that Israel's glory will no longer include all that God once said it would include that it will be other than he said it would be. If that is unsettling, still more so is the revelation that the Messiah will be an ambivalent liberator, one destined for the fall as well as the rise of many in Israel, and that "a sword shall pierce through thy own soul also." When Gabriel first visited Mary, he said nothing of this sword.

Historically, early Christianity faced a difficulty, if not a scandal, in the fact that Christ, for whom it was making such large claims, had gone so nearly unnoticed during his lifetime. Yes, he had attracted followers in some number, as well as a few powerful enemies, but neither his nation nor the world had been brought to a stunned halt by his arrival. In interestingly different ways, all four of the canonical Gospels make literary art of this lack of recognition by pitting Jesus' own knowledge of who he is against the ignorance of even those closest to him: his family and his disciples. The interactions that result from this create much of the forward narrative momentum in the Gospels as the reader begins to strain forward psychologically, seeking an interlocutor who will finally realize the truth. This effect is enhanced by three factors.

First is the fact that somewhere between Jesus' knowledge of himself and others' bafflement stands the partial knowledge of privileged third parties like Gabriel, Simeon, and, paradoxically, Satan. Their statements are always pregnant with a knowledge that they never fully share. They provide the associates of Jesus a hint or a clue and then pass from the scene.

Suspense is served, in the second place, by the fact that what these privileged observers do reveal often has something menacing about it: Simeon's sword, the demon's shriek, or—in the Gospel of Matthew—Herod's attempt to kill the infant Christ by killing every male child two years old or younger. An angel warns Joseph in time, but the reader is reminded of what Jesus' parents, unaided, cannot see—namely, that murderous intentions toward Jesus are written into the script. Of Herod's slaughter, Matthew writes:

> Then was fulfilled that which was spoken by Jeremy the prophet, saying:
>> In Rama was there a voice heard,
>> lamentation, and weeping, and great mourning,
>> Rachel weeping for her children,
>> and would not be comforted
>> because they are not.
>
> (KJV; Matt. 2:17–18, quoting Jer. 31:15)

His adding this quote does nothing, immediately, to clarify the identity of Jesus, but it does much to darken the mood. At this early moment, Jesus is already being hunted.

The third factor complicating the dialogue between knowledge and ignorance that so shapes the Gospel narrative is the intermittent, though always ambivalent, suggestion that Jesus may not fully apprehend his own divine identity. We have seen his odd restraint in dealing with the Devil at the time of his desert temptation. Was he refraining from the use of his power, or was he uncertain himself just how much power he had? We have seen as well his reluctance to perform miracles on request. He faults the petitioners, but does he, despite his confident—not to say arrogant—manner, have some buried doubt about himself? In the Gospel of Mark, he warns the demons who address him as "Son of God" not to make him known (3:12) and gives the same warning repeatedly to his own disciples. Of course, standing in danger of assassination from so early a point, Jesus has a plausible enough motive for secrecy; yet he seems to have deeper, more personal reasons for reticence. On the one hand, he is his own most compelling topic. He brings himself up again and again, saying, for example, to the Samaritan woman: "If you only knew . . . who it is who says to you, 'Give me a drink'" (John 4:10). On the other hand, when his words or deeds attract the spotlight, he wants it turned off. His ambivalence and the reader's uncertainty about what that ambivalence implies deepen both the mystery and the suspense that surround him.

The impression that Jesus' awareness of his own identity progresses through the course of his life is nowhere clearer than in the episode that ends the so-called hidden life of Jesus:

> Now his parents went to Jerusalem every year at the feast of the passover. And when he was twelve years old, they went up to Jerusalem after the custom of the feast. And when they had fulfilled the days, as they returned, the child Jesus tarried behind in Jerusalem; and Joseph and his mother knew not of it. But they, supposing him to have been in the company, went a day's journey; and they sought him among their kinsfolk and acquaintance. And when they found him not, they turned back again to Jerusalem, seeking him.
>
> And it came to pass, that after three days they found him in the temple, sitting in the midst of the doctors, both hearing them, and asking them questions. And all that heard him were astonished at his understanding and answers. And when they saw him, they were amazed: and his mother said unto him, Son, why hast thou thus dealt with us? behold, thy father and I have sought thee sorrowing. And he said unto them, How is it that ye sought me? wist ye not that I must be about my Father's business? And they understood not the saying which he spake unto them. (KJV; Luke 2:41–50)

Jesus, who in his twelfth year believes that he "must be about [his] Father's business," evidently did not entertain this belief about himself when he was eleven. He knows something about himself now that he did not then. Almost equally revealing is the fact that, naively, he expects his parents to know about him what he knows about himself; he expects them not to be surprised. Mature self-understanding always includes a hard-won appreciation of what others are likely to miss of what one knows about oneself. In a single, subtle stroke, Luke tells us that Jesus lacks that kind of maturity. Later, dealing with others, even other intimates, he will anticipate ignorance as here he anticipates knowledge. Later, on the stormy visit to the Temple that we have already reviewed, he will anticipate rejection as here he anticipates acceptance. But at twelve he is different. For now, the boy who can astonish the Temple rabbis with "his understanding and answers" is still just a boy.

HE REPUDIATES HIS WARRIOR PAST

"Is this not Joseph's son?" the men of the synagogue asked when Jesus proclaimed at his inaugural appearance in the Nazareth synagogue, "Today this scripture is fulfilled even as you listen" (Luke 4:21–22). But more, we saw, was involved than the fact that "a prophet is without honor in his own country" (John 4:44). Jesus, reading their minds, knew that they were not pleased that his miraculous cure in neighboring Capernaum had come at the request of an official working for Rome. His response to their resentment had been not to apologize but to compound his offense by reminding them that, centuries earlier, Elijah and Elisha had performed miracles for a Phoenician woman and a Syrian man. Though this was true, the meaning that he seemed to draw from these precedents so enraged them that they attempted to throw him off a cliff.

During the ensuing weeks, Jesus has preached in various Galilean synagogues, performed other miracles, and attracted a growing number of disciples. He has also begun to attract disapproving attention from "the Pharisees and their scribes," the leaders and scholars of a religious movement stressing strict decorum and exact observance of Jewish law. The Pharisees and scribes object, for example, that

> "John's disciples are always fasting and saying prayers, and so also the disciples of the Pharisees, but yours keep eating and drinking." Jesus replied, "Surely you cannot make the bridegroom's friends fast while the bridegroom is yet with them. Still, the time will come when the bridegroom is taken from them. And in those days, they will fast." (Luke 5:33–35)

Though weddings are occasions for joy and festivity, this bridegroom is a marked man. The effect of Jesus' foreboding allusion is to render the scene both darker and more mysterious than it would be as merely a discussion of asceticism versus indulgence. Jesus is clearly becoming something of a celebrated figure, yet he is preoccupied with his own demise. What is his mission? Does he intend to remain in Galilee indefinitely, preaching in one synagogue after another, curing one invalid after another, until his enemies overcome him? If he is the Messiah, the fulfillment of the prophecy that he has claimed to be, then he must intend something more than that, but what will it be? And if this "bridegroom" is not the Messiah, then who or what is he?

The answer comes only when the question has reached critical mass. Because of Jesus' fame as a healer, a great crowd has gathered "to hear him and to be cured of their afflictions. People tortured by unclean spirits were cured as well, and everyone in the crowd was trying to touch him since a power came out of him that healed them all" (6:17–19).

The demons tormenting the possessed should be imagined as shrieking like the demon in the Capernaum synagogue. As for the physically afflicted, Luke tells us that they have come from as far south as Jerusalem and as far north as Phoenicia. In all their distress, these people have been on the road for days. A great crowd of such sufferers not patiently waiting their turn but all trying to touch Jesus at once makes for a scene of extreme emotional and physical agitation.

Mingling with these suffering pilgrims is the growing number of Jesus' local disciples. Just before addressing the throng, he has spent a night praying in the hills and then selected from among them twelve whom he calls "apostles," or emissaries, recalling—inevitably in this Jewish context—the twelve sons of Jacob for whom the twelve tribes of Israel are named, and thereby endowing his personal vocation and this already charged moment with national significance.

In the Nazareth synagogue, the prophecy of Isaiah that Jesus said was being fulfilled even as he spoke was

> The spirit of the Lord is upon me,
> for he has anointed me
> to bring good news to the afflicted.

Since the base meaning of the word *messiah* is "anointed," a defensible translation of Isaiah 61:1 is "He has made me Messiah to bring good news to the afflicted." Very well, the afflicted have gathered in unprecedented numbers: What good news does this messiah have for them in the public address that Christian tradition regards as the most important statement of his ethical teaching?

The news he has for them, whether it can be called good or not, is little short of astonishing, for it is a virtual repudiation of what on innumerable previous occasions God has taught his people to expect of him. Addressing his disciples directly but surrounded by the diseased and insane, Jesus says:

> Blessed are you who are poor, for yours is the kingdom of God.
> Blessed are you who now hunger, for you shall have your fill.
> Blessed are you who now weep, for you shall laugh.

Blessed are you when people hate you, shun you, insult you, and slander your name for the sake of the Son of Man. Rejoice when that day comes, and dance for joy, for, lo, your reward shall be great in heaven. This is the way their forebears treated the prophets.

But woe to you who are rich, for you have had your consolation.

Woe to you who are sated, for you shall hunger.

Woe to you who now laugh, for you shall mourn and weep.

Woe to you when all speak well of you, for thus did their forebears treat the false prophets. (Luke 6:20–26)

In Deuteronomy 27–28, speaking through Moses, God served notice on Israel that if it was obedient, it would be blessed, and if disobedient, cursed. The nature of the blessings and curses, however, could not be more unlike the blessings and "woes" listed above. Obedient Israelites were not to be blessed in the two stages that Jesus speaks of. They were not to be, first, poor, hungry, weeping, hated, shunned, and slandered; then, later, sated, laughing, and joyful. On the contrary, God guaranteed them prosperity and hegemony from the start:

The Lord shall make you abound in possessions: in the fruit of your womb, in the fertility of your herd and in the yield of your soil, in the land that he swore to your forebears that he would give to you. For you the Lord will open heaven, his treasure house of rain, to give your land rainfall in due season, and to bless all your labors. You shall lend to many nations, yet borrow from none. The Lord shall put you at the head, not at the tail; you will always be on the top and never on the bottom, if you heed the commandments of the Lord. (Deut. 28:11–13)

As for the curses on the other side of the ledger, God swore to inflict a bloodcurdling assortment of horrors if Israel transgressed against him, and he listed the transgressions he had in mind. To name just a few:

Accursed be anyone who moves a neighbor's boundary marker. . . .

Accursed be anyone who leads a blind man astray on the road. . . .

Accursed be anyone who violates the rights of the alien, the orphan, or the widow. . . .

Accursed be anyone who has sexual relations with his father's wife. (27:17–20)

The list of possible transgressions was long and detailed, but wealth, satiety, joviality, and good repute—the "woes" of Jesus' list—were not on it.

Speaking through various prophets, God has decried the abuse of wealth, but he has never denounced wealth itself. Through Amos, for example, God said:

> For three transgressions of Israel, and for four,
>   I will not revoke the punishment;
> Because they sell the righteous for silver,
>   and the needy for a pair of shoes,
> They trample the face of the poor into the dust of the earth,
>   and force the afflicted off the road.
>
> (Amos 2:6–7)

But one may search in vain among all God's earlier utterances for a statement like "Blessed are you who are poor" without the promise that God will someday make these poor rich. And as for the poor, so, analogously, for the hungry, the mournful, and the scorned. Though smug self-satisfaction and a self-righteous sense that one is beyond the reach of judgment are condemned, usually because they accompany other, more serious offenses, satiety, happiness, and good repute are consistently regarded as blessings.

It may be objected that Jesus does not really invert the traditional values; he simply expands the time frame in which God may deliver good and ill to all according to their merit. Punishment will still be punishment, on this reading, and reward will still be reward; the delivery of each will simply come in heaven rather than on earth. Yet if even this much is true, Jesus must be seen to have sharply revised the emerging meaning of his miraculous cures. The diseased and disturbed have gathered in such numbers because they expect immediate relief. The claim that Jesus has made for himself is that, more than an ordinary healer, he is the fulfillment of the grandest promises that God has made to his people rather than yet another postponement of it. Those already suffering so grievously have surely not come so far simply to be told that their misery is their blessing inasmuch as, further along, their reward will be so great. Can this redefinition of weal and woe really be the fulfillment of the promise the Lord made through Isaiah?

Jesus, preaching frankly against the promise, does not hesitate to say that indeed it is. His words serve notice, in effect, that he has not come to perform mass healings or mass exorcisms. His healings are mere demonstrations. Most of those who are racked with illness or tormented by demons should not look to him for miraculous healing; rather, they should embrace their affliction as analogous to the mistreatment that his own disciples will encounter for their devotion to "the Son of Man."

Whatever his miracles portend, it is not simple, direct, or, least of all, universal relief from pain.

What follows on this surprise, however, is a far greater one:

> But to you who are listening I say this: Love your enemies, do good to those who hate you, bless those who curse you, pray for those who scorn you. If someone slaps you on one cheek, turn the other cheek as well. If someone takes your outer garment from you, let him have your undergarment as well. Give to anyone who asks of you. If someone takes your property, do not ask for it back. Treat others as you would like them to treat you. If you love those who love you, what credit is that to you? Why, even sinners love those who love them! And if you do good to those who do good to you, what credit is that to you? Again, even sinners do that much. . . . Instead, love your enemies, and do good to them, and lend without any hope of return. Then you shall have a great reward, and you shall be children of the Most High, for he himself is kind to the ungrateful and the wicked.
>
> Be merciful as your Father is merciful. Do not judge, and you will not be judged; do not condemn, and you will not be condemned; forgive, and you will be forgiven. Give, and it will be given to you . . . because by the measure that you use will you be measured. (Luke 6:27–38)

In this sermon, Jesus preaches what he will practice when his enemies come for him and he does not resist them. "Turn the other cheek" has rightly been taken to be his signature teaching. The phrase is used by millions who might not be able to quote anything else that Jesus said and by millions more who do not know that it was he who first said it. It defines him didactically as the Crucifixion defines him dramatically. Yet the popular reception of this sermon, for all the fame it has conferred upon Jesus, has been such as to obscure his deeper originality and his more radical revision of the tradition he inherited.

This has been so because discussion of his ethic of nonresistance to evil has so consistently focused on the application of this ethic rather than on its premise—namely, that human beings must do thus *because God does thus*. But does God in fact do thus? This is a question that interpretation of this passage generally does not ask. Jesus assumes a positive answer to that question without ever asking it, but his assumption elides a drastic revision of the divine identity. When we recall how God has in fact conducted himself in the face of opposition or insult from past enemies, it becomes clear that, though Jesus speaks as if God is now as he always has been, he is in fact revealing (or enacting) an enormous change in God. ☛

God, to repeat, is the model whom Jesus would have us believe that we imitate when we love our enemies, do good to those who hate us, and so forth. If we do all this, he says, we "shall be children of the Most High, for he himself is kind to the ungrateful and the wicked." When urging mercy, Jesus does not say "Be merciful because mercy is better than vengeance." What he says is "Be merciful as your Father is merciful." But how merciful has the Father shown himself to be in his previous career? How kind has the Most High typically been when confronted with the ungrateful or the wicked?

God's classic early characterization of himself comes at Exodus 34:5–7:

> The Lord passed before [Moses] in the cloud and stood with him there, and proclaimed the name of the Lord. The Lord passed before him, and proclaimed, "*Yahweh! Yahweh!* A god merciful and gracious, slow to wrath, and abounding in steadfast love and faithfulness, keeping steadfast love unto the thousandth generation, forgiving iniquity, transgression, and sin, but letting nothing pass and visiting the sins of the parents upon the children and children's children unto the third and the fourth generation."

In this statement, inasmuch as God's love abides "unto the thousandth generation," an unimaginably long time, while his punishment reaches only unto the third and fourth, he may seem to be more loving than wrathful. Even here, however, it is clear that, for him, forgiveness by no means precludes punishment. Sinners may be forgiven, yet their children and their children's children must pay the price. Punishment is never commuted. God lets nothing pass.

It is not principally, however, what God says but what he does that makes him seem a being other than the one whose benignity and neutrality Jesus invokes. The Lord's actions speak much louder than his deeds. Between the Israelites' Exodus from Pharaoh's Egypt and their entry into the promised land of Canaan, to consider only Israelite sinners and only that forty-year period, the Lord executes at least thirty thousand of them. He sees to it that three thousand are put to the sword after the episode of the golden calf in Exodus 32. Later, in Numbers 16, he buries alive some 250 rebellious Levites and Reubenites, along with their wives, their children, and the other members of their households. At a conservative twelve per household, counting concubines and slaves, the total put to death comes to another three thousand. Later still, the Lord fatally poisons an unstated but evidently large number of Israelites when, angry over their complaints of hunger and thirst, he sends "fiery serpents" against them (Num. 21). Finally, after Israelite men consort sexually with the priestesses of a Canaanite god, he slaughters twenty-four thousand (Num. 25). At no point during Israel's desert wanderings does the Lord seem slow to wrath. At one point, much to the contrary, he contemplates exterminating ungrateful Israel altogether and beginning a new nation from the loins of Moses (Num. 14:12). Moses shames him out of this by warning him that he will ruin his reputation back in Egypt and by quoting to his face the "slow to wrath" language of Exodus 34:6.

So much for the Lord's conduct toward his friends. What of his conduct toward his enemies? How does Jesus' characterization of him square with, for example, his characterization of himself to the prophet Habakkuk? In the timber-rattling battle poem found at Habakkuk 3, the Lord portrays himself as a colossus of war who has turned his powers of creation into weapons of destruction, shaking the mountains, gouging riverbeds into the earth, trampling the sea, and terrorizing the very sky. The prophet who receives this vision of cosmic rampage trembles with fear as he alternately describes and prays to the divine warrior who is allegedly coming to his rescue:

> Pestilence goes before him,
>   and plague follows close behind.
> He stands, and the earth quakes,
>   he glances, and the nations quiver.
> The ancient mountains buckle,
>   the ageless hills collapse. . . .
> You carve torrents across the land;
>   the mountains see you and tremble,
> The great floods rush past,
>   the abyss roars aloud,
>   flinging high its waves.
> Sun and moon hide in their houses,
>   take flight at the flash of your arrows,
>   at the glint of your lightning lance.
> In rage you stride across the land,
>   you trample the nations in anger
> As you advance to save your people,
>   to rescue your anointed one.

You stave in the sinner's roof beams,
    you raze his house to the ground.
You split his skull with your bludgeon,
    His warriors you blast away,
They whose joy it was to take us,
    like some poor wretch, to devour in their lair.
With your horses you trample the sea,
    you stir the mighty waters.
When I heard, I was shaken to the core,
    my lips quivered at the sound;
My bones were wrenched loose,
    my legs gave way beneath me.
Numb, I await the day of anguish
    Which will dawn on the people now attacking us.

                        (Hab. 3:5–6, 9–16)

Though Habakkuk's is a uniquely vivid evocation of the divine warrior in action, the Lord offers essentially identical self-characterizations in dozens of speeches to other prophets. And Israel did not fail to take the point but learned to pray to the Lord as just the fearsome warrior he claimed to be. Thus, to choose a typical passage from the Book of Psalms:

God is for us a god of deliverance;
    Lord Yahweh opens an escape from death.
God smashes the heads of his enemies,
    the hairy head of him who walks in guilt.
My Lord said, "I will bring you back from [the mountains of]
    Bashan,
    will retrieve you from the bottom of the sea,
That your feet may wade through blood;
    that the tongue of your dogs may have its portion of your
    enemies."

                        (Ps. 68:20–23)

If what Jesus is saying is correct, then such prayers can no longer be offered. The Lord can no longer be praised for smashing the heads of his enemies, for he is no longer a head-smashing kind of god. But there is no denying that the Lord *has been* a head smasher—both by performance and in endlessly repeated aspiration. If he is such no longer, then he must have changed, but what accounts for the change?

One possible answer is that there will be no answer because the Lord intends that there should be none. Though he insisted, when speaking to Moses, on the clarity and transparency of his words and intentions (Deut. 30:11–12), God has grown more remote and more mysterious as the centuries have passed. During Israel's Babylonian Captivity, he began saying for the first time things like "As the heavens are high above the earth, so are my ways above your ways, my thoughts above your thoughts" (Isa. 55:9). Often enough, Jesus talks the same way. And whether or not God Incarnate will choose to make himself humanly comprehensible, God has certainly never acknowledged at any earlier point any slightest *obligation* along those lines. If we grant that Jesus is God Incarnate, then we must grant as well that he has the right to announce a deep change in God— which is to say, in himself—without quite calling the change by that name and without otherwise troubling to explain it. The Lord of All the Earth does as he pleases.

Yet there is no mistaking—particularly in Matthew's version of the sermon quoted above—that Jesus does indeed intend to claim the authority of God for what he is saying, and in his own way he does indeed wish to explain himself. If Jesus were merely a prophet speaking by divine authorization, we would expect to read: "And then the Word of the Lord came to Jesus of Nazareth, saying, 'Say unto the people of Israel, "Thus says the Lord. . . ."'" But both Matthew and Luke read otherwise. On no authority but his own, Jesus boldly characterizes God and proceeds to derive an arresting new morality from his characterization. The crowds are understandably "astonished at his teaching, for he taught them as one in authority, and not as their scribes" (Matt. 7:28).

Jesus emphasizes that his authority is his own by his repeated contrastive use of the phrase "But I say this to you" to underscore the fact that what he is announcing is an unabashed revision. He says, for example:

> You have heard how it was said, "You will love your neighbor and hate your enemy." *But I say this to you:* Love your enemies, and pray for those who persecute you, so that you may be children of your Father in heaven, for he causes his sun to rise on the wicked as well as on the good, and he sends down rain on the just and the unjust alike (Matt. 5:43–45, italics added)

In Leviticus 19:18, part of which Jesus cites in the passage just quoted, God does not in fact say "you will hate your enemy," but neither does he say "you will *not* hate your enemy." What he says, to quote the verse in full, is "You shall not take vengeance on or bear any grudge *against your countrymen*. Love your neighbor as yourself. I am the Lord." The context is clarifying. Directly contradicting what Jesus implies about him, the Lord most certainly did take vengeance on and bear grudges against his enemies, his enemies being in every case Israel's; and he both expected and, on various occasions, directly commanded Israel to do the same, imposing obligations upon them that were consistent with his vengeful and grudge-bearing character.

The point may be illustrated by the story of the Lord's long-running grudge and ruthless vengeance against Amalek. When Moses led the Israelites from Egypt to Canaan, Amalek was the first of several nations to attack Israel en route. After the attack was repulsed, the Lord swore to Moses: "Record this in writing, and recite it in Joshua's hearing, that I will utterly wipe out the memory of Amalek from under heaven" (Exod. 17:14). Moses built an altar to witness the oath, saying: "The Lord will be at war with Amalek from generation to generation" (17:16). What the Lord swore and Moses solemnly witnessed was, in more modern language, an oath of genocide. The Lord swore that he would exterminate the Amalekites, however long it took. Over the ensuing two centuries, far longer than the four generations of Exodus 34, the Amalekites and the Israelites were, as predicted, repeatedly at war with each other, but Israel gradually grew stronger. Finally, the Lord decided to fulfill his ancient vow to the letter. He summoned King Saul: "I intend to avenge what Amalek did to Israel—laying a trap for him on the way as he came up from Egypt. Now, go and crush Amalek. Put him under a curse of total destruction, him and all that he possesses. Do not spare him, but slay man and woman, child and babe, ox and sheep, camel and ass" (1 Sam. 15:2–3). Saul carried out the order without hesitation, sparing only—for later demonstrative execution and ritual sacrifice in the Israelite shrine city of Gilgal—Agag, king of Amalek, and the prize livestock of the slaughtered tribe. The Lord, however, was indignant that anything Amalekite had been left breathing. He wanted his vengeance enacted exactly as ordered. In his wrath, the Lord stripped Saul of his kingship, leaving the prophet Samuel to complete the genocide:

> Samuel then said, "Bring me Agag, king of Amalek!" Agag came forward on unsteady feet, saying, "And now, the bitter taste of death!" Samuel replied: "As your sword has left mothers bereaved, so shall your mother be left bereaved among women." Samuel then butchered [that is, dismembered] Agag before the Lord at Gilgal. (15:32–33)

The Lord did to the last Amalekite (the mother who would have been left bereaved is already dead) only what Amalek would presumably have done to the last Israelite, given the chance. The point to be made is that when the Lord said, through Moses, "Love your neighbor as yourself," he was not saying anything that Moses or he thought incompatible with the Lord's earlier vow "I will utterly wipe out the memory of Amalek from under heaven." The story of Amalek from first attack to last defeat can quite coherently be read as a gloss on Leviticus 19:18, demonstrating, among other things, that the reference group for the word *neighbor* in that verse is Israel alone. Leviticus 19:34 graciously extends the circle to include aliens peacefully resident in the Land of Israel, but enemies are another matter.

The story of Amalek need not necessarily mean, of course, that Israel is allowed, much less that it is commanded, to hate its enemies to quite the violent extreme that God hates his. The Lord concludes his "love your neighbor" commandment, as typically in the Book of Leviticus, by saying, "[You will] love your neighbor as yourself. I am the Lord." He does not say: "You will love your neighbor as yourself because I, the Lord, love my neighbors as myself, and you must be like me." Conceivably, Israel could be held to a stricter standard of forbearance than the Lord intends to impose on himself. The more natural assumption, however, given the fact that Israel's friends and enemies are essentially indistinguishable from the Lord's, has to be that the Amalekite principle is no less valid for Israel than it is for the Lord.

This would seem to be the point of a revealing episode in 1 Kings 20. The Lord has promised Ahab, the king of Israel, victory over Ben-Hadad, the king of Aram. The battle goes just as promised, but aides to Ben-Hadad advise him: "We have heard that Israelite kings are merciful. Let us dress in sackcloth with cords around our heads [the traditional garb of penitence] and go out to meet the king of Israel; maybe he will spare your life" (1 Kings 20:31). Ahab shows himself merciful indeed, making a generous peace settlement and sparing Ben-Hadad's life. The Lord, however, is furious at this conduct. "You will pay with your life," he tells Ahab, "for having set free a man who was under my curse of destruction. It will be your life for his life, and your people for his" (1 Kings 20:42).

From this, it would seem to follow that God wants his people to be no more merciful (or no less vindictive) than he is. In the Books of Samuel and Kings, no less than in the Gospels, God is the model. And it would seem further to follow that Jesus captures the spirit of the ancient commandment accurately enough when he says: "You have heard how it was said: 'You will love your neighbor and hate your enemy.'"

What Jesus would substitute for this conduct, which at its root is no more than the spontaneous and natural discrimination that everyone past early childhood learns to make between friend and foe, is an unspontaneous and unnatural refusal to discriminate. His followers are called on to treat everyone alike, taking the sun as their model, which God makes to shine without discrimination "on the wicked as well as on the good." If this noble refusal to discriminate would be problematic anywhere in the world, it is doubly so in Israel, for Israel was brought into existence as a nation by an act of undisguised and, in fact, proudly proclaimed discrimination on the part of God. What Moses held up as the pinnacle of divine greatness could not be more remote than it is from the indifferent shining of the sun:

> Did ever a people hear the voice of a god speaking from the heart of fire, as you have heard it, and yet live? Has it ever been known before that a god intervened to bring one nation out of another by such trials, signs, and wonders—war waged with mighty hand and outstretched arm, horrendous terrorism—as the Lord your God has done for you in Egypt before your very eyes? . . . But he loved your forebears and, after them, chose their descendants, and for their sake he personally conducted you out of Egypt, showing forth his mighty power, dispossessing for you nations who were larger and stronger than you, to make room for you and to give you their country as your inheritance. (Deut. 4:33–34, 37–38)

God's covenant with Israel *is* this act of discrimination, and he never equates Israel with other nations except when afire with rage.

Yes, rarely, as through Amos, he may snarl in his fury something like:

> "Are not you and the Ethiopians all the same to me, children
>   of Israel? . . .
> "I brought Israel up from Egypt, oh yes,
>   and the Philistines from Caphtor,
>   and the Aramaeans from Kir.
> "Beware! Lord Yahweh's eyes are on the sinful kingdom.
>   I shall wipe it off the face of the earth!
>   (although I will not destroy the House of Jacob completely),"
>   declares the Lord.

> (Amos 9:7–8)

When he talks this way, the Lord aggressively and insultingly secularizes what Moses has declared sacred. He normalizes what Moses has declared exceptional. Did God bring Israel out of Egypt? Yes, but so what? God is always bringing somebody out of somewhere, is he not? Are the Israelites so vain as to think that they are his special favorites because of a mere population transfer?

But when the Lord talks this way, he taunts Israel only to make a point. The idea that the Exodus was just another population transfer is not one that he entertains for long. As the half-retraction of the closing parenthesis shows, the idea that Israel might be for him just one among the peoples of the world is finally not one he is prepared to act upon. Even on this occasion, even pushed—as he imagines himself—to this extreme, he cannot bring himself to present perfect neutrality as his own behavior in its ideal form. And on innumerable other occasions, he boasts of himself as by no means neutral but, on the contrary, openly and passionately discriminatory.

So, then, what has come over him, now incarnate as Jesus of Nazareth, that he presents himself so differently? As God Incarnate, Jesus surely remembers quite well what he once did to the Amalekites. Surely he remembers as well that he promised no less to Israel's later oppressors. What has driven him to forswear those oaths and assume so utterly different an attitude? The root of the change, as we have seen, is something more radical than an intensified commitment to the mercy, patience, and steadfast love of Exodus 34:6–7, something more than a mere muting of transgenerational revenge. No, Jesus exhorts his hearers to a profoundly counterintuitive, cost-what-it-may disregard for the most basic of human differences, the difference between amity and hostility. What makes this ideal inherently and massively disruptive for God no less than for Israel is the fact that at the time when Jesus preaches it, he has behind him a two-thousand-year career based on acknowledging and exalting one difference above all others—namely, the difference between Israel, the people with whom he has established his covenant, and all other peoples. Israel has been everything to the Lord. Since the time when he first narrowed his focus from mankind in general ("Be fruitful, and multiply") to Abraham ("I will make your offspring like the stars of the sky"), his every word, his every action, has revolved around his chosen people. What could possibly induce him to level to nothing a distinction upon which he has based so defining a personal commitment?

The answer is, in two words, extreme duress. In the greatest crisis of his life, God makes heroic virtue of dire necessity. To appreciate what he faces and how he responds to it, we may consider first how he conducted himself during a similar if somewhat less life-defining time—namely, the time leading up to the destruction of Jerusalem by Babylonia and the abduction of much of his people to their infamous Babylonian Captivity. This was an event that, in principle, could have left Israel without a god, and God without a people. The covenant between them, having been established by God's victory over Pharaoh, was predicated on God's guarantee that no other king or god-king would do as Pharaoh had done: subjugate Israel. By rights, then, once Babylonia did just that, the covenant should have become moot.

It did not become moot, because God had made his protection conditional. It was guaranteed only if Israel would "listen to the commandments of the Lord your God, which I lay down for you today, and then keep them and put them into practice, not deviating to the right or the left from any of the commandments that I impose upon you today, by following other gods and serving them" (Deut. 28:13–14). If Israel was guilty of any deviation, then "the Lord will raise against you from the far ends of the earth a nation like a raptor in flight, a distant nation strange of speech, grim of face, ruthless toward the old, and pitiless toward the young" (28:49–50). By the time of the alien eagle's final victory, the besieged towns of Israel, God warned, would be so desperate for food that "the most dainty and fastidious of your women" would be reduced, after giving birth, to eating their own afterbirth (28:56–57).

Israel did indeed deviate from fidelity to the Lord. According to the sixth-century prophets and the Books of Kings, most Israelites were worshipping other gods at the time of the Babylonian Conquest. The fall of Israel, then, did not reflect negatively on the power of God. This was what he had said would happen. God did not simply withdraw his protection and allow Israel's enemies to have at her. The Babylonian victory, like the earlier Assyrian victory, was not something that had simply befallen Israel, and therefore him. No, he insisted, it was something that he had actively and purposefully *inflicted* on Israel using these seeming conquerors as means to his end.

The Babylonian Captivity was a calamity, then, for which theoretical provision had been made; yet it still felt like something new, unprecedented, and terrible when it finally came about, scarcely less so for the Lord than for Israel. Speaking to the prophet Habakkuk, God said in wonderment at his own employment of Israel's enemies:

Cast your eyes over the nations,
  gape and be amazed to stupefaction.
For I am doing something in your own days
  Which you would not believe if told of it.
Behold, I am stirring up the Chaldeans [Babylonians],
  That fierce and fiery nation
Who march across miles of countryside to seize the homes
    of others.

(Hab. 1:5–6)

Later in that brief but scathingly eloquent book of prophecy, the Lord sends Habakkuk a second vision, in which, as we have seen, the divine warrior marches back into Canaan to wreak vengeance on these very marching and pillaging Chaldeans. The Lord's intent was to establish beyond any shadow of a doubt that both ends of this transaction—both Israel's initial, crushing humiliation and her ultimate, glorious vindication—were his doing and no one else's. But in taking this means to his end, he had to wonder at himself.

Did he achieve his goal? Not necessarily, or entirely, or permanently. True, it may be more painful to imagine that there is no god or that, if there is, you are beneath his notice than to imagine that your god is ruthlessly punitive. After all, a god who punishes may later reward. A god who is in control of the world order, whatever it is, may someday improve it. If this is comfort, however, it is cold comfort; and there were clearly some in ancient Israel who were not willing to wait for it indefinitely. To say this is to recall that the second half of God's punishment-and-rehabilitation promise was never kept. He never delivered the reward that he said would follow on punishment. Yes, some of the Babylonian exiles returned to Israel, but many did not. Yes, a very limited kind of national sovereignty was reestablished, but it did not even include all of traditional Judea, much less all of Israel. In due course, a modest new temple was built, but the divine giant never came striding forth from the mountains of the south, shaking the earth and terrifying the sky as he had said he would. Despite an interlude of relative independence, Israel seemed to be on a road leading downward toward permanent subjugation, worsening, at the whim of its rulers, into outright and brutal oppression.

The psychological cost of this state of affairs, as decades lengthened into centuries, is set forth with grim and grieving clarity in Psalm 44:

God, we have heard for ourselves,
our ancestors have told us,

of the deeds you did in their days,
in days of old, by your hand.
    To establish them in the land you drove out nations,
to make room for them you harried peoples.
It was not their own sword that won the land,
not their own arms which made them victorious,
but your hand it was and your arm,
and the light of your presence, for you loved them.
    You are my king, my God,
who decreed Jacob's victories;
through you we conquered our opponents,
in your name we trampled down those who rose up against us. . . .
Our boast was always of God,
we praised your name without ceasing.
    Yet now you have abandoned and humiliated us,
you no longer take the field with our armies,
you leave us to fall back before the enemy,
those who hate us plunder us at will.
    You hand us over like sheep for slaughter,
you scatter us among the nations,
you sell your people for a trifle
and make no profit on the sale.
    You make us the butt of our neighbours,
the mockery and scorn of those around us,
you make us a by-word among nations,
other peoples shake their heads over us.
    All day long I brood on my disgrace,
the shame written clear on my face,
from the sound of insult and abuse,
from the sight of hatred and vengefulness.
    All this has befallen us though we had not forgotten you,
nor been disloyal to your covenant,
our hearts never turning away,
our feet never straying from your path.
Yet you have crushed us in the place where jackals live,
and thrown over us shadow dark as death.
    Had we forgotten the name of our God
and stretched out our hands to a foreign god,
would not God have found this out,
for he knows the secrets of the heart?
For your sake we are being massacred all day long,
treated as sheep to be slaughtered.
    Wake, Lord! Why are you asleep?
Awake! Do not abandon us for good.

> Why do you turn your face away,
> forgetting that we are poor and harassed?
>   For we are bowed down to the dust,
> and lie prone on the ground.
> Arise! Come to our help!
> Ransom us, as your faithful love demands.
>
> (NJB; Ps. 44:1–5, 8–26)

The remnant that reestablished a national life in Israel was a genuinely faithful remnant; and the greater its fidelity, the less plausible the interpretation of continuing foreign oppression as divine punishment. If the congregations that recited or perhaps sang the poignant words of Psalm 44 knew this, then did God not know it as well? And as he heard it, did it not remind him of his own broken promise, made through so many different prophets, that he would restore Israel to its former glory?

How could it not? But if we imagine that God was not, as Psalm 44 imagines, asleep but simply too weak or that he was for some other, still more mysterious reason no longer willing to impose his will on history, then we have in hand a motive for Jesus' revolutionary sermon. The prospect facing God is that if, on the one hand, he cannot defeat Israel's enemies and, on the other, he can no longer claim that when they slaughter his sheep they are doing his bidding, then he must admit defeat. He must admit that, because of his failure rather than Israel's, the covenant between him and his people has definitively lapsed. His failure will be only the more ignominious for his many boasts that Israel's enemies are nothing but a pack of dogs he has whistled up for his hunt (Isa. 5:26). If those boasts are now exposed as vain, then God may, at most, be honored for his past services. He can no longer be respected for his present power.

God does have, however, one alternative to simply bringing his storied career to an ignominious close. Instead of baldly declaring that he is unable to defeat his enemies, God may declare that *he has no enemies,* that he now refuses to recognize any distinction between friend and foe. He may announce that he now loves all people indiscriminately, as the sun shines equally everywhere, and then urge—as the law of a new, broadened covenant—that his creatures extend to one another the same infinite tolerance of wrongdoing that henceforth he will extend, individually and collectively, to all of them.

Gentiles may imagine that their own goodness, their own attractiveness, was a sufficient motive for God's decision to bring them into the covenant that he had once reserved for the Jews. But if we approach this change from God's side, taking seriously a Bible that presents his covenant with Israel as dwarfing all else in its importance to him, then we must seek the reason for the eventual expansion of the covenant in the troubled state of his role within it. The covenant had to be changed because God could not keep its terms and because, on the eve of a new national catastrophe for Israel, he chose to stop pretending that he could.

The objection may be raised—indeed, must be raised—that it is one thing for God, safe in heaven, to resolve his dilemma by declaring that his erstwhile enemies are now friends, and quite another for human beings, imperiled on earth, to be required to do the same. Clever though it may be for God to excuse himself from the chore of defeating his enemies by declaring that he has none, this is cleverness on the cheap, or so the objection must insist, for it costs him nothing while imposing an unbearable burden on his creatures.

This objection is beyond logical refutation. The radical rejection of human difference, including the difference between friend and foe, does come on the cheap for God—unless and until God becomes a human being and suffers the consequences of his own confession. But in the story we are reading God has become a human being, and we may now begin to see why he has done so. Israel will be slaughtered like sheep, but God has become a lamb. He has made virtue of necessity, yes, but the virtue is real virtue. It is the heroic ideal of universal love.

INTERLUDE: THE ROMAN *SHOAH* AND THE DISARMAMENT OF GOD

Why did God become a Jew and subject himself to public execution by the enemy of his chosen people? He did so in order to confess that, by choice or of necessity, he was a god disarmed. He knew that genocide against his chosen people was imminent and that he would do nothing to prevent it. The one thing he could choose to do, as the Jew he became, was to break his silence about his own scandalous inaction.

God revealed to the seer Daniel at the court of the king of Babylon that when Babylon fell, the kingdom of God would not come immediately. Instead, there would come—in a succession symbolized in Daniel's vision (Dan. 7) by a series of beasts—the kingdoms of the Babylonians, the Medes, the Persians, and the Greeks of Alexander the Great. Only then would God's kingdom come, symbolized in the vision by "one like a son of man." But as the Gospel opens, instead of God's kingdom, there has come the kingdom of the Romans, and the iron fist of this new Babylon is tightening around Judea in the last decades before a catastrophic rebellion. If, as the Book of Daniel makes clear, God foresees the historical future in detail, then he knows that he will not rescue his people from the defeat that lies ahead. Rome, enraged by Jewish rebelliousness, will perpetrate genocide, and God will do nothing. The one thing he can do—and does do as Jesus of Nazareth, God the Son—is break his silence about his own inaction.

The word *genocide* above refers to the ferocious escalation of violence that took place in the generation immediately after the execution of Jesus and came to its first climax with a Jewish revolt against Rome in 66–70 C.E. The Jews were a formidable opponent for imperial Rome. They were, more than is sometimes remembered, populous, well organized, well financed, and passionately motivated. Rome did not finally defeat them and suppress their rebellion until after it peaked for a second time, in 132–135 C.E. After this final Jewish revolt, an uprising led by the messiah Simon Bar Kokhba, Rome changed the name of Jerusalem to Aelia Capitolina and made it a capital offense for any Jew to set foot in the erstwhile City of David. Jewish sovereignty in the Land of Israel then came to an end for fully eighteen centuries.

Rome's imperial agenda did not extend to the extermination of all the Jews of the empire. In that one regard, the Roman suppression of world Jewry's bid for freedom differed from the Nazi "Final Solution" of 1941–45. In two other regards, however, Rome's victory in its sixty years' war with the Jews may plausibly bear the grim designation *genocide*. First, the Roman intent in destroying the Jewish Temple was to end the distinctive national life that the Jewish people had led as a nation within the empire. Second, the portion of the world Jewish population that perished in the first of the Jewish Wars alone is comparable to the portion that perished in the Nazi *shoah*.*

Contemporary estimates of the world Jewish population in the first century range from a low of 5.5 million to a high of more than 8 million. Of these, 1 million to 2.5 million lived in Palestine; 4.5 million to 6 million lived in the diaspora. In the years before the doomed uprisings, the Jews of the Roman empire, notwithstanding worsening oppression within their homeland, were more numerous, more powerful, and better

---

*I use this Hebrew noun, which means simply "catastrophe," in preference to the more usual *holocaust,* a word that some find offensive because its original setting is in the Jewish religion itself. *Shoah* is the noun most commonly used in Israel to refer to the slaughter of the Jews of Europe during World War II.

organized within the greater multinational social order of their day than were the Jews of Europe before the outbreak of World War II. Their remarkable unity—all Jews looking to Jerusalem as their spiritual capital and all supporting the Temple by the payment of a Temple tax—mimicked the organization of the Roman empire itself. This political coherence was admired by the other, less autonomous peoples of the empire, but it was understandably suspect in the eyes of the imperial authorities themselves.

Perhaps because of latent Roman resentment of Jewish success within the empire, not to mention various officially conceded Jewish legal exemptions and privileges, the Jewish revolts were put down with exceptional violence. The first-century historian Josephus, a Romanized Jew, reports that 1.1 million died in Titus's siege of Jerusalem in 70 C.E. The Roman historian Tacitus estimates six hundred thousand dead. Though many modern historians have regarded these numbers as exaggerations, Josephus in reporting his figure recognizes that it will seem incredible and explains that Passover pilgrims from the diaspora had swollen the resident population of Jerusalem to a degree that, though not out of the ordinary for this pilgrimage city, might well seem unbelievable to outsiders. He then engages in a surprisingly modern back-calculation from the number of animals slain for the feast—256,500—to a Passover population of 2,700,200 at the time the siege began.

Jerusalem in that era, it must be remembered, was like Mecca in our own: the site of an astounding annual concentration of pilgrims, overwhelmingly male, for whose ritual purposes an equally astounding number of animals were slaughtered. When the Roman siege began, the temporary population of Jerusalem was further swollen by refugees from parts of Palestine where Roman forces had already, and with great force, been putting down the Jewish rebellion for three full years. In view of all this, the large casualty figures quoted by Josephus and Tacitus are not as implausible as they might otherwise seem.

Even adjusting those figures downward, however, it seems clear that the first-century slaughter of the Jews of Palestine was large enough to be comparable in its impact to the twentieth-century slaughter of the Jews of Europe. The destruction of the Temple in and of itself would have had a major psychological impact, but this loss came coupled with staggering casualties; mass enslavements and ensuing depopulation in the promised land; and, not least, the memory of hideous atrocities. Generally faulted for obsequiousness toward Rome, Josephus does not flinch from reporting terror-crucifixions outside the walls of Jerusalem—mass crucifixions aimed at driving the defenders of the city to despair and panic—or from reporting that when some of the defenders did flee, Roman mercenaries took to disemboweling them in search of swallowed gold coins until stopped by the Roman commander himself.

Tales like these bear comparison with the grisliest from the Nazi concentration camps. The memory of them, combined with so devastating a loss of life in the Promised Land and with major pogroms against Jews in a number of cities within the Roman empire, can scarcely fail to have raised many of the radical or desperate questions about God that, to some, seem to have arisen for the first time in the twentieth century. As for radical or desperate answers to those questions, one seems to have been the Christian vision of the divine warrior self-disarmed.

Historically, there is little doubt that the Jews who rose against Rome expected that their God would come to their assistance, as he had in the historic victories whose celebration remains central to Judaism. There can be equally little doubt that these rebels, as they imagined the God who would assist them, imagined him as knowing the future in detail. This is the image of God expressed so vividly in the Book of Daniel. Literary criticism attending to the character of God within the Old Testament and the New is free to accept this understanding of God (as well as the time and place of the Book of Daniel as given in the text) and then to stipulate about God, as we have done earlier in this book, that, from the Babylonian exile onward, his character is such that he knows the future in the detailed way that human beings know the past.

Yet to imagine a first-century Jew imagining God in this way, even before the disastrous Jewish Wars, is to imagine a Jew in distress. Instead of the predicted kingdom of God, there has come the kingdom of the Romans, and its oppressiveness dwarfs that of all previous oppressors. What was a devout first-century Jew reading the Book of Daniel in a trusting, straightforward, precritical way to think as he or she noted its disconfirmation by events? Had God been mistaken? Had he failed to foresee the rise of Rome? What the radical reversal in the divine identity implied by the pacifist preaching of Jesus suggests is that a Jewish writer of powerful imagination projected this crisis of faith into the mind of God, transforming it into a crisis of conscience. God had broken his own covenant, and the fact that he had broken it had to matter to him. He knew he should have stopped Rome. He knew he had not done so. From that simple notion, a composition of enormous complexity could be derived.

A good many historical critics, it should be noted, have based their reading of the Gospels on speculation about the historical consciousness of Jesus. Beginning with Albert Schweitzer in 1901, many have believed that Jesus—living under Roman rule, intensely aware of Jewish tradition, and experiencing what we would call cognitive dissonance between the two—inserted himself into the apocalyptic mythology of his day by personifying the "son of man" image of Daniel 7 and then identifying himself as the personage in question. Jesus believed, Schweitzer concluded, that by his own agency and, finally, his own death, Rome would fall, history would end, and God's Kingdom would be established for all time.

More recent scholarship tends to believe that this and related, more or less learned scriptural identifications were made not by Jesus during his lifetime but only about Jesus after his death. So it may well have been, yet the protagonist of the Gospels as we encounter him on the page acts *as if* he has made these identifications himself, and on this literary datum may be grounded an interpretation in which historical speculation about the remembered mind of Jesus yields to literary speculation about the imagined mind of God at that historical juncture. For literary purposes, in other words, it does not matter whether the historical Jesus referred to himself as "Son of Man" or not, so long as the literary character Jesus Christ does so on the page. Nor need it matter that the effect this character produces on the page, as the page is read by some contemporary interpreter, may not have been intended by all or even by any of the writers who produced the Gospels. It is proper to a literary classic that it touch readers generation after generation, century after century, in ways that transcend the intentions of the originating author.

But having gone thus far in claiming space for a literary reading of the Gospels, let me immediately concede that nonhistorical readings vary in the degree to which they are informed by history. A fantastical or mystical or morally didactic reading, for example, might prescind almost entirely from historical information. The reading offered in this book, by contrast, admits history roughly to the extent that it is admitted in the interpretation of a historical novel. Moreover, though one does not read a historical novel in order to extract history from it, a general awareness of historical time and geographic place colors and contributes to the aesthetic effect, which, as interpreted, may be historically suggestive without entailing any outright historical claim.

Against the usual Christian spiritualization of the Old Testament, the interpretation offered here is, then, a relative materialization of the New Testament, in which God's real-world, land-and-wealth-and-offspring promises to the Jews are expected to remain on his mind—which is to say, on Jesus' mind—and in which they are allowed, without shame, to remain on his hearers' minds as well. What such an interpretation of the Gospels suggests about the historical situation behind them is that a theodicy—a moral justification of the behavior of God—whose plausibility had survived several centuries of fluctuating foreign oppression finally came into crisis under the steadily worsening Roman oppression of the first century.

According to the received theodicy, first formulated after Israel was conquered by Assyria and Babylonia, that double defeat did not mean what it seemed to mean. The Lord's victory over Egypt had been a real victory, but his apparent defeat by Assyria and Babylonia was not a real defeat. No, Assyria and Babylonia were actually tools in the hands of the Lord, who, far from defeated, was in perfect control of events and merely punishing Israel for its sins. Painful as it might seem to accept the claim that a national god who had once been so favorable had now turned hostile, the alternative was the loss of that god as a potential future support and protection. Since Israel's sense of itself as a people had become inseparable from its sense of covenant with the Lord, life with him even in an angry and punitive mood was preferable to life altogether without him.

By the expedient of attributing its enemies' victories to the action of its own god, Israel saved that god from suffering the same kind of defeat that Israel itself had suffered. But the price of this expedient was high. It required a massive inculpation of the people of Israel—a blaming of the victim, if you will—and an uncomfortable emphasis on anger and vindictiveness in the characterization of the god. Even at the start, these features of the theodicy were felt to be so costly that it was necessary to add, when presenting it, that God would not always conduct himself thus. Israel's national good fortune would be restored before long, and with it a much happier relationship between the god and his people.

But for how many centuries of continuing oppression, especially as different oppressors succeeded one another, could this revision of the covenant remain adequate? The historical suggestion implied by the literary reading of the Gospels offered here is that for a significant segment of the Jewish population, a further revision came to seem necessary. It became necessary to concede the obvious and to redefine the Lord as a god whose return to action as a warrior was not just delayed but altogether canceled, and then to adjust his warlike character accordingly. Not the least part of this adjustment was a revision of his relationship to the other nations of the world; for if the Lord could no longer function effectively as anybody's enemy, then he was necessarily everybody's friend. And if his covenant love was now indiscriminate and universal, then so also must be the love of his covenant partner.

Israel, as God's partner in the original covenant, was expected to demonstrate its status as such by its exclusive devotion *to the Lord*. As the new covenant is proclaimed, Israel's sin, its infidelity and failure to be exclusive in its devotion, is more forgotten than forgiven. The God who will no longer reward or punish his covenant partners as he once did can no longer require of them what he once required. Henceforth, it is not their devotion to him but their devotion to one another and, even more remarkably, to strangers that will signal their status as his. To the extent that they keep this one commandment, to that extent the divine warrior will be excused from ever again taking up arms. Israel will have no enemy because no one will have an enemy other than Satan, the enemy of all.

God Incarnate does indeed understand himself to be, as to his human identity, the "Son of Man" of Daniel 7. But in this capacity, rather than establish the Kingdom of God by military force, he preaches military renunciation: He urges his followers to turn the other cheek. Going dramatically beyond even that, he reveals what he will *not* do—what no one any longer must expect him to do—by going without protest to his own execution on the gallows of the oppressor. The covenant revision is communicated, in sum, not only by prophetic preaching but also by a traumatic, cathartic, climactic, and, not least, ironic sacred drama in which the central role is played by God himself.

Did the historical Jesus actually foresee the worst for his nation, despair of anything like divine rescue, and then—by a bold but conceivable modification of Israelite prophecy—infer that, rather than the prophet of God, he was God himself become incarnate to turn the bad news into an ironic kind of good news? As noted, the all-but-universal assumption on the part of contemporary historical critics is that others turned Jesus into Christ and then into God after his death.

I myself, rather than suppose that Jesus was a simple preacher drafted, as it were, against his will into a larger role, find it historically more plausible to suppose that he was complicitous in his own mythologization, a messenger who intended somehow to become the message, a provocateur who stimulated others to further provocation. Israel Knohl* and Michael O. Wise† claim, on evidence from the Dead Sea Scrolls, to have

The Messiah Before Jesus: The Suffering Servant of the Dead Sea Scrolls (Berkeley: University of California Press, 2000).

† *The First Messiah: Investigating the Savior Before Christ* (San Francisco: HarperSanFrancisco, 1999).

identified historical figures who, before Jesus, believed themselves or were believed by their followers to be divine, suffering messiahs. One need not accept the exact identifications they propose to recognize that, on the evidence they adduce, the idea of combining these elements— divinity, suffering, and messianism—had grown religiously plausible in Palestinian Jewry well before its Christian enactment.

The new research has attracted as much attention as it has because a chasm separates the claim that the Messiah must suffer from the far bolder claim that the suffering messiah is God Incarnate. And, to be sure, even though Jesus makes this claim in the Gospel of John, it remains possible that the idea behind the claim may not in fact have emerged until decades after his death—that is, until closer to the time when the Gospel of John was written. A careful and conservative scholar, the late Raymond E. Brown, asked forty years ago in his great commentary on John

> whether there is any likelihood that Jesus made such a public claim to divinity as that represented in [John 8:58, "Before Abraham was, I AM"], or are we dealing here exclusively with the profession of faith of the later Church? As a general principle it is certainly true that through their faith the evangelists were able to clarify a picture of Jesus that was obscure during [his] ministry. However, it is difficult to avoid the impression created by all the Gospels that the Jewish authorities saw something blasphemous in Jesus' understanding of himself and his role. There is no convincing proof that the only real reason why Jesus was put to death was because he was a social, or ethical, reformer, or because he was politically dangerous. But how can we determine scientifically what the blasphemous element was in Jesus' stated or implied claims about himself? In the clarity with which John presents the divine "I AM" statement of Jesus, is he making explicit what was in some way implicit? No definitive answer seems possible on purely scientific grounds.

There, as it seems to me, the matter still rests. I am content, however, to leave further discussion of this point to the historians, for the explosion of religious and literary creativity that turned material defeat into spiritual victory is no less remarkable as the achievement of Jesus' Jewish contemporaries after his death than as his own creation. The spectacle of the Lord of Hosts put to death by the enemy ought, in principle, to have ended forever a covenant predicated on the Lord's ability to protect his friends and defeat their foes. In practice, for those who made the commemoration of that awful spectacle a covenant ritual, its meaning was that a new covenant between God and mankind had taken effect that was immune to defeat, a covenant that could withstand the worst that Satan, standing (as in the Book of Revelation) for all historical enemies past or future, could inflict. Whatever provoked this brilliant adjustment of the idea of covenant (and scholars, significantly, are unanimous that the Gospels were all written after the destruction of Jerusalem in 70 C.E.), it is conceptually analogous to the adjustment made when the victories of Assyria and Babylonia were defined as the punitive actions of God. The far-reaching implications of this revision are a matter to which we shall return at the start of Part Four. What the revision creates, in the end, is a new theodicy, a new way of maintaining that there is still a god and that he still matters in the face of historical experience to the contrary.

While I was at work on this book, Rabbi Ovadia Yosef, the spiritual leader of Israel's right-wing Shas party, created a scandal by suggesting in a sermon that the Jews who suffered and died in the Nazi Shoah may have died because of Jewish sin. When this statement came up in conversation in Los Angeles, a friend of mine recalled with anger and sadness that, as a boy in the 1940s, he had heard the rabbi in his Orthodox *shul* preach this interpretation of the Shoah not just once but repeatedly. Reactions *against* such statements—including both my friend's anger and the scandal that erupted in Israel over Ovadia Yosef—are, of course, as much a part of contemporary Jewish thought as are the statements themselves, but the sadness and the scandal are instructive for anyone attempting to make sense of Jesus.

How did the divine warrior end up preaching pacifism? Christian theology has tended to speak of this change as spiritual growth in God, though rarely using a phrase like "spiritual growth." The answer suggested here is that God made a new human virtue of his divine necessity. He found a way to turn his defeat into a victory, but the defeat came first. For some, to be sure, no divine defeat is so devastating as to extinguish forever the hope of victory. But for others, considering the number and magnitude of the defeats, a different conclusion has seemed inevitable: If God must be defined as a historical-time, physical-world warrior whose victory has simply been postponed indefinitely, then there might as well be no such god. Indefinite postponement is tantamount to cancellation. Effectively, after such a conclusion, the only choices left are atheism or some otherwise unthinkably radical revision in the understanding of God.

This is a question that is called with devastating starkness in Elie Wiesel's *Night* (1958):

The SS hanged two Jewish men and a youth in front of the whole camp. The men died quickly, but the death throes of the youth lasted for half an hour. "Where is God? Where is he?" someone asked behind me. As the youth still hung in torment in the noose after a long time, I heard the man call again, "Where is God now?" And I heard a voice in myself answer: "Where is he? He is here. He is hanging there on the gallows."

If God will not rescue us, then is there a god? If there is and he still will not rescue us, then is he a weakling or a fiend? It should go without saying that Wiesel did not write this scene as an apology for Christianity. But the scene cannot fail to evoke the Crucifixion for Christian readers, and Wiesel cannot have failed to notice and intend this.

In sum, the disarmament of the divine warrior in the first century mirrors, though with different consequences, his disarmament in the twentieth century. The dedication to *The Prophets,* the most widely read of the books of the late Abraham Joshua Heschel, the most influential Jewish theologian of the twentieth century, reads:

TO THE MARTYRS OF 1940–45

All this has come upon us,
Though we have not forgotten Thee,
Or been false to Thy covenant.
Our heart has not turned back,
Nor have our steps departed from Thy way
. . . for Thy sake we are slain. . . .
Why dost Thou hide Thy face?

—*from Psalm 44*

Heschel had every reason to think of these lines—from Psalm 44, quoted in full above (pp. 106–08)—when thinking of the martyrs of 1940–45, but other Jews nineteen centuries before him, thinking of other martyrs, had no less reason to turn to the same Psalm. And one of them, whether or not the one in question was Jesus himself, may have gone on—like the Jew witnessing the hanging in *Night*—to imagine that the Jew on the gallows, this time, was truly God himself.

THE PRICE OF HIS PACIFISM: JOHN IS MURDERED

At the time when Jesus declared that the prophecy "He has sent me to proclaim liberty to captives" was "fulfilled even as you listen," John the

Baptist was an actual captive hoping for a proclamation of liberty. Herod Antipas, the ruler of Galilee, had had him arrested for daring to criticize Herod's incestuous marriage. If Jesus was all that John had said he was at the Jordan, not to speak of all that Jesus himself had claimed to be in Nazareth, then was John's freedom at hand?

Before Jesus' sermon, John might have raised that question hopefully. Afterward he raises it with a clear undercurrent of anxiety. If Jesus is telling him to love the treacherous Herod, emulating God the Father, who allows his sun to shine equally on debauched kings and ascetic preachers, then has John been mistaken about Jesus? Was he deluded when he said, "I am unfit to loosen the strap of his sandal," and predicted, "He will baptize you with the Holy Spirit and fire"? Or did he fail to realize just what he was saying when, in a very different vein, he saluted Jesus as "the Lamb of God"? A prophet speaking the word of God rather than simply his own words may not always grasp the full import of everything the Holy Spirit prompts him to say. That phrase came from nowhere and, at the time, seemed to go nowhere. Does John begin to see where it can lead?

The implications of Jesus' words may escape some, but they will not have escaped John, who, immersed in Jewish tradition, cannot expect the divine warrior to declare himself a noncombatant. As for Jesus, as this query reaches him, though he respects John as the last and finest flower of the tradition he is revising, he does not defer to him—an aloofness that John and his followers cannot fail to sense. "Through the time of John," Jesus will later say, "it was the Law and the Prophets. From that point forward the Kingdom of God has been preached, and the world has been challenged to enter it" (Luke 16:16). John's preaching ("The axe is laid to the root" and so forth) assumed that God did indeed have enemies and would unhesitatingly treat them as such. If Jesus is now saying something disturbingly different, John cannot miss the implications for his own grim situation. Capricious murder has been the hallmark of the Herodian dynasty, and John is at the mercy of a Herod.

In the immediate aftermath of his sermon, Jesus briefly resumes his activity as an itinerant healer. Then there comes a terse query from the desert prophet who had baptized not only Jesus but all his disciples as well:

John, summoning two of his disciples, sent them to the Lord to ask, "Are you the one who is to come, or are we to expect someone else?" When the men reached Jesus, they said, "John the Baptist has sent us to you to ask, 'Are you the one who is to come or are we to expect someone else?' At that very time [Jesus] was healing many people of illnesses and afflictions and of evil spirits, and bestowing sight upon many who were blind. So he answered them, "Go and tell John what you have seen and heard: The blind see, the lame walk, lepers are cleansed, the deaf hear, the dead are raised to life, the good news is preached to the poor. Blessed is he who finds me no hindrance to faith." (Luke 7:18–23)

No hindrance to faith! Jesus evades the question but correctly guesses its motive. Though he tries to make the question answer itself, he concedes that to someone like John, the work of Jesus, interpreted as Jesus himself has lately been interpreting it, could indeed be an obstacle to faith and worse: a crushing disappointment. That is, Jesus' preaching could arouse doubt that God was coming in power to liberate his suffering people.

John and Jesus understand each other well, though they couch their exchange in the veiled language that might be expected when one man is behind bars and the other might at any time be accused of sedition. Jesus knows to whom John's oblique (at least to the Romans) "one who is to come" refers. John hears the silence when Jesus omits "and prisoners are set free" from his long list of authenticating signs. Jesus offers his miracles as his authentication, yet the frame he places around them suggests an agonizing reappraisal of just what it is that Israel—and John— should hope for from God.

Knowing that his words will hurt John when they reach him in his cell at Herod's sumptuous court, Jesus speaks of John to his own disciples admiringly, ruefully, and defensively—but not before John's disciples have left:

What did you go out into the desert to see? A reed trembling in the breeze? No? Then what did you go out to see? A man dressed in fine clothes? Look, those who dress in finery and live in luxury are to be found at royal courts. Then what did you go out to see? A prophet? Yes, I tell you, and more than a prophet. It is of him that it is written: "Behold, I send my messenger in advance to prepare a path before you." I tell you, of all those born to women, there is none greater than John. . . . And yet, the least in the kingdom of God is greater than he." (7:24–28)

God, even God Incarnate, does not apologize. From the first word of Genesis to the last word of Revelation, his manner bespeaks perfect moral certitude. God never admits doubt about any word he ever says or any action he ever takes. What he does allow himself to express, on rare occasions and in sometimes veiled language, is regret, and this is one of those occasions. In the clutches of Herod, a quisling whom even his Roman paymasters despise, John is an all-too-perfect personification of Israel under Roman rule abetted by Jewish collaboration. Moreover, John's plight all too precisely reflects the setting of at least half the Psalms: An innocent man in danger turns to God for help, imploring the Lord of the covenant to unleash his fabled powers and avert disaster. Jesus receiving a plea with a Psalm written between its lines from an exceptionally good man in exceptional peril is all too like God hearing Israel's pleas and failing to answer them.

John is laconic, but his situation speaks for itself, and what it says—to borrow a verse from a typical Psalm—is:

> O Lord, be not far off.
> O my strength, come quick to my aid.
> Save my life from the sword,
> my one and only life from the fangs of their dogs.
>
> (Ps. 22:19–20)

John presents in person the devastating cost of Jesus' revision of the covenant. From prison, the Baptist sends for a clarification, and, to his sorrow, he gets one. In this exchange, he is the representative of Israel, the devout Jew par excellence, hearing from God the painful news that the covenant promises will not be kept, or will be kept only in so different a way that they amount to an entirely new covenant.

God has alluded before to the possibility of a new covenant based on something other than the kind of military victory that began the old covenant and might portend the rescue of a prisoner like John, but *alluded* is indeed the right word. This possibility has been marginal, almost theoretical, an exception scarcely expected to become a new rule. Speaking through Jeremiah, in measured prose rather than in the excited poetry usual on such occasions, God did once foresee such a state of affairs:

> Behold, a time is coming when I will make a new covenant with the House of Israel and the House of Judah. It will not be like the covenant I made with their forebears when I took them by the hand to bring them out of Egypt (a covenant that they broke, even though I was their Lord). For this will be the covenant that I will make with the House of Israel when the time comes—I will plant my law *within*

them, writing it in their hearts. Then I shall be their God, and they will be my people. No longer will they need to teach neighbor or brother, saying, "Heed the Lord." For they will all heed me, from the least to the greatest, since I shall have forgiven their iniquity and will never again call their sin to mind. (Jer. 31:31–34)

This "new covenant" does not begin, as the old one did, with victory over an oppressor, and no reference is made to punishment, only to forgiveness. Among so many other passages (no less in Jeremiah than in other books of prophecy) that foresee the return of the mighty hand and outstretched arm of Deuteronomy, this passage stands out for its hint—it is no more than a hint—that a covenant between God and Israel might continue to exist even if, for whatever reason, God were to lay down his arms.

Jesus' message to John need not be cause for absolute despair, then, and yet it cannot fail to be a bitter disappointment. What Jesus is telling John is that he who so eloquently preached the Lord's return in power may well die at the hands of his captors. And this is exactly what happens next:

[Herod had had John] chained up in prison because of Herodias, his brother Philip's wife [and his own niece], whom he had married. For John had told Herod, "It is against the law for you to have your brother's wife." As for Herodias, she was furious with [John] and wanted to kill him, but she was not able to do so because Herod was in awe of John, knowing him to be a good and upright man, and he gave him his protection. When he heard him speak, he was greatly troubled, yet he liked listening to him.

Herodias got her chance on Herod's birthday, when he gave a banquet for the nobles of his court, for his army officers, and for the leading figures in Galilee. When the daughter of the same Herodias came in and danced, she delighted Herod and his guests; so the king said to the girl, "Ask me anything you like and I will give it you." And he swore an oath to her: "I will give you anything you ask, even half my kingdom." She went out and said to her mother, "What shall I ask for?" And she replied, "The head of John the Baptist." The girl at once rushed back to the king and made her request: "I want you to give me John the Baptist's head, immediately, on a platter." The king was deeply distressed, but, thinking of the oath he had sworn and in front of his guests, he was reluctant to go back on his word to her. Next thing, the king sent one of the bodyguards with orders to bring John's head. The man went off and beheaded John in the prison; then he brought the head on a platter and gave it to the girl, and the girl gave it to her mother. When John's disciples heard about this, they came and took his body and laid it in a tomb. (Mark 6:17–29)

The story of the murder of John the Baptist is as sparing in detail and restrained in tone as the story of the binding of Isaac. When a detail is included, such as the platter that the girl asks for, it attracts attention by its very isolation. In Richard Strauss's expressionist opera *Salome,* the young dancer actually cradles the bleeding head in her arms as she sings to it of decadence and desire. In Mark, more realistically, she asks that it be brought on a platter. She cannot have been eager to handle it before delivering it to her monstrous mother—or so we are left to guess. (How did the guests react? the reader wonders. Mark, in his biblical way, holds his tongue.)

Style aside, the murder of John is as much a gloss on Jesus' "Love your enemies" as the story of the Amalekites is a gloss on Moses' "Love your neighbor." It matters that John not only loses his life but loses it in a hideous way to contemptible people. Herodias is worse than a Lady Macbeth. Herod Antipas is worse than, or less than, a Macbeth. He is a man of idle curiosity whose simpering good intentions crumble under pressure like a sugar sculpture. Herod's willingness to turn murder into entertainment would strike a Jewish audience as quintessentially and revoltingly Roman. So too, perhaps, might his effete susceptibility to his wife's manipulation: "Give not your strength to women," the Book of Proverbs says, "your ways to those who ruin kings" (31:3). As for Herodias, her cynicism in making her own child an accomplice to assassination is the worst possible indictment of the debauched, deracinated subculture to which she belongs.

Yet the deepest, most traumatic transaction in this episode is the one that takes place silently between John and Jesus: John, who appears only as a severed head carried in on a platter, and Jesus, the price of whose teaching is here on display even as his own death is foreshadowed. When the guards seized John in his cell, did he resist them? Did he bare his neck voluntarily to the executioner's sword, or did he struggle? Jesus, who said, "If someone takes your outer garment from you, let him have your undergarment as well" (Luke 6:29), had stopped short of saying, "And when they come to behead you, bare your neck," because he could not yet continue such a statement by saying, ". . . for your Father in heaven, when they came to kill him . . ." The moment for that blasphemous suggestion is not far in the future as John's blood drains from his jugular; but until it comes, John's passing stands as a grim prophetic pantomime of Jesus' own end and the price of his new revelation.

A WHORE DEMONSTRATES HIS STRATEGY OF SHAME

Jesus' pacifist vision might seem to entail that he himself should have an obliging, complaisant, generally uncontentious and pacific personality, but he does not. The Jesus of the Gospels, especially of the Gospel of John, is more often peremptory than solicitous, and this with his supporters no less than with his opponents. When he is asked for material help, his first instinct is not to be obliging but to be irritated and dismissive. He never backs away from a dispute, nor does he ever allow disagreement to be papered over with a soothing cliché like the Samaritan woman's "I know that Messiah is coming; and when he comes, he will explain everything." In all these unamiable ways, Jesus is in considerable characterological continuity with his own past. The thesis, then, that God's character has changed requires a mental asterisk. He has indeed changed, but some of his old traits live on. There is reason, in particular, to suspect that his break with violence does not entail the renunciation of all forms of resistance. This is a point that may be taken away from, of all things, his public celebration of the unrecognized virtue of a fallen woman.

* One should know, to appreciate the scene that follows, that in first-century Palestine guests at a formal meal typically dined reclining on couches with their heads pointing inward around a U-shaped table. Servants came and went bringing food and drink through the open end of the U. An uninvited guest in this story waits until the invited guests have settled onto the couches around the U. Then she approaches one of them at the foot of his couch.

> One of the Pharisees had invited [Jesus] to a meal; and when he arrived at the Pharisee's house, he reclined in his place at the table. A woman of the town, who had a bad name, had heard he was dining with the Pharisee. Having brought with her an alabaster flask of perfumed oil, she waited behind him at his feet, weeping, and began to bathe his feet with her tears and dry them with her hair. She covered his feet with kisses and anointed them with the fragrant oil.
>
> When the Pharisee who had invited him saw this, he said to himself, "If this man were a prophet, he would know who and what sort of woman it is who is touching him and what a sinner she is." Then

Jesus took this up and said, "Simon, I have something to say to you."
He replied, "Say it, Teacher." "There was once a creditor who had
two men in his debt. One owed him five hundred days' wages, the
other fifty. Neither could pay, so he let both off. Which of the two
will love him more?" Simon answered, "The one who was let off
more, I suppose." Jesus said, "Right you are."

Then he turned to the woman and said to Simon, "Do you see this
woman? When I came into your house, you provided no water for my
feet, but she has bathed my feet with her tears, dried them with her
hair. You gave me no kiss, but she has been covering my feet with
kisses ever since I came in. You did not anoint my head with oil, but
she has anointed my feet with perfumed oil. That she shows so much
love proves that her sins, many as they are, have been forgiven. It is one
who is forgiven little who shows little love." Then he said to her,
"Your sins are forgiven." Those who were with him at table began to
ask among themselves, "Who is this man, that he even forgives sins?"
But he said to the woman, "Your faith has saved you. Go in peace."
(Luke 7:36–50) ☙

Why is this woman weeping? Is she weeping tears of joy that her sins
have been forgiven? Is she weeping tears of sorrow for those sins? Do the
tears count with the flask of perfumed oil as an expression of her love for
Jesus? Has he then already met with her, heard her confession, and forgiven her, so that his closing words to her in Simon's house merely ratify
or reveal to the dinner guests what he and she already know? Or is she
for some reason grieving over him, consoling him for something that he
is suffering and that perhaps only she knows about?

A woman weeping for an unknown reason attracts all eyes to herself.
If, while she weeps, she begins to undress (the meaning, in this culture,
of letting down her hair), her behavior becomes obscene, an obscene
demonstration. But of what? Jesus interprets her action, quite apart from
what it may say about her relationship to him, as a statement about
Simon. She is engaging in shameful behavior so as to shame. She is hum-
bling herself so as to humiliate another. The object of her action is not
just to honor and comfort Jesus but also to shame and discomfit Simon.

Did she really intend this? How can we know? She never speaks. For
that matter, we know only through Jesus' interpretation that she is showing love toward him because much has been forgiven her and not for
some more mundane reason. Simon, whose reaction recalls that of Jesus'
disciples in Samaria, is surprised to see Jesus so at ease as he receives
physical attention of an intimate sort in a public place from a woman of
ill repute. Does Jesus' calm as he receives this attention suggest that he

has received it before? His serenity, like her tears, might have any of several explanations and, by remaining unexplained, raises the emotional temperature of the episode. One thing, however, is clear—namely, that he approves of her shaming behavior. He has no desire to lower the temperature or spare Simon further embarrassment. On the contrary, he wants to keep the heat on and intensify the embarrassment. If the story of John's beheading is a gloss on "Turn the other cheek," so is the story of the whore in Simon's house. The two are complementary. John exhibits the madness in Jesus' method; the whore exhibits the method in his madness.

What Jesus said, to quote the shocking line again and this time in Matthew's more revealing formulation, is "If someone strikes you *on the right cheek,* turn the other to him as well" (Matt. 5:39, italics added). Supposing a right-handed attacker, the blow should fall on the left cheek. That it falls on the right means that it is a backhanded slap, the kind delivered by a master to a slave or a ruler to a subject. If the victim then turns his left cheek toward his attacker, he places the features of his face where his right cheek had been when the first slap landed. He dares his master, his ruler, or whoever it is who has insulted him to insult him further by landing a second blow squarely on his nose and mouth. Thus does the victim shame the victimizer, forcing insolence into consciousness of itself and then, perhaps, into repentance.

In a second illustration, using, significantly, the Latin word for *mile,* the word that the occupying Romans would use, Jesus says, again in Matthew's version: "If a man presses you into service to go one mile, go with him two" (5:41). What is being alluded to is not just any importunate acquaintance but an arrogant soldier of the occupying Roman army forcing a Jew to carry his pack. But soldiers can be shamed too. They may be, more than appears, pained to be causing pain. If one of them abuses his strength, force him into a worse abuse, and you may shame him into mercy.

Finally, most obviously because most ludicrously, Jesus says, "If anyone wants to sue you for your undergarment, let him have your outer garment too" (5:40). It was the costlier outer garment that might be taken as security from a poor person rather as, in our day, a student might leave a credit card as security when renting a bicycle. (The use of clothing as security is alluded to at Exodus 22:26 and at Deuteronomy 24:12, where the humane provision is added that a pledged cloak would have to be returned at nightfall lest the poor person have nothing to sleep in. In the era before the mass manufacture of clothing, a substantial outer garment was an object of no slight value.) But the undergarment? No one would take that in pledge. The idea is more than slightly indecent. Luke's version (6:29) of Jesus' comparison reverses the position of the two garments: "If someone takes your outer garment from you, let him have your undergarment as well." In Luke as in Matthew, the victim shames the victimizer by standing naked before him. But in Matthew the victimizer is both more "respectable," because he goes to court to get what he wants, and more contemptible, because what he wants is a man's underwear. In any event, supposing that such a lawsuit were to take place, a defendant who chose to hand over his outer garment as well as his undergarment would show up the shameful—and indecently petty—conduct of the plaintiff. Like the whore in Simon's house, he would strip away his opponent's dignity by stripping away his own.

None of these behaviors is retaliation, but none, either, is simple capitulation. What Jesus has discovered, and the discovery is to have a long and explosive history in the West, is the power of the victim against the victimizer. Yet if it is possible to imagine, as he does, scenes in which, while doing no harm, striking no blow, delivering no outright insult, the victim wins, it is equally possible to imagine counterscenes in which the victim loses because there is no flicker of grace in the soul of the victimizer. If it had been Jesus rather than John who condemned Herod, perhaps he would have found a more arresting, more droll, or simply more politic formulation than John's blunt and artless "It is against the law for you to have your brother's wife" (Mark 6:18). Still, it takes little to rile a petty tyrant. There may have been no way for John to say what he had to say cleverly enough to escape with his life.

Yet the story of John's beheading, considered in this light, suggests another way in which the victim can win. If instead of looking for victory only in the victim's personal gains or losses we broaden the context, then one who loses for himself may win for others. John's truth-telling cost him his head, but then what happened? Did Herod move on without a backward glance? No; he remained troubled by the thought that John might rise from the dead. He was persuaded that Jesus, a new censor whose fame was reaching his court, might be John come back to life. In short, Herod, after John's death, was changing. A man without a conscience was being led, however haltingly and nervously, to develop one—to the potential gain of all Galilee.

If the Romans shocked the Jews by making death a form of entertainment, the Jews who founded Christianity were about to shock the Romans by taking hold of the idea of martyrdom and making death an unprecedented form of protest from one end of the Roman empire to the other. The death of John the Baptist, a prophet slain for speaking truth to power, is a moment in the genesis of Jewish martyrdom. Historically, this genesis was a complex process whose earliest fully conscious biblical antecedent may be found nearly two centuries earlier, in the martyrdoms of 2 Maccabees 7. In that chapter, seven brothers, one following another, accept death after hideous torture rather than desert their ancestral religion. The Hellenistic tyrant who is overseeing their execution wavers in his bloody resolve after the sixth dies and tries to cajole the seventh and youngest into compliance. He urges the boy's mother, who has witnessed the entire gory spectacle, to persuade him to save his own life. She feigns cooperation but then, speaking to the boy in Hebrew or Aramaic, which the tyrant does not understand, exhorts him to die bravely. The passage ends as follows:

> "I too [the seventh brother says], like my brothers, offer up my body and life for the laws of my forefathers, imploring God quickly to take pity on our nation, and by trials and afflictions to bring you to confess that he alone is God, so that through my brothers and myself the Almighty may bring to an end the wrath that he has rightly loosed on our whole nation."
>
> The king fell into a rage and treated this one more cruelly than he had the others, for he was stung by the young man's scorn. Thus, the last brother met his end unsullied and with perfect faith in the Lord. The mother was the last to die, after her sons. (2 Macc. 7:37–41)

Two of the elements of the victim strategy as Jesus has taught it are in evidence here. First, torture is accepted not simply to demonstrate courage but to change the mind of the torturer, and the tactic is not without effect: The tyrant is "stung by the young man's scorn." Second, vindication beyond the grave is assumed. When the second brother accepts death rather than eat pork, his dying words make this particularly clear: "You accursed wretch, you may discharge us from this present life, but the King of the World will raise us up to live forever, since it is for his laws that we die" (2 Macc. 7:9).

On two other points, however, there is a difference. First, the seventh son assumes that the Greek tyrant's presence in the land is temporary. He is no more than a part of God's punishment of Israel, which will end in due course. Despite the fact that the tyrant is subjectively iniquitous, the oppression he visits upon Israel is objectively "the wrath that [the Almighty] has rightly loosed on our whole nation." This is the sort of thing that Jesus never says, and the omission could not be more striking than it is. Second, the Maccabees are a Hellenized Jewish warrior clan that, by making an alliance with Rome, will succeed in defeating the Hellenistic tyrant and establishing an independent Jewish kingdom that will last a full century—essentially, until Rome is strong enough to move in and take over. Accordingly, the martyrs of 2 Maccabees 7 do not renounce violence but eagerly anticipate military vindication by their own victory on the battlefield. The fifth brother's dying words are "Do not think that God has deserted our race. Just wait, and you will see in good time how his mighty power will torment you and your descendants" (7:16–17). In the Books of Maccabees, moral resistance does not preclude military resistance but only pursues it by other means, like propaganda or "psy-op" (psychological operations) in modern warfare. In the Gospels, moral resistance entirely replaces military resistance.

In some form, then, the notion of martyrdom is known to the audience that Jesus addresses, yet he redefines the role of martyr even as he redefines the role of messiah. Martyrdom, as he envisions it, is not battlefield heroism in another form but demonstrative suffering of a kind that even a prostitute can manage. Any victim, however humble, who manages to make his pain a form of speech can turn himself from a simple victim into a martyr, or so Jesus suggests. In our own culture, where this form of speech is deeply rooted and instinctively understood, the powerful are constantly on guard against having the pain they inflict create martyrs whose voices can be heard speaking against them. In Jesus' day, though all of Hellenistic culture honored valor and though influential currents of moral philosophy such as Stoicism honored suicide as well, martyrdom understood as Jesus understood it was a novelty that would become a cultural weapon only after his death.

Even within the Gospels themselves, martyrdom is not treated as a well-understood or generally accepted idea. On the contrary, though all four Gospels include early allusions to it, their pervasive assumption is that this idea shocks even Jesus' closest disciples. Jesus treats his own future martyrdom as a disturbing and fearful secret—in effect, a scandal, to be disclosed only to a few and only with the greatest caution. John in Herod's prison and the whore in Simon's house are moments in that gradual disclosure. Jesus' praise for her exceeds any that he has spoken for anyone except John, and in fact the two eulogies have a deep link and raise the same pressing question.

For if the strategy of shame requires, at the extreme, that the victim shame his opponent by surrendering his very life, and if this strategy is now the principal strategy of the divine warrior, then what lies ahead for Israel? John acclaimed Jesus as the Lamb of God, but now it is John himself who has been butchered. Are the disciples to see in John's fate an illustration of Jesus' new tactics? Does Jesus want to produce a nation of lambs? Does he really expect to redeem Israel from oppression merely by shaming her oppressor? It was not by such means that the Lord God of Hosts ever promised to save Israel!

HE FEEDS A MULTITUDE

The identity of Jesus is, of course, the question whose answer changes everything. The angels, at his birth, referred to him as "Christ *the Lord,*" using a title that, as noted earlier, is reserved in the Old Testament for God. The demon whom Jesus expelled from a madman in the Capernaum synagogue addressed him as "the Holy One," using a similarly reserved title. But has any mere human being entertained the thought that Jesus might be God Incarnate?

The odd fact is that Jesus has often seemed determined to conceal rather than reveal his identity. His caution only grows more pronounced after the death of John. From that point on, his parables in Galilee take on a significantly darker, more guarded, more coded character—more like the language he used at the start in Judea:

> As a large crowd gathered and people from every town found their way to him, he told this parable:
> "A sower went out to sow his seed. Now as he sowed, some fell on the edge of the road and was trampled underfoot; and the birds of the air ate it up. Some seed fell on rock; and when it sprouted, it withered for lack of moisture. Some seed fell amid thorns, and the thorns grew with it and choked it. And some seed fell into good soil, where it grew and produced a hundredfold." Saying this, he cried: "If you have ears to listen, then listen."
> His disciples asked him what this parable could mean, and he said, "To you it has been given to understand the secrets of the kingdom of God. For the others, it remains in parables, so that [quoting Isaiah]
>
> > *they may look but not see,*
> > *listen but not understand.*
>
> Here, then, is what the parable means: The seed is the word of God."
> (Luke 8:4–11)

Jesus explains the parable, but only to a chosen few; and the explanation matters less than the fact that, as God Incarnate, Jesus is concealing his own message just as God did at Isaiah 6:9, the passage that he quotes. He is speaking and yet seeing to it that he is not understood until the events that he is arranging, the events that will say more than any words, have come to pass. By quoting Isaiah, he reminds his disciples that this is how God sometimes proceeds, but his conduct remains paradoxical, for he reminds them of God at a highly paradoxical moment in God's past.

What Jesus conceals for the moment but must soon reveal is, above all, his own divinity. Actions of his that might suggest blasphemous presumption in a mere human being—actions like casting out demons and forgiving sins—have certainly been wondered at, but the enormity of divinity as their true explanation has been psychologically out of reach. As Jesus approaches the moment when he will perform his most spectacularly godlike miracles, perhaps the one man still alive who has an inkling of the full truth is Nicodemus. The eminent Jerusalem leader, dumbstruck at first, may later have understood that Jesus, with his talk of "water and the Spirit," was laying claim to nothing less than God's own power to create worlds and destroy them. Jesus has not otherwise attempted to bring anyone so far into his confidence. But this is about to change.

Shortly before the execution of John, Jesus, taking charge of his mission in a new and more organized way, sends his disciples out, two by two, to cast out demons in his name, heal the sick, and preach repentance. The mission goes well, but the grim news of John's death reaches him just as the disciples return, and Jesus calls for a tactical retreat.

He said to them, "Come away by yourselves to some isolated spot and rest for a while." There had been so many people coming and going that they had had no time even to eat. So they headed offshore toward an isolated spot where they could be by themselves. But people had seen them leaving, and many recognized them. And so from every town they all hurried to the same spot on foot and reached it before they did. The result was that when Jesus came ashore, he found a large crowd waiting. But his heart went out to them because they were like sheep without a shepherd, and he set about teaching them many things.

When it grew late, his disciples came up to him and said, "This place is remote, and it is getting late. Send them away now so that they can go to the farms and villages in the area to buy themselves something to eat."

He answered, "Give them something to eat yourselves."

They said, "Are we to go and spend several months' wages buying bread for them?"

He asked, "How many loaves have you? Go check."

When they did, they said, "Five, and two fish as well."

Then he ordered them to settle everyone in groups on the grass, and they sat down in groups of hundreds and fifties. Then he took the five loaves and the two fish, raised his eyes heavenward while saying the blessing, then broke the loaves and began handing them to his disciples to distribute among the people. He also divided up the two fish among them all.

They all ate their fill, and twelve baskets of bread scraps and fish pieces were collected afterward. Those who had eaten the loaves numbered five thousand men. Right away he made his disciples get into the boat and go on ahead to the other side near Bethsaida, while he himself dismissed the crowd. |

Seeing the sign that he had done, the people said, "This must surely be the prophet who is to come into the world." Jesus, when he realized they were coming to take him by force and make him king, fled alone into the hills. (Mark 6:31–46 | John 6:14–15) ✒

While this is obviously the most spectacular and the most public miracle Jesus has yet performed, it is the interpretation he places upon the miracle that makes it a further revelation of his identity. Central to his interpretation is that he sees the crowd who have come seeking him as "sheep without a shepherd." The murder of John has robbed Israel of a leader sent by God. Rome is the real murderer, and what has happened to John will happen again with steadily increasing frequency until it culminates in the genocidal slaughters of 70 C.E. and 135 C.E. Then, indeed— and God Incarnate foresees this—the Jews will be sheep without a shepherd.

The phrase "sheep without a shepherd" has further, highly suggestive associations, however, for someone who bears the name Joshua (as Jesus does in his own Aramaic language)—and who knows well what the name Joshua means. Moses, just before his death, said to the Lord: "Let the Lord . . . appoint a leader for this community to be at their head in all that they do, a man who will lead them out and bring them in, lest the Lord's community be *sheep without a shepherd*" (Num. 27:16–17, italics added). God honors this request, instructing Moses to appoint Joshua as leader; and Joshua goes on to become the greatest warrior in Israelite history, even greater, perhaps, than David. It was Joshua who defeated the Canaanites and conquered, with the Lord's help, the land that the Lord had promised. Joshua was the Lord's chosen shepherd.

The name Joshua—alternately *yehoshua'* or *yeshua'* in Hebrew—is *Iēsous* in the ancient Greek translation of the Hebrew scriptures, the same Greek name that, when it occurs in the Gospels, is conventionally translated "Jesus," though it could just as easily be translated "Joshua." In other words, Jesus' real name effectively *is* Joshua. Though the name *yeshua'* has acquired a certain currency in recent popular books about Jesus and though that name accurately reproduces the form of this name that he most likely used, *yeshua'* effectively muffles all the associations that Jesus' contemporaries heard in either the Greek or the Hebrew form of that name, all of the warlike, heroic, and salvific associations that modern Bible readers hear in "Joshua."

The duties of a shepherd in ancient Israel, through the time of Jesus, were not confined to placidly herding and feeding the sheep. In those days, the habitat of the Asiatic lion included the Jordan Valley, and wolves roamed the hills of Galilee and Judea. Armed only with hand weapons, a shepherd had to defend his flock against these predators as well as against human thieves. A "good shepherd" needed the skills of a warrior, and military historians have long noted that these skills, combined with an animal butcher's knowledge of anatomy, would again and again make pastoral peoples formidable in combat.

When the Lord sees his people as "sheep without a shepherd," therefore, he is seeing them not just as lost or needy but as defenseless before ravenous predators. When he spoke to King Ahab through the prophet Micaiah of a coming great defeat, Micaiah's vision was of "all Israel scattered on the mountains, as sheep without a shepherd" (2 Chron. 18:16)—scattered sheep as an image of military defeat. In the coming great defeat by Rome, Israel will be scattered like shepherdless sheep throughout the Roman empire; the wanton murder of John the Baptist, fresh in Jesus' mind, is a bitter foretaste of that horror and a reminder to God Incarnate of what he will *not* do on that day of darkness.

To say all this is not to deny the element of simple, immediate compassion in Jesus' reaction to the hungry crowd or, for that matter, the connection of this reaction to the further associations of the phrase "Shepherd of Israel" (Ps. 80:1). The tender, emotive side of God's covenant with Israel as a people is endlessly evoked through this metaphor, and even the individual Israelite may say with perfect confidence, "The Lord is my shepherd" (Ps. 23:1). When the early, culturally Jewish church represented Christ as a young shepherd bearing a lamb on his shoulders, it was consciously portraying God as well: Such had been God's relationship to Israel; Jesus as God Incarnate merely enlarged the flock.

This may seem a great deal to load onto a turn of phrase that could be read much more simply, but the occasion, after all, is one on which Jesus demonstrates divine power by performing a miracle that goes far beyond any faith healing. If in this of all moments his followers seem to him like sheep, then he must seem to himself in the same moment like their shepherd, with all the associations that this relationship summons up.

When God spoke through Isaiah, in the same passage that Luke quotes in telling the story of Jesus' baptism, he promised that he would soon come to the rescue of his people as a warrior shepherd:

> Go up on a high mountain,
>> O messenger to Zion!
> Lift up your voice,
>> O messenger to Jerusalem!
> Shout it boldly,
>> saying to the towns of Judah,
> "Behold your God!"
>> Behold the Lord Adonai coming with power,
> He rules by his mighty arm,
>> his reward he brings with him,
>> his prize precedes him.
> *Like a shepherd, he feeds his flock,*
>> *gathering the lambs in his arms,*
> *Holding them against his breast*
>> *and gently leading the mother ewes.*
>
> (Isa. 40:9–11, italics added)

Speaking through Jeremiah, he reacted with the same mix of anger and tenderness to the fact that his flock was without a shepherd:

> This is what the Lord, the God of Israel, says about the shepherds who shepherd my people: "You have scattered my sheep; you have driven them away and have not cared for them. So then I will punish you for your misdeeds—the word of the Lord! But the remnant of my flock I myself will gather from all the lands where I have driven them, and I will bring them back to their pasture. (Jer. 23:2–3)

When God Incarnate sees a crowd of Jews as "sheep without a shepherd," his reaction is inevitably a comment not just on them but also on their leaders, their negligent shepherds. But his motive in replacing those shepherds with himself is not just that the sheep should enjoy safety and plenty but also that they should recognize him as their shepherd—that is, as their God. After making, through Ezekiel, the same promise to replace Israel's greedy and careless shepherds with himself, he concluded: "And they shall know that I, the Lord their God, am with them, and that they, the house of Israel, are my people, says the Lord God. And you are my sheep, the sheep of my pasture, and I am your God, says the Lord God" (RSV Ezek. 34:30–31 with modifications).

When Jesus himself was hungry, after fasting in the desert, and the Devil challenged him to turn a stone into a loaf, he declined. That is, he declined to perform a food miracle in the desert for himself as he had once done for the Israelites under Moses. Had he provided himself manna in the desert at the Devil's instigation, he would have performed his miracle for one witness alone. Now, keeping to his own schedule, he performs such a miracle for five thousand witnesses, demonstrating that, to paraphrase Ezekiel, they are his sheep, the sheep of his pasture, and he is their God.

The story of the feeding of the multitude well illustrates the mixed literary style of biblical narration, a style the Gospels do not invent but merely continue. The miracle proper could be at home in a fairy tale or, if the frame of reference were made large enough, a myth, but here the setting is a real place, the crowd is an ordinary crowd experiencing ordinary hunger, and the scraps are collected afterward as after any large human repast. Most strikingly, perhaps, the miracle worker himself, when the crowd seeks to make him king against his wishes, does not cast a spell upon them or turn himself into a swan and fly away. He simply flees from them into the nearby hills as any ordinary man might do.

To say this, however, is not to suggest that the mixed style of the Gospels is an adequate explanation for Jesus' behavior. If Jesus is a new Joshua, if this is what he reveals by so spectacularly exhibiting his power, then why is he running away? Does the good shepherd, the brave shepherd, flee the flock?

HE STILLS A STORM

Jesus' disciples attempt to cross the Sea of Galilee to Bethsaida, as he has instructed them, but the wind is against them. From his hiding place in the hills, Jesus watches them struggle.

During the night, when the boat was well out from the shore and he was alone on the land, he could see that they were struggling to stay on course, for the wind was against them. Sometime between three and six in the morning, he came toward them, walking on the sea. He would have passed them by; but when they saw him walking on the sea, they thought it was a ghost and cried out. They all saw him and were terrified. But at once he spoke to them. "Take heart, I AM," he said, | and he rebuked the wind and said to the sea, "Silence! Be still!" The wind dropped, there followed a great calm, | and immediately they were at the place on the shore they had been heading toward. |

He said to them, "Why are you so frightened? Have you still no faith?" They were overcome with awe and said to one another, "Who can this be? Even the wind and the sea obey him." . . . The reason they were dumbfounded was that they had not grasped the import of the miracle of the loaves. Their minds were closed. (Mark 6:47–50 | Mark 4:39 | John 6:21 | Mark 4:40–41, 6:51–52)

The list of questions about Jesus that already contains

> *Who is this that casts out demons?*

and

> *Who is this that forgives sins?*

as well as

> *Who is this son of Joseph to declare himself the fulfillment of prophecy?*

acquires here another entry:

> *Who is this that the wind and the sea obey him?*

Power over the sea is the signature power of God. This is the power he deployed when he created the world, as we recalled when discussing Jesus' words to Nicodemus about "water and the Spirit." This is also the power that he used to part the Red Sea and the Jordan River before the advancing Israelites. In the Psalms, storms at sea stand poetically for all the tribulations that face Israel as a nation and the individual Israelite turning to God in prayer. God's power to still the storm is, par excellence, his power to rescue the oppressed. Thus:

> They cried out to the Lord in their affliction,
>   and he delivered them from their distress.
> The tempest he made to be still,
>   and the waves to be silent.
> They were glad then because of the quiet,
>   and he brought them to the haven they sought.
>
> (Ps. 107:28–30)

Had the disciples recognized that when Jesus multiplied the loaves and fishes he was demonstrating divine power, they would not have been surprised at this further demonstration of his divinity. But they did not recognize it then, and so he has now given them a more awe-inspiring, truly godlike demonstration of what he can do.

Yet a disturbing shadow lies across this scene. Jesus lets the storm rage for some time before coming to his disciples' rescue. More disturbing still, when he comes to them walking on the raging waves, *he makes as if to walk past them.* When he finally comes close enough for them to see that it is he and not a ghost, the words he says are the mysterious name I AM that God gave himself when speaking to Moses from the burning bush. He will do the same at several later moments of high drama. But what dread meaning is to be conveyed by the fact that the incarnate I AM allows his disciples to entertain the thought, for a terrifying moment, that his divine powers will not be exercised to save them, that he may, in fact, allow them to drown in the Sea of Galilee? They receive an answer to that question not long after they disembark, shaken to the core by their narrow escape from shipwreck, but the answer they receive merely deepens their confusion.

HE SPEAKS OF DRINKING BLOOD, AND MANY DESERT HIM

The next day, not finding Jesus and having seen his disciples leave for Capernaum in their boat, some of the crowd follow in boats of their own.

> When they found him on the other side, they said to him, "Rabbi, when did you come here?" Jesus answered:
>
> > Truly I tell you,
> > you are looking for me

> not because you saw the signs
> but because you had all the bread you wanted to eat.
> Do not work for food that spoils,
> but work for food that keeps unto eternal life. . . .
> I am the bread of life.
> Your forefathers ate manna in the desert
> and they [eventually] died . . .
> I am the bread of life which has come down from heaven.
> Anyone who eats this bread will live forever.
> But the bread that I shall give
> is my flesh, for the life of the world.

Then the Jews started arguing among themselves: "How can this man give us his flesh to eat?" Jesus replied to them:

> Truly I tell you,
> if you do not eat the flesh of the Son of Man
> and drink his blood,
> you will have no life within you.
> Whoever eats my flesh and drinks my blood
> has eternal life,
> and I will raise him up on the last day.
> For my flesh is true food
> and my blood is true drink.
> Whoever eats my flesh and drinks my blood
> lives in me
> and I in him. . . .

After hearing this, many of his followers said, "This is intolerable talk. How can anyone accept it?" Jesus was aware that his followers were complaining about it, and he said: "Does this upset you? What if you were to see the Son of Man ascending to where he was before?" . . . Thereafter, many of his erstwhile disciples went away and accompanied him no more. (John 6:25–27, 48–56, 60–62, 66)

What kind of man gives you his flesh to eat and his blood to drink? Whatever else this shocking speech refers to, it must refer somehow to Jesus' death. It also serves notice to those who have flocked to him because he fed them that it is not his vocation simply to be a cornucopia. Yes, he fed a crowd on that one occasion, but crowd-feeding is not what he is about. In just the same way, he saved his followers from drowning, but rescue—whether from the real waves of the Sea of Galilee or from the metaphorical waves of unspecified tribulation—is not his mission either. Somehow, his mission is to be discharged by his own death—a violent death, he suggests; a death like John's. And this alone, this even if his "bread of life" speech were not as physically and spiritually repellent as it is, would be enough to drive people from him. If he cannot save himself, what hope is there that he can save or otherwise serve them?

Beyond that motive for disaffiliation, however, there should be no doubt whatsoever that Jesus' speech is viscerally repugnant to his hearers' Jewish sensibilities. John writes their reaction into his account of the speech, but one could guess it had he not written it. What Jesus speaks of seems to be, to give it a plain name, cannibalism, a practice that is repugnant in most cultures. Even granting that many or most of his hearers realize that he must be speaking of a symbolic action of some sort, the symbolism is only somewhat less repugnant than the real thing—and most especially so to Jews.

In the Garden of Eden, Adam and Eve were vegetarians. Though they were free to eat of the fruit of every tree but one, they were given no comparable freedom to eat the flesh of every, or any, animal. This came only after the great flood, when God made a new covenant with Noah and his descendants:

> Every living thing that moves will be yours to eat, no less than the foliage of the plants. I allow you everything, with one exception: You must not eat flesh with life—that is to say blood—still in it. And I shall demand an account of your lifeblood as well. I shall demand it of every animal, and of man. Of man as regards his fellow man, I shall demand an account for human life:
>
> > *Shed no man's blood,*
> > *Or by man will your blood be shed,*
> > *For in the image of God*
> > *Is man made.*
>
> (Gen. 9:3–6, italics added)

Homicide is an offense against the God whose image mankind bears—except when God himself commands it. As for the meat of animals, it may be eaten only after the blood has drained from it into the earth, for blood, like breath, has life in it, and life belongs to God alone. It is from this verse that the practice of kosher butchery descends. Meat is kosher—that is, fit for consumption in accordance with God's law—only when the blood has been drained from it. How shocking, then, that Jesus should propose miming the consumption of a human corpse. And how unutterably, unspeakably shocking that the corpse should be that of the Messiah.

Israel knew about cannibalism. The Lord had promised to drive Israel's enemies to just this extreme. "They will be as drunk on their own blood as on new wine," he had exulted (Isa. 49:26). He had sworn that if his own people disobeyed him, the enemy he would send against them would do even worse to them:

> During the siege and in the distress to which your enemy will reduce you, you will eat the fruit of your own bodies, the flesh of the sons and daughters given to you by the Lord your God. The gentlest and most refined of your men will begrudge his brother, and the wife whom he embraces, and his surviving children, any share of the flesh of the child he is eating. (Deut. 28:53–55)

But these were horrors recognized as such and rhetorically employed as such. The notion that God Incarnate should propose even the symbolic drinking of his own blood is so obscene as to seem almost deranged—a charge that has been made against Jesus already and will be made again. But Jesus knows quite well what he is doing.

Why did he perform the two spectacular miracles he has just performed if he did not intend to perform others like them? His motive in thus demonstrating his power was to make it clear that the shocking things he is now beginning to say are truly being said by God. With many, perhaps most, of his hearers, he does not succeed. With a few, he does: "Then Jesus said to the twelve, 'What about you, do you want to go away as well?' Simon Peter answered, 'Lord, to whom shall we go? You have the words of eternal life. We believe—and have come to know—that you are the Holy One of God.'" (John 6:67–69). Peter's loyalty is clear, but does he know what he is saying? Certainly as regards Jesus' scandalous speech, Peter gives no sign of prescience or exceptional penetration. He does not declare himself, for example, prepared to eat his master's flesh and drink his blood. All the same, he does acclaim him with the title "the Holy One of God," a phrase hitherto applied to Jesus only by a demon in the synagogue of Capernaum. No human being has yet dared so far. Jesus, perhaps recalling that agitated but knowing devil, reacts to Peter's declaration by saying: "'Did I not choose the twelve of you? Yet one of you is a devil.' He meant Judas, son of Simon Iscariot, since he was the man, one of the twelve, who would betray him" (John 6:70–71).

HE APPEARS IN SUDDEN GLORY ON A MOUNTAINTOP

Blocked, after John's death, in his first attempt to withdraw to a remote location, Jesus succeeds on his second try. With a group of his disciples, he sets out for Caesarea Philippi, several days' journey to the north, at the foot of snowcapped Mount Hermon. By far the most impressive mountain in the entire region, Mount Hermon lies well outside Galilee and therefore outside the jurisdiction of Herod Antipas. Jesus is prepared to die, but he does not intend to die at the hands of the puppet king who slew John.

During the course of a grueling, twenty-five-mile uphill walk, out of earshot of the authorities and strung out along the road as hikers always are on a long trek, Jesus and his disciples talk.

> He put this question to his disciples, "Who do people say I am?" And they told him, "Some say John the Baptist, others Elijah, still others one of the prophets." "But you," he asked them, "who do you say I am?" Peter spoke up and said to him, "You are the Messiah." And he gave them strict orders not to tell anyone about him.
>
> Then he began to teach them that the Son of Man was destined to suffer greatly, and to be rejected by the elders and the chief priests and the scribes and to be put to death, and after three days to rise again. He said all this quite openly. Peter, taking him aside, then tried to rebuke him. But, turning and looking toward his disciples, he rebuked Peter, saying to him, "Out of my sight, Satan! You are thinking as men think, not as God thinks." (Mark 8:27–33)

Is Jesus speaking to Peter, merely calling him "Satan," or is he speaking, in fact, to Satan himself, aggressively rejecting a temptation seductively offered through Jesus' leading disciple? The conduct that Peter urges, if not quite as self-serving as what Satan urged earlier, is, at the very least, not much different from what the crowd so recently had in mind when it sought to anoint Jesus king of Israel. Loyal and pious as he is, Peter believes that he knows from scripture what Jesus must do if he is to be the Messiah. Peter is mistaken, but his is not an ignorant mistake. Though the concept of messiah was fluid in some regards, the future that Jesus sketches for himself clearly violates it. The Messiah was not to be rejected, much less slain, by the people he would come to save. On the contrary, he would rally them, just as Joshua and David did, against enemies holding the promised land against God's will. Peter has solid traditional grounds on which to object, but Jesus will not be rebuked. He halts the caravan, allows the disciples to gather, and says to them and to anyone else within earshot, in plainer language than any yet used, what he requires of them.

> • He called the crowd and his disciples to him and said, "If anyone wants to be a follower of mine, let him renounce himself and take up his cross and follow me. Whoever wants to save his life will lose it; but whoever loses his life for my sake, and for the sake of the Gospel, will save it. What good is it to win the whole world and forfeit life itself? What indeed can be offered in exchange for one's life? If anyone in this sinful and adulterous generation is ashamed of me and of my words, the Son of Man will also be ashamed of him when he comes in the glory of his Father with the holy angels." And he went on to say: "Truly I tell you, there are some standing here who will not taste death before they see the Kingdom of God coming in power." (Mark 8:34–9:1) •

Jesus preemptively rebukes any disciple who, like Peter, would rebuke him for proceeding as he intends to proceed. In so doing, he evokes both larger losses and larger, more personal gains than they have yet heard him evoke: on the one hand, death on the cross, the Romans' hideous instrument of torture and death; on the other, a mysterious victory that will come so soon that some of them will never die at all.

More now than ever before hangs on the identity of Jesus. When he preached the renunciation of violence and yet insisted, in answer to the doomed John's inquiry, that he was indeed "he who is to come," he was shattering hopes that had been entertained on the highest authority for hundreds of years. Who was he to go so far? And had he anything to offer but surrender? Shocking as it would be for God to revoke his earlier promises, it would be blasphemous for any human being to do so. Any prophet claiming that this was his prophetic message would be a false prophet. Is God's word not irrevocable? But in this speech, I AM Incarnate seems to be saying, first, that the kind of victory he used to promise, up to and including the winning of the whole world, is worthless in comparison with "life" and, second, that "life" can only be saved by losing it.

The multiplication of the loaves, the walking on water, and now these predictions of suffering, death, followed only *then* somehow by the triumph of the Kingdom of God—all of this is the further explication of Jesus' paradoxical sermon against violent resistance. God has become man to win a great victory by enacting that sermon, or so it seems. Crucifixion first and then . . . what? The Son of Man coming down from heaven in glory and surrounded by his angels? Even if he can cure the sick and forgive sins, even if he can feed multitudes and give orders to the wind and the sea, does the son of Joseph have anything remotely approaching the authority to make predictions and demands like these?

> Now about eight days after this, he took with him Peter, John, and James and went up a mountain to pray. And as he was praying, the appearance of his face changed, and his clothing became dazzling white. And suddenly two men were there talking to him. They were Moses and Elijah, appearing in glory, and they were speaking of the exodus that he was to accomplish in Jerusalem. Peter and his companions had been overcome by sleep, but now they awoke and saw his glory and the two men standing with him. As they were leaving him, Peter said to Jesus, "Master, it is good for us to be here, so let us make three shelters—one for you, one for Moses, and one for Elijah." He did not know what he was saying. As he was saying this, a cloud came and overshadowed them; and when they went into the cloud, the disciples were afraid. And a voice came from the cloud, saying, "This is my Son, my Chosen One. Listen to him." And after the voice had spoken, Jesus was found alone. The disciples kept silent and, at that time, told no one what they had seen. (Luke 9:28–36)

The eight-day lapse indicates that Jesus and his disciples have arrived at Caesarea Philippi. This Roman shrine city was built adjacent to an earlier Greek shrine, the Paneion, honoring the god Pan; and the Greek shrine, built where the headwaters of the Jordan River emerge from a natural grotto, paid silent homage to an older, Canaanite tradition according to which Mount Hermon was the abode of the gods, the Mount Olympus of the Canaanite pantheon. In Israelite tradition, Mount Zion, site of the holy city of Jerusalem, was not a place where God had lived from time immemorial but only one where God at a certain point in time had chosen to abide. Until David captured Jerusalem from the native Jebusites and made it his capital, Mount Zion had not been holy to the Lord. Heaven was most often named as the Lord's home, but several mountains were named as places where he was wont to sojourn or, in one way or another, make his glory manifest. Mount Sinai was the most famous of these; Mount Horeb, evidently another name for Mount Sinai, was another; Mount Seir in the south is a third; and an unnamed "mount of assembly" in the far north, mentioned at Isaiah 14:13 and at

Psalm 48:2, was a fourth. This sacred northern mountain is undoubtedly Mount Hermon, Israel having appropriated, as so often in its poetry, an indigenous Canaanite tradition.

The place to which Jesus brings his three most important apostles is, then, richly suggestive and would be so even if he did no more than speak to them there with appropriate solemnity. What happens, instead, is that he is joined by the spirits of two giants from Israel's past, to each of whom the Lord appeared on a mountaintop: to Moses, on Mount Sinai; to Elijah, on Mount Horeb. But does the Yahweh Elohim now appear to Jesus as he did to Moses and Elijah? No, it is *Jesus himself* who appears— his face transfigured and his clothes shining with a preternatural white-ness—to Moses and to Elijah. They speak to him as if they know him, and they clearly know as well of the passing, or exodus (the Greek word used is *exodos*), that awaits him in Jerusalem. All this happens, and the three apostles awake to find it in progress. They see the glory of the Lord Christ just as Moses saw the glory of the Lord God on Mount Sinai and as Elijah did on Mount Horeb. Then a cloud appears—again, just as it did atop Mount Sinai when the Lord appeared to Moses—and from the cloud a voice speaks: "This is my Son, my Chosen One. Listen to him!" The voice of God? But when they look, they see no one but Jesus.

On whose authority, to repeat the question that the three disciples brought with them up the mountain, does the son of Joseph presume so drastically to reinterpret the promises of the Lord God to his chosen people? The answer, they now know, is this: He does so on his own authority. The Father has become his own Son. The voice from heaven is his own voice, as it was when it said at his baptism, "You are my Son. This day have I begotten you." The glory of the Lord made manifest on the sacred mountain of the north is Jesus' overwhelming reply to Peter's rebuke. Yet, awestruck as Peter is, stammering out his incoherent won-derment, can he, can any of the three, yet make sense of the coming col-lision of divine glory and human agony?

PART THREE

The Lord of Blasphemy

During the few weeks that precede his execution, Jesus spends his time in and near Jerusalem. Once reluctant to perform miracles even when asked, he now performs them even when not asked. Once secretive when talking about either his divinity or his doom, he now talks openly of both, often linking them. Once a preacher and healer in rural villages and "lonely places," he now works in the precincts of the Temple in the heart of Jerusalem. Once acclaimed as king of Israel only by a lone disciple, he is now about to hear that phrase shouted by a huge crowd: Jews from around the world assembled in Jerusalem for the Passover feast. Yet once disparaged only as "Joseph's son" and seriously threatened only by a band of Nazareth neighbors, he is now aggressively dismissed as a Samaritan, a Galilean, a madman, or a demoniac and made the object, finally, of an assassination plot conceived at the highest levels.

The effect is that of a gathering before a shattering, as when a wave hangs poised before it breaks on a rocky shore, yet Jesus never indicates for even a fleeting moment that events are running out of his control. Nothing surprises him. He foresees the worst and embraces it. Others are dismayed or confused. God Incarnate is lordly and serene.

HE FLAGRANTLY VIOLATES THE LAW OF SABBATH REST

After this there was a Jewish festival, and Jesus went up to Jerusalem. Now in Jerusalem next to the Sheep Gate there is a pool, called

Bethesda in Hebrew, which has five porticoes. Under these lay a large number of sick people—the blind, the lame, and the paralyzed. One man there had been ill for thirty-eight years; and when Jesus saw him lying there and knew he had been ill for so long, he said, "Do you want to recover?" The sick man replied, "I have no one, sir, to put me into the pool when the water stirs. While I am yet on the way, someone else gets down there before me." Jesus said, "Arise, pick up your mat, and walk." At once the man was cured, and he picked up his mat and started walking.

Now that day happened to be the Sabbath, so the Jews said to the man who had been cured, "This is the Sabbath. You are not allowed to carry a mat." He answered, "The man who cured me told me, 'Pick up your mat and walk.'" They asked him, "Who was this man who told you to pick it up and walk?" The man who had been cured had no idea who it was, since Jesus had slipped into the crowd. Later Jesus met him in the Temple and said, "Now that you are well again, leave off sinning, lest something worse happen to you." So then the man went back and told the Jews that it was Jesus who had cured him. It was because Jesus did such things on the Sabbath that the Jews started harassing him. His answer to them was, "My father does not stop working, and neither do I." But that only made the Jews more intent on doing away with him, for not only was he breaking the Sabbath, but he also spoke of God as his father in a way that made him equal to God. . . .

✒ [Jesus challenged the crowd,] "Why do you want to kill me?" The crowd replied, "You're crazy. Who wants to kill you?" He answered, "I do one work, and you are all amazed at it. Moses instructed you to practice circumcision, and you circumcise on the Sabbath. Well, if the law of Moses is not violated when you fix a penis on the Sabbath, why are you upset with me for fixing a whole body on the Sabbath? Don't go by what looks right. Go by what *is* right."❧

—John 5:1–18, 7:19–24

In the episode quoted above, Jesus heals an invalid on the Sabbath, thus violating the traditional practice by which most normal work ceased on the seventh day of the week because on that day the Lord himself had observed a day of rest after creating the world. A physician or healer might break the rule of Sabbath rest to save the life of someone mortally ill, but the invalid at Bethesda—a spot just to the northeast of the Temple—is merely handicapped. He has lived with his affliction, whatever it is, for thirty-eight years. There is no reason, then, why Jesus might not have waited a day to cure him. He has not asked to be cured. Even when Jesus offers to cure him, he does not accept the offer eagerly.

He seems scarcely to understand the question. Nor is there any evident reason why Jesus should require the man, simply because he has been cured, to violate the Sabbath by carrying the burden of his sleeping mat. The man could keep the Sabbath for another few hours in the place where, it seems, he has already spent many days and then gather up his belongings and leave.

The grounds that Jesus gives for first healing the man and then ordering him to pick up his mat and walk are that God, contrary to traditional belief, does not actually rest on every Sabbath, even though he may have rested on that first Sabbath. And if God keeps working on the Sabbath, then Jesus and anyone acting at Jesus' behest may do so as well. Yet who but God himself can say whether or not God rests on the Sabbath? Once again, Jesus dares to announce a change in God or, as it may be in this case, the previously unknown truth about God.

In comparing Sabbath healing, which is forbidden, to Sabbath circumcision, which is permitted, Jesus uses the traditional Jewish *a fortiori* style of legal reasoning against his adversaries, but this is no more than intellectual byplay. His real strategy, as we have seen before, is to shame his opponents. Whatever the technical requirements of Sabbath observance, who would not be ashamed to object when a lifelong invalid is restored to health? Who, hearing such an objection made, would not be inclined to side with the healer against the authorities? Who can believe that God would object, the God who once said:

> Say to the fearful at heart,
> 　"Be strong, dread not!
> Behold, your God!
> He shall come with vengeance,
> 　with terrible retribution.
> 　He shall come and save you."
> Then shall the eyes of the blind be opened,
> 　and the ears of the deaf unstopped.
> Then shall the lame leap like a stag,
> 　and the dumb tongue sing for joy.
>
> 　　　　　　　　　　　(Isa. 35:4–6)

Not every observer realizes just how much hostility this kind of provocation can arouse, but Jesus himself does. "You're crazy," some bystanders say when he claims to have become the object of a murder plot, but he has been anticipating the hostility that he will arouse. The hostility is, in fact, a part of his plan.

SCANDAL SPREADS, AN ARREST ATTEMPT FAILS

At the start of his short career, Jesus was faced repeatedly with people who thought they knew who he was. Even when they held a high opinion of him, his response was typically to suggest that he was either more than or other than what they thought he was. As his career draws near its violent close, the talk about him in Jerusalem makes it clear that he has succeeded quite decisively not just in making his identity a public question but also in making it a public occasion for the raising of other disputed questions:

> At this time some of the people of Jerusalem were saying, "Is this not the man they have been trying to kill? Here he stands, speaking openly, and they say nothing to stop him! Could it be true the authorities have concluded that he is the Messiah? But then, we all know where he comes from, and when the Messiah appears, no one will know where he comes from." . . .
> They wanted to arrest him then and there, but no one could lay a hand on him because his hour had not yet come. There were a good many in the crowd, however, who believed in him; and they were saying, "When the Messiah comes, will he give more signs than this man has?" When the Pharisees and chief priests heard that talk about him was taking this turn and spreading among the people, they sent the Temple police to arrest him.
> Then Jesus said:
>
> > For a short time I am with you still,
> >   but then I return to him who sent me.
> > You will look for me
> >   but you will not find me,
> > For where I AM,
> >   you cannot come.
>
> So the Jews said to one another, "Where is he going that we shall be unable to find him? Does he intend to go abroad into the diaspora and teach the Greeks?" . . .
> Some who had been listening said, "He must be the prophet." Others said, "He is the Messiah." Still others said, "Would the Messiah come from Galilee? Does not scripture say that the Messiah must be descended from David and come from Bethlehem, the town of David?" So people could not agree about him.
> Some wanted to arrest him, but no one succeeded in laying a hand on him. The police returned to the chief priests and Pharisees, who said to them, "Why haven't you arrested him?"

The guards replied, "No one has ever spoken like this man."

"Have you too been led astray?" the Pharisees retorted. "Has any one in authority come to believe in him? Any of the Pharisees? This rabble knows nothing about the Law—damn them."

One of them, Nicodemus—the same man who had earlier come to Jesus—objected to them, "But does our Law judge a man without first giving him a hearing and learning what he is doing?"

To this they answered, "Are you a Galilean too? Look into the matter, and see for yourself: Prophets do not arise in Galilee." (John 7:25–27, 30–35, 40–52)

Jesus is presented here as the center of a tangle of disagreements. There are authorities who want to arrest him and put him to death, but opinion even at the top is divided about him—a fact that does not escape notice below, where opinion, though more favorable, is also divided. Is he the Messiah? The question stirs up conflicting expectations about the Messiah. Some think that when the Messiah comes, no one will know his origin; others think that he must be identifiable not just as a descendant of David but also as a resident of Bethlehem, David's ancestral village.

And then there is the matter of signs. Some, who evidently expect the Messiah to prove his claim to that role by working miracles, are impressed by Jesus' miracles. But others think that if Jesus is a miracle worker, then this proves that he is, in fact, not the Messiah, the Son of David, but rather "the Prophet," the second Moses whom Moses had promised would someday come. David was not a miracle worker, but Moses was, and his miraculous powers were granted him precisely in order to prove to the Israelites that his was the voice of God and must be heeded:

"But what if they will not believe me or attend to my words [Moses said to the Lord] and say to me, 'The Lord has not appeared to you'?"

The Lord then said, "What is that in your hand?"

"A staff," he said.

"Throw it down on the ground," the Lord said.

Moses threw it down on the ground. The staff turned into a snake, and Moses recoiled from it.

The Lord then said to Moses, "Reach out your hand, and grasp it by the tail."

He reached out his hand, grasped it, and it turned back into a staff in his hand.

"Thus shall they come to believe that the Lord, the God of their forebears, the God of Abraham, the God of Isaac, and the God of Jacob, has appeared to you." (Exod. 4:1–5)

If Jesus had offered many signs, then perhaps the proper inference should be: "He must be the Prophet!"

Jesus' own comment addresses neither the claims made for him nor the doubts raised about him. Brief as his words are, they allude both to an identity that transcends even the boldest claims made about him and to a destiny that will be accomplished sooner than they guess. The statement "Where I AM, you cannot come" is audibly askew. Logically, it should read "Where I go, you cannot come." But I AM is the name of God. When Jesus speaks of where he is going (as in "I return to him who sent me"), he is speaking—less blatantly at this point than he will a bit later— of who he is. But with the irony that grows ever more intense as the Gospel of John nears its conclusion, he is also speaking of his own death, which few if any in the crowd realize is only "a short time" away.

This second meaning, this progressive revelation of an identity, con- ceals something of a third meaning. Though the ultimate meaning of Jesus' execution will be inseparable from his identity, the proximate rea- son for it is the wisdom of his preaching, a wisdom that the world cannot comprehend. In Proverbs 1:24–28, God speaks as Wisdom personified, a feminine voice, the anima to God's usual male animus:

> Because I have called and you would not listen,
>   have stretched out my hand and no one cared,
> Because you have ignored all my advice
>   and rejected my correction,
> I will laugh at your calamity
>   and mock when panic grips you,
> When panic rakes you like a storm
>   and your downfall descends like a whirlwind,
>   when distress and anguish come upon you.
> Then they will call upon me, but I will not answer.
>   They will look for me, but they will not find me.

Jesus is not referring only to the fact that, after his death, people will look for him and not find him. He is also referring to the coming destruction of Jerusalem and to the fact that, on that dread occasion too, people will look for God to rescue them and will not find him. Jerusalem will be abandoned in her hour of need just as Jesus will be in his.

But is it because Jerusalem is rejecting God Incarnate that he will abandon them to the Romans? It may as easily be the other way around: Because God knows that he will abandon Jerusalem to the Romans, he must arrange for Jerusalem to abandon him to the Romans first. They must abandon their God to the enemy so that he may be exonerated when, as it will seem to them, he abandons them to the same enemy. The destruction of Jerusalem, like the death of the Messiah, will be preceded by raucous Jewish quarrels—in fact, by a true civil war—and followed by a deathly silence. The first atrocity is a gloss, in advance, on the second.

At moments like these, Jesus seems to locate himself in the eternity whence he comes ("In the beginning was the Word"). That the Temple auditors hear so little suggests to the reader that perhaps, even with the best will, no one can hear everything that is being said. Some of them think, with a naive literalism, that if Jesus is going so far away that he cannot be followed, then he must be leaving Judea for the Greek-speaking diaspora around the Mediterranean. Their guess misses all that is dark and vast about Jesus' statement, yet—irony within irony—they are right by being wrong. The word *Greeks* as they use it need not imply *Gentiles,* any more than the word *Galileans* does. Just as there are Galilean Jews, or Galileans accepted as children of Israel, so also are there Greek Jews. In other words, the word *Greeks,* deliberately ambiguous, may refer either to Greek-speaking Jews of the diaspora or to the much larger population of Gentiles in the huge Greek-speaking Mediterranean world. But in either sense, the mistaken guess of those who listened to Jesus is true in a way they do not guess, for Christianity will spread around the Mediterranean by traveling, at first, from synagogue to synagogue through a network of Greek-speaking Jewish communities, only later spreading outward from those communities into the larger Gentile world. Paul will do what those listening to Jesus guess that he himself may be about to do.

Meanwhile, in the eyes of the Jewish authorities, any full-blooded Jew who would defend this Galilean risks being damned as an ignorant Galilean himself—ignorant of the law and therefore doomed to break it and to fall under the Lord's curse: "Accursed be anyone who does not uphold the words of this law by observing them" (Deut. 27:26). Nicodemus tries to fight Deuteronomy with Deuteronomy, alluding to Deuteronomy 1:17: "You shall not be partial in judgment; you shall hear the small and the great alike" (RSV). His efforts fail, but the failure matters little: Jesus' enemies are powerless against him, for "his hour [has] not yet come" (John 8:20), and it will not come a moment sooner than he wishes.

HE REFUSES TO CONDEMN AN ADULTERESS

Under the Jewish law of Jesus' day, adultery was a sin with a different meaning for men and for women. If a married man had sexual relations with an unmarried, unbetrothed woman, he was not guilty of adultery; but if a married woman had sexual relations with any man other than her husband, she *was* guilty of adultery and would be stoned to death if caught. As for the unmarried, a woman observant of the law was allowed no sexual relations before marriage, and her abstinence was enforced by her family. A man observant of the law faced no comparable prohibition, though in general the only unmarried women culturally available for sex were prostitutes.

Consent played no role in these reckonings. Sexual access to a young woman was a family asset, and he who stole that asset risked reprisal, even if the young woman was willing. The greater peril by far, however, was hers. A bride who could not produce the blood proof of her virginity on her wedding night could be stoned to death. A man risked death only when the woman he slept with was married or betrothed to someone else and when he was caught in the act by two eyewitnesses.

Circumstantial evidence was not enough to convict either a man or a woman of adultery. However, here too there was a double standard. In the absence of the required eyewitness testimony, a husband suspicious of his wife could bring her before a priest, who would require her to drink "the water of bitterness," water mixed with dust from the floor of the Tabernacle or Temple. If she was guilty, the Lord would strike her "thigh" (a euphemism for her genitals)—that is, she would suffer a painful urinary infection—and she would say "Amen, Amen," admitting her sin. At this point, she would fall under the Lord's curse against adultery and could be put to death (Num. 5:12–31). No provision was made for a suspicious wife to require her husband to drink the water of bitterness.

Despite what this double standard might seem to suggest, adultery was not seen ultimately as the betrayal of a husband by a wife but as an offense against God. Accordingly, a wronged husband did not have the right to commute the death sentence of an adulterous wife to some smaller punishment. Adultery was close to an unforgivable sin. Only apostasy matched it in gravity, an equation that explains, in part, why these two sins were so closely associated in ancient Israelite prophecy.

Against this background, what is the already endangered Jesus to say when a woman caught in the act of adultery is brought before him in the Temple itself?

> At dawn, Jesus appeared in the Temple again. All the people gathered around him, and he sat down and began to teach them. The scribes and Pharisees brought a woman who had been caught in the act of adultery. Forcing her to stand there in the middle, they said to Jesus, "Teacher, this woman was caught in the very act of committing adultery. Now in the Law, Moses has ordered us to stone women like this. What say you?" They asked him this as a test, seeking a charge to use against him. But Jesus bent down and started writing in the dust with his finger. When they persisted in their questioning, he rose up and said, "Let him among you who is without sin cast the first stone at her." Then he bent down again and resumed writing in the dust. When they heard this, they went away one by one, beginning with the eldest, and Jesus was left alone, and the woman still standing there in the middle. Jesus stood up and said, "Woman, where are they? Has no one condemned you?"
>
> "No one, sir," she replied.
>
> "Neither do I condemn you," said Jesus. "Be on your way, and from now on sin no more." (John 8:2–11)

In the classic manner of biblical narrative, this episode stops just short of making perfect sense, forcing the reader by its economy to complete its sense by answering the questions it leaves unanswered.

A first and obvious question: Is the woman innocent or guilty? Jesus is not asked to make that determination. The scribes and Pharisees present her as unquestionably guilty, a woman who has literally been caught in the act. But are they telling the truth?

An answer is suggested by the fact that Jesus begins writing on the ground. From writing on the ground, it is a small step to writing on the wall. What Jesus may intend to bring to the mind of the scribes, experts in scripture, is the scene in the Book of Daniel in which writing appears ominously on the wall at a feast held by a doomed Babylonian monarch. If the words that Jesus writes on the ground are the famous (and quickly written) Aramaic words *mene, mene, teqel,* and *parsin* (Dan. 5), then there may come quickly to the scribal mind the fact that Daniel had once rescued a woman falsely accused of adultery. On that occasion (Dan. 13), two of the most respected elders in the community had hidden themselves in the beautiful Susanna's locked garden, accosted her as she bathed, and said that unless she lay with them, they would report that they had come upon her in the garden lying with a young man who had escaped when discovered. She refused them, they carried out their threat, and her stoning was about to begin when Daniel broke in to expose inconsistencies in their testimony. In the end, Susanna was spared, and the perjured elders were stoned to death in her place.

As we noted earlier, Jesus reads minds. Like Daniel, he has the powers of a seer. As he delays his reply and writes on the ground (the one and only time Jesus is described as writing), is this the chain of association he wants to call to their minds?

Other questions arise. For one, why does Jesus bend down? To write on the ground, one must look down, of course, but Jesus may have had a second reason. A convicted adulteress was stripped naked before her stoning. A woman caught in the act of adultery might be unveiled humiliatingly for her trial (as Susanna was) or even stripped to the waist. After writing what he writes, Jesus looks up only long enough to speak a single sentence to the scribes and Pharisees, then looks down again. By the time he looks up for the second time, the men are gone; and if her clothes were disheveled, the woman has had time to rearrange them. Speculative? Of course. Historical? Certainly not: The story of the adulteress brought to Jesus in the Temple is a very late addition to the Gospel of John with a particularly weak claim to historicity. But it is impossible to exclude it from the imagination and therefore from a literary reading of this episode.

Stoning was a form of execution designed not to exclude the community at large, as is the case today with the sanitized barbarity of capital punishment in the United States, but to involve it both physically and emotionally. There was no designated executioner. The men of the community did the killing themselves, all participating in the same way at the same time, a rule that, in a close-knit community, must have served as a deterrent, rather than an incentive, to the use of capital punishment. There was just one exception to the rule of execution by universal, simultaneous action, but it happens to bear directly on Jesus' response. In the case of an apostate convicted by at least two eyewitnesses, according to Deuteronomy 17:5–7, the stones were not to be thrown all at once. The witnesses were required to throw the first stones; only then could the other men of the community join in.

Is this a clue to Jesus' strategy when he speaks so unexpectedly of the throwing of the first stone? Under Mosaic law, when an adulteress as distinct from an apostate was to be stoned, the eyewitnesses, of whom the husband would almost always be one, were *not* required to throw the first

FIRST PLACE ME MILES
MRS INTRODUCED POLITICS &
TOO BAD HE FELT ME NEED.

stone. The law that did not permit a husband to spare an adulterous wife did, at least, provide that he would not himself have to take the lead in bashing her to death. But is Jesus intensifying the law, rather than breaking it, in the paradoxical way we have seen him manage before? Could this be what is meant when he says, "Let him among you who is without sin cast the first stone at her"? Is the import, in other words, "Let the innocent party—the wronged husband—begin the execution of the guilty party"? If so, then Jesus is once again employing his strategy of shaming by paradoxical hyperagreement. The younger men might not take the point immediately, but the older men certainly would. They might appreciate that even a husband who wanted to see his cheating wife die in an anonymous hail of rocks would not want to throw the first rock himself, with the eyes of his fellows—not to speak of her eyes—fixed upon him.

A fourth question arises. What if, instead of this paradoxical hyperagreement with the Law of Moses, Jesus had put himself in routine and uncontroversial agreement with it? What if he had replied simply, "If the Law of Moses says to stone her, then do what you must do"? What sort of "charge to use against him" would that reply occasion? If the scribes and Pharisees are laying a trap, how does the trap spring shut?

Elsewhere, the Gospel of John 18:31 states that under the Roman occupation, Jewish authorities have been deprived of the right to inflict capital punishment. Granting that this is the case, if Jesus takes it upon himself to say that the adulteress should be stoned, he will have broken the laws of Rome. But if Jesus says the woman should be spared or even brought before the Roman authorities, he will have broken the Law of Moses. Either way, he will have provided his enemies an accusation to use against him. Either way, he will have been stopped.

The scribes and Pharisees, protecting themselves against the Romans, do not say, "Join us in stoning this sinner." They stop short of saying even "We believe that she should be stoned. What do you believe?" But subtle as his opponents are, Jesus is subtler still. In the end, it is they who must retreat, and so it happens once again that the bridegroom of Israel finds himself alone with a woman of questionable—or, at any rate, questioned—reputation. In the stunned privacy of the moment he could say anything he wanted, about adultery or anything else. What does he choose to say?

Strikingly, though he says nothing either to affirm her innocence or to diminish the gravity of adultery as a sin, he chooses not to condemn her, even privately. Recall that he is God and that the rule of stoning is a rule that he himself established. Why has he broken it? What explanation can be offered when he says, "Neither do I condemn you," other than that he has grown more merciful?

According to Exodus 34:6, a passage already quoted, the Lord is "a god merciful and gracious, slow to wrath, and abounding in steadfast love and faithfulness, keeping steadfast love unto the thousandth generation, forgiving iniquity, transgression, and sin, but letting nothing pass and visiting the sins of the parents upon the children and the children's children unto the third and the fourth generation." But God has never, in his long life, allowed his mercy to overcome his justice as Joseph, in the Book of Genesis, does when he spares Judah, the half-brother whose idea it had been to sell the boy Joseph into Arab slavery for twenty shekels of silver. The triumph of mercy comes when Judah, not recognizing the now grown Joseph, offers himself as Joseph's slave in exchange for the freedom of Benjamin, Joseph's full brother. Joseph in that moment (Gen. 44–45), touched by Judah's selfless courage, spares him when, in accordance with the law, he might have had him put to death. These actions set a standard of mercy that God himself has so far never met. But he meets it with this woman. Is God changing?

Between the lines of more than a few Psalms, Israel hoped that God would change. For example, a softened, poetic expansion of Exodus 34:6 is offered in Psalm 103:8–14 (italics added):

> The Lord is merciful and gracious,
>   slow to wrath and abounding in steadfast love.
> He will not always chide,
>   nor will he hold his anger forever.
> *He does not deal with us by the measure of our sins,*
>   *nor requite us in proportion to our iniquities.*
> For as high as the heavens are above the earth,
>   so great is his steadfast love for those who fear him.
> And as far as the east is from the west,
>   so far does he remove our transgressions from us.
> As a father pities his children,
>   so the Lord pities those who fear him,
> *For he knows our frame,*
>   *he remembers that we are dust.*

If we grant that the alleged adulteress is an actual adulteress and that she has been brought before God Incarnate, then the Psalmist's hope seems not to have been in vain. Men, speaking for the Lord, were prepared to deal with her according to her iniquity. The Lord himself has chosen to remember that she is dust.

The long-suffering Job yearned to see such a moment, a moment when righteous men, men who presumed to speak for God, would be struck dumb as God spoke simply but eloquently for himself. To God's presumptuous defenders, Job—tempted to (and accused of) blasphemy—said:

> Will you speak falsehood for God,
>   and lie on his behalf?
> Do you presume to do favors for him,
>   and make his case for him?
> Will it go well for you when he finds you out?
>   Or do you think to fool him as you fool men?
> Will he not expose you
>   if you hide your bias?
> Will his majesty not terrify you,
>   and dread of him overwhelm you?
>
> (13:7–11)

The Lord tarried long before vindicating the supposedly blasphemous Job, but in the end he rebuked those who presumed to defend God just as Job had dreamed he would. "You have not spoken rightly of me," the Lord said to them, "as has my servant Job" (42:8).

If the Lord has grown more merciful, then those who think to do his will by stoning an adulteress proceed on a false premise. Moreover, those who, figuratively speaking, would stone Israel, saying that the nation's infidelity has made its continuing oppression well deserved, serve him equally ill. The husband of the adulteress was not the only innocent party in the circle of men standing around her. If stones were to be thrown, surely Jesus himself met his own criterion. Surely he was sinless enough to have thrown the first stone, but he chose not to do so. As he refrains from condemning her, will he now, as God Incarnate, refrain as well from condemning Israel?

Hitherto, the perfect innocence of God has been the premise for all the abuse that he has seen fit to heap upon Israel. He was the faithful bridegroom, she the faithless bride. But is the premise still adequate? In his relations with Israel, the Lord has been like an outraged husband who, just before he rips off his wife's blouse and smashes her in the mouth, screams out the damning word "Slut!" He insisted that the Assyrians and the Babylonians were not battering Israel, *he* was doing so, but then had he not every right? What husband, wronged as he had been wronged, would do less? Once, God spoke that way, but does he still?

Just what *are* the rights of a cuckolded husband? On an earlier occasion, some Pharisees had approached Jesus and, "to put him to the test, said, 'Is it against the Law for a man to divorce his wife on any pretext whatever?'" Some taught that adultery was the only ground for divorce. Others admitted other, less weighty grounds. What position did Jesus take?

> He replied, "Have you not read that the Creator from the beginning *created them male and female* and that he said: *This is why a man leaves his father and mother and cleaves to his wife, and the two become one flesh*? So then they are no longer two, but one flesh. Therefore, what God has joined together, let no man put asunder."
> They said to him, "Why then did Moses establish that by a writ of dismissal a man could divorce his wife?" He said to them, "It was because you were so hard-hearted that Moses allowed you to divorce your wives, but it was not like this in the beginning." (Matt. 19:4–8)

Asked to offer grounds for divorce, Jesus instead, quoting Genesis in the words italicized above, offers the deep and original ground for marriage and challenges his questioners to respect it. He faults them for the hard-heartedness—and such it surely was in that era—that would turn a respectable married woman into a social outcast with no means of support but prostitution or servitude. The Old Testament, significantly, often calls for kindness to the widow but never once for kindness to the divorcée. Whatever the divorcée suffered, so the implicit message ran, she deserved it. Jesus, whatever social critique may be implied, unmistakably claims the right not merely to interpret but to revise the Law of Moses and to do so by invoking the revised intentions of the Creator as if he were the Creator himself. By invoking the Garden of Eden against Mount Sinai, Jesus alludes, as in his conversation with Nicodemus, to the coming of a new creation: a return to Eden or, indeed, an improved Eden. The curse of sexuality as we know it is to be lifted no less than the curse of mortality. Outside the Garden, the provision Mosaic law makes for divorce may be reasonable, but God is not going to bar mankind from the Garden forever.

Jesus has now spoken on his own authority, as God Incarnate, for mercy and against cruelty; but then he goes on to do something even more astonishing. Having rescued a fallen woman from sure death, he speaks, astonishingly but revealingly, *as if he himself has become a defendant* and is seeking witnesses in his defense. The Lord God is indeed a defendant, and he knows of what he can be accused, but his way of asking for mercy is to extend mercy.

When Jesus spoke to the people again, he said:

> . . . You judge by human standards;
>> I judge no one.
>> Yet if I do judge, my judgment will be true.
> For I am not alone:
>> He who sent me is with me.
> In your law it is written
>> that the testimony of two witnesses is reliable.
> I testify on my own behalf,
>> but the Father who sent me testifies on my behalf as well.

They asked him, "Where is your Father, then?"
Jesus answered:

> You know neither me nor my Father.
> If you knew me,
> you would know my Father as well.

He spoke these words while teaching near the Temple treasury. No one arrested him, because his hour had not yet come. (John 8:12, 15–20)

John adds the comment "No one arrested him" because once again Jesus is claiming equality with God, and it is just this that has previously led to arrest attempts. In one sentence, Jesus says that his Father and he are two witnesses. In the next, he says that to know him is to know his Father. Coming after the sparing of the adulteress, these words have the effect of underscoring the fact that it is God himself who has spared her and therefore God himself whose attitudes on this and related matters must be changing. The meaning of his line "I judge no one" is "I condemn no one," a meaning that may become clearer if we recall the famous line (Matt. 7:1) "Judge not, that you be not judged." The God of Israel made his reputation as a judge who would by no means ever say, "I condemn no one," but God is changing before our eyes. Having turned the tables on the husband in two instances of marital casuistry, God the Husband now turns the tables on himself. In his relationship with Israel, not all the wrong, not all the excess, has necessarily been on her side.

Even if God's sins are largely of omission, even if they consist in a failure to rescue his abused wife, and even if the worst omissions lie in the future, they are sufficient in the aggregate to direct attention, his own attention, away from her to himself. In a word, confronting his sinful but suffering people, God may be not just merciful but also penitent.

"IS HE GOING TO KILL HIMSELF?"

If God neither condemns evil nor resists it, it would seem to follow that he can neither rescue others nor protect himself. The lordly equanimity alluded to earlier has about it a quality that in a Greek tragedy would be called fatalistic. But fate is not an actor in this tragedy; or if that role exists at all, then God himself is playing it. Though the God of Israel cannot be said to have had everything under his control at every moment, it certainly cannot be said that any other power has exerted a control more pervasive or complete than his. Satan, despite the extent to which his influence has grown, cannot be said to have overtaken God. More important, there is no impersonal force to which both God and Satan are both subject—no karma, no ineluctable destiny. If Jesus seems doomed, it can only be because God has doomed himself.

But what word do we use of someone who dooms himself? In the Gospel of John, some of Jesus' contemporaries ask aloud if he intends to kill himself. The word *suicide* has not yet been coined, but in the language of our day this is indeed what they ask about. And as so often with popular interpretations of Jesus in that Gospel, they are both wrong and right to ask.

> Again he said to them:
>
>> I am going away; you will look for me,
>> but you will die in your sin.
>> Where I am going, you cannot come.
>
> At this the Jews said among themselves, "Is he going to kill himself, that he says, 'Where I am going, you cannot come'?" (John 8:21–22)

The brief answer Jesus gives on the spot becomes a more searching explanation a bit later when he says:

> I am the good shepherd.
> The good shepherd lays down his life for his sheep.

A hired hand, when he sees a wolf coming,
abandons the sheep,
since he is not the shepherd
and the sheep are not his.
He runs away,
and the wolf attacks and scatters the sheep.
He runs away because he is only a hired hand
and does not care about the sheep.
I am the good shepherd.
I know mine and mine know me,
just as the Father knows me
and I know the Father.
I lay down my life for my sheep.
And I have other sheep
that are not of this fold,
and I must lead them too.
They too must hear my voice,
and there will be one flock, one shepherd.
The Father loves me
because I lay down my life
in order to take it up again.
No one is taking it from me.
I lay it down of my own accord.
I have the power to lay it down,
and I have the power to take it up again.
This is the commission that I have received from the Father.

These words caused renewed division among the Jews. Many said, "He is possessed! He is out of his mind! Why do you listen to him?" Others said, "This is not the voice of demonic possession. Could a devil open the eyes of the blind?" (John 10:11–21)

So, then, those listening to Jesus are correct to a point in their suspicion that he intends to kill himself, but he understands his death to be, somehow, for their sake. He may not die by his own hand, but his own death will nonetheless be of his own doing:

No one is taking [my life] from me.
I lay it down of my own accord.

True, when God Incarnate does such a thing, there is a difference. Though any man might choose to lose his life, only God can "take up again" a life once lost. Only he can employ death, his own death, to

make a point and survive to see the point made. But even if a resurrection is to follow, why should God inflict human dying upon himself in
the first place?

As we noted when discussing the multiplication of the loaves and
fishes, the shepherd in Israelite tradition was a figure of heroism and
valor. The king of a nation was like the shepherd of a flock not in nur-
ture alone but also, and perhaps most important, in physical courage. It
was his task to fight off hostile foreigners as a shepherd fought off wolves.
In the Twenty-third Psalm, which opens "The Lord is my shepherd," the
most important verse is the fifth (italics added): "You prepare a table for
me *in the presence of my enemies.*" The wolves are out there, but the divine
shepherd has the strength to keep them at bay. The claim that Michelangelo's muscular *David* portrays the Israelite hero as a Greek god, though
true enough at the level of art history, does not make the work untrue to
the Bible once one recalls that Israel's God was a shepherd understood to
have muscle enough to kill when the occasion required. The earliest
Christian image of Christ, that of a youthful, beardless shepherd carrying
a lamb on his shoulders, is emotionally akin to the image of an infantry-
man holding a lost child in time of war. But that image, as inherited
equally from Israel, was also an image of God himself. This is what God
at his best was like: young, fearless, tender, and heroic.

Recalling this, we should expect God Incarnate, when speaking of
the good shepherd, to say not what he says in the passage quoted above
but, rather, something like this:

> A hired hand, when he sees a wolf coming,
> Abandons the sheep and runs away.
> I am the good shepherd.
> When I see a wolf coming to attack my sheep,
> I kill the wolf.

How are sheep served by a dead shepherd? Such a consideration, naive
and literal-minded as it may seem, might well prompt those listening to
Jesus to suppose that, suicidal or not, the man is deranged. The thought
that would make sense of Jesus' words—the *only* thought that can make
sense of them—is that of divine self-martyrdom, but this is a thought too
shocking to consider.

The Greek word *martys,* from which the word *martyr* is derived,
means "witness." The martyr who suffers and dies for his faith witnesses
before his fellow men to the depth of his devotion to God. But when
God suffers and dies, to whom does he testify? And can he thus demon-

strate his devotion to his human creatures? Why not do so by rescuing them instead of punishing himself? A martyr proves, after all, not just his devotion but also his trust that the divine power for which he dies will ultimately prevail. What is to be made of a martyrdom in which divinity seems to demonstrate only its weakness?

Jesus forces this very question by first defining himself as shepherd and then announcing that, rather than protect his sheep from the Roman wolf, he will let the wolf kill him, their shepherd. As a demonstration for the benefit of Israel and of the "other sheep / That are not of this fold," this martyrdom cannot fail to suggest with the utmost vividness that God will not save his people even from annihilation at the hands of the Roman oppressor.

Notably, however, even when speaking of his own impending defeat, Jesus does not speak of the Romans. He speaks instead, at the most crucial moments, of Satan; in so doing, he identifies his enemy not as Rome or some other earthly power, least of all Israel, but as death itself. This shift could not be more important than it is for the revision of God's identity. When Jesus dies, death wins, and the Devil wins for the moment; but when Jesus rises from the dead, life wins, and the Devil loses for all time. By rising from the dead, God Incarnate will surely not defeat Rome, but he just as surely will defeat death. He will win a victory of a new sort, over a newly identified enemy, and in the process he will redefine the traditional covenant terms of victory and defeat. Victory under the traditional covenant was victory over the likes of the pharaoh of Egypt. Were God to win such a victory in Jesus' time, it would be a victory over the Caesar of Rome. But what did victory over Egypt matter in the end when the victors—those Israelites who looked on while the pursuing Egyptian army drowned—eventually died anyway? By the same token, what would victory over Rome matter, supposing that God could win such a victory? Well, then, if victory over any given nation does not matter, then neither does defeat by any given nation. The battle moves to a new battlefield where God, by rising from the dead, will lay claim to a new kind of invincibility:

> No one is taking [my life] from me.
> I lay it down of my own accord.
> I have the power to lay it down,
> and I have the power to take it up again.

This is his new boast, replacing "I am the god who brought you out of Egypt with mighty hand and outstretched arm."

That this is how God resolves the crisis in his own life will not become fully evident in the New Testament until after Jesus has risen from the dead—more accurately, until after his disciples have realized what his resurrection means for them. His crossing from death to life will function henceforth as the crossing of the Red Sea did when he was still a god out to win conventional battlefield victories. His own resurrection will be the miracle that establishes his credibility and defines his identity. But this revision of God's identity entails, scandalously, that before his victory God should first suffer a physical horror equivalent to the horror that impends for his chosen people. He must allow Roman soldiers to do to him what Roman soldiers will soon do to his covenant partner. So it is that in speaking of himself as a shepherd, Jesus inverts the traditional biblical image in a way that allows him to reveal the shocking truth only to those few who may be ready to hear it while concealing it from those who are not ready. When God quits the battlefield, God's people are left defenseless. If this is not to be seen simply as abandonment and betrayal, he must show, first, that he himself is willing to pay the price this change will exact of them and, second, that this defeat presages another kind of victory.

Martyrdom, as we saw in discussing that of the seven Maccabee brothers (pp. 128–29), had begun to be celebrated in Israel during the last pre-Christian centuries, but it was never God who was martyred. A demonstration of self-annihilating courage that could be edifying in God's saints would be unthinkable in God himself. Accordingly, the more nearly godlike the claims Jesus makes for himself, the more unacceptable, a priori, becomes the suggestion that he is about to die by self-martyrdom. The rhetorical question "Will he kill himself?"— to which the effective answer is yes—belongs, for those who ask it, with the opinions "He is possessed, he is raving." Suicide, madness, demonic possession—all these are forms of dismissal. If any of these charges is true, then Jesus' larger claims are false. Those who make these charges do so as if to excuse themselves from listening further, but their own dismissals do not quite work, for "Could a devil open the eyes of the blind?"

INTERLUDE: THE SUICIDE OF GOD
INCARNATE IN CHRISTIAN THEOLOGY

The interpretation of the New Testament offered in this book is literary rather than historical or theological. It is literary, however, without indifference to history or prejudice against theology. And in that connection, it is worth recalling that the concept of the suicide of God has a history stretching back to the very first Christian theologians. Its presence in the Gospel of John, the Letter to the Philippians, and the Letter to the Hebrews might in itself be sufficient to establish its antiquity, but these canonical works are, in fact, just the beginning. In a Greco-Roman world whose habitual ideas about suicide were so far from our own, the suicide of Christ was, in effect, more nearly a boast than a scandal.

Pierre-Emmanuel Dauzat makes this point in the opening paragraph of *Le Suicide du Christ,* his intellectually probing historical survey of the use of the idea in Christian thought:

> The theme of these pages is born of a double astonishment: that the notion of a Christ who would commit suicide should have been born so early, as early in fact as the Gospel of John; and that this notion should owe virtually nothing to the anti-Christian polemic of the first centuries. The idea of the suicide of Christ will have been, before all else, a Christian if not indeed a Christological idea.

Early Christianity knew a quasi-anatomical, virtually suicidal interpretation, Dauzat reports, of the Gospel verse in which Jesus "said 'It is fulfilled' and, bowing his head, gave up his spirit" (John 19:30):

> Christ first bows his head, then dies, when ordinarily it is the opposite order that should obtain. The bowing of the head is normally a consequence of death. Up to the moment of death, Jesus remains the subject of an active verb: "Bowing his head" (Greek, *klinas ten kephalen*), he gives up his spirit. Otherwise put, Jesus voluntarily gives up his spirit because, as Origen [185–254 C.E.] would later say, it was inconceivable that God should be at the mercy of the flesh as any ordinary mortal would be.

Origen's contemporary Tertullian spoke in a similar vein, stressing the fact that Jesus died on the cross with such abnormal rapidity that he could only be understood to have died as and when he chose.

Of even greater importance, perhaps, than the voices of these early Christian witnesses is the silence of Celsus, a scathing second-century critic who missed no opportunity to mock Christianity. ("A religion for worms," he called it, inasmuch as its adherents claimed to draw eternal life from a corpse.) Celsus evidently saw nothing to be gained in disparaging Jesus as a suicide: The associations of suicide in his day were so positive that such disparagement could all too easily seem praise. Anti-Christian polemicists like Celsus were far more likely to mock Jesus for fearing death than for embracing it with suspect eagerness. Jesus' bloody sweat on the eve of his execution and his prayer "*Abba,* Father! For you everything is possible. Take this cup away from me" (Mark 14:36) were, in pagan eyes, grotesquely unbecoming a hero, much less a god. Cowardice was a disgrace. Suicide could be a proof of courage.

Suicide could also be an expression of sheer devotion, as can be seen in a remarkable passage in Paul's Letter to the Philippians:

> Life to me, you see, is Christ, but in that case death would be a positive gain. But on the other hand, if to be alive in the body gives me an opportunity for fruitful work, *I do not know which I should choose.* I am caught in this dilemma: I want to be off with Christ, and this is by far the stronger desire—and yet for your sake to stay alive in this body is a more urgent need. (NJB; Phil. 1:21–24 with modifications, italics added)

Like Socrates, Paul believed that a heedless or irresponsible suicide was wrong, but that a moral, fully pondered suicide was conceivable. One could not take one's life in disregard of God's wishes, but God might well acquiesce in or even actively approve of such an action, just as he might acquiesce in or actively approve of martyrdom. The theoretical similarities, during this period, among Platonism, Judaism, and Christianity are greater than their differences, though there was wider divergence in practice.

The self-martyrdom of God Incarnate was an inspiration for Christian martyrs during the first three centuries of church history. Imperfectly distinguished from martyrdom, suicide did not become a theoretical problem for Christianity until martyrdom itself became a practical problem for the church. This happened when the Roman empire became Christian and dissident Christians began using martyrdom against the now established church as effectively as their forebears had used it against the empire. It was only then that a sharp distinction between glorious martyrdom and shameful suicide began to be actively propagated. The great change owes most to the philosopher and theologian Augustine of Hippo (354–430 C.E.), a bishop of the established church in whose diocese heretical martyrs were winning converts. It was Augustine's influence that brought about the revision in Christian thought whereby martyrdom in any but an approved cause could be judged to be self-homicide and therefore, like any other homicide, an offense against God.

By this time, however, the ideal of sacred suicide had had three hundred years to put down social as well as intellectual roots in Christianity. To be sure, the socially and even ecclesiastically disruptive power of the idea was enormous, but then this aspect of it had been grasped long before Augustine. Two centuries before his day, the Christian theologian Clement of Alexandria was prepared to dismiss certain Christian martyrs as mere "athletes of death." But how far could Clement or Augustine or any Christian theologian go in this direction before skirting the possibility that Jesus himself was a mere athlete of death? Had his death not been unwelcome to established religious authority? And so the question remained unresolved. Against Clement, Origen honored martyrdom as "a second baptism in blood." In the persecution of Christians that broke out in the third century, his was understandably the more appealing idea. When the persecution passed, it lost some of its appeal, and so on, back and forth.

In the end, however, the ideal of sacred suicide was too well established in Christian behavior, beginning with Jesus himself, and too well documented in scripture to be altogether suppressed, even when opposed by the brilliance of an Augustine. It could be and was muted, submerged, softened, and rationalized, but it could not be and never has been entirely eliminated. Instead, it has lived a kind of stop-and-start life in theology, repeatedly forgotten, repeatedly revived. As Dauzat puts it, "Both the durability of the theme and the circuitous, fragmentary, or, if you will, episodic approach that it inspired were quick to appear."

Dauzat offers *Le Suicide du Christ* as a kind of "theological novel," revisiting the kinds of theology that have been written in each chapter of Christian history, starting with the earliest. Strikingly, what was true back then has remained true: The "lost" idea has been rediscovered and reexplored by Christian theologians far more often than by anti-Christian polemicists. What might be the consequences of a revival in our own day? Dauzat suggests that both conservative and radical theology will be undercut if and when this marginal idea begins to move toward the center. Conservative "atonement" theology, according to which God sacrifices Jesus so as to make amends to himself for the sins of mankind, will be undercut when God is understood to be sacrificing himself. Radical "death of God" theology will be undercut when the Incarnation is understood to be not a conceptual culmination but simply a premise for the drama in which God subjects himself to human dying.

In his distinctly sardonic style, Dauzat writes: "From the agnostic side, they crowd around the gate. It's a question of who will get to deliver the fatal blow. From the side of the theologians, the same silly airs, the like intrigues. Pilate, Judas, our sins, the Romans, the too famous 'Jews' of John: Everyone has his place in this macabre *mise en scène* for courtroom buffs. Except God." Dauzat's own, postmodern way of bringing God onto the "macabre *mise en scène*" may be suggested by the title of his introduction, "Theology Stripped Naked by Her Bachelor, Even." That title echoes the title of Marcel Duchamp's epoch-making *The Bride Stripped Naked by Her Bachelors, Even*. The meaning this endlessly discussed painting acquired (whatever Duchamp intended) was that the art of painting was itself about to change. For Dauzat, theology's bachelor is God himself, the one and only one of his kind in the universe. Theology will change, or could change, Dauzat implies, when the self-sacrificing, suicidal, cosmic bachelor takes the place in contemporary Christian consciousness that he had in early Christian consciousness. In the postmodern manner, Dauzat's theology goes backward and forward at will, assuming that any new chapter in the ongoing "theological novel" of the West may draw as eclectically as it chooses on all the previous chapters. The history of theological thought, like the history of all thought, is a story whose entire plot must stir in its sleep as each subsequent chapter is written.

Traditional biblical theology has been ideological criticism of the text of the Bible and as such has been far more deferential toward its subject than, for example, the comparable criticism of the plays of Shakespeare has been toward its. From Shakespeare's plays alone, even without detailed study of the playwright's historical setting, it is possible—if one is determined to do so—to infer an entire worldview. Rarely is it suggested, however, that once the ideology of a Shakespeare or any other author is established, it should be taken as normative. In recent decades, quite to the contrary, ideological criticism has been used more often to belittle than to aggrandize the major writers of the Western canon. In this regard, ideological criticism of the Bible—that is, biblical theology—has remained at a striking remove from other ideological criticism, for its assumption has continued to be that the thought of the Bible should indeed be normative or, if not normative in every regard, then at least relevant by definition for the conduct of personal and political life. To a point, the Bible, rationalized by biblical theology, still functions in just this way for a large religious constituency. It continues to do what imaginative literature, at its most ambitious and evangelically "humanistic," had begun to do for a secular constituency in the West until a loss of secular faith brought that kind of humanism to a close at the end of World War I. Perhaps biblical theology will continue to function in some such normative way, but if so, what new challenge must it meet?

In 1942, Albert Camus opened *The Myth of Sisyphus* with the famous line "There is only one serious philosophical problem—the problem of suicide." At the turn of the twentieth century, the Netherlands became the first country in modern times to legalize euthanasia. Dauzat suggests that the way in which Christianity imagines the suicide of God may have much to do with how the ongoing philosophical question of suicide, and the many questions to which it relates, will be engaged in the twenty-first century. To say this is not to sketch the outline of a theology but only to name a starting point. New starting points, however, may be what theology needs most.

For the modest purposes of this book, no overarching theological thesis need be advanced. It should be enough to note that strange as the idea of the suicide of Christ may seem to some, it is an idea that a Christian, even a devout Christian, can entertain. Among many possible illustrations of this point, one must suffice, an example of particular clarity and poignancy taken from the career of one of Shakespeare's contemporaries, the poet and theologian John Donne.

In 1610, Donne wrote *Pseudo-Martyr,* a dismissal of the dissident Catholic martyrs of the early seventeenth century as deluded suicides. Then, just a year later, he wrote *Biathanatos,* a defense of outright suicide in which Jesus himself is chief among the exemplary suicides of the past. *Biathanatos*—so daring in its day that it could be published only after Donne's death—is a tour de force of authentic intellectual passion. A fiercely brilliant scholar who once confessed a "sickely inclination" to become a *biathanatos* (that is, a suicide: the Greek word means "one dead by violence, especially self-inflicted"), Donne was paradoxically strengthened by his pathology to trace Christian martyrdom to its source in the suicide of God Incarnate. *Pseudo-Martyr,* by contrast, seems a politically expedient work of conventional religious propaganda. Yet who is to say that Donne did not believe what he wrote both times?

The ambiguity of the question resides in the fact that Christ is a suicide by metaphysical definition, whether or not he is a suicide in some more ordinary sense of the word. That is, if Jesus is God Incarnate, then no one can have taken his life away from him against his wishes. His suicide is, in this regard, as deeply built into the Christian story as the doctrine of the Incarnation. Thus, for Thomas Aquinas, Jesus was the cause of his own death as truly as a man who declines to close a window during a rainstorm is the cause of his own drenching. Thomas strongly implies, moreover, that those who actually killed Jesus, or conspired to kill him, were less than fully responsible agents, that they were tools in the hand of God, a species of human rainstorm drenching God because God wished to be drenched. There is support for the latter view in the New Testament itself. From the cross, Jesus says of his executioners, "Father, forgive them, for they know not what they do" (Luke 23:34). Peter, preaching in the Temple after Jesus' death, says, "Now I know, brothers, that neither you nor your leaders had any idea what you were really doing; but this was the way God carried out what he had foretold when he said through all his prophets that his Christ would suffer" (Acts 3:17–18).

But granting that Jesus is a suicide at least in this unique sense, is he a suicide in any more ordinary sense? Can his death be linked with the despair that precedes "private" suicide? Or was the ignominious suicide of Judas, Jesus' betrayer, added to the Gospel story precisely as a reminder that a chasm separates ordinary human suicide from the suicide of the God-man? Dauzat, building on the contemporary philosophical debate over suicide, wants to see an overlap such that what is said theologically about Christ's suicide can bear philosophically on the discussion of suicide in general. Voluntary, self-inflicted death, he says, typically represents the rejection of a marred or strangled life in the name of "*une vie dont on ne meurt pas,*" "a life you don't die of." One thinks of the dying dream of the purged communist in Arthur Koestler's 1941 novel *Darkness at Noon*. Did the disturbing eagerness of some early Christians for martyrdom perhaps express their political rejection of the Roman empire no less than it expressed their identification with the slain Redeemer? Were the Roman emperors who persecuted them not essentially correct in recognizing their martyrdom as a political threat? Did the martyrs not, in the end, defeat Rome as the armed insurrections of Judea could not?

Perhaps so, but just there the complications begin. Donne, a kind of prophet for our own day, managed both to defend the British crown in its need for order, as Augustine might have done, and to defend the human soul in its sickness unto death, as Kierkegaard would and as Christ might have seemed to do when he said, "Unless the grain of wheat falls into the earth and dies, it remains only a single grain." Donne was torn between these two views, just as Christianity itself has been torn and as perhaps it must always be torn whenever it allows itself to look this inherently disruptive question in the eye.

HE RESOLVES THE GREAT CRISIS IN HIS LIFE

In Jerusalem more than in Galilee, when Jesus appears in public, he often seems to be alone. This is particularly true as his life nears its end, and true above all in the Gospel of John. Except at the time of his triumphal entry into Jerusalem just before Passover, no enthusiastic crowds gather to hear him speak as they did in Galilee. Individual, anonymous voices do express wonder, but the people he addresses in the Jerusalem Temple—typically referred to as "the Jews," perhaps in contradistinction to "the Galileans," perhaps from the perspective of an ethnically mixed Christian community outside Palestine—respond to him with skepticism that escalates into hostility, and he contributes to the escalation. They wonder aloud whether he intends to kill himself. He insists that they are out to kill him. They say that he is possessed by a devil. He counters that they are servants of the Devil. They call him a Samaritan—that is, not a descendant of Judah, not a Jew. He counters that, in spirit, they are sons of Ishmael, not sons of Isaac—in effect, Arabs. The confrontation climaxes when he speaks of himself using the sacred, unspeakable proper name of God, and they take up stones to execute him on the spot for blasphemy. His engagement with them grows steadily more hostile, yet he succeeds in changing the terms of that engagement, terms that are— though they do not yet see this—the terms of their covenant with God.

The escalation from skepticism to hostility begins innocuously enough when Jesus says:

> If you take shelter in my word,
> you will be my disciples.
> You will come to know the truth,
> and the truth will set you free.
>
> (John 8:31–32)

Finding his promise of freedom presumptuous, they rebuke him: "We are descended from Abraham and have never been anyone's slaves" (8:33). Why do they need Jesus to set them free? The obvious answer, never spoken aloud by either side in this exchange, is "Because you are the oppressed colony of a foreign power."

Jesus gives, instead, an answer that transforms the meaning of freedom as well as of Abrahamic descent and, in the process, transforms the nature of God's acknowledged obligation to them:

Truly I tell you,
anyone who commits sin is a slave.
Now, a slave has no permanent standing in the household,
but a son belongs to it forever.

(8:34–35)

Why does Jesus make this reference to the differential standing of a slave
and a son in a household? Because, taking up their reference to Abraham,
he wishes to allude to the fact that the legendary patriarch had two sons:
Isaac, by his wife, Sarah, and Ishmael, by her slave and his concubine,
Hagar. The Jews understand themselves to be the legitimate descendants
of Abraham through Isaac. But by equating slavery and sin, Jesus equates
Jewish sinners with Abraham's descendants through Ishmael, whose
mother was a slave. He turns Jewish sinners, in other words, into spiritual
slaves.

"I know that you are descended from Abraham," he explains,

but you are seeking to kill me
because my word finds no reception in you.
I speak of what I have seen in *my* Father's presence.
You do what you have learned from *your* father.

(8:37–38, italics added)

For Father Abraham, Jesus now abruptly substitutes God the Father.
Somewhat surreptitiously, he also introduces a "Satan the Father" without yet saying the words *God* or *the Devil*. He taunts them by a rhetorical
sleight of hand. Lagging a step behind him, they continue to insist "Our
father is Abraham" (8:39), but Jesus drives his point home:

If you are children of Abraham,
do as Abraham did.
As it is, you are seeking to kill me,
a man who has told you the truth
as I have heard it from God
["*my* Father"].
This is not what Abraham did.
You are doing *your* father's work.

(8:39–41, italics added)

As they begin to catch his drift, they reply defensively that they are children of God the Father no less than he is: "The only father we have is

God" (8:41). What other father could he be referring to? But Jesus now confronts them more bluntly. It is not he but they who are under the Devil's control:

> If God were your father, you would love me,
> since I have come from God and am here.
> I am not here on my own.
> He sent me.
> Why do you not understand what I say?
> The fact that you cannot accept my words
> means that you must be from your father, the Devil,
> and you prefer to do as your father wishes.

> (8:42–44)

In God's innumerable past denunciations of Israel, his claim was invariably that they had turned away from him and were worshipping Baal, Asherah, Moloch, or some other of the gods of Canaan. They were thus violating the covenant commandment to "love the Lord" (Deut. 6:5), which was, more exactly, a commandment to remain strictly loyal to the Lord. In John 8, God Incarnate's denunciation of "the Jews" for not listening to him is structurally identical to those ancient complaints but for the fact that the role of Baal is now being played by the Devil. The Lord's people do not love him; instead, they "prefer to do as [their] father [the Devil] wishes."

But what is it that the Devil wants? The question matters crucially, because by defining his own mission in opposition to the Devil's, Jesus will redefine the mission of God himself. What the Devil wants, according to Jesus, is death. He is a murderer, a bringer of death. If God is now to be defined as the Devil's enemy, then God must be a savior, a bringer of life. And God's ancient command that Israel "choose life" (Deut. 30:19) by accepting his Torah becomes a new command to choose life by accepting "truth"—namely, the preaching of Jesus.

> Your father, the Devil, . . . was a murderer from the start.
> He stands outside the truth;
> there is no truth in him.
> When he lies,
> he betrays his true nature,
> for he is a liar, and the father of lies.
> But it is because I speak the truth
> that you do not believe me.

> (John 8:44–45)

By the defeat of Caesar, God might retake the land of Canaan, but that is not the war he chooses to fight. He has chosen, instead, by the defeat of Satan to defeat death itself and to lead his people into the new promised land of eternal life.

But who are his people? In this history-transcending, cosmic vision, where does historical Israel fit in? Jesus' hearers call him a Samaritan, challenging his ethnic legitimacy for a reason: He must be a Samaritan, for no true Jew would demonize them as he does; even worse, "Are we not right to say that you are a Samaritan and possessed of a devil?" (8:48). Replying to them, Jesus completes the provocation that, at this point, he has only half-made. He has defined the Devil's mission as murder and death. He now defines his own:

> Truly I tell you,
> whoever keeps my word
> will never see death.

> (8:51)

Rome may win, but what will that matter if death loses? And if Rome is the last thing on his hearers' angry minds, then he has only succeeded the more. Their anger consolidates his success in establishing life and death—rather than victory or defeat on the battlefield—as the future terms of God's relationship with them. His outrageous new claim quite effectively obliterates that embarrassing old failure. They are outraged, but by their very outrage they confirm his success in changing the subject:

> Now we *know* that you are possessed. Abraham is dead, and the prophets as well, and yet you say, "Whoever keeps my word will never taste death." Are you greater than our father Abraham, who died? The prophets are dead too. *Who are you claiming to be?* (8:52–53, italics added)

❦ This is the climax. They have asked, in the Temple itself, the question that Jesus must answer if God is to shed his old military identity as conqueror of Egypt and Canaan and robe himself in his new identity as bringer of eternal life. Jesus responds provocatively, as if defying *them* to tell *him* that he is their God in person:

> Your father Abraham rejoiced to see my day.
> He saw it and was glad.

They reply derisively, "You are not fifty yet, and you have seen Abraham!"

He counters, climactically:

> Truly I tell you:
> Before Abraham was,
> I AM.
>
> (8:56–58)

As we noted earlier, what matters about the Crucifixion is not what is suffered—the Romans crucified Jews by the thousands—but who suffers it. By applying to himself the sacred, unspeakable name of God—the I AM that Moses heard from the burning bush (Exod. 3:14)—Jesus gives an intolerable answer to their objection and reveals at last his own identity. Speaking this way, in public, on the Temple grounds, to an audience that cannot fail to take his point, Jesus leaves them only two choices: They must either accept him as God Incarnate or execute him as a blasphemer in obedience to God's commandment at Leviticus 24:16: "He who utters the name of the Lord shall be put to death: All the congregation shall stone him. Whether resident alien or native, the penalty for uttering the Name shall be death." The crowd chooses to obey Torah rather than humble themselves to this stranger: "At this they picked up stones to stone him, but Jesus hid himself and left the Temple" (John 8:59). •

I n intellectual history, when a question is left unanswered long enough, it tends to be abandoned. In Jewish intellectual history, the question of when the Lord would come again to restore Israel to sovereign greatness would become such a question. A tradition born in the Lord's seeming victory over the army of Pharaoh, the god-king of Egypt, would come to its climax, its death cry, in the disastrous uprisings of 66–70 and 132–135 C.E. of Judea against Rome. There were many in this climactic period who thought they could calculate the date of the Lord's coming intervention, among them the great Rabbi Akiba, who acclaimed Bar Kokhba, the leader of the second uprising, as messiah. Had either of those uprisings succeeded, the identity of the God of Israel as a war god would have come through its crisis in a different way. But the uprisings failed, and God's identity only went deeper into crisis.

Most of the large literature announcing that God would come again in power, and soon, was excluded from the Jewish and the Christian scriptural canon alike. Though Rabbinic Judaism and Christianity were both significantly affected by apocalypticism, each, in the end, was more profoundly affected by its separate repudiation of it. Those repudiations left the question of imminent national restoration under an army led by God effectively abandoned by both traditions. Each in its own way went on to other questions, other concerns, other hopes, and other ambitions. Each went on, as well, to a new spiritual space replacing the physical space of the razed Temple. For Judaism, this was the mystical space of Torah; for Christianity, the mystical body of Christ.

How can a process of identity revision like this one be given dramatic expression? How can it be turned into a story with characters and interpersonal conflicts and a resolution that allows its central character to live on in some way? In the Gospels, the dynamic of the unanswered, then abandoned, then replaced question shines forth every time Jesus talks about what he wants to talk about rather than about what his disciples or his questioners, friendly or hostile, want him to talk about. He is like a savvy politician who, when asked an embarrassingly unanswerable question, changes the subject and eloquently answers the question he would prefer to have been asked. The Incarnation creates the condition for this dramatization of a political moment in the life of God. By bringing the Lord God face-to-human-face with his "constituency"—the people for whom the embarrassing question When will the Lord come again in power to free us from bondage? is so omnipresent that it scarcely needs to be asked at all—the Gospels force him either to answer it directly or to change the subject. Because the true answer to the question When? is Never, he has no choice but to change the subject. But if his change of subject is to have any chance of succeeding, then the new subject must be so engaging, so shocking, so controversial, and yet so exciting and promising that the old question, compelling as it is, will simply fade from the mind. Moreover, as he changes the subject, the Lord must make it clear that it is *he* who is changing the subject.

This is a feat that, in its entirety, is only accomplished in the New Testament as a whole through the gradual assimilation of the meaning and promise of the Resurrection. It is complete in outline, however, by the end of the fourth Gospel (John); and within that Gospel, the outline is visible with particular clarity—with scandalous clarity—in John 8, the chapter that we have been examining. Here, by the tactical use of three inherently gripping subjects—adultery, suicide, and slavery—John distracts his Jewish readers' attention from God's traditional obligations and Israel's traditional expectations and redirects it to a new set of obligations and expectations that reflect a profound transformation in the identity of God.

The first of these distractions-to-a-point is adultery. The woman dragged before Jesus at John 8:2–11 has been captured in the act of illicit copulation, and her sentence is to be death by stoning. Jesus saves her life by rescuing her from the punishment that, under the law, she may well deserve. "Has no one condemned you?" he asks her. "No one, sir," she replies. "Neither do I condemn you," he says, suggesting, to riveting effect, that there is no longer any sin—in particular, any sexual sin—from which God cannot, at will, rescue the sinner. At this point, the scene, with its promise of a more abundant mercy, becomes not just gripping in itself but consoling in its implications, and yet God seems no longer the same god.

The second subject is suicide. Jesus, who has repeatedly claimed that he is threatened by murderers, may in fact be on the verge of killing himself, a possibility that makes the scene compelling in quite a different way. Though John 8:12–30 deals with other subjects en route, it crests at the Jews' question "Is he going to kill himself, that he says, 'Where I am going, you cannot come'?" When God is in constant danger of being killed or, possibly, of killing himself, his aura of military invincibility vanishes.

The third subject is slavery. Jesus, still facing the crowd that (he insists) wants to kill him, broaches at long last the unmentionable divine embarrassment: the bondage from which, after half a millennium, the Lord has not freed the Jews. He speaks of bondage only to redefine it immediately as bondage to sin. But if bondage is now bondage to sin rather than to Rome, then liberation is liberation from sin rather than from Rome. And what liberation now leads to is not the unencumbered, uncolonized, free possession of a promised land but eternal life. This is the boon by which God now defines himself.

The core objection to all this redefinition of God—namely, that only God can define God—is, positively, the core requirement for it. The quintessential Gospel scene, the scene enacted again and again with different subject matter for different audiences, is the scene in which Jesus and his audience clash over who he is and what he must do. As the Messiah, he might be expected to accept the classic terms for divine intervention, merely making an obvious set of contemporary substitutions. Thus,

for Pharaoh,	Caesar;
for bondage in Egypt,	oppression by Rome;
for the conquest of Canaan,	the reconquest of Judea;
for Moses and David,	the Messiah as prophet and king.

Instead, he proposes new terms for divine intervention in a way that would exceed the authority of anyone but God himself. Thus,

for Caesar,	the Devil;
for oppression by Rome,	bondage to sin;
for the reconquest of Judea,	eternal life;
for the Messiah as prophet and king,	the Messiah as God Incarnate.

True, the subject of Rome does not come up, but then the subject ought not come up when the very point is to change the subject. The kind of engagement by which the Lord had once so centrally defined both his own identity and that of Israel, his covenant partner, is here swept aside. And as if to authorize the sweeping transformation and place the new terms of engagement beyond question, there comes the climactic, all-silencing line "Before Abraham was, I AM."

It is by this scandalous line that Jesus of Nazareth—the all-forgiving murder target, the could-be suicide who promises eternal life to those who receive him as "the light of the world" (John 8:12)—claims to be none other than the Lord himself in person. Let those who still care about the old battlefield games play them. The Lord is playing for higher stakes. In this passage he makes plain what he meant on an earlier occasion when he said of Caesar, the god-king of the latest empire, "Render to Caesar the things that are Caesar's, and to God the things that are God's" (RSV; Luke 20:25). The monumental central subject of all Israelite history has been successfully changed. The unanswerable question has been deliberately abandoned. Though the full price is yet to be paid, the crisis in the life of God has been resolved.

HIS NEW COMMANDMENT: KINDNESS TO STRANGERS

Adultery, suicide, and death are not conventionally ethnic or political subjects, but as Jesus takes them up in turn in the chapter just discussed, each acquires a distinct ethnic and political coloration. It must be so, for the Lord is in the process of redefining his own political responsibilities to a distinct ethnic group and, in the same process, redefining his own identity. These are two sides of the same coin. Israel is Israel because of him, and he is himself because of Israel.

When the Lord refuses to condemn the adulteress, violating his own law, he carries his mercy to such an extreme that it would be reasonable to infer that he must not be the Lord. He has done something clearly out of character—unless his character has changed. But the rescue of the adulteress is simultaneously a story about Israel as a people defined by its covenant relationship with him. If his character as God is changing, then theirs as the people of God cannot remain untouched. The preservation of the identity of Israel as a distinct endogamous group with a unique relationship to God requires the close monitoring of pregnancies. This is why adultery is understood not simply as a violation of an Israelite husband's marital rights but also, and more importantly, as an offense against God. But can occupied Israel impose its own adultery law upon occupying Rome? If the answer is no, then no is also the answer to the background question of whether the divine warrior will ever end the Roman occupation that is so inimical to his own intentions. When Jesus spares the adulteress, his mercy toward her allows Torah, the code of his own covenant with Israel, to be defeated by the law of the foreign oppressor. Israel, under Roman law, may not execute such a woman. God Incarnate declines to intervene. He says, in effect, that if Israel is under foreign rule, so be it; and his jealous prior claim on the firstborn from every Israelite womb expires at that moment.

It is as if the calendar has been turned back to the sixth day of creation. Once again, the first couple have been told to "be fruitful and multiply," and God, once again, enters no claim of ownership on their offspring. He is once again like the sun, shining indiscriminately on the sexual reproduction of the wicked and the good.

As for Jesus' impending suicide-by-execution, it too has a surprising ethnic or geopolitical dimension. Recall that the words "Where I am going, you cannot come" or the equivalent are spoken twice. On the second occasion (John 8:21–22), the crowd asks, not inappropriately, "Is he going to kill himself?" But on the first occasion (7:34–35), they ask, "Does he intend to go into the diaspora and teach the Greeks?" There is, in fact, an inescapable connection between the suicide of the shepherd of Israel and the merger of his flock with the "other sheep [I have] / That are not of this fold" (10:16). This is so because once God has excused himself from defending any one portion of the flock against oppression by any other portion (he will die for his sheep but not kill for them), his relationship to all portions cannot fail to become the same. But this is a cataclysmic change; for if God will not fight to maintain the distinction between Israel and other nations, then there cannot be a distinction. His national covenant with Israel, given his universal military neutrality, must either lapse or become a world covenant by default of the divine action necessary to maintain it as national. ●

Finally, once God defines freedom not as freedom from bondage to an Egypt or a Rome but rather as freedom from bondage to sin and death, he removes the most important bar to the extension of his covenant to all mankind. All men cannot live in Canaan; Canaan cannot hold them. But all are equally prey to sin and equally subject to death; and the land of the living has room for them all. The leveling character of God's new promise explains why in the third section of John 8, two apparently unrelated topics—death and descent from Abraham—intertwine so strangely. By linking bondage to sin and death with genealogical illegitimacy, God Incarnate spiritualizes the meaning of genealogical legitimacy and thereby of nationality to the point that he need never again go forth to do battle for any actual, physical nation.

The ancient debate over "supersessionism"—that is, over whether any new spiritual Israel can or should "supersede" the old ethnic Israel in God's plan—has one meaning with reference to the two historically related communities and another with reference to God. The shift of perspective that occurs when attention is redirected from God's covenant, as restricted or not, to his character, as dictating or precluding restriction, is analogous to the shift that occurs when one says that neither the Jews nor the Romans killed Jesus but, rather, that God killed himself. Taking this view, we may see God expanding membership in his covenant simply because he cannot do otherwise. But if he cannot do otherwise, then it is not the Jews who have failed him but he who has failed the Jews. By the terms of the new covenant, God is excused from the old responsibilities that he has failed to meet, while assuming new responsibilities that, terrible as their cost may be to him, he seems confident he can meet. On the terms by which, starting at his victory over Pharaoh, he himself has defined his divinity, he has failed. Unless some adjustment of those terms can be made, then he cannot continue to be God. The adjustment he makes, his own disarmament, entails an expansion of membership in his covenant. But he brings about this expansion not, first, out of love for the Gentiles, much less out of hatred for the Jews, but, rather, to reconstitute his own identity. ◄

Though this resolution of God's crisis may seem complex, it was anticipated in a very simple story that Jesus told in Galilee when his popularity was at its peak. In it, the themes of death, life, and ethnic conflict intertwine just as they do more intricately in John 8.

> Now a lawyer stood up and, to test him, asked, "Teacher, what must I do to inherit eternal life?" He said to him, "What is written in the Law? What is your reading of it?" He replied [quoting a mix of Deut. 6:5 and Lev. 19:18; italics added], "*You must love the Lord your God with all your heart, with all your soul, with all your strength,* and with all your mind, *and your neighbor as yourself.*" Jesus said to him, "You have answered correctly. Do this, and life will be yours."
>
> The man had a point to make, however, and he said to Jesus, "But who is my neighbor?" Jesus replied, "A man on his way down from Jerusalem to Jericho fell into the hands of robbers. They stripped him, beat him, and then made off, leaving him half-dead. Now a priest happened to be traveling on the same road, but when he saw the man, he crossed to the other side of the road and passed him by. In the same way a Levite who came to the spot saw him, crossed to the other side, and passed him by. But a Samaritan traveler was moved with pity when he saw him. He went up to him and bandaged his wounds, bathing them with oil and wine. He then hoisted him onto his own mount and bore him to an inn, where he looked after him. The next day, he took out two denarii and gave them to the innkeeper with the instruction, 'Look after him, and on my way back I will compensate you for any extra expense you have.' Which of these three, do you think, proved himself a neighbor to the man who fell into the robbers' hands?" [The lawyer] answered, "The one who took pity on him." Jesus said to him, "Go, and do likewise." (Luke 10:25–37)

What is the ethnicity of the waylaid traveler? Jesus does not say; and even if Jesus knows, the Samaritan of the story cannot in the nature of things know whether he is saving another Samaritan or a Jew or even a Roman. The traveler, after all, is not just unconscious, beaten nearly to death, but also stripped of his clothing and the identification that they might provide. Though Jesus provocatively tells his Jewish questioner a story in which a Samaritan performs well and two Jews—in fact, two Jewish religious officials—perform badly, the message of the story goes far beyond any suggestion that Jews should have more respect for Samaritans than they do.

Recall that the story is told to answer the question "Who is my neighbor?" in clarification of God's commandment "You must love your neighbor as yourself." In the context of Leviticus 19:18, "your neighbor" is *not* defined as anyone you come across. But "anyone you come across" is just the definition that Jesus gives in this story, and his definition is of a piece with the earlier, explicitly revisionist statement on which so much depends:

> You have heard how it was said, "You will love your neighbor and hate your enemy." But I say this to you: Love your enemies, and pray for those who persecute you, so that you may be children of your Father in heaven, *for he causes his sun to rise on the wicked as well as on the good, and he sends down his rain on the just and the unjust alike.* (Matt. 5:43–45, italics added)

In the parable of the good Samaritan, Jesus gives an ethnic version of his earlier statement, as if to say of God, "He causes his sun to rise on the Samaritan as well as the Jew, and sends down his rain on the foreigner as well as the native." But it is crucial to recognize that what is being promulgated, rather than ad hoc generosity toward an opponent, is uniform treatment of all. And this rule, new for Israel, is drastically new as well for God himself. It is a repudiation of the jealousy that he made his defining characteristic in the first words of his revelation at Mount Sinai:

> I am the Lord thy God, which brought thee out of the land of Egypt, from the house of bondage. Thou shalt have none other gods before me. Thou shalt not make thee any graven image, or any likeness of any thing that is in heaven above, or that is in the earth beneath, or that is in the waters beneath the earth: Thou shalt not bow down thyself unto them, nor serve them; for I the Lord thy God am a jealous God, visiting the iniquity of the fathers upon the children unto the third and fourth generation of them that hate me, And shewing mercy unto thousands of them that love me and keep my commandments. (KJV; Deut. 5:6–10)

The God who now defines himself by comparing himself to the sun, which is not jealous of its rays but sheds them indiscriminately on all, including those who worship another god than him, has in effect given himself a new commandment: Thou shalt not covet thy neighbor's worshippers.

Can any greater change be imagined? Can this truly be the import of what Jesus is saying? What, in practical terms, would be the consequences if God himself were to so revise Leviticus 19:18 that there would no longer be any need to distinguish Israel from the other nations of the world? Jesus gave an answer to that question in a parable that rings changes on the verse that immediately follows the "love your neighbor" verse in Leviticus. That verse (19:19) reads with more coherence than might first appear: "You shall not let your cattle breed with a different kind; you shall not sow your field with two kinds of seed; nor shall you put on a woven garment made of two kinds of yarn." These separations—one breed of cattle from another, one kind of seed from another, and so forth—are a symbol, woven into the texture of everyday life, of how God has separated the people of Israel from the other peoples of the world:

> I am the Lord your God, who have separated you from the nations. You shall therefore make a distinction between the clean and the unclean beast, and between the unclean and the clean bird. You shall not make yourselves abominable by beast or by bird or by anything swarming on the ground, which I have designated for you to hold unclean. You shall be holy to me; for I the Lord am holy, and I have separated you from the peoples to make you mine. (20:24–26)

The reference to love of neighbor at Leviticus 19:18 must be understood in this context; and so understood, its aesthetic unity with 19:19 becomes clear. Love of neighbor does not obliterate the distinction between the Israelite and the other but, in fact, expresses that distinction, for it is, above all, the Israelite neighbor who is to be loved.

But if that was God's old regime, is it also his new regime? Teaching in Galilee, Jesus answered that question in the negative not directly, by speaking about the mingling of peoples, but indirectly, by speaking about the mingling of crops. In effect, he commented on Leviticus 19:18 by commenting on 19:19:

> The Kingdom of God may be compared to a man who sowed good seed in his field. While everyone was sleeping an enemy came, sowed weeds among the grain, and fled. And when the young grain sprouted and began to ripen, weeds appeared as well. The owner's workers went to him and said, "Sir, was it not good seed that you sowed in your field? If so, where do weeds come from?" He told them, "An enemy has done this." And the workers said, "Do you want us to pull them out?" "No," he said, "because in pulling out the weeds, you might pull out the grain with them. Let them both grow until the harvest. Come the harvest, I will tell the reapers: 'Gather the weeds first, and tie them in bundles to be burned. Then gather the grain into my barn.'" (Matt. 13:24–30)

Asked privately by his disciples to give a fuller, less parabolic explanation of his meaning, Jesus complied:

> The sower of the good seed is the Son of Man. The field is the world. The good seed is the children of the kingdom. The weeds are the children of the Evil One. The enemy who sowed it is the Devil. The harvest is the end of the world. The reapers are the angels. As the weeds are gathered up and burned in the fire, so it will be at the end of time. The Son of Man will send his angels, and they will gather out of his realm all who cause others to sin and all sinners, and then throw them into the fiery furnace, where there will be weeping and gnashing of teeth. Then shall the upright shine like the sun in the kingdom of their Father. (13:37–43)

"The harvest is the end of the world," he says, but, very significantly, the great separation will come only then. Until then, weeds will be treated like grain, sinners like the just, and, to return to the parable of the good Samaritan, a wounded stranger like a wounded countryman.

The parable of the sower and the seed is a tale that Jesus told to make sense, perhaps first to himself, of a shocking comment he had just made about his own family. He had been speaking in a synagogue when unexpectedly,

> his mother and his brothers were standing outside and wanted to speak to him. A man told him, "Your mother and your brothers are standing outside; they want to speak to you." But his response to the man was "Who is my mother? Who are my brothers?" And gesturing toward his disciples, he said, "Here are my mother and my brothers! Whoever does the will of my father in heaven is my brother and sister and mother." (Matt. 12:46–50)

"The land is mine, I consider you just resident aliens," God said in one of his darker moments. Jesus seizes that moment and radicalizes it. The point is not that Jesus' human family means nothing to him as a man but that God Incarnate (who, significantly, never promises anybody a baby) is prepared to extend the precious privileges of family to all mankind regardless of consanguinity.

Under the old regime, Israel and its one God were separated in myriad ways from the other nations and their many gods, and the means of the separation were as old as the Sinai covenant itself. Under the new regime, there is still a separation, but the criterion for it is ethical rather than ethnic. As Peter, who fought hard against this unnatural idea, would later put it: "Now I understand that God does not play favorites. In every nation, whoever fears him and does what is right is acceptable to him" (Acts 10:34). The criterion is in place, then, but the actual separation is to come at the end rather than at the beginning. God can still tell the difference between his friends and his foes, but he chooses not to act on the difference, and he commands those who would ally themselves with him to abstain from hostile action just as he abstains. He stops short, in other words, of giving himself the commandment Thou shalt not covet the Devil's worshipers. In the long run, there is to be no sympathy for the Devil. Those who will not serve God will eventually be destroyed. But all the intermediate steps against evildoers—all the interventions that might accomplish the timely defeat of an Egypt or a Babylonia or a Rome—are dispensed with.

When acclaiming Jesus at the start of his career, John the Baptist used the same metaphor—harvest as a last judgment—that Jesus uses in this parable. John said: "The winnowing-fork is in his hand, to clear his threshing floor and to gather the grain into his barn. The chaff, however, he will burn in an eternal fire" (Luke 3:17). Jesus agrees with John about himself, but a question arises: How near is the harvest? At some moments in his preaching, Jesus, like John, implies that the harvest is at hand. At other moments, and the telling of the weeds-and-grain parable is one such moment, he implies that the grain has barely sprouted and the harvest is far in the future. However slow it may be in coming, the fact that weeds and grain are now to be allowed to grow up side by side, unchecked by the action of God or anyone acting in the name of God, resolves the crisis in the life of God.

HIS NEW PROMISE: VICTORY OVER DEATH

In God's new regime as Jesus has preached it, the rule of fidelity to God in worship is secondary to the rule of kindness to strangers. That change, hinted at in the parable of the good Samaritan, was spelled out more explicitly in another Galilean parable that, like that of the weeds and grain, summons up a vision of how the Son of Man will finally judge his human creatures:

> When the Son of Man comes in his glory, and all the angels with him, then will he seat himself on the glory throne. With all the nations gathered round him, he will separate people from one another just as a shepherd separates sheep from goats. The sheep he will place on his

right hand, and on his left the goats. Then the King [note how interchangeable are "shepherd," "Son of Man," and "King"] will say to those on his right, "O blessed of my Father, come, take as your inheritance the kingdom prepared for you since the foundation of the world. For I was hungry and you gave me to eat, I was thirsty and you gave me to drink, I was a stranger and you took me in, naked and you clothed me, sick and you tended me, a prisoner and you visited me." Then the just will say to him in reply, "Lord, when was it that we saw you hungry and gave you to eat, or thirsty and gave you to drink, a stranger and took you in, or naked and clothed you? When was it that we knew you to be sick or in prison and visited you?" And the King will answer, "Truly I tell you, whatever you did for the least of these my brethren, you did it for me." Then will he say to those on his left, "Depart from me, and be damned to the eternal fire prepared for the Devil and his minions. For I was hungry and you gave me no food, I was thirsty and you gave me no drink, I was a stranger and your door was closed, naked and you left me so, sick and in prison and you came not to my aid." Then they in turn will ask, "Lord, when did we see you hungry or thirsty, a stranger or naked, sick or in prison, and did not come to your aid?" Then he will answer, "Truly I tell you, whatever you failed to do for the least of these my brethren, you failed to do for me." Then will they depart to eternal punishment, but the just to eternal life. (Matt. 25:31–46)

"I was a stranger and you took me in." The kindness that defines the new covenant is kindness to strangers—like that of the Samaritan to the stranger whom he found wounded and naked and in need of food and drink. Those who perform this act bind themselves to God and will be rewarded at the Last Judgment. They themselves do not recognize as they perform it that it is a covenant act. They see it only as a human act. God, however, who makes no mention of the duty of worship, sees it as something more—something, indeed, rather mysteriously more—and it is his view that matters.

What the divine king says to the company of those who, during the entire course of human history, have been defined by their kindness to strangers is "Take as your inheritance the kingdom prepared for you *since the foundation of the world*" (italics added). What inheritance was prepared for all mankind at the foundation of the world? What else but Earth itself, the open garden that Earth was before the Creator chose to confine the first couple in an enclosed garden? The king harks back to the moment when Earth was turned over to its human trustees, the moment when God said:

"Let us make man in our image, after our likeness; and let them have dominion over the fish of the sea, and over the birds of the air, and over the cattle, and over all the earth, and over every creeping thing that creeps upon the earth." So God created man in his own image, in the image of God he created him; male and female he created them. And God blessed them, and God said to them, "Be fruitful and multiply, and fill the earth and subdue it; and have dominion. . . ." And God saw everything that he had made, and behold, it was very good. (RSV; Gen. 1:26–28, 31)

The path back to that original kingdom, the kingdom prepared since the foundation of the world, lies, paradoxically, through anonymous and nondiscriminatory kindness. The just are not to segregate themselves from the sinners. They are not to attempt to distinguish the deserving poor from the undeserving or an innocent waylaid stranger from a wounded bandit who got what was coming to him. God can make these distinctions, and he will do so, at the end of time. But God's people are not to make them in the interim, no matter how long the interim lasts.

If kindness and generosity, even and especially to strangers, are the defining virtues of the new regime, the defining vices are violence and envy, even and perhaps especially toward family. When Jesus, during the Temple confrontation that we have already considered, refers to the Devil as "a murderer from the start" (John 8:44), he alludes to the first murder in the Bible, a murder that Satan sought.

Now Abel kept sheep and Cain tilled the soil. Time passed, and Cain brought the Lord an offering of the fruit of the ground, and Abel brought of the firstlings of his flock and of their fatty parts. And the Lord favored Abel and his offering over Cain and his. So Cain grew wrathful, and his face fell. The Lord said to Cain, "Why are you wrathful, and why has your face fallen? If you mean well, will you not be accepted? But if you do not mean well, Sin crouches, a demon at the door, craving you. And will you master him? Will you?"

Cain said to Abel his brother, "Let us go out into the field." And when they were out in the field, Cain set upon his brother Abel and killed him. (Gen. 4:2–8)

Death entered the world when, led on by the serpent, Adam and Eve disobeyed the Lord, and the Lord cursed them with mortality. Murder entered the world when Cain slew Abel, but did the Devil not play a role here too? The text is obscure, but there seems to be a moment when God and Sin fight for mastery over Cain. Only a few modern translations personify Sin, the crouching thing that God exhorts Cain to resist, but a well-established Jewish tradition, to which Jesus alludes, made just that identification. "God created human beings to be immortal," we read in the Book of Wisdom, which reflects this tradition:

> He made them as an image of his own nature.
> Death came into the world because of the Devil's envy,
> as those who are the Devil's discover to their cost.
>
> (Wis. 2:23–24)

And as Cain discovered to his cost. Those who continue to reason as Cain did, Wisdom says, "do not know the *hidden things* of God" (2:22, italics added).

The moment when Jesus identifies the Devil as an actor in the last act of his own life is a moment when his brothers threaten his life as Cain threatened Abel's. Their motive, like Cain's, is religious. Jesus' offense, like Abel's, is the appearance—in his case, the claim—of an intimacy with God greater than theirs. To kill for religion (Cain) or to rescue without regard for religion (the Good Samaritan)—in contemporary terms, these are the alternatives. The Devil's domain is defined as one of life-wasting rivalry, especially over religion, and even within the family. The Lord's domain is defined as one of life-saving forbearance, especially with regard to religion, and even beyond the family.

Why did Jesus speak in parables like these? He did so, according to Matthew, who quotes Psalm 78:2:

> to fulfill what was spoken by the prophet:
> *I will speak to you in parables,*
> *I will utter things hidden since the foundation of the world.*
>
> (Matt. 13:35, italics added)

What is it that has been hidden since the foundation of the world? Matthew sees fit to make this comment just before Jesus explains the parable of the weeds and grain. The new revelation is one of anonymity, nondiscrimination, the repudiation of rivalry, and—by no means least— the nonresistance that follows inevitably on that repudiation.

But innocent people will die if they do not resist! They may even die as John the Baptist died, his capital punishment turned into an obscene amusement for his oppressors. Does God not realize this? He does in- deed; but it is because he does that he becomes human, subjecting himself to a death he could have avoided, pointedly refusing to defend himself, in order to make it clear both that such is truly the new regime that he wishes to establish and that, accordingly, he will not and must not intervene as he would have under his old regime. Were any mere prophet to deliver such a message, he would be rejected as a false prophet. Indeed, at the Transfiguration, Peter rebuked Jesus for saying just such things. Jesus responded, "Out of my sight, Satan!" (Mark 8:33), because Peter, like Satan just after Jesus' baptism, was tempting him to turn back. What Jesus was saying was scandalous, given everything that God had said up to this point in his long history; but the scandal was intentional, and he remains prepared to pay its price even as he demands that his followers do the same. God's promise, hidden since he laid the foundation of the world, is that by paying the same price, he will lead the world back past the murderous envy that the Devil introduced when he led Cain to murder Abel, back past the mortality that God introduced into the world when the Devil led Adam and Eve to disobey him, back to the world in which God had "created human beings to be immortal"—back, in a word, to paradise.

HE RAISES A DEAD FRIEND TO LIFE AS A SIGN

After escaping unscathed when his blasphemous "Before Abraham was, I AM" provokes a crowd to attempt to stone him in the Temple, Jesus avoids the Temple for a time. Then, in some adjacent region of Judea, he restores sight to a blind man. This miracle—unique among all those attributed to Jesus—does not stimulate immediate acclaim but, rather, a hostile investigation (John 9). It survives the investigation and later underlies a popular rejoinder, already quoted, to the charge that Jesus is possessed: "Could a devil open the eyes of the blind?" (John 10:21).

In any event, Jesus soon ventures into the Temple again, but the previous confrontation quickly recurs when he provokes the crowd with another blasphemous remark.

> The Jews gathered around him and said, "How much longer are you going to leave us hanging? If you are the Messiah, say so openly." Jesus replied:
>
> > I have said so, but you do not believe.
> > The works I perform in my Father's name are my proof,
> > But you do not believe
> > Because you are not my sheep.

The sheep that belong to me hear my voice.
I know them, and they follow me.
I give them eternal life.
They shall never perish.
No one shall ever snatch them from my hand. . . .
No one shall ever steal them from the Father's hand.
The Father and I are one.

The Jews picked up stones to stone him. Jesus said to them, "I have shown you many good works from my Father. For which of them are you stoning me?" "Not for doing a good work," the Jews answered him, "but for blasphemy. Though you are only a man, you are claiming to be God." Jesus answered: . . .

If I am not doing my Father's work,
you need not believe me.
But if I am,
then even if you do not believe in me,
believe in the work I do.
Then you will know for sure
that the Father is in me and I am in the Father.

(John 10:24–34, 37–38)

They make another attempt to arrest him, but again he escapes; and this time he withdraws farther, to the far side of the Jordan River, to the spot where John the Baptist had worked and where his own public career had been inaugurated. "Many people came to him, and they said, 'John performed no sign, but all he said about this man was true.' And many believed in him" (John 10:42). What John said of Jesus was cryptic when he said it and remains cryptic. He said that Jesus was the Lamb of God who takes away the sin of the world, that he would baptize with the Holy Spirit, and that he was the bridegroom "who comes from above." Even at this late point in the story, Jesus cannot be said to have demonstrated the meaning, much less the truth, of any one of these three contentions. If people are beginning to believe what John said about Jesus, it can only be because they expect that the proof and the clarification will come in due time. And theirs may be an expectation linked to the theme that has been growing steadily more prominent in Jesus' discourse: the recovery of eternal life that he promises to accomplish, somehow, by his own death.

This was the theme that he first struck when Nicodemus visited him by night after Jesus' first, aggressive confrontation with the Temple authorities. He said then that Nicodemus would have to be born anew in water and the Spirit. How would this happen? Speaking perhaps to himself, Jesus said that it would come about when he was "lifted up" like the serpent that Moses had lifted up in the desert. Now, no longer speaking in such indecipherable code, no longer at a private meeting under cover of darkness but in public and within the Temple precinct, he has promised that "whoever keeps my word / will never see death" (John 8:51). His maximally public and highly controversial restoration of sight to a blind man has given a kind of advance credibility to this larger, far less easily credible promise. New disciples are coming to him in such numbers that some synagogues have threatened their members with expulsion if they consort with him (9:22). Nicodemus, though not mentioned, is still an influential figure in Jerusalem and cannot be unaffected by this ferment.

At this moment of heightened promise and heightened threat, word is sent across the Jordan to Jesus: "Lord, the man you love is ill" (11:3). The man in question is Lazarus, who lives with his sisters, Mary and Martha, in Bethany, not far from Jerusalem. Jesus' followers are reluctant to see him expose himself to new danger: "Rabbi, it is not long since the Jews were trying to stone you; are you going back there again?" (11:8). Jesus knows as the message reaches him that Lazarus is dead, but he delays his departure for two days, and the journey to Bethany on foot takes another two days. As he nears the village, Lazarus has been in the tomb for four days, and it is Martha who comes to the outskirts of the village to greet Jesus:

> "Lord, if you had been here, my brother would not have died, but even now I know that God will grant whatever you ask of him." Jesus said to her, "Your brother will rise again." Martha said, "I know that he will rise again at the resurrection on the last day."
> Jesus said:
>
>> "I am the resurrection and the life.
>> Whoever believes in me, even if he has died, will live.
>> And whoever lives and believes in me will never die.
>
> Do you believe this?"
> "Yes, Lord," she said. "I believe that you are the Christ, the Son of God, the one who was to come into this world." (11:21–27)

As they proceed together toward Lazarus's tomb, Mary comes toward Jesus, throws herself, weeping, at his feet, and says:

"Lord, if you had been here, my brother would not have died."

At the sight of her tears and those of the Jews who had come with her, Jesus, greatly distressed, shuddered and said, "Where have you put him?"

They said, "Lord, come and see."

Jesus wept, and the Jews said, "You can see how much he loved him!"

But some remarked, "He opened the eyes of the blind man. Could he not have done something to prevent this man's death?"

Shuddering once again, Jesus reached the tomb, which was a cave with a stone across the entrance. He said, "Take the stone away."

Martha said to him, "Lord, by now he will stink. This is the fourth day since he died."

Jesus replied, "Have I not told you that if you believe, you will see the glory of God?" So they took the stone away. Then Jesus lifted up his eyes and said:

> Father, I thank you for hearing me.
> I know that you always do,
> but I speak for all those who are standing near me
> that they may believe that it is you who have sent me.

When he had said this, he cried in a loud voice, "Lazarus, come forth!" The dead man came forth, his feet and hands bound with burial bands, and a cloth covering his face. Jesus said to them, "Unbind him. Let him go free." (11:32–44)

When Mary, a dear friend, addresses Jesus as *kurios,* the word cannot be translated as "sir"; it can only be rendered as "Lord." And even though the word as used here cannot be equated without qualification with *kurios* as used of the Lord God in the Old Testament, the echoes of that usage are both loud and intended.

In short, lest there be any doubt that Jesus meant what he said when he claimed identity with God at his last appearances in the Temple, any doubt that his promise of life was to be taken at full strength, he dispels it at this moment and by this act. Those who remark "He opened the eyes of the blind man. Could he not have done something to prevent this man's death?" are reacting just as he intends them to react. Yes, he could have prevented Lazarus's death. There is a great deal that God could prevent but does not. Yes, it is a fair inference that one who could grant sight to a man born blind might be able to raise the dead. The miracle, coming just after Jesus' astounding promise of eternal life, is intended to make that point. And Martha is not mistaken, either, when she says that her brother "will rise again at the resurrection on the last day." This remains the resurrection that matters. But to make his point, to make his meaning clear and his power unmistakable, Jesus allows Lazarus to die, waits until his corpse is putrefying, and then restores him to life. What "Before Abraham was, I AM" and "The Father and I are one" are in words, the raising of Lazarus is in act. It is a claim outrageous and unbelievable but also arresting and thrilling.

HE IS MARKED FOR DEATH, THEN EXALTED AS KING

Many of the Jews who had come to visit Mary, and had seen what he did, believed in him, but some of them went to the Pharisees and told them about it. Then the chief priests and Pharisees called a meeting of their council. "This man is performing many signs," they said. "What should we do? If we let him go on in this way, everyone will believe in him, and the Romans will come and destroy both our Temple and our nation." But one of them said, "You still haven't grasped the real situation. You don't see that it is more to your advantage that one man should die for the people than that the whole nation should perish". . . . From that day on, they were determined to kill him. (John 11:45–50, 53)

Israel, now so brutally oppressed by Caesar, came into existence as a nation through a fabulously successful revolt against Pharaoh. The memory of that triumph is a memory with politically explosive potential. The Jerusalem religious leadership tacitly takes it as a given that, should a revolt break out against Rome, God will not drown Caesar's army in the Mediterranean as he drowned Pharaoh's in the Red Sea. Any "messiah" who provokes the nation to think otherwise, they clearly believe, will only lead it to destruction. The leaders dare not repudiate the old hopes, but they dare not trust them either. And in their caution, the leaders make no mistake. They are right in what they expect of the Romans. They are equally right in what they no longer expect of God. The choice Rome has offered them is the classic oppressor's choice: Either you police yourselves or we police you. In defense of the bargain he has made, Caiaphas offers the classic collaborationist argument: Fewer will die if we do our own killing.

Historically, fewer did die so long as the collaboration lasted. When a religiously fueled popular uprising finally broke out in earnest a few decades later, the Romans did just what Caiaphas here predicts they will do.

Though it took them, significantly, fifty years to fully defeat the Jews, the defeat, when it finally came, was close to absolute. After the elimination of the last military messiah, with the Temple long since razed, the Romans gave Jerusalem a new Latin name, Aelia Capitolina, and made it a capital offense for any Jew to set foot in the place. Caiaphas and his colleagues have reason to fear that, given the highly political religious tradition of their nation, religious enthusiasm, once roused, will inevitably, and fatally, take a political turn. They are defending the nation against a danger that Jesus does not actually pose, but their assumption about the kind of enthusiasm he is generating is more than plausible.

And their misunderstanding, of course, becomes a part of the Gospel plot. Within that plot, the protagonist fully intends to be misunderstood. Official misunderstanding of him both moves the action along and functions as commentary on it in the manner of a chorus commenting on the action in a Greek tragedy. John characterizes Caiaphas as a prophet in spite of himself when he says that it is better that one man die than that the entire nation perish. "He did not say this on his own," John says. "He was [unwittingly] prophesying that Jesus was to die for the nation—and not for the nation only, but also to gather into one the scattered children of God" (John 11:51–52). God is the only real agent here. Caiaphas is functioning as God's tool, just as Nebuchadnezzar of Babylon did when he defeated Judea and destroyed the Jerusalem Temple. The difference is that, this time, it is God in person upon whom the defeat will be inflicted; it is the temple of his body, rather than the Temple of Solomon, that will be destroyed.

The raising of Lazarus creates a sensation, just as the leaders have predicted; and when Jesus arrives in Jerusalem for Passover, he is hailed as a king in cries that quote a Psalm and a prophecy (see passages in italics below). On this occasion, rather than deliver another ironic speech, Jesus engages in an ironic pantomime:

The next day the huge crowd of people who had come up for the [Passover] festival heard that Jesus was on his way to Jerusalem. They took branches of palm and went out to receive him, shouting:

> *Hosanna!*
> *Blessed in the name of the Lord is he who comes* [Ps. 118:25–26]:
> the king of Israel!

Jesus found a young donkey and mounted it—as scripture says:

Do not be afraid, O daughter of Zion.
Behold, your king approaches,
riding on the foal of a donkey [Zech. 9:9].

(John 12:12–15)

The palm was a familiar symbol of victory, long used as such by Jewish royalists. The Greek word *hosanna,* in the verses quoted from the Psalm, reproduces a Hebrew or Aramaic imperative (the literal meaning is "Save!") in a special form associated with entreaties directed toward God or toward a king. The phrase "the king of Israel" does not occur in the Psalm but is added by the inflamed crowd, which is politicizing Jesus' miracle just as Caiaphas and his party were sure it would.

Jesus himself, by arriving on a young donkey, contributes to this politicization, for his action mimes an image used by the prophet Zechariah in a passage predicting the victory of Israel over Greece.

Since Greek was the common language of the eastern half of the Roman empire, Jews in Palestine had the habit of referring to everyone who belonged to the common Greco-Roman culture as Greek. Whether as actual Greeks, cultural Greeks, or Greek-speaking Romans, these were the people who had been the principal enemy of Israel for two centuries. But the passage to which Jesus alludes has more in it than a promise of victory:

> Rejoice greatly, O daughter of Zion!
>> Shout aloud, O daughter of Jerusalem!
> Lo, your king comes to you;
>> triumphant and victorious is he,
>> humble and riding on an ass,
>>> on a colt the foal of an ass.
> "I will cut off the chariot from Ephraim
>> and the war horse from Jerusalem";
> and the battle bow shall be cut off,
>> and he shall command peace to the nations;
> his dominion shall be from sea to sea,
>> and from the River [Euphrates] to the ends of the earth.
> "As for you also, because of the blood of my covenant with you,
>> I will set your captives free from the waterless pit.
> Return to your stronghold, O prisoners of hope;
>> today I declare that I will restore to you double.
> For I have bent Judah as my bow;
>> I have made Ephraim its arrow.

I will brandish your sons, O Zion,
     over your sons, O Greece,
     and wield you like a warrior's sword."

                                   (RSV with modifications; Zech. 9:9–13)

When Assyria took Israel and Babylonia destroyed Jerusalem, God referred to them as the weapons that he was brandishing against his chosen people. Since then, Israel's "prisoners of hope" have never abandoned the dream of a day to come when Israel would once again be the weapon that the Lord would brandish against her oppressor as he had done at the Exodus from Egypt. When the Nazarene who has just demonstrated his power over life and death arrives in Jerusalem triumphant and riding on the foal of an ass, this is the long-deferred hope that is summoned up. In the excitement, no one is slowed by the thought that he comes "humble" or that what he promises may be to "cut off . . . the war horse from Jerusalem" and "impose peace upon the nations" rather than war. Even less does anyone look for a hidden meaning in "the blood of my covenant with you."

Must they? Why should they? One may read a citation like this one ironically, as a pacifist, subverting its usual meaning, but one may just as easily countersubvert the subversion and read the verse, less ironically, as a militarist. In any event, one must "get" any ironic reading the way one "gets" a joke. Whence the explanatory comment in the text: "At first his disciples did not understand these things, but later, after Jesus had been glorified, they remembered that what had been written about him was what had then happened to him" (John 12:16). As for the Greeks, against whom Judah was to be the bow and Ephraim (Samaria) the arrow:

Among those who went up to worship at the festival were some Greeks. They approached Philip, who came from Bethsaida [a Greek-speaking town] in Galilee, and said, "Sir, we should like to see Jesus." Philip went to tell Andrew, and Andrew and Philip together went on to tell Jesus. Jesus answered:

     Now is the hour
     for the Son of Man to be glorified.
     Truly I tell you:
     Unless a grain of wheat falls into the earth and dies,
     it remains but a single grain.
     Yet if it dies, it yields a rich harvest.
     Whoever loves his life will lose it.
     Whoever hates his life in this world

> will keep it for eternal life. . . .
> Now my soul is troubled.
> What shall I say:
> "Father, save me from this hour"?
> No, for this is the very reason why I have come to this hour.
> Father, glorify your name!

Then came a voice from heaven: "I have glorified it, and I will again glorify it."

The bystanders, hearing it, said it was thunder, though some said, "It was an angel speaking to him." Jesus said in answer,

> It was not for my sake but for yours
> that this voice came.
> Now is sentence rendered on this world.
> Now will the Prince of This World be driven out.
> But I, when I shall have been lifted up from the earth,
> Will draw all people to myself. . . .

Having said this, Jesus left them and went into hiding. (12:20–32, 36)

The Greeks do not speak to Jesus. All the Greeks will, in due course, be part of the "rich harvest," but first the grain of wheat, Jesus himself, must fall into the earth and die. The sword spoken of in Zechariah is not to be wielded against them or against the Romans but against God himself. The blood of his covenant is his own blood, which is about to be shed. And the voice from heaven that spoke at his baptism speaks again in ratification.

Jesus does not need to hear this voice, for it is his own, but his disciples do, for what he has just said is deeply disturbing. He who has so recently demonstrated his power over life and death is choosing death over life for himself. But by his doing so, "the Prince of This World," the Devil, will be driven out and paradise will be regained. Thus does the public ministry of Jesus, the ministry that began with his public repentance, come to an end. The Prince of This World, who retreated after skirmishing with him in the desert, is on the march. The battle has been joined. There remains only to win it.

PART FOUR

The Lamb of God

The spectacle of the Lord of All the Earth dying in agony on a Roman cross is a huge and horrifying surprise. That this happens at all is a shock, given his powers. That he endures it without protest is a second shock, because his temperament is the temperament of a warrior. It has been the thesis of this book that so problematic a turn in the life of God, problematic despite the fact that his execution is followed by a resurrection, can only be explained by supposing a prior problem for which this enormity may seem the resolution. Before turning to the climax of the Gospel, then, we turn again to that prior problem. The title given to a late anthology of writings by Samuel Beckett was *I Can't Go On, I'll Go On.* Something like that might be the title as well of this last chapter in the life of God.

THE CHANGING OF THE MIND OF GOD

God came into being as an amalgam of several of the Semitic gods and goddesses whom Israel had encountered in its originally nomadic history. As monotheism progressively supplanted polytheism in Israel, the powers, responsibilities, and related personality traits of these deities, rather than being simply suppressed, tended to accrue by reattribution to Yahweh Elohim, Israel's god. The literary precipitate of this process—God as we encounter him on the pages of the Old Testament—is a character of great complexity and inner tension. God is like an actor who has been called on to replace an entire cast. The virtuosity of his performance is both compelling and disturbing, and the memory of it deeply marks even the many parts of the Old Testament from which he is absent.

Semitic polytheism had divided the roles of creator and destroyer. Israelite monotheism required its god to play both those roles. As creator, he is the god of order; as destroyer, the god of chaos. Semitic polytheism had divided the responsibilities of national defense and international order: Every nation went to war led by its own god, but above them all there was a lordly judge and lawgiver whom no nation could easily claim. The god of Israel is both: on the one hand, Israel's national god and its captain in time of war; on the other, the international arbiter and impartial lawgiver to whom all mankind owes honor. Semitic polytheism had assigned the task of personal protection or advocacy to a flexible category of personal gods or guardian spirits whose limited powers and responsibilities did not extend to the national level, much less to the international or the cosmic. The god of Israel, despite his larger national, international, and cosmic duties, is understood in the Old Testament to hear the most private prayer of any and every Israelite. Finally, none of the Semitic gods was celibate, and the goddesses of the Semitic pantheon equaled the gods in their variety and importance. The god of Israel, though he may have had a consort at some stage in the evolution of Israelite monotheism, eventually absorbed her functions as fully as he had those of the other deities whom he supplanted; and though he remains male, and celibate in his uniqueness, he has, particularly in discharging certain functions, a distinctly female aspect.

Conflict among these several functions and their matching personality profiles defines some of the most memorable moments in the Old Testament. Thus, the Lord as creator breathes life into the first man in Genesis 2, then as destroyer curses him with death in Genesis 3. Thus, again, he tells the first couple to be fertile and "fill the earth" in Genesis 1, then blights their labor and sexual desire and at Genesis 7 covers the earth with a great flood to drown the results of their fertility. It is, however, the tension between the roles of cosmic creator and national protector that proves most consequential in the long run.

After retreating from indiscriminate support of human fertility, God lends his support preferentially to Abraham, with the result that the Israelites, Abraham's offspring, once they move to Egypt, threaten to outnumber the Egyptians themselves. When Egypt turns against them,

enslaving them and killing their firstborn males, God comes to their rescue as their national god, but he captains an army whose soldiers are
forces of nature. It is only after he has turned the Nile River to blood and
covered the Egyptian countryside with vermin that the Lord sends an
armed lieutenant, his Angel of Death, to slaughter the firstborn sons of
all Egypt. Similarly, the Lord who saves the fleeing Israelites from the
pursuing Egyptian army does so not by fielding his own army against
Egypt's but by unleashing the Red Sea against his opponent.

The mood thereafter in the Old Testament is one of pervasive and
often exhilarating confidence that Israel's god is far more than just a
national god. The god of Israel, unlike the limited or (later) truly nonex-
istent gods of other nations, is the almighty creator and lord of the cosmos; and his supremacy lends both him and his chosen people an air of
triumphant invincibility. Israel is the one nation in the world whose god
is *God*! Let the lesser deities squabble among themselves like courtiers
in the corridors of his palace. The Lord of Heaven and Earth is irre-
sistible. His enemies—be they as powerful as Egypt, the mightiest empire
known—are as nothing before him. Why, the "divine" Pharaoh's very
thoughts are under the Lord's control! When the Lord goes into battle
alongside David, Goliath is doomed. When David's heirs must surrender
the kingdom to Assyria and Babylonia, the proud conquerors are, all
unknowing, mere tools in the Lord's hand. He can repeal what they have
done whenever he wishes, he assures his prophets, and he promises that
he will do so soon: The days of the conquerors are numbered.

Yet, as the victories of Assyria and Babylonia go unreversed for centuries, the inference drawn so confidently from the Lord's epoch-making
inaugural victory over Egypt becomes difficult to sustain. The same
combination of traits and functions that has been a source of confidence
becomes increasingly a source of consternation. For some, the hope remains alive—as in the prophet Habakkuk's vision of the divine warrior
rampant—that God will once again turn his power over nature to military use and once again demonstrate his invincibility, flexing his "mighty
hand and outstretched arm" as he did so memorably in Egypt. But little
by little, as centuries pass and vindication does not come, pressure
becomes detectable for revision, and this in more directions than one.

One form of creeping revision is a qualified and gradual retreat from
monotheism. As the power of Satan is slowly admitted to be a real one—
not equal to God's own power, to be sure, but by no means negligible—
an explanation emerges for the postponement of the victory God promised. Though it remains a scandal that God has not kept his promise and

restored Israel to its Davidic glory, the scandal acquires a mitigating factor: God is facing, as may be seen in the Book of Daniel, some formidable opposition after all: enemy angels playing in dead earnest the hostile
role once played by the gods of Canaan. Though still powerful, God
comes to be seen as far less in control than he was when he brought Israel
out of Egypt. Whether or not he has changed in any more intrinsic way,
he is no longer unopposed.

A second hint of future revision is a slight but significant change in
the relationship between God's roles as king of Israel, on the one hand,
and as ruler of the world, on the other. In principle, yes, God's immense
powers as ruler of the world may one day be deployed again in military
service to his covenant partner, Israel; but in practice, a new way of con-
ceiving the ancient covenant begins to be faintly discernible. Rather than
immediately making the nations of the world his messiah's footstool (Ps.
110:1), God may be content for a long while to define Israel as his light
unto the Gentiles (Isa. 49:6). Israel's victories have always had a secondary,
demonstrative effect: Besides doing good for Israel, they have always
manifested the greatness of God to the world at large. But if this secondary effect should become primary, then a corollary question will emerge:
Can a comparable demonstrative effect not be achieved by other means
than war? If so, then the painful postponement of God's promised military intervention may become less painful as God finds other means to
his (adjusted) end. In the Book of Daniel, for all the coded talk of divine
intervention on the field of battle, the reader cannot suppress the suspicion that what most engages the writer is his vision of Jews arousing universal admiration at an imperial court for their piety, their compassion,
their courage, and above all their wisdom. In their wisdom and the
admiration it inspires, there is the suggestion, still undeveloped, of a new
way to preserve the dignity of God without resorting to war. The god of
war is poised to become a god of wisdom.

And as if to suggest that with wisdom comes a measure of detach-
ment, the notion begins to emerge that the Lord himself is more an
international observer than Israel's furiously engaged commander in
chief. In Psalm 33, for example, we read:

> The Lord looks down from heaven;
>   he sees all humankind.
> From where he sits enthroned he watches
>   all the inhabitants of the earth—
> he who fashions the hearts of them all,
>   and observes all their deeds.

A king is not saved by his great army;
  a warrior is not delivered by his great strength.
The war horse is a vain hope for victory,
  and by its great might it cannot save.
Truly the eye of the Lord is on those who fear him,
  on those who hope in his steadfast love,
to deliver their soul from death,
  and to keep them alive in famine.
Our soul waits for the Lord;
  he is our help and shield.
Our heart is glad in him,
  because we trust in his holy name.
Let your steadfast love, O Lord, be upon us,
  even as we hope in you.

(33:13–22)

The Psalmist hopes for immortality and economic security (salvation from famine) but not for military victory. And what the Lord sees as he "looks down from heaven" and "sees all humankind" is not glorious victory for his friends and abject defeat for his foes but something quite different and unprecedented: the folly of trust in armed strength. He sees this because he "fashions the hearts of them all." Psalm 33 repudiates nothing, at least directly, but its emphases are new and portend a way for God's military inaction to be conceived as something other than simple failure.

The third form of revision flows from the second. If God, for whatever reason, is not going to demonstrate his power and his relationship with Israel by making Israel victorious in battle, then the purely personal and more or less private dimension of his covenant relationship with his people comes to the fore almost by default. By the cultivation of that relationship through personal piety on the part of each Jewish family individually rather than by all Israel on the field of battle, Israel may win a new kind of victory and demonstrate the greatness of the Lord in a new way. Jewish piety endlessly replicated will become the wonder and the edification of the whole world, as Daniel is the wonder and the edification of the Babylonian court. This heroism of virtue rather than of valor may even, it is hinted, be a heroism of study. In Daniel 9, the practice of Bible reading—that is, of the private study of scripture—makes its groundbreaking first (and only) appearance in the Tanakh as the great sage is found reading the Book of Jeremiah, the very prophet to whom the Lord spoke of "planting my Law within them, writing it on their hearts" (Jer. 31:33). In this scene, the harbinger of a huge history to come, Torah is to be understood not just as obedience to the Lord but also as intimacy with him. Combining reading with prayer and fasting, Daniel is the very picture of study as a form of worship; and he is rewarded with a visit from an angel. This angel, however, giving another kind of clue to the future than the one he intends to give, is an exegete whose function might easily be discharged by an inspired human being like Daniel himself. It is as if, with the whole world to edify, the Lord must employ a holy faculty of rabbinic angels and angelic rabbis. He himself, "the Ancient of Days," may seem increasingly remote, but they will implant his Law in the hearts of their students; and as their students learn, the world will slowly be led to wisdom. If God is no longer so alone as once, it is not just because he has acquired an enemy worthy of the name but also because the voice of the Lord, once heard in solo visitations, is now heard in choral exegesis.

The second and the third of these pressures derive, to a considerable extent, from the refinement and rationalization of monotheism itself. To an extent, life is simpler for Israel when its God is not quite the only god but merely (though by far) the strongest and most important god. At Judges 11:24, an Israelite leader, speaking to his counterpart from Ammon, on the far side of the Jordan, says: "Do you not own what Chemosh your god has given as yours? So we will own all that the Lord our God has given as ours." The working peace that this diplomatic polytheism allows between territorial neighbors can have its convenient analogue even when neighbors are more theological than territorial. Life is simpler when they have their gods over there, and Israel its God over here. Life is simpler, in other words, when Israel is spared from thinking much either about them or about their gods. Unfortunately, that kind of simplicity and the simplicity of strict monotheism are mutually exclusive. If there truly is only one god and if that one god is the God of Israel, then everybody has Israel's God whether Israel likes it or not, and Israel as a result has to deal somehow with everybody. The second and third pressures for revision in the understanding of God are accommodations to the increasingly inescapable task of dealing conceptually with everybody.

The most natural way to reconcile the tension between monotheism and national election—that is, the "chosenness" of Israel—was to envision Israel at the pinnacle of a sacred empire encompassing the whole world. Rather than simply a way to make Israel's enemies her footstool, this was a vision of all nations entering a covenant with God. In Isaiah 2:3, the nations of the world are imagined to say:

Come, let us go up to the mountain of the Lord,
    to the house of the God of Jacob;
that he may teach us his ways
    and that we may walk in his paths. (RSV)

The conjunction of world empire and national election is very ancient and, by this late date, it may seem almost inevitable that when a nation grows wondrously in power, it should attribute its growth to divine election. Older editions of the Anglican hymnal contain the so-called "National Hymn," with music composed by George William Warren in 1892 for lyrics written by Alexander Pope in 1712:

Rise, crowned with light, imperial Salem, rise!
Exalt thy towering head and lift thine eyes!
See heav'n its sparkling portals wide display,
And break upon thee in a flood of day. . . .

See barbarous nations at thy gates attend,
Walk in thy light, and in thy temple bend:
See thy bright altars thronged with prostrate kings,
While every land its joyous tribute brings. . . .

But even very ancient ideas have a beginning. The idea of empire arose with the rise of Assyria—effectively, the world's first multinational empire —in the ninth century B.C.E. As for divine election, if that idea was not unique to Israel, it was Israel's form of the idea that was to have the longest reach in human history. When the eighteenth-century English poet speaks of "imperial Salem," Salem being a synonym for Jerusalem, he speaks of imperial England in terms borrowed from the Jewish scriptures. For the first-century inhabitants of Jerusalem itself, however, the abstract appeal of sacred empire as an idea was badly battered by half a millennium during most of which Israel had not been an empire embracing all nations but merely one of many nations embraced by others' empires.

The fourth and final revision is an enlargement of the field of battle from the land of Israel to the cosmos and from time to eternity. On this new battlefield, there is a new way for God to win. As we read in the Book of Wisdom:

The souls of the righteous are in the hand of God,
    and no torment can touch them.

To the foolish, they seemed to die,
    their passing was thought a catastrophe,
    but they are at peace.
If to us they seemed to suffer punishment,
    their hope is rich with immortality.
Small was their correction,
    great will be their blessing.
God was putting them to the test,
    and he has found them worthy to be with him.

(3:1–5)

Immortality is not necessarily the negation of history. There is still room and still reason for God to restore the temporal fortunes of Israel if and when the right moment arrives. Nonetheless, a certain pressure is undeniably eased by the opening of this alternative form of redress. For all those Jews for whom restoration by force of arms will arrive too late, here is blessed vindication of another sort. The brutality of foreign oppression—the terror crucifixions by which Titus sought to panic the defenders of Jerusalem during the Roman siege, the evisceration of Jewish refugees by Roman mercenaries in search of swallowed gold, the whole ghastly catalog of atrocities—may be seen in retrospect to have been just a test. God will gather the pious of Israel to himself and keep them forever "beyond torment." And if this proves in the end to be the last and only victory that he wins, will it not be enough? God may not humble his earthly enemies as once he humbled Pharaoh, but what will it matter if his people are secure in a heavenly refuge that no earthly power can storm?

In each of these four areas, Rabbinic Judaism and Christianity both saw fit to revise the character of God as it was understood as late as the destruction of the Jerusalem Temple in 70 C.E., which marked the demise of every *other* variety of official or unofficial Judaism. In doing so, both built on such intellectual foundations as those just sketched, all of which were laid before the Temple was destroyed. While these foundations were being laid, it must be noted, a large and noisy apocalyptic literature was being written, of which many examples have survived to instruct scholars in modern times. Apocalypticism was emphatically *not* a revision of the character of God, however, and certainly not a revision in the direction suggested above, but, rather, an emotionally fevered and intellectually clouded theological conservatism. The longer God's promised military intervention was postponed, the more grandiose, horrific, and overwhelming—the more "apocalyptic," to use the word in its modern sense—that intervention became in the imagination of the architects of this conservatism. The more gargantuan God's intervention became in imagination, the greater, in turn, became the pressure to pin it to the calendar, but the greater, as well, became the fear that any date set would become yet another date missed. The result of this contradictory pressure to both set the date and escape it was a literary subgenre of oracular calendar coding, aimed at preserving "deniability" for the deity, whatever happened or failed to happen by the encrypted date. Though both Rabbinic Judaism and Christianity were marked at the start by such apocalypticism, both movements were, as already noted, more deeply marked in the long run by their repudiation of it. The voluminous apocalyptic literature has been, in the main, excluded from both the Jewish and the Christian canon, and this not by oversight but by design, for what the movement led to, historically, was utter catastrophe.

By contrast with sterile apocalypticism, more liberal, fertile currents within world Jewry began even before 70 C.E., a revision in their understanding of God and of the historical hopes and social boundaries that had been linked to that understanding. The destructions of 70 C.E. and of 135 C.E. accelerated this revision, with the Christian revision entering its most creative period shortly after 70 C.E. and the Rabbinic shortly after 135 C.E. The Gospel story, a story in which the Jewish God is condemned, tortured, and executed by the foreign oppressor of the Jews, is a particularly violent and dramatic way to announce that that God is no longer a warrior prepared to rescue the Jews from foreign oppression but, rather, a savior who has chosen to rescue all mankind from death. The New Testament story as a whole—combining the Gospel story with the story of the early church—is a particularly radical and disruptive way to announce that God has exchanged warfare on behalf of the Jews for missionary teaching through the Jews. But neither of these ideas, not even the "supersessionist" second one, can possibly have occurred first to Gentiles. The world did not—until certain radical Jews issued it an invitation—have any designs on the identity of the Jewish God, nor did the world aspire to membership, however qualified, in the Jewish nation. Extreme as these "Christian" ideas are, they can only have been at their conception a Jewish response to an excruciating and uniquely Jewish dilemma, one to which Rabbinic Judaism was required to develop—and did develop—its own distinct and equally original response. And these new ideas, like all new ideas, can only have been fabricated from available revisionist resources, including at least the four varieties indicated above.

Just as Christ (not "the" Christ) is the Word Incarnate of Christianity, so Torah (not "the" Torah: one does not use the article when the word is being used as a proper name) is the Word Incarnate of Rabbinic Judaism, scripturalization being a terrestrialization and, to that extent, an incarnation of the divinity. Each of these two entities, Christ and Torah, is inseparable from God, and yet somehow each can be and was used to revise God. Christ is the more blatant revisionist of the two: "You have heard it said . . . but I say unto you . . ." Torah as the object of the radically intensified study that developed after the destruction of Jerusalem—is, in comparison, more subtle, more analytic, more gradualist, more comprehensive, and above all less dramaturgical, but it achieves in the end an analogous outcome.

Is the New Testament compatible with the Old Testament? The question is ill-conceived. One might as well ask, for the question would be exactly parallel: Is the Talmud compatible with the Tanakh? Is any revision compatible with that which it revises? Though neither the New Testament nor the Talmud admits the fact except obliquely, and though both can easily be quoted in denial of the fact, each is a revision of the older Hebrew scriptures. And the revisions are clearly incompatible with each other. As for the older scriptures, as twice edited and doubly owned, they are socially and textually incorporated into two parallel responses to a single religious, political, and intellectual crisis. The great subject, the epic argument, of the Bible in its second, Christian edition, is the changing of the mind of God. But the great subject of Torah and Talmud, taken together, is the same subject pursued in a different manner.

A SECOND PASSOVER

Before the festival of the Passover, Jesus, knowing that the hour had come for him to pass from this world to the Father, having loved those who were his in the world, loved them to the end.

—John 13:1

The aesthetic distinctiveness of the Christian revision of the identity of God is that it is a dramaturgically realized revision—a theatrical revision that fuses the four kinds of novel thinking listed above into a literary work with scenes, characters, dialogue, and action. As the Lord gathers with his followers on the last night of his life, the script that they will follow is the script for a reenactment of the Passover, the miracle that defined God as the Lord of Israel a millennium earlier. In the words and actions of this script, the four areas of conceptual revision mentioned above find interlocking and mutually intensifying dramatic expression.

First, Satan, whose power explains in no small measure why God has not kept his ancient promises to the Jews, is a character in this reenactment, though he never speaks. The role that he plays is comparable to that of Pharaoh at the first Passover. It is he who must finally be subdued; it is he who must finally be forced to acknowledge the manifest superiority of the Lord. The victory that the Lord wins over Satan by rising from the dead is only a victory in principle. In practice, Satan's power will continue for a long, long while to come. Yet the Lord's people win through the Lord's resurrection a foretaste of victory now and the assurance of total victory later—along with, crucially, an explanation of why total victory cannot be immediate. They must be persecuted as the Lord has been persecuted before they too can triumph as he has triumphed.

Second, at every step in this second Passover, the Lord is a teacher. He controls the flow of words and actions as a pedagogue must. The Word of God presents himself to his followers as, in effect, a text to be read. Repeatedly, he states that what he is doing for them or in their presence is an example to be taken as such. Jesus is, in person, "the light of the world" (John 8:12), God's light unto the Gentiles in person, but his disciples must carry this light to the world. They may be frightened now, they may feel that he has left them orphaned, but after his death, his Spirit, the "Paraclete," will enter them and embolden them to continue his instructive and redemptive work.

Third, their reward as members of his new covenant will be, in the first instance, their intimacy with him, an intimacy that will bring them into intimacy with one another as well. They are to express their love for him not directly but indirectly, by loving one another. This is, in fact, his covenant command to them. As the First Letter of John will later put it: "Beloved, let us love one another; for love is of God, and he who loves is born of God and knows God. He who does not love does not know God; for God is love" (RSV; 1 John 4:7–8). If God is love, then God Incarnate is love incarnate. What makes brotherly love not just a commandment but a covenant commandment is that the brethren are collectively to incorporate and so continue the Incarnate God's love for them. They are to love one another as he loved them—that is, with more than the force of spontaneous human affection. The same act by which they are to inspire and attract the world will comfort them with an experiential glimpse of the reward that awaits them after their eventual victory over Satan.

Fourth, as for that victory, it will be achieved only when God corrects and repairs his own creation. Satan, whom Jesus has called "a murderer from the start," will not be finally defeated until the Lord revokes, for everyone, the curse of mortality that he spoke against his human creatures after their disobedience. By "passing over" from death to life, Jesus, who has taken the ancient curse upon himself, will be the first to prove that this reconciliation has truly come about. But where he has gone, they will follow.

Each of these four revisions of the character of God has been under way throughout the Gospel, but the four come together at the conclusion of the Gospel of John as four subjects in a great fugue. They are held together and made to work polyphonically by the character, Jesus himself, who "performs" them all simultaneously.

At the first Passover, the Lord played a role that, were he to play it again now as God Incarnate, would have him sending his disciples before Caesar (not Pilate) to demand the liberation of the Jewish people. On the eve of such a second Passover, Jesus would be found not in Jerusalem or even in Judea but on the far side of the Jordan River, on a mountain somewhere in the desert, awaiting his liberated people. If Caesar, despite a series of admonitory, empirewide afflictions, were to ignore Jesus' demand, then Jesus would order his people to flee to him. In preparation for their flight, their escape from Roman bondage, each Jewish household would slay a lamb, splash its blood on the lintel, and then eat it at a meal rehearsing what would become a perpetual commemoration of this second liberation. Jesus would then send an avenging angel to slay the firstborn of the Romans throughout the empire, from the palace of Caesar down to the lowliest slave in a Roman galley. The Jews alone would be spared in this slaughter, for the blood of the second Passover lamb, splashed on their lintels, would save them, signaling the Lord's angel to "pass over" them. After they crossed the Jordan River en route to his holy mountain, the pursuing Roman legions would drown in a flash flood of epic proportions that would turn the Jordan Valley into a torrent of death.

So the story would unfold were the Lord of Hosts to return in power, but the Lord will never return with that kind of power. That he will not is the premise, if not in fact the central point, of this second Passover. To make that point, the role the Lord himself chooses to play in this Passover is, shockingly, the role of Passover lamb. The blood of this paschal lamb will save his disciples, as the blood of the original Passover lamb saved the Israelites in Egypt, not from death in a single massacre but from the curse of mortality itself. Rather than being splashed on lintels, the Lord's blood will be symbolically drunk as the sign of a new covenant. Thereafter, by subjecting himself to the full force of the curse that he swore against his first human creatures, the Lord in effect will repent of it, atone for it by his death, and begin a new creation that will correct the old. At his resurrection, as the firstborn of this new creation, Jesus will "pass over" from death to eternal life, leading the way for his followers as the Lord led Israel from Egypt to Canaan. Having become one with him by symbolically eating his flesh and drinking his blood, his disciples have his word that they will pass over into the eternal life of the new creation just as he has done. This is his covenant promise to them, the promise that will be sealed and solemnized once and for all by the shedding of his own blood.

The blood of other sacrificial lambs has symbolized entrapment in the human condition. The blood of this sacrificial lamb will symbolize liberation from it. "I desire mercy and not sacrifice," the Lord said through the prophet Hosea (6:6), but it is the Lord himself, because of his ancient lack of mercy, for whom mercy is now most required. The disobedience of the first humans was a sin; yet it was not the enormity of that sin but, rather, the ruthlessness of God's curse that brought death into the world. Thus, though sinners, for their own good, need to repent and be forgiven, it is God, in the end, who must atone for his vengeful and destructive reaction to their sin by restoring their immortality. God's own ancient and long-running vengeance is the sin that, as the Lamb of God, the Lord himself takes away when he replaces the curse of death with a blessing of eternal life.

Once he demanded that they offer sacrifice to him; now he sacrifices himself for them. Once he demanded that they serve him; now he serves them. Once he demanded that they love him; now he loves them "to the end" and instructs them that the mark of their covenant with him shall be not their devotion to him but their devotion to one another. It is through this that they will teach the world and through this that the world will know that he is Lord. Finally, he who once insisted endlessly on separation and difference now insists endlessly on unity. His final prayer for them is that they should be one—one with him, one with his Father, one with one another.

"Take heart," he says, moments before his arrest; "I have conquered the world" (REB; John 16:33). Has he in fact conquered the world? He has certainly not conquered it in the way that he once conquered Canaan. Of his enemies back then, no one—man, woman, or child—was left breathing. Now it is he, not his enemies, who will draw his last breath in torment. What would seem more obvious than that the world, in the person of the Romans who rule the world, has conquered him? Yet he has redefined conquest and in so doing redefined himself. He has given the crisis of his life a literally human form, and in that form, as the human being who embodies the crisis, he is carrying through his resolution of the crisis "to the end."

Has he conquered the world? The legendary dying words of Julian, the last Roman emperor to attempt (and fail) to reinstate paganism, were, in Greek: "*Nenikēkas, Galilaie,*" "Thou hast conquered, Galilean!" Julian used the same Greek verb for "conquer" that Jesus does. Though Rome's concession, through Julian, will be three centuries in coming, the claim may surely be made that the Jewish God will win more in defeat, at the second Passover, than he won in victory at the first. The gods who will disappear as Christianity spreads throughout the Mediterranean are beyond counting. John Milton, in his "On the Morning of Christ's Nativity," compares the fading of those gods to the fading of shadows before the rising sun. They are all, for him, Satan's "damnèd crew," and they begin immediately to "troop to the infernal jail" when Christ is born. Milton delights in listing them: Cynthia, the moon goddess of Greece, and Apollo, the sun god; the Lars and Lemures of Rome; the Baalim and Asheroth of Palestine; Hammon of Libya; Thammuz and Astarte of Phoenicia; Moloch of Canaan; and the animal-headed gods of the Nile. The last to go are Osiris of Egypt and Typhon, the hundred-headed dragon god of chaos (probably Semitic in origin), whom Greek mythology imagined lurking beneath Mount Etna:

> [Osiris] feels from Judah's land
> The dreaded Infant's hand,
>   The rays of Bethlehem blind his dusky eyn;
> Nor all the gods beside
> Longer dare abide,
>   Not Typhon huge ending in snaky twine:
> Our Babe, to show his Godhead true,
> Can in his swaddling bands control the damnèd crew.

Milton wrote sixteen centuries after his namesake John the Evangelist, for whose first readers the claim that their contemporary—an obscure Jewish dissident executed as a Roman traitor—had somehow conquered the world and banished all its gods was surely far more difficult to credit than it was for the first readers of the Puritan poet. The line "Take heart, I have conquered the world," spoken on the threshold of the most abject physical and mental degradation, produces an effect of daredevil defiance, an extravagance of self-confidence that is, at first, more intoxicated than intoxicating. Nothing is easier to credit than the reports that Jesus was regarded by some of his contemporaries as insane. Nothing is less surprising than that after his arrest he should have been abandoned by all but one of his followers.

"Blessed are the meek," he has said previously, "for they shall inherit the earth" (Matt. 5:5). In secular terms—the terms, as it were, of political science—his line might be called a reflection on the fall of many empires, the thought that the arrogant invariably lose the earth serving as precursor to the thought that it may be, after all, the meek who inherit the earth. To be sure, the step from implicit antimilitarism to explicit pacifism—from the Lord looking down from heaven and seeing that the war horse cannot save to "Blessed are the meek"—is not logically necessary, but it is psychologically possible; and, depending on the circumstances, some such adjustment may have become psychologically necessary as well. In the dramatic and religious terms of the Gospel as a story, the pacifist thought that appears at the beginning as a promise returns at the end as a boast. Jesus promises his followers, as his career begins, that by their meekness, they shall inherit the earth. He boasts, just hours away from the terminal humiliation of his own meekness—from the moment when the "promise" of the beheading of John the Baptist is realized for him—that he has conquered the world. The promise and the boast are equally dramatic, but neither is sustainable unless it is God who speaks. The drama within the drama is that, yes, it is God who speaks, but who could have dreamed that his promises and boasts could ever lead to this result?

THE LAST TESTAMENT OF THE LORD

Several of the greatest figures of the Old Testament—Abraham, Isaac, Jacob, Moses, and David—deliver long speeches just before their deaths. These "last testaments" mingle visionary prediction with pondered, if sometimes mysterious, advice. The last and greatest of these last testaments is that of the Lord himself, which takes the form of a dialogue (more accurately described, perhaps, as an interrupted monologue in the Johannine manner). Twice during this dialogue, Jesus resorts to the theatrical gesture of a ritual action.

1. *He washes his disciples' feet*

Jesus knew that the Father had given everything into his hands, that he had come from God and that he was returning to God. And so he got up from the table, removed his outer garment, and, taking a towel, wrapped it around his waist. Then he poured water into a basin and began to wash the disciples' feet and to wipe them with the towel he was wearing. . . .

When he had washed their feet and put on his outer garment again, he went back to the table. "Do you understand what I have done for you?" he said. "You call me Teacher and Lord, and rightly so, for such I am. But if I, the Lord and the Teacher, have washed your feet, then you must wash each other's feet. I have given you an example so that you may imitate what I have done for you. . . . Now that you know this, blessed are you if you behave accordingly." (John 13:3–5, 12–15, 17)

To a proud people, few of the consequences of foreign occupation are so humiliating as being required to feed and wash the foreigners. But it is this of all manifestations of oppression—a service performed in his day by the lowliest of slaves—that Jesus chooses to mime. He presents himself to his disciples not in the guise of a kind friend but in the guise—that is, in the working attire—of an outright slave.

To the Romans, the Jews are a subject people who, should they resist their subjugation, may be reduced at any moment to outright slavery. By miming that subjugation and then telling his followers to accept it in imitation of him, the Lord delivers a milder form of the same message that he delivers when he allows the Romans to execute him. He will not spare them what he does not spare himself.

Yet the aptness of the scene as a metaphor for political oppression meekly accepted rather than violently resisted is its burden rather than its strength. Its strength is the touching beauty of the action itself. As traditionally defined, God is no one's servant but, rather, everyone's lord. Servitude, to put it mildly, does not become him. But in this scene he finds a way to make the unbecoming becoming and, indeed, irresistibly attractive. He achieves a profound revision of his own identity by what seems the simplest, most spontaneous of gestures. The frame that he places around the whole is not at first glance the frame of adjustment to defeat but that of love taught by example. As he has loved them and taught them to love, so they will love and teach love to others:

No one has greater love
  than he who would lay down his life for his friends.
You are my friends
  if you do what I command you.
I no longer call you servants,
  because a servant does not know what his master is about.
I call you friends,
  because I have revealed to you
  everything I have heard from my Father.
You did not choose me.
  No, I chose you, and I have charged you
To go forth and bear fruit,
  fruit that will last,
So that my Father will give you
  whatever that you ask him in my name.

(15:13–16)

In the Old Testament, the word *friend* is poignantly rare in connection with God. In the Book of Exodus, the Lord is said to have spoken face-to-face with Moses, "as a man speaks to his friend" (33:11). Once, speaking through Isaiah, the Lord refers to Abraham as his friend (41:8). Otherwise, the Lord is—certainly to any modern sensibility—strangely and painfully friendless. He may demand perfect sincerity—the sincerity of the "circumcised heart" (Deut. 10:16). He may promise perfect constancy in return. But he neither asks nor ever offers simple friendship. God Incarnate, offering and asking friendship, shows God to have become, to be sure, someone whom one might have imagined him becoming, but much of the best that can be imagined never comes to pass. It is a stunning surprise to find the Lord of All the Earth washing anyone's feet.

2. He foresees betrayal but preaches love

Having said this, Jesus was deeply troubled and declared, "Truly I tell you, one of you is going to betray me."

The disciples looked at one another, wondering whom he meant. The disciple whom Jesus loved was reclining next to him. Simon Peter motioned to him to ask who it was he meant, and so, leaning back against Jesus' chest, he said, "Lord, who is it?"

Jesus replied, "It is he to whom I will give this piece of bread after I dip it in the dish." And when he had dipped the piece of bread, he gave it to Judas, son of Simon Iscariot. As soon as Judas had taken the bread, Satan entered him. Jesus then said, "What you are about to do, do quickly." None of the others at the table understood why he said this. . . . When he had gone, Jesus said: . . .

> Little children, I shall not be with you much longer.
> You will look for me, but as I told the Jews,
> where I am going, you cannot come.
> I have given you a new commandment:
>   Love one another.
> You must love one another
>   just as I have loved you.
> It is by your love for one another
>   that all will know that you are my disciples.

Simon Peter said, "Lord, where are you going?"

Jesus answered, "Where I am going you cannot follow me, but later you will."

Peter said to him, "Why can I not follow you now? I will lay down my life for you."

"Lay down your life for me?" answered Jesus. "I tell you truly that three times before the cock crows you will have denied knowing me." (John 13:21–28, 31, 33–38)

At the several points earlier in the Gospels where Jesus deals with demonic possession, the demons who possess human beings as Satan now possesses Judas do not afflict them at the command of God. Although God is far from powerless against these demons, they are less than fully under his control. So it is here. Jesus does not employ Satan as his passive tool but rather outsmarts Satan so as to make the seduction of Judas produce a good effect that Satan cannot foresee. But to say that Jesus' strategy is in place and working as intended does not mean that its implementation is not costly. Judas and Peter are a part of the price. Jesus' preaching is a picture incomplete without its frame of betrayal and abandonment, for he is commanding his disciples to love one another even when they find themselves betrayed and abandoned by one another. If they remember Judas and Peter when they remember his new commandment, they will better understand what he demands of them.

Later, while Jesus is in custody in the palace of the high priest, his prediction about Peter comes true:

> Simon Peter and another disciple followed after Jesus. This disciple, who was known to the high priest, went with Jesus into the high priest's courtyard, but Peter stayed outside the gate. So the other disciple, the one known to the high priest, went out, spoke to the gate-

keeper, and brought Peter in. The girl on duty at the door said to Peter, "Aren't you another of that man's disciples?" [The first disciple evidently has admitted this about himself.]

He answered, "I am not." Now it was chilly, and the servants and guards had started a charcoal fire and were standing around it, warming themselves. Peter stood there too, warming himself like the others. . . .

As he stood there warming himself, someone said to him, "Are you not another of his disciples?"

He denied it, saying, "I am not."

One of the high priest's servants . . . said, "But didn't I see you in the garden with him?"

Again Peter denied it, and at once a cock crowed. (18:15–18, 25–27) ✍

What matters most about Jesus' prediction of Peter's denial is that he makes it *and then stops.* He does not condemn or expel Peter. He does not treat Peter as Peter will treat him. The evangelist's account of the denial is explicit and circumstantially detailed. He makes the fact of the denial unmistakable, but then he too falls silent. The kind of belief that Jesus has sought in his disciples has been personal commitment, attachment to him as a model and a friend rather than concurrence with some discrete set of teachings. Peter's denial of acquaintance with Jesus reverses just that kind of commitment. He does not deny the teachings but the teacher. He detaches himself from the friend to whom he has just professed himself so attached.

Jesus, in a real struggle with Satan, needs and wants disciples. If he seemed detached toward his disciples at the start, he is ardently attached to them at the finish. Speaking through Isaiah, the Lord had said mournfully, centuries earlier:

> The ox knows its owner,
>   and the ass its master's crib;
> But Israel does not know,
>   my people does not understand.
>
> (RSV; Isa. 1:3)

But of the apostles, his tiny, hand-chosen flock, he had said, "I am the good shepherd. / I know mine and mine know me" (John 10:14). Yet the bond between these sheep and their fond shepherd turns out to be painfully fragile. At the end of the meal, when they all leave for the Mount of Olives, he will say to them: "You will all desert me tonight, for as the scripture says, 'I shall strike the shepherd, and the sheep of the flock will be scattered'" (Matt. 26:31, quoting Zech. 13:7).

Yet Jesus' use of this image is not bitter but, even at this moment, bathed in compassion and forgiveness. In Isaiah's day, when Israel denied God as Peter has denied Jesus, God was prepared to inflict severe punishment. Jesus, in sharp contrast, is prepared to let Peter's cowardly offense, his act of wounding disaffiliation, go uncondemned and unpunished. The betrayals of Judas and Peter are to the betrayals of Adam by Eve, Abel by Cain, Abraham by Laban, Esau by Jacob, and so forth as the incarnation of God in the New Testament is to the anthropomorphism of God in the Old. The betrayal of God Incarnate by his closest friends brings the biblical betrayal story, the archetypal story-type of the entire Bible, to its final pitch of intensity. As the leader of the twelve apostles, Peter stands collectively for the twelve tribes of Israel and is a perfect symbol for all the faithless kings of Israel and Judah who of old did "what was displeasing in the sight of the Lord," deserting him and leading the people to desert him. It was their infidelity that prompted the Lord to send Babylonia swooping down from the north to lay waste to Jerusalem. But though Peter is as faithless as they, Jesus allows him to retain his position of leadership. On this night of role reversals, it is the Lord, not the vassal, who must be punished.

3. The supper of the Lamb

> As they were eating he took bread, and when he had said the blessing, he broke it and gave it to them. "Take it," he said, "this is my body." Then he took a cup, and when he had given thanks, he gave it to them, and they all drank of it. He said to them, "This is my blood, of the new covenant, which is poured out for many. Truly I say to you, I shall not drink again of the fruit of the vine until that day when I drink it new in the kingdom of God. | I am going now to prepare a place for you; and when I have done so, I will return to take you with me. . . . I will not leave you orphans but will come to you. In a short while, the world will no longer see me, but you will see that I live, and you will live as well. On that day, you will know that I am in my Father, and you in me, and I in you." (Mark 14:22–25 | John 14:2–3, 18–20)

Jesus enacts a Passover meal that begins, for him, in this world but ends only in the next. After symbolically offering his own body and blood, he proclaims his faith in his coming resurrection. When "that day" comes, he says, the world will see him as dead and gone, but his followers will see, with the eyes of faith, that he is alive and that his triumph over death is the promise of their own triumph. And one day, perhaps soon, he will return to take them to himself. Then and only then will he drink with them again.

It is exceptional for Paul to quote Jesus verbatim, but Paul's report of this moment in the life of the Lord is one of the exceptions. His version of "the Lord's Supper," from one of the two or three oldest documents of Christianity, is striking for its closing reference to the Lord's return:

> For I have received from the Lord what I now pass on to you, that the Lord Jesus on the night when he was betrayed took bread and, when he had given thanks, broke it, and said: "This is my body, which is for you. Do this in remembrance of me." And the cup as well, in the same way, after supper, saying, "This is the new covenant in my blood. As often as you drink this, do it in my memory."
> *For as often as you eat this bread and drink the cup, you proclaim the Lord's death until he comes.* (1 Cor. 11:23–26), italics added

Paul's closing comment reminds his congregation that when they perform the ritual of remembrance, they look not just back to the ceremony that the Lord conducted on the night before he died but also forward to his second coming, when their participation in his resurrection will be realized.

By transforming himself symbolically into a lamb slain and eaten on the occasion of this new Passover, the Lord makes his human death a saving death. Eating the body of the Passover lamb was a part of the existing Passover ritual, but drinking or otherwise consuming the blood was not, for God had forbidden Israel to eat "flesh with life, that is to say blood, in it" (Gen. 9:4). The Israelites in Egypt did not consume the blood of the paschal lamb (the adjective *paschal* comes from *pesach,* the Hebrew word for Passover) but splashed it on their lintels. It was only in that way, as a signal to God's angel, that it saved them. The blood of the new paschal lamb saves in a new way. At the second Passover, the blood of the Lamb of God must be drunk for the same reason that, ordinarily, blood must not be drunk—that is, precisely *because* it has life in it. Yes, life belongs to God, but God Incarnate has chosen by this extraordinarily vivid symbol, the symbolic drinking of his own blood, to show that he intends to share his eternal life with his people. His is the life-giving, life-carrying blood that will henceforth be the sign of his covenant with humankind, and after this ultimate sacrifice none other need ever be conducted.

The covenant ritual will consist not of repeated sacrifices but of the repeated commemoration of this single, inherently unrepeatable and unsurpassable sacrifice. At one level, the rite will be utterly simple, civil, and quiet—just the sharing of a loaf of bread and a cup of wine. At another, it will be the revival and perpetuation of the visceral power of the basins of ox blood that Moses flung over the heads of the assembled Israelites in the Book of Exodus. And because the blood, in this case, will symbolically be human blood, the rite will be even darker and wilder than the Exodus covenant-ratification rite, for it will evoke the earlier covenant drama in which God asked Abraham to spill the blood of his son, Isaac, as a proof of devotion (Gen. 22). Because this time the sacrifice will not have been aborted, the rite that will commemorate it will capture the buried, prerational hunger for human sacrifice. Yet the rite will tame what it captures. The commemoration will require no further bloodshed. The cup of the new covenant will never be filled with real blood, animal, human, or divine, but only with wine and memory. Nothing will be lost. Everything will be carried forward. And yet everything will be transformed.

Were anyone but God himself to create such a rite, it would be not just obscenely close to human sacrifice and cannibalism, but also sacrilegiously free with God's own person. But desperate needs beget desperate measures. The impossible challenge facing God is somehow to revoke the expectations aroused in his people by the Exodus from Egypt—expectations that he knows he will never again meet—without altogether destroying his relationship with them. He must save himself as well as them, and his means to this end is a new event intended to transcend the Exodus on every level: a grander promise, a more poignant and heart-stopping story, a more vivid and unforgettable liturgy of commemoration, and finally a new means of corporate identity for them and self-incorporation for himself.

When the Hebrew scriptures are read in the Jewish order, few comparisons seem so instructive as that between the second and the thirty-fourth of the thirty-nine canonical books. In Exodus, the second book, a hostile king, Pharaoh of Egypt, threatens Israel with genocide. In their peril, the Israelites cry to the Lord, who rescues them with a spectacular display of his power over nature. In Esther, the thirty-fourth book, a hostile king—this time it is the king of Persia—again threatens Israel with genocide. But this time, in their peril, the Jews do not cry to the Lord; God is not even mentioned in the Hebrew text of Esther. Rather, by a combination of virtue and valor, they rescue themselves from their oppressor. In Esther, in other words, Israel plays collectively the same

[margin handwritten note: AND THUS, Communion]

role that the Lord plays in Exodus. It is very much as if Israel has become a corporate version of the Lord—loyal to him, to be sure, certainly never denying him, but doing for itself what he once did.

At the Last Supper, Jesus mediates a similar transfer of functions. Earlier, he has preached (to the scandal of many):

> My flesh is truly food,
> and my blood is truly drink.
> Whoever eats my flesh and drinks my blood
> lives in me and I in him.
>
> (John 6:55–56)

By the life that he will live in them, he will acquire their earthly or temporal lives and their human capacities. When the human lifetime of Jesus ends, his earthly work will continue through them. His absence will be bearable because of their corporate presence to one another. Like the Jews of the Book of Esther, they will provide one another what he once provided them. Of the various names by which the sacrament established at the Last Supper will later be called, one will be *Holy Communion,* because those who are brought into union with the Lord by eating his flesh and drinking his blood—"Of his fullness we have all received," John promised in his prologue (1:16)—will understand themselves to be brought into communion with one another by the same means. Down to the present, the image of the lamb is commonly stamped on the communion wafer. Finally, because the same link that joins them together in their mortality also binds them to him in his immortality, the rite that symbolizes unity also symbolizes victory in the only battle that finally matters: the battle with death.

4. *"Take heart, I have conquered the world"*

> I have told you these things while still with you,
> but the Paraclete, the Holy Spirit,
> whom the Father will send in my name—
> he will teach you everything and remind you of all I have
>   told you.
> Peace I leave with you,
> my own peace I give to you.
> A peace that the world cannot give.
> This is my gift to you. . . .
> If the world hates you,
> know that it hated me before it hated you. . . .

Remember what I told you:
A servant is not greater than his master.
If they persecuted me,
they will persecute you too. . . .

His disciples said, "Now you are speaking plainly and not in figures of speech. We realize now that you anticipate everything and do not need the questions first; because of this, we believe that you have come from God."

Jesus answered them:

You believe for the moment.
But wait: a time will come—indeed it has come already—
when you will be scattered, each going his own way
and leaving me alone. . . .
In the world you will face persecution,
but take heart,
I have conquered the world.

After saying this, Jesus raised his eyes to heaven and said:

Father, the hour has come!
Glorify your Son that your Son may glorify you!
You have given him power over all mankind
so that he may win eternal life for all those you have entrusted to him. |
I will not speak with you much longer
because the Prince of This World approaches.
He has no power over me,
but the world must recognize that I love the Father
and that I do just as the Father has commanded.
Come now, let us be on our way.

> (John 14:25–27; 15:18, 20; 16:29–17:2 |
> 14:30–31; italics added)

❧ When the children of Israel, oppressed in Egypt, cried out to the Lord to rescue them, the Lord did not reply: "A servant is not greater than his master. If they persecuted me, they will persecute you too." The Lord could not give such a reply. Who had ever persecuted him? Nor could he say: "Take heart, I have conquered the world." When had the world not been his? Unless and until opposed, as in Egypt he was opposed for the first time, the Lord had nothing to conquer and therefore no call to become a warrior. From this night on, however, the Lord will always be able to decline when his people cry to him for warlike assistance. This is the context that must be recalled to give full meaning to what Jesus said on his last appearance in the Temple:

Now my soul is troubled.
What shall I say:
"Father, save me from this hour"?
No, for this is the very reason why I have come to this hour.
Father, glorify your name!

wow!

(John 12:27–28)

God has "come to this hour," placing himself in this condition, despite its enormous cost to him, so that he may be able to answer the prayers of the persecuted in the future as he has not been able to answer them in the past—namely, by saying, "If the world hates you, know that it hated me before it hated you." ✏

To a very considerable extent, this is how prayer has come to be understood in the West. It has remained possible, of course, to offer prayer for the success of one's nation on the battlefield. Such prayers were offered with great public solemnity in the West at least as late as World War I. But private and even public prayer has become, far more frequently, prayer for something like the secret assistance of a Paraclete, prayer that the Lord, if he cannot eliminate the persecution or other affliction, may through his Spirit provide the strength to bear it. This spiritualization of hope in the Lord would have been rejected as purely and simply an impoverishment of hope unless the Lord had been able somehow to provide a rationale for it and unless he had been able to endow himself with a new moral authority in proposing it. The new rationale is victory over Satan, leading in the end to the possession of eternal life. The new moral authority is his own persecution, suffering, and death: If hope must now give way to courage, God has first demanded this courage of himself.

As we recalled when considering the murder of John the Baptist, the Book of Psalms, the prayerbook of Israel, presents persecution—typically the Psalmist's private experience of prejudice and injustice—as that to which the Lord, if he is the God the Psalmist believes him to be, must respond. In a few of the greatest Psalms, private sorrow is replaced by national tragedy, and the Lord is approached in a mood of hope deeply scarred by grief. How can the Lord *fail* to respond when the cause is so just?

✏This is precisely—but *precisely*—the question that must be answered. How indeed can the Lord fail? *The Lord needs a way to fail*—without ceasing altogether to be the Lord. The way he settles on—his new Passover, to which the whole world is invited—is the passion, death, and resur-

rection of his incarnate self. Henceforth, no unrighted wrong, no un-
vindicated innocence, will be so great that this sacred drama cannot
accommodate it. Human hope and divine honor will have been re-
deemed together at a single transcendent stroke.

HE IS ARRESTED, TRIED, SCOURGED, AND SENTENCED

In a posthumously published lecture, Jorge Luis Borges says that the
world's greatest stories—for him, these are *The Iliad, The Odyssey,* and the
Gospel—invite endless retelling. Yet, "in the case of the Gospel," he says,
"there is a difference: The story of Jesus Christ, I think, cannot be told
better." Borges does not imply that the Gospel story should not be retold.
He knows that it has been retold as endlessly as *The Iliad* and *The Odyssey,*
and he expects that it will continue to be retold. But he is surely right that
the Gospel, for anyone who feels invited to retell it, does seem quickly to
retract its own invitation, to defy or defeat what it first provoked. The
writer who attempts the retelling immediately senses this.

In no part of the Gospel is this sense of mysterious finality more pal-
pable than in the narration that begins with Jesus' arrest and ends with
his death, and in none of the accounts more so than in the last. Through
the length of the Gospel of John before the arrest, a brief narration is
typically followed by long, rhetorically flamboyant interpretation. John's
account of the miracle of the loaves and fishes, for example, is ten verses
long, while his account of the "bread of life" discourse that follows the
miracle is forty-four verses long. But from the arrest on, Jesus says very
little and then only in the shortest of sentences. Jesus has just said, "I will
not speak with you much longer" (John 14:30), and he keeps his word.

He has by this point explained so much to his disciples that he has
little to add. As for his opponents, he has no further desire for the verbal
jousts with them that have loomed so large earlier in the Gospel. When
Judas Iscariot left the supper chamber to betray him, Jesus said, "What
you are about to do, do quickly" (13:27). A certain deliberate speed marks
the narration of John 18–19. What Jesus says may be bold, but it is always
terse as well. He does nothing to slow his own progress toward the end,
and at three key moments seems to accelerate it. The Last Supper ends
with Jesus' lengthy prayer to his Father for his disciples, and the mood
thereafter is such that the action seems not a climax but only a denoue-
ment, as if Jesus himself is psychologically in the company of his Father
rather than of the human beings whom he is required to address. That

the Son and the Father are identical gives Jesus' prayers a peculiarly con-temporary cast inasmuch as he is praying to himself or bringing himself to a focused presence to himself. Can God pray? To whom would God address a prayer? The Gospel answer to that question is: God prays as a son would pray, addressing a father whom he knows to be himself. In the Gospel of John, Jesus seems to place himself in this state just before his arrest and, in effect, never leaves it again. This mood makes those moments, from that point on, when others address him or he is required to address them seem like interruptions or self-interruptions.

The first of the moments when Jesus seems to hasten the action comes in the garden, when an arrest party including Temple guards and a Roman cohort arrives "all with lanterns and torches and weapons" (18:3). Jesus does not wait to be singled out but comes forward and asks whom they seek. When they say, "Jesus of Nazareth," he answers, "I AM," speaking aloud the sacred name of the Lord, and they tumble backward, falling to the ground (18:4–6). Then Jesus says, less porten-tously, "I am the one you are looking for; let these others go" (18:8), and they apparently do so.

Jesus is then bound and taken to the palace of a former high priest, Annas, who attempts to engage him in conversation about his disciples and his teaching, but Jesus declines to be engaged: "I have always taught in synagogues or in the Temple, where all the Jews gather. I have said nothing in secret. Why ask me? Ask my hearers about my teaching. They know what I said" (18:20–21). A guard slaps Jesus for so affronting a sen-ior priest, but the interview is over. Jesus is taken, still bound, to the palace of Annas's son-in-law, the incumbent high priest Caiaphas, who had earlier called for his death, and then is led, after daybreak, to the Praetorium, the law court of the Roman governor. No charge has yet been brought against him.

When Pilate asks what the charge is, Jesus' Jewish captors respond, "If he were not a criminal, we would not have turned him over to you," to which Pilate replies, "Take charge of him yourselves, and try him in accordance with your own law" (18:30–31). But they object that Rome has forbidden them to impose capital punishment. Pilate then has Jesus taken into Roman custody, inside the Praetorium, and brought before him for interrogation. "Are you the King of the Jews?" he asks. Jesus, guessing (or knowing) that this is the charge that has been privately brought against him, asks, more like a lawyer than like the accused, "Do you ask that question of your own accord, or have others suggested it to you about me?" Pilate, irritated, retorts: "Am I a Jew? It is your own nation and the chief priests who have turned you over to me. What have you done?" (18:33–35).

The question of what God will do about Roman oppression of the Jews has been the unspoken background subject of the entire Gospel. As the Gospel of John comes to its climax, that subject moves dramatically to the foreground. The most momentous question in the history of Israel is called with maximum starkness. This is truly "the hour" of which Jesus has spoken. The divine warrior of the Exodus must now either deploy or renounce his fabled powers. Jesus' confrontation with Pilate at this second Passover is the equivalent of a face-to-face confrontation between Yahweh and Pharaoh at the first Passover. This time, of course, it is Yahweh who is in bondage, but will he break his bonds?

If he does break them, on whose behalf will he act? The question arises because at this Passover the Lord's enemy is not just foreign but also Israelite. Jesus is in peril not just from Romans but also from Jewish collaborators with Rome. The charge on which the Jews have had Jesus arrested is treason against Rome, but for a Jew to bring such a charge against another Jew, *any* Jew, is to collaborate with Rome. Such Jewish collaborators are the Jews whom John, at times, seems most pointedly to have in mind when he speaks of "the" Jews. Officially pious, "the Jews" in this sense are manipulators of the Roman system, insiders with well-tended Roman connections, the kind of Jew, in sum, whom pious Jewry conventionally loathed. The conversation continues: "Jesus replied, 'My kingdom is not of this world; if my kingdom were of this world, my followers would be fighting to prevent my being turned over to the Jews. As it is, my kingdom is elsewhere.' Pilate said, 'So, then, you *are* a king.' Jesus replied, 'It is you who say that I am a king'" (18:36–37). Jesus dissociates God from the overthrow of Rome on the one hand, and from corrupt Jewish accommodation to Rome on the other. Later, at the time of the Jewish rebellions against Rome, there will be those who maintain that a Jew who is not a "zealot," that is, a rebel, is a collaborator. And it will not be immediately clear—God himself has left it unclear for centuries—that any middle ground exists. But Jesus intends to open such a middle ground for the Jews and for their God alike. His confrontation with Pilate marks the birth of the Western tradition of nonviolent resistance. By winning for God the right to fail at war, Jesus wins for him simultaneously the right to succeed at peace. In other words, he creates a nonmilitary profile of political success.

That Jesus' otherworldly definition of kingship makes a mockery of the Lord's usual kingship claims is a charge built into the story. As the day of his death wears on, while Jesus is condemned before Pilate by "the Jews" for claiming to be the Son of God, he is mocked in private by the Roman soldiers for claiming to be some sort of king. Pilate has had Jesus scourged, normally a prelude to crucifixion. After the scourging, the soldiers—the same, presumably, who have been guarding him all day and so have overheard his conversation with Pilate—twist thorns into a crown, put the crown on his head, dress him in a purple robe, and cry, "Hail, King of the Jews!" as they slap him around (19:1–3).

Jesus' new notion of kingship *does* make a mockery of the old notion. Unless this potentially grotesque aspect of his revision is grasped, its full cost cannot be appreciated. The execution of John the Baptist was turned into a hideous Roman entertainment, and now something similar is happening to Jesus. When violent resistance to evil is renounced, there is no guarantee that dignity or decorum will be retained. Mockery is a particularly pointed inclusion in this account because the linkage between laughter and vindication is so frequent in the Old Testament. Psalm 37:12–13 is one of a very large number of passages that could be cited in this connection:

> The wicked plots against the righteous,
>   and grinds his teeth at him;
> but the Lord laughs at the wicked,
>   for he sees that his day will come.

When (as often enough happens) the wicked laugh at the righteous, the righteous complain to the Lord, confident that he will put the laughter back in the right mouth. This complaint is the most conventional of poetic tropes. But now God himself is being laughed at, and God's people, as he has told them just a few hours earlier, should expect to endure no less than he is enduring. Henceforth, when they find themselves laughed at, they can no longer call on God to save them from the cruelty of ridicule. If God has not spared himself ridicule, his people cannot expect that he will spare them. The psalmbook has to be read in a new way. The servant, as he has reminded them, is not greater than the master.

"Where are you from?" Pilate asks when the bloodied Jesus is again brought before him. The question could not be more open-ended or multilevel. If Jesus had wished to delay his own demise, he would not, even in this condition, have been at a loss for rhetorically expansive responses. However, at this second of the moments when he hastens rather than slows the action, Jesus declines to respond, as he earlier declined to respond to Annas.

> Pilate then said to him, "Do you decline to speak to me? Do you not realize that I have the power to release you or to crucify you?"
> Jesus replied, "You would have no power over me at all if it had not been given you from above. That is why the one who turned me over to you has committed the greater sin." (19:10–11)

Pilate does not rule by the power of God, whatever the phrase "from above" might seem to suggest, but by the power of Satan, the Prince of This World. Pilate would not have Jesus in his custody were it not for Judas's surrender to Satan. Pilate's words recall Satan's words in the desert about the power that "has been handed over to me, for me to give to whom I choose" (Luke 4:6). Jesus' reply to Satan on that occasion, quoting Moses, was "You must worship the Lord your God; him alone must you serve" (Luke 4:8). Power does come ultimately from the Lord, but Jesus did not then deny that Satan had for the time being the power he claimed to have, any more than he denies now that Pilate has the power that he claims to have. Yet Pilate is disturbed:

> From that moment Pilate sought to release him, but the Jews shouted, "If you release him, you are no friend of Caesar's. Anyone who claims to be a king is Caesar's enemy."
> Hearing these words, Pilate brought Jesus out and seated him on the chair of judgment at a place called the Pavement (in Hebrew, Gabbatha). It was about noon on the Day of Preparation. "Here is your king," said Pilate to the Jews.
> But they shouted, "Away with him, away with him! Crucify him!"
> Pilate said, "Shall I crucify your king?"
> The chief priests answered, "We have no king but Caesar."
> At that Pilate handed him over to be crucified. (John 19:12–16)

If the Israelites had said to the Lord on the eve of the first Passover, "We have no king but Pharaoh," would the Lord have freed them from bondage anyway? Jesus' kingdom "not of this world" may be a sorry joke for his detractors, but they turn themselves into a grotesque caricature of political sagacity when their defense of the nation—recall that it was for the good of the nation that, according to Caiaphas, Jesus had to be put to death—requires them to declare, "We have no king but Caesar."

The "Day of Preparation" that John mentions in an aside is the day of preparation for Passover. According to tradition, it was at the sixth hour on that day, or about noon, that the slaughter of the lambs to be consumed on the following day began. Jesus, the Lamb of God, is handed over to be crucified at the same hour of the day when the Passover lambs are being handed over to the butchers.

> Then they took Jesus, and, carrying his own cross, he went out to the Place of the Skull (in Hebrew, Golgotha), where they crucified him with two others, one on either side and Jesus in the middle. Pilate wrote out a placard and had it fastened to the cross. It read, "Jesus the Nazarene, King of the Jews." This notice was read by many of the Jews, because the place where Jesus was crucified was not far from the city and because the writing was in Hebrew, Latin, and Greek.
>
> So the chief priests of the Jews said to Pilate, "Do not write 'King of the Jews' but 'He said "I am King of the Jews."'"
>
> Pilate answered, "I wrote what I wrote." (19:17–22)

For the Jews, Jesus' crime is that of falsely claiming to be the Messiah, the King of the Jews. For the Romans, the defendant is guilty only if the claim is true. So Pilate seems to say to Caiaphas that he understands the game that is being played. He seeks to remind Caiaphas that when such games are played, Rome always wins. Caiaphas has gambled and won. He has the prize he came for. But Rome is the casino, and by casino rules, the house never loses.

But has the Roman casino really won? When Nathanael acclaimed Jesus as "King of Israel," Jesus declined the acclamation, saying, "You are going to see greater things than that" (John 1:49–50). Rather than merely the King of Israel, Jesus saw himself as the Son of Man to whom was given "dominion and glory and sovereignty, that all races, nations, *and languages* should serve him" (Dan. 7:14, italics added). Crucifixions were normally done along public thoroughfares, the better to deter potential criminals. The roads leading to Jerusalem are filled with pilgrims coming for Passover from throughout the Roman empire. Pilate labels Jesus "King of the Jews" in Hebrew, Greek, and Latin. He brings about a first, partial fulfillment of Daniel and also of Jesus' repeated statement in the Gospel of John that when he is "lifted up," he will draw all men to himself. At the moment when Jesus ended his public ministry, some

"Greeks"—possibly Gentiles, more likely Greek-speaking Jews—had wished to speak to him. He had gone into seclusion before that conversation could take place. Now those Greeks and others may see him labeled "king" in their own language and may take word about him to their distant homes.

Moreover, and more profoundly, if Jesus is in truth the Messiah, if he is in truth King of the Jews, and if he is now being executed as a criminal, then all who have any understanding of the expectations that these designations have traditionally evoked must now drastically revise their expectations. Whatever Pilate intends, this is what the Lord intends: "This is the very reason why [he has] come to this hour" (John 12:27). He has taken the role of the Messiah, King of the Jews, upon himself so that as such he may be executed as a criminal among other criminals.

In the Psalms and the prophets, misfortune is frequently stated by reference to those with whom one is "numbered"—with the living, with the dead, with the righteous, with wrongdoers, with the blessed, with the cursed, and so forth. Jesus' execution with criminals means that he is "numbered" with them, and this permits an unmarked but exceptionally far-reaching allusion to the prophet Isaiah. To quote what would become, for Christianity, perhaps the most celebrated single poem in the Old Testament:

> He had no form or comeliness that we should look at him,
>   and no beauty that we should desire him.
> He was despised and rejected by men;
>   a man of sorrows, and acquainted with grief;
> and as one from whom men hide their faces
>   he was despised, and we esteemed him not.
> Surely he has borne our griefs
>   and carried our sorrows;
> yet we esteemed him stricken,
>   smitten by God, and afflicted.
> But he was wounded for our transgressions,
>   he was bruised for our iniquities;
> upon him was the chastisement that made us whole,
>   and with his stripes we are healed.
> All we like sheep have gone astray;
>   we have turned every one to his own way;
> and the Lord has laid on him
>   the iniquity of us all.
> He was oppressed, and he was afflicted,
>   yet he opened not his mouth;

> like a lamb that is led to the slaughter,
> > and like a sheep that before its shearers is dumb,
> > so he opened not his mouth.
> By oppression and judgment he was taken away;
> > and as for his generation, who considered
> that he was cut off out of the land of the living,
> > stricken for the transgression of my people?
> And they made his grave with the wicked
> > and with a rich man in his death,
> although he had done no violence,
> > and there was no deceit in his mouth.
> Yet it was the will of the Lord to bruise him;
> > he has put him to grief;
> when he makes himself an offering for sin,
> > he shall see his offspring, he shall prolong his days;
> the will of the Lord shall prosper in his hand;
> > he shall see the fruit of the travail of his soul and be satisfied;
> by his knowledge shall the righteous one, my servant,
> > make many to be accounted righteous;
> > and he shall bear their iniquities.
> Therefore I will divide him a portion with the great,
> > and he shall divide the spoil with the strong;
> because he poured out his soul to death,
> > *and was numbered with the transgressors.*

> (RSV; Isa. 53:2–12, italics added)

It was not generally thought that the Lord's Messiah would be numbered with transgressors, much less that he himself, as Messiah, would be so numbered. But was such a thing wholly inconceivable? Had the Lord given absolutely no indication that such a disturbing eventuality might come to pass? No, Isaiah 53 had long since been a poem to give pause. By "lifting up" the King of the Jews between criminals, by thus "numbering" him with transgressors, Pilate perpetrates, against any intention of his own, a mimed allusion to Isaiah.

The Messiah, the King of the Jews, has come with the silence of a lamb, not the roar of a lion. "Like a lamb that is led to the slaughter, and like a sheep that before its shearers is dumb, *so he opened not his mouth*" (Isa. 53:7, italics added). Yet the poem in which the Lord may have imagined this hour of silent anguish describes, by its end, not a defeat but a wondrous victory.

HE IS CRUCIFIED AS KING OF THE JEWS

When the soldiers had crucified Jesus, they took his clothes and divided them into four shares, one for each soldier. His undergarment was seamless, woven in one piece from the top down, and so they said to one another: "Instead of tearing it, let's throw dice to decide who will get it." Thus were the words of scripture fulfilled:

> *They divided my garments among them*
> *and for my clothes they cast lots.*

That is what the soldiers did. (John 19:23–25, italics added)

Since it is in prayer that Israel expressed its expectations of God and since the Book of Psalms is the prayerbook of Israel, this book looms large at that moment in the Gospel—namely, the Crucifixion—when ancient expectations are being most visibly revised. The quoted verses, "They divided my garments . . . ," come from Psalm 22 and point again to the theme of the mockery of the Jewish Messiah, who is naked and dying, by the soldiers of his enemy, who are gambling over his clothing. The full stanza (22:16–18) can be translated:

> Dogs surround me,
>   a gang of criminals harasses me
>   like a lion at my hands and my feet.
> I can count all my bones;
>   *they divide my garments among them*
>   *and for my clothes they cast lots.*

Another part of the same Psalm (6–8) reads:

> I am a worm, not a man,
>   scorned by my kind, despised by my nation.
> All who see me mock me;
>   they make faces at me, they wag their heads.
> "Let him trust in the Lord, let him deliver him,
>   let him rescue him, then, if he delights in him!"

This is the passage that Mark alludes to when he writes:

Those who passed by derided him, wagging their heads, and saying, "Hah! You who would destroy the Temple and build it in three days! Save yourself! Come down from the cross!" The chief priests and scribes mocked him as well, saying among themselves, "He saved others; himself he cannot save. Let the Messiah, the King of Israel, come down now from the cross for us to see and believe." Those who were crucified with him taunted him too. (Mark 15:29–32)

Matthew and Mark (but not Luke or John) quote the opening words of Psalm 22, "My God, my God, why have you forsaken me?" as words that Jesus himself speaks from the cross. The two present him (each a bit differently) quoting the Psalm in some blend of Aramaic and Hebrew: *Eli, Eli* (or *Eloi, Eloi*), *lama sabachtani?* The line can be interpreted in two almost diametrically opposed senses. Taken alone, it can be heard as a cry of despair. Taken as a quotation from the Psalm, a quotation perhaps inspired by Jesus' observing his executioners gambling for his undergarment, it can take on the meaning of the Psalm as a whole. It is the latter interpretation that seems more in character for the dying Jesus in all four Gospels. In not one of them does he beg for mercy, scream in pain, or otherwise seem to lose control. His royal or divine serenity may be more complete in Luke and John, but he is extraordinarily restrained in Matthew and Mark as well. In John, as we shall see, Jesus' very last words may be yet another allusion to Psalm 22.

More than mockery or the transcendence of mockery is involved, however, when reference is made to Jesus' chiton, his seamless tunic or undergarment, for in his day another kind of seamless chiton was worn by the high priest. By noting that Jesus went to his death wearing a priestly garment, John was able to suggest to his original Jewish audience that Jesus was not just the lamb who was sacrificed at this Passover but also the priest who was performing the sacrifice. The Letter to the Hebrews—a book of the New Testament written around the same time as the Gospel of John and, it would seem, under the same circumstances—develops this idea at great length. For the theologian who wrote the Letter to the Hebrews, it is God's literal self-sacrifice that accomplishes the defeat of Satan and wins eternal life for mankind, serving, along the way, as a reminder to Jesus' persecuted followers that they need have no fear of death:

By his death he was able to set aside him who held the power of death—that is, the Devil—and liberate all those who had been held in lifelong slavery by the fear of death. For it was not the angels that he came to help but the line of Abraham. He had to become like his brothers in every way so that he could become a merciful and trust-

worthy high priest for them before God, able to expiate the sins of the
people. For the suffering he himself endured while being put to the
test enables him to help others who are being tested. . . .

And he did not need to offer himself again and again, as the high
priest goes into the sanctuary year after year with the blood that is not
his own, or else he would have had to suffer over and over again since
the world began. As it is, he has appeared once and for all, at the end
of the last age, to abolish sin *by sacrificing himself.* (Heb. 2:14–18, 9:25–26,
italics added)

A priest who is his own sacrificial lamb, a lamb who is his own sacrificing priest, a father who is his own son, an Isaac who is his own Abraham,
with the dagger in his own hand—it is by this fusion of identities that the
crisis in the life of God is resolved. And it is this fusion of identities, as
God Incarnate "sacrifices himself," that leads to the daring claim of the
Letter to the Hebrews that the death of Christ was self-inflicted.

Jesus speaks his dying words to his mother, to a beloved disciple, and
at last to his Father—or to himself:

At the cross of Jesus stood his mother and his mother's sister, Mary the
wife of Clopas, and Mary Magdalene. Seeing his mother and the disciple whom he loved standing beside her, Jesus said to his mother,
"Woman, behold your son." Then he said to the disciple, "Behold
your mother." And from that hour the disciple took her into his home.

After this, Jesus knew that everything had now been completed,
but so that the scripture should be completely fulfilled, he said, "I
thirst." A jar full of sour wine stood there. Putting a sponge soaked in
the wine on a branch of hyssop, they held it up to his mouth. When
Jesus had taken the wine, he said, "It is accomplished," bowed his
head, and gave up his spirit. (John 19:25–30)

If the words, "After this" are taken to refer back no further than to
the episode that immediately precedes, then a link exists between this
scene and Jesus' conclusion that "everything had now been completed."
Recalling that love was the theme of the Lord's last testament and that
this is the disciple whom he most loves, it may be that the Lord sees his
love living on through this disciple. If Jesus' mother still has her son, then
somehow Jesus is not dead. Through Jesus' love for his disciples and
theirs for him, his work—including even his care for his own mother—
will continue. The beloved disciple becomes, at this moment, the first
Christian.

As for Jesus' thirst or, more exactly, his decision to say "I thirst," this seems to be yet another allusion to Psalm 22, in which at one point the Psalmist's mouth "is dried up like a potsherd." Psalm 22 reads as an ascent from the abyss of its opening "My God, my God, why have you forsaken me?" In its exultant closing stanzas, vindication comes not for the Psalmist but for God himself:

> All the ends of the earth shall remember,
>   and turn to the Lord;
> and all the families of the nations
>   shall bow before him.
> For kingship belongs to the Lord,
>   and authority over the nations is his. . . .
> Posterity shall serve him;
>   his fame shall be told for generations to come.
> They shall proclaim his justice
>   to a people yet unborn
>   for he has acted.

> (22:27–28, 30–31)

The last words of the Psalm are, in Hebrew, *kiy 'aśah*—*kiy* meaning "that" or "because," and *'aśah* meaning "he has done (it)" or simply "he has acted." In either Hebrew or Aramaic, the verb can be converted to *na'aśah,* a one-word sentence meaning "it is done" or "the action is complete." The last word that the dying hero speaks from the cross may allude, then, to the last word of the Psalm. A common English translation of this word (it is a single word in Greek as well) is "it is accomplished," but one could easily substitute the one-word sentence "Done."

Done! What has God done by the desperate extreme of inflicting a maximally traumatic human death upon himself? He has rescued an imperiled vision. Through his Incarnation and now through his death, he has found a way to infuse the closing stanzas of Psalm 22, as well as the innumerable other statements in the Old Testament expressing what those stanzas express, with a new meaning that transcends rather than negates the old meaning. It has cost him everything to make this cataclysmic change, but he has made it, and—*na'aśah*—it is accomplished. He bows his head and breathes out his last breath.

HE RISES TO LIFE, INCORPORATES,
ASCENDS TO HEAVEN, AND MARRIES

Nicodemus and Joseph of Arimathea give Jesus a hurried burial in a tomb chosen because it is nearby. It is Friday, the eve of Passover. All Jewish holy days begin at sundown. The two men succeed in their intent to have the body interred before Passover officially begins. The corpse remains in the tomb Friday night, Saturday, and Saturday night. Early on Sunday morning (his third day in the tomb, counting Friday and Saturday), Mary Magdalene goes to visit the tomb. Finding the stone rolled away from its entrance and fearing that the body has been stolen, she runs to tell Peter and an unnamed second disciple, usually taken to be John. They come running, enter the tomb, find it empty, and hasten home. Neither sees Jesus, and we read: "As late as this moment, they had still not understood the scripture and that he must rise from the dead" (John 20:9). When the two men leave, Jesus appears to Mary, who has returned to the garden where the tomb is located. She reports his appearance, but it is unclear whether anyone believes her.

Then, still on the same Sunday,

two of them were on their way to a village called Emmaus, seven miles from Jerusalem, and they were talking together about all that had happened. And it happened that as they were talking together and discussing it, Jesus himself came up and walked by their side; but their eyes were prevented from recognizing him. He said to them, "What are all these things that you are discussing as you walk along?" They stopped, their faces downcast.

Then one of them, called Cleopas, answered him, "You must be the only person staying in Jerusalem who does not know the things that have been happening there these last few days." He asked, "What things?" They answered, "All about Jesus of Nazareth, who showed himself a prophet powerful in action and speech before God and the whole people; and how our chief priests and our leaders handed him over to be sentenced to death, and had him crucified. Our own hope had been that he would be the one to set Israel free. And this is not all: two whole days have now gone by since it all happened; and some women from our group have astounded us: they went to the tomb in the early morning, and when they could not find the body, they came back to tell us they had seen a vision of angels who declared he was alive. Some of our friends went to the tomb and found everything exactly as the women had reported, but of him they saw nothing."

Then he said to them, "You foolish men! So slow to believe all that the prophets have said! Was it not necessary that the Christ should suffer before entering into his glory?" Then, starting with Moses and going through all the prophets, he explained to them the passages throughout the scriptures that were about himself.

When they drew near to the village to which they were going, he made as if to go on; but they pressed him to stay with them saying, "It is nearly evening, and the day is almost over." So he went in to stay with them. Now while he was with them at table, he took the bread and said the blessing; then he broke it and handed it to them. And their eyes were opened and they recognized him; but he had vanished from their sight. Then they said to each other, "Did not our hearts burn within us as he talked to us on the road and explained the scriptures to us?" (REB; Luke 24:13–32)

The Jesus who appears to the two disciples on the road to Emmaus may fairly be compared to the angel Gabriel appearing to the sage Daniel. What the angel performs for Daniel is not a miracle but an exegesis, and exegesis is also what Jesus offers the two disciples on the road. And just as Daniel will do for others as Gabriel has done for him, so also will the two disciples do for others as Jesus has done for them. Philip will do for the Ethiopian eunuch what Jesus does for these downcast disciples. They had been hoping for someone "to set Israel free" and had wanted to believe that Jesus would be the one. What he shows them is that God has not disappointed them (or himself) after all but has devised a new way to set Israel free. Jesus *was* the one, and is the one, if they can but understand their own scriptures aright. Creative exegesis was nothing new in Judaism. Christianity began—and is seen beginning at this moment—as just another school of Jewish exegesis, reading the received texts in a new direction but with a familiar intensity. When he breaks the bread, beginning the commemorative ritual that is itself an exercise in exegesis, they recognize him, and he immediately vanishes: The completion of the ritual is theirs to accomplish.

The two of them immediately head back to Jerusalem and, arriving presumably after dark, find the eleven apostles and their companions assembled and with a piece of exciting news: The Lord has appeared to Peter. They proceed to tell their own story, and just as they finish it, Jesus appears and greets the group with the words "Peace be with you."

And after saying this, he showed them his hands and his side. The disciples were filled with joy at seeing the Lord, and he said to them again, "Peace be with you. As the Father sent me, so am I sending you." After saying this he breathed on them and said:

> Receive the Holy Spirit.
> If you forgive anyone's sins,
>   they are forgiven;
> if you retain anyone's sins,
>   they are retained.

Thomas, called the Twin, who was one of the Twelve, was not with them when Jesus came. So the other disciples said to him, "We have seen the Lord," but he answered, "Unless I can see the holes that the nails made in his hands and can put my finger into the holes they made, and unless I can put my hand into his side, I refuse to believe." Eight days later the disciples were in the house again and Thomas was with them. The doors were closed, but Jesus came in and stood among them. "Peace be with you," he said. Then he spoke to Thomas, "Put your finger here; look, here are my hands. Give me your hand; put it into my side. Do not be unbelieving any more but believe." Thomas replied, "My Lord and my God!" Jesus said to him:

> You believe because you can see me.
> Blessed are those who have not seen and yet believe.

(NJB; John 20:20–29)

Jesus has kept the promise he made at the Last Supper. He has returned to breathe his own spirit, the Paraclete, into his apostles. Henceforth, when they speak, it will be his breath that issues from their lips. When they act, it will be he who acts through them. In all they do, they will do as he has done and be as he has been. The apostles who receive his spirit have been born again from skepticism to belief, as fully as the dry bones in Ezekiel's valley. Though they have all been calling him "Lord," Thomas brings the Gospel of John to a culminating pitch of awestruck recognition by addressing him as "My Lord and my God!"

Jesus remains among them for forty days more. Then, at the last possible instant, there comes a jolt of something approaching levity: "Now it happened that they had come together, and they asked him, 'Lord, will you now restore sovereignty to Israel?'" (Acts 1:6). Who is it, one wonders, who at this late hour asks the Lord whether he is about to restore sovereignty to Israel? Is it perhaps Jude, who asked him at the Last Supper, "Lord, what has happened that you intend to show yourself to us and not to the world?" (John 14:22). Jude, who would be honored centuries later as the patron saint of lost causes and impossible cases, stopped just short on that earlier occasion of beginning his question "Lord, what has gone wrong that you . . . ?"

Many a teacher has had the experience, perhaps on the very last day of class before the examination, perhaps while conducting a routine review of the material covered, of hearing a student ask a question so dumbfoundingly elementary, so heartbreakingly basic, that the teacher concludes that nothing, truly nothing, has been effectively conveyed. Of all the writers in the New Testament, Luke (the author of the Acts of the Apostles) is the one who just conceivably might have timed the placement of a final note of incomprehension to produce a rueful smile in the reader. But experienced teachers also know that the student who asks the stupid question often miraculously focuses many months of learning for the entire class and forces the teacher himself to come at last to the point. The question "Will you now restore sovereignty to Israel?" is the defining question of the Gospels, as it was the besetting question for Israel under a Roman occupation that had led, around the time Jesus was born, to an uprising put down only after two thousand crucifixions. The answer to the question is "No"—if not no in principle, then at least no in practice; if not no forever, then at least no for the duration of an indefinitely long postponement. But, as we have seen, rather than simply answer the old question, the Lord—for good reason, though at supreme cost to himself—has preferred to change it.

When the old question is posed one last time, Jesus, with nothing further to gain or lose, replies gently:

> "It is not for you to know times or dates that the Father has determined by his own authority, but you are going to receive power as the Holy Spirit comes upon you, and you will be my witnesses not only in Jerusalem but throughout Judea and Samaria, and to the farthest ends of the earth. | Go then and make disciples of all nations, baptizing them in the name of the Father and of the Son and of the Holy Spirit and teaching them to observe all that I have commanded you. And remember, I am with you always, to the end of time." | As he said this, he was lifted up, and a cloud took him from their sight. They were still staring into the sky when suddenly two men in white were standing beside them, who said: "Why do you Galileans stand here looking into the sky? This Jesus who has been taken from you up into heaven will return in the same way as you have seen him go up." (Acts 1:7–8, Matt. 28:19–20, Acts 1:9–11)

Jesus is floating up to heaven, and they *still* don't get it.

But then they do. They return to the Temple and, against every expectation aroused by their conduct after Jesus' arrest, they begin preaching and arguing his cause just as boldly as he did while with them. The disciples—through their spiritual offspring, of whom the most notable will be Paul of Tarsus—do become his witnesses to the farthest ends of the earth. Jesus does not return, but the time of his return begins to be counted among those times and dates that "it is not for you to know."

If such is the continuation of their story, many of them eventually dying as martyrs, the continuation of his story is in heaven. The Book of Revelation, by the visionary John of Patmos, follows the Lamb of God to heaven. Early in his vision, as John weeps in fear of what may lie ahead for the church on earth, a heavenly elder tells him: "Do not weep. Behold, the Lion of Judah, the Root of David, has conquered, and he will open the scroll [of the future] and its seven seals" (Rev. 5:5). The Lion of Judah (Gen. 49:9) turns out to be the Lamb of God, but the scroll of the future, terrifying as its contents prove to be, belongs to this Lamb. John is to take heart: Appearances to the contrary notwithstanding, the Lamb has conquered the world.

Before the Lamb opens the seals of the scroll and a horrendous vision unrolls of the time between now and the second coming of Christ, a rite of cosmic triumph is performed in language for which the "Hallelujah Chorus" of Handel's *Messiah* has become the unofficial score. As the Lamb comes forward to open the scroll,

> I beheld, and I heard the voice of many angels round about the throne and the beasts and the elders: and the number of them was ten thousand times ten thousand, and thousands of thousands;
>
> Saying with a loud voice, Worthy is the Lamb that was slain to receive power, and riches, and wisdom, and strength, and honour, and glory, and blessing.
>
> And every creature which is in heaven, and on the earth, and under the earth, and such as are in the sea, and all that are in them, heard I saying, Blessing, and honour, and glory, and power, be unto him that sitteth upon the throne, and unto the Lamb for ever and ever. (KJV; Rev. 5:11–13)

Irony is the last word that the "Hallelujah Chorus" brings to mind, and yet the enthronement of the Lamb is a supremely ironic outcome. This is not how God's work in the world was supposed to culminate, and yet, ironically, this is just what was predicted. This is not the glorious victory that the Lord promised to Judah, and yet, ironically, it meets every criterion for that victory. The Bible is a divine comedy in both the high and the low sense of the word *comedy*. The enthronement of the Lamb is truly both sublime and ridiculous. Yield to it in just the right way, with just the right music playing, and you will be swept away. Catch it at a slightly crooked angle, with the sound system off, and you will laugh out loud.

The scene as "every creature which is in heaven, and on the earth, and under the earth, and such as are in the sea" gathers round to applaud the enthroned Lamb invites the skills of the Walt Disney studio, if taken as low comedy; but if taken as the highest of high comedy, then the scene is the fulfillment of the Lord's celebrated promise through Isaiah:

> The wolf shall dwell with the lamb,
> and the leopard shall lie down with the kid,
> and the calf and the lion and the fatling together,
> and a little child shall lead them.
> The cow and the bear shall feed;
> their young shall lie down together;
> and the lion shall eat straw like the ox. . . .
> They shall not hurt or destroy
> in all my holy mountain;
> for the earth shall be full of the knowledge of the Lord
> as the waters cover the sea.
>
> (RSV; Isa. 11:6–7, 9)

"The lion shall eat straw like the ox"—Disney could have a little fun with that one too. But this joke is more than a joke, or deeper than a joke. If there is about all religious faith an element of going along with the gag, these passages provide the religious gag with klieg lights and a Dolby system.

And the enthronement of the Lamb comes at the *beginning* of Revelation. By its conclusion, the sublime and the ridiculous have collided with an even louder crash as, first, the Word of God, appearing this time as the archetypal man-on-a-white-horse, rides off to the war that truly ends all wars.

And I saw heaven opened, and behold a white horse; and he that sat upon him was called Faithful and True, and in righteousness he doth judge and make war. His eyes were as a flame of fire, and on his head were many crowns; and he had a name written, that no man knew, but he himself. And he was clothed with a vesture dipped in blood: and his name is called The Word of God. And the armies which were in heaven followed him upon white horses, clothed in fine linen, white and clean. And out of his mouth goeth a sharp sword, that with it he should smite the nations: and he shall rule them with a rod of iron: and he treadeth the winepress of the fierceness and wrath of Almighty God. And he hath on his vesture and on his thigh a name written, KING OF KINGS, AND LORD OF LORDS. (KJV; Rev. 19:11–16)

At the end of the ensuing battle, Satan is chained in the abyss for a thousand years, after which, it is revealed, he will be released to wreak havoc again but only for "a little season" (KJV; 20:3) before being "cast into the lake of fire and brimstone, where the beast and the false prophet are, and shall be tormented day and night for ever and ever" (KJV; 20:10).

Christian militarism has fed on the imagery of these passages for two millennia, but how much serious militarism or military seriousness is to be realized from the story of a war that is won by a lamb? The Book of Revelation surely does express the honest horror of early Christianity at the consequences of unarmed resistance to the armed might of Rome. Its *Sturm und Drang* is an elaborate expansion of the dismay buried in John the Baptist's question to Jesus from his own Roman captivity: "Are you the one?" But the book, for all its excesses, effectively conveys a confidence that the Lamb of God has indeed won and, whatever the historical moment may suggest, won definitively.

And so it happens that the comic epic of Christianity ends, as so many comedies do, with a gala wedding. The Lamb Triumphant arrives at long last at his wedding day, taking to himself his eternal intended, the human race itself:

> I heard what seemed to be the voices of a mighty throng, like the surging of the sea or the rumble of thunder, answering:

> Hallelujah!
> For the Lord God Omnipotent reigns.
> Let us rejoice and be glad
> And give glory to God,
> For now comes the wedding day of the Lamb.
> His bride has made ready.
> She has dressed herself in fine linen,
> Dazzling white because made of the good deeds of the saints.

> (Rev. 19:6–8)

The beasts, we presume, are all invited to the reception—the flying, the hopping, the swimming, and the burrowing. As for the invitation, it will be engraved—in gold, of course—with a text from the prophet Hosea:

> I will make for you a covenant on that day
>> with the beasts of the field,
>> with the birds of the air,
>> and with the creepers on the ground.
> The bow, the sword, and war I will banish from the land.
>> I will make them lie down in safety.
> And I will marry you forever,
>> I will marry you in righteousness and justice,
> I will marry you in faithfulness,
>> and you shall know the Lord.
>
> (Hos. 2:18–20)

It is all too much, but then is mystical experience ever temperate? Is it ever just enough?

> Then I saw a new heaven and a new earth. The old heaven and the old earth had passed away, and the ocean no longer existed. I saw the holy city, a new Jerusalem, coming down out of heaven from God, arrayed as a bride adorned for her husband. Then I heard a loud voice calling from the throne, "Behold, God now lives among human beings. He shall make his home among them. They shall be his people, and he shall be their God, their God-with-them. He shall wipe the last tear from their eyes. There shall be no more death, and no more mourning or sadness or pain. The world of the past has gone." (Rev. 21:1–4)

No more death, no more mourning, no more sadness or pain. The world of the past left behind. The last tear wiped away. The ultimate epiphany of bliss.

> The Spirit and the Bride say, "Come!"
> Let everyone who listens answer, "Come!"
> All who thirst, let them come.
> All who thirst for the water of life shall drink it
> and drink it free. (22:17)

Water and the Spirit. . . .

At the start of his public ministry as a human being, God submitted to a rite of repentance in the waters of the Jordan and, speaking from heaven, with his Holy Spirit hovering visibly over his human brow, he declared himself well pleased with what he had done and who he had become. He had become a lamb, and he was pleased as he had not been since the last day of creation.

Repentance in the Greek of the Gospels is *metanoia,* a changing of the mind. The changing of the mind of God is the great subject, the epic argument, of the Christian Bible. Having blighted his own work and cursed his own image with misery and mortality, God faced an immense challenge. He had to restore his masterpiece. He had to redeem those whom he himself had exiled from paradise. For his own sake and not just for theirs, he had to recover the lost crown of his creation. But instead of becoming again the calm and sure creator he had been at the start, he became, for long centuries, an angry and anxious warrior. He won his first battle in Egypt, and effortlessly at that: What weapon avails against an opponent armed with nature itself? A few centuries later he seemed to suffer defeat at the hands of Assyria and Babylonia, but he assured his people Israel that, in truth, he was only losing so as to inflict pain and punishment on them. Soon, he said, he would wreak against their new enemies the same spectacular havoc that he had wreaked in Egypt, ravaging the landscape, laying waste to the flora and the fauna, decimating the human population, and so forth. They would be victorious, and grateful, and—a matter obsessively on his mind—the world would know beyond any doubt that he was Lord.

He was going to do all that again; but somehow, mysteriously, when the time came, he couldn't go through with it. His mind had changed. In the end, what would such a victory accomplish? After it, the deeper consequences of his own inaugural violence—a catastrophe for mankind far more devastating than any mere military defeat, more devastating even than slavery—would remain as unending punishment for them and a silent indictment of him.

So he broke his promise. He allowed himself and his people to suffer a still more catastrophic defeat; but before that doom descended, he joined them, suffering in advance all that they would suffer, and creating out of his agony a way for them to rise from the dead with him and return to paradise, bringing all nations with them.

Adam and Eve did not speak of themselves as God's children, and God did not speak of himself as their father. That came later, for God had to learn how to be a father. He had to learn how to be a spouse as well: the Lord God as the bridegroom of the universe and husband of the human race. Most of all, he had to learn how to win by losing. It took a long time, and Satan has not yet been entirely vanquished, but the Lamb of God has won the only victory that really matters. The Good News of the Gospel is the news of how he did it.

On Writing the
Lives of God

A literary reading of the Bible may take any of a variety of forms. Of these, one is a discussion of God as the protagonist, the central character, of this classic of world literature. In an earlier book entitled *God: A Biography,* I attempted such a discussion for the God of Judaism's Bible, the Tanakh, a collection of sacred scripture that coincides largely but not entirely with Christianity's Old Testament. In this book, I have attempted the same sort of discussion for the God of Christianity's Bible, comprising both the Old Testament and the New.

The interpretive strategy in *God: A Biography* had two simple rules, based on two premises:

The first rule was that conflict in the divine character as it is found on the pages of the Tanakh should be regarded as real for the purposes of literary discussion rather than, after the manner of historical criticism, explained away by reference to the various human authors of the Tanakh and their historically differing views. The premise behind this rule was a literary appropriation—rather like a transposition from one musical key to another—of the age-old Jewish belief that "the Lord is our God, the Lord alone" (Deut. 6:4). The effect that God produces on the page owes much to tension among his mutually contradictory character traits, but the condition for this tension is that the character be always the same character. When historical criticism dissolves the dynamic tension of monotheism by tracing different character traits to different ancient sources, one may understand better how the composite character came into existence, but the character himself is gone, dissolved into a polytheism of component parts.

The second rule was that conflict in the divine character, rather than being described or analyzed systematically, as in theology, should emerge in the course of the narrative. The premise behind this procedure was that internal complexity in the character of God could be shown to develop over time in response to vicissitudes in God's long-running relationship with mankind and, in particular, with the nation of Israel. In this way, though there would be no birth or death, there could be a coherent passage from God's first words and deeds on the page to his last. There could be character development and, in a word, biography.

In Christianity's edition of the Jewish scriptures that it inherited, a revised conclusion, the New Testament, radically revises the meaning of God's life as a whole. I have attempted, in this second book, to read that revised meaning from the revised conclusion. Once again, God has been taken neither as the object of religious belief nor as a topic in ancient history but as the central character in a work of literature. Once again, the interpretive strategy has had two premises and two matching rules.

Just as the first premise of *God: A Biography* was a literary appropriation or transposition of the core Jewish belief that "the Lord is our God, the Lord alone," so the belief appropriated or transposed here has been the classic Christian belief that "Jesus is Lord" (Rom. 10:9)—the dogma, foreshadowed in the New Testament and formally defined at the first ecumenical councils, that Jesus Christ was and is God Incarnate, God in the flesh. The interpretive rule that follows from this premise is that everything that Jesus says, does, or suffers in the New Testament should be regarded as said, done, or suffered by God. Moreover, tension within the character of Jesus—beginning with the troublesome fact that he speaks sometimes as God and sometimes as a man—should not be relaxed, as in historical criticism, by referring different Jesuses to different ancient writers and their different constituencies. For literary as distinct from historical purposes, there should be only one Jesus, and he should always be both divine and human.

The second rule, matching the second rule of *God: A Biography,* has been that the complexity of this character, with his double identity, rather than being described or analyzed systematically, as in theology, should again emerge in the course of the narrative. Having become human as Jesus of Nazareth, God lays claim—not all at once but gradually as the New Testament unfolds—to every function that he ever discharged through a human intermediary. He is Adam, the image and likeness of himself and the firstborn of a new creation. He is Moses, revealing a new *torah,* a new teaching, for all of mankind. He is David, inaugurating a new kingdom "not of this world." He is Elijah, resolving all disputes with miraculous insight and foretelling all history until the end of time. Once God spoke his Word through others; now his Word "has become flesh." Once he adopted Solomon so as, through him, to become the adoptive father of all Israel; now he has become his own son—"I and the Father are one," Jesus says (RSV; John 10:30)—and is prepared, through him, to adopt the whole world. The character who results from this multiplication of identities is full of swirling tensions that are resolved only when the traumatic death of Jesus resolves a much deeper, prior conflict in the character of God. The second premise, then, of this reading of the New Testament has been that this fusion in one man of all God's prior interactions with mankind could be shown to emerge—this emergence being quintessentially the art of the New Testament—in the narrative of Jesus' interactions with his fellow men during his life and even after his death.

What difference does it make, page by page, to read the New Testament as the continuation of the biography of God to a revised conclusion in which, at the end of his already extraordinary career, he becomes a human being?

In the first place, when one reads in this way, many vivid scenes are recovered for the characterization of the protagonist that, because they did not happen, historical criticism must read as the self-characterization of an author. Did a heavenly host of angels sing praise at Jesus' birth as Luke reports? For historical purposes, the answer must be no: Angels have no place in secular history. For literary purposes, however, even secular literary purposes, the answer may and indeed must be yes. For the historian, the angels' unhistorical song tells you something about an ancient author, whom you may call Luke if you wish, but nothing about the historical Jesus. For the literary critic, the song of the heavenly host, no matter that it is unhistorical, enhances the angel messenger's characterization of the newborn Jesus as "a savior who is Messiah and Lord" (Luke 2:11). What matters for the literary effect is not that the account cannot be verified (a laughable notion) but that it wakes echoes of a dozen exultant Psalms, among them Psalm 148:1–2:

> Praise the Lord from the heavens,
>   praise him in the heights above.
> Praise him, all you angels,
>   praise him, you heavenly hosts.

And as for Jesus' birth, so also for the rest of his life as God in the flesh. Did he raise the dead, walk on water, still the storm, and converse on a mountaintop with Moses and Elijah? After his resurrection, did he ascend bodily into heaven before the wondering eyes of his disciples? Once returned to heaven, did he, as the enthroned Lamb of God, open a scroll revealing the course of all history until the end of time? And did the Lamb then marry? Since "the historical Jesus" did none of this, historical criticism must turn the wine of such conduct—God Incarnate's dramatic self-characterization on the page—back into the grape juice of the supposed historical agenda of one (postulated) author or another. Literary criticism is free to drink the wine. This is the first difference.

The second difference, and a more important one, is that when one takes the protagonist of the Gospels to be God Incarnate, his every interaction has behind it not just the prior life of Jesus of Nazareth but also the prior life of the Lord God with his chosen people, everything that he has done to them and they to him during the course of (his image for it) their long and difficult marriage. As God the Son, Jesus incurs all the old debts of God the Father. Every hope the Father ever kindled in the Jews becomes the Son's to extinguish or inflame. The stakes are high for him as well as for them.

On the page, as a result, the Incarnation can seem, at any given moment, almost like a reincarnation. A characterological doubling takes place because *God has been here before.* Now that he is back, every place he goes, every remark he makes or hears, is charged with ancient memories and associations, and many episodes are charged as well with dramatic irony because of God's own broken promises.

There is no single necessary or correct way to read the New Testament, as there is no single necessary or correct way to read any great literary classic; but when the divinity of Christ the Lord is embraced as a literary opportunity rather than resisted as a theological imposition, the protagonist of this work can seem illumined from within. The classic Christian view, first expressed in the prologue to the Gospel of John and in the Letter to the Hebrews, has long been that though God spoke many words through the prophets, Jesus is his last word, his Word in person. But the corollary to this view is that, Jesus being God Incarnate, all of

God's earlier words were Jesus' words as well and may—indeed, must—be taken into account as evidence about his character. An interpretation that takes those words seriously as God's words and, at the same time, takes him seriously as God Incarnate is forced to entertain the hypothesis that an ironic transformation of the divine character must have been in progress of which he is the unlikely late expression and the result.

Irony—because it deals in double meanings and reversals of meaning, because it talks behind people's backs and over their heads, because it pretends to be sincere, then pretends to be insincere, because it half-expects not to be understood and will not stoop to explanation—seems to have no place in religious literature. But when long-standing expectations about the very premise of a religion are suddenly reversed, there is indeed a place for irony in religion. The famous literary critic who said that it is absurd to imagine Abraham as either sincere or insincere was only half-right: It may be absurd to imagine Abraham as simply insincere, but it is not absurd at all to imagine him as ironic. What is true of Abraham is true, in a similar but denser and more tangled way, of Jesus. Because nearly everything that Jesus says recalls something else, nearly everything he says has more than one meaning. And therein lies much of his mysterious appeal.

*G*od: *A Biography* asserts that the life story of God comes to a fully satisfying conclusion in the Tanakh. Its sequel does not retract that assertion, yet a text can permit what it does not require. That the New Testament is, in literary terms, unnecessary does not make it uninteresting. Christianity rearranged the canon that it had inherited from Judaism by moving the prophets to the end and by appending to that arrangement a radically revisionist final chapter to the life of God. The result is, in critic Harold Bloom's sense of the phrase, a strong misreading or "poetic misprision" of the Jewish edition and, as such, is right in a way that does not make its predecessor wrong.

Charles Gounod wrote his "Ave Maria" as a melody above the harmony of the first prelude in J. S. Bach's *Well-Tempered Clavier*. Some may dislike what Gounod wrote, regarding it simply as an adulteration of Bach's work. But even those who admire the "Ave Maria" do not believe that it negates or supersedes Bach's composition—as if Bach uncompleted by Gounod could no longer be performed—but only that it realizes a melodic possibility that would have been there awaiting realization whether or not Gounod had ever lived. Jesus of Nazareth, in a similar way, realizes a possibility in the character of God that would have been there whether or not Jesus had ever lived. Bach's composition is still itself after Gounod. The Tanakh is still itself after the New Testament. But in either case, something that was only potential has been made actual.

The autonomy of the Tanakh aside, there are two ways to take up the question Why does the New Testament exist at all? Historical criticism typically rephrases that question as some version of Who wrote the New Testament? The motive behind the New Testament, the reason it exists, is then stated as the sum of the temporally and locally conditioned motives of the authors of the New Testament and their several ancient audiences. Literary criticism as I have attempted it here prefers to remain within the assumptions of the story and to rephrase the question as Why does God do it? Why does he become a man?

Why *does* he do it? And why, if he has to become a man at all, does he choose to become the unlikely man he becomes? When the lion behaves like a lamb, there is certainly every reason for incredulity. God's power was such that, in his prime, he annihilated in minutes the mightiest army in the world. More than once, he compared himself to a great marauding beast. Why does he become a defenseless peasant who, when the authorities sentence him to death, offers no resistance and ends his life as a convicted criminal? Does the Incarnation not begin to seem, as Nietzsche might have put it, the greatest misfortune ever to befall the Lord God of Hosts? Rather than a further development of God's character, does Jesus, the Lamb of God, not seem its terminal collapse?

Yes, he does, and the condition for a literary appreciation of the New Testament is a willingness on the part of the reader to see this ending as a horrifying or ludicrous surprise. God the Son is not at all the kind of man one would expect God the Father to become. Jesus' own first followers are appalled to discover that their leader, alongside all the other roles he has been assuming, intends to assume the role of sacrificial animal. But the strangeness of the New Testament is the key to why there is a New Testament in the first place. As merely a grand reprise of the Tanakh, the New Testament would surely be superfluous. What makes the surprise subjectively urgent as well as logically possible for God, given his previous life, is that he has something appalling to say that he can say only by humiliating himself.

The Lord of All the Earth, to use the grandest of all his Old Testament titles, arranges to have himself put to death as the King of the Jews not to destroy hope as he destroys himself but only to replace a vain hope with one that can still be realized. The old hope predicated on invincible military power must yield to a new hope predicated on the inevitability of military defeat but anticipating the kind of victory that arms cannot win. Christ's double nature makes it possible for him to use his own death demonstratively and instrumentally as no other human being can and as God himself could not unless he had first become a human being. As God he cannot cease to exist, but as man he can undergo the ordeal of a human death so as to dramatize a message too violent for words alone to convey. Defeated by Rome, God thus accomplishes what he tried and failed to accomplish when defeated by Babylonia: He turns the defeat into a triumph, the humiliation into an exaltation. As he is led off to die, he says, to recall his words one last time, "Take heart, I have conquered the world" (REB; John 16:33).

Historical criticism is free to object that Jesus of Nazareth did not interpret his own death beforehand in these words, that others put them into his mouth after his death, and so it well may have been. But the writer who dared to put such radical words into the mouth of the Creator was a great writer, and his words stayed where he put them, defining for all time the astonishing literary character who stands at the heart of the New Testament.

There has been something Promethean about the critical labor of turning Christ the Lord back into Jesus of Nazareth, but the transgressive daring of the historical critique must not eclipse the enormity of the original literary offense itself. And that offense, that effrontery, cannot be appreciated unless the God of Israel has first been confronted in all his untamed and terrifying intensity. That of all gods *this* god should be imagined to have become of all men *this* man; and that, repudiating everything he had always seemed to be, he should have had himself put to death by the enemy of his chosen people—this is a reversal so stunning that it changes everything back to the beginning. The Rock of Ages cannot die as God; but as God Incarnate, the Rock can be cleft. God, shattered, can descend to death; and when he rises to eternal life, he can lift his human creatures up with him. Victory is postponed in the Christian revision of the Jewish epic no less than in the Jewish original. Yet because that victory is assured, even the poor, even the meek, even the grief-stricken and scorned who in this world must hunger and thirst for justice may count themselves blessed. Theirs, because he made himself one of them, is the kingdom of heaven.

Appendices

Appendix I

ONE BIBLE FROM MANY SCRIPTURES
(HOW IT HAPPENED AND WHY IT MATTERS)

How it happened

Unlike most other literary classics, the Tanakh—the sacred scripture of the Jews—is written in not one but two original languages. Ancient Israel's first language was Hebrew; but when Israel was reduced to Yahud, a province of the Persian empire, in the sixth century B.C.E., Aramaic, the business language of the empire, became the second language of the Jews even for the writing of sacred scripture. Parts of the latest books in the Tanakh are written in Aramaic, and the Aramaic alphabet replaced the original Hebrew alphabet for the writing of Hebrew itself.

Later, in the fourth century B.C.E., when Yahud became Ioudaia, a province within the set of culturally Greek sister-empires that succeeded the Persian empire, Greek, the language of the new empires, came into use alongside Hebrew and Aramaic, again for sacred as well as for secular purposes. As a part of this process, a Greek edition of Jewish scriptures was produced in the second century B.C.E. for the Greek-speaking Jews of Egypt. This edition, called the Septuagint, included not just translations of Hebrew and Aramaic works (including a few that were later excluded from the still fluid collection in Palestine itself) but also a few works written originally in Greek. These works—whose inclusion in the Greek Bible was analogous to the inclusion of untranslated Aramaic works in the emerging "Hebrew" Bible—make the literary autonomy of the collection clear. It was an edition, not just a translation, and it reflected the evolution of Judean Jewry during the Hellenistic period into a world Jewry in which many more Jews spoke Greek than spoke either Hebrew or Aramaic.[1]

Hellenistic Jewry regarded the Jewish scriptures in Greek as literally miraculous in origin—the translation was seen as an act of God—and as no less divinely inspired than the Hebrew. When belief in Christ spread from the Greek-speaking Jews of Palestine to the Greek-speaking Jews of this populous Mediterranean diaspora (a population perhaps five times larger than the Jewish population of Palestine), the Greek scripture was already in place "waiting" for it. In short order, the Septuagint became the scripture of the new movement,[2] and its New Testament, written with the Septuagint intensely in mind, would become Hellenistic Jewry's greatest contribution to world literature. All but one of the authors of the New Testament were ethnic Jews, but only one, at most, was a Palestinian Jew living in Palestine at the time he wrote. The Mediterranean Jewish Diaspora, not Palestine, is the home country of the New Testament, including, very emphatically, the Gospels. Even the Gospel of John, whose rhetorical affinities with the Dead Sea Scrolls have suggested that its author could conceivably have been a Palestinian Jew, is written in Greek and has the subculture of Hellenistic Jewry as its principal frame of reference.

After 70 C.E., when Rome destroyed Jerusalem, deported much of the population of Judea, and ended even limited political autonomy for the Jews, the Hebrew and Aramaic languages became a newly important line of religio-ethnic demarcation in the Roman empire. This was so because Hellenistic Jewry had already become a major source, if not *the* major source, of converts to Christianity. Sociologist Rodney Stark argues persuasively that Christianity remained a majority-Jewish movement until long after the New Testament canon was complete. We must recall that this new Jewish sect migrating outward from Palestine was, at the start, very small by comparison with the Jewish diaspora already in place. If 80 percent of diaspora Jewry declined the Christian invitation, Stark argues, the acceptance of it by the remaining 20 percent—presumably the most Hellenized fifth—would have sufficed to create a movement with 1 million members by 250 C.E. even in the absence of any Gentile converts.[3] There were, of course, many Gentile converts, but conversion to early Christianity did not seem a renunciation of ethnicity to Jews. In fact, the opposite was the case: It seemed a relative renunciation of ethnicity to Gentiles. To practitioners of Greco-Roman polytheism, conversion to Christianity seemed, understandably, like affiliation with a movement that was overwhelmingly Jewish both in content and by membership. For reasons too complex to go into here, this was, in fact, part of its appeal.

With regard, more narrowly, to the understanding or understandings of the Bible that were taking shape at this time, Rabbinic Judaism—with Christianity, one of the two forms of Palestinian Judaism that had survived the cataclysm of 70 C.E.—increasingly saw the scripture in Greek as the Christians' scripture or, more accurately perhaps, as the apostates' scripture. Among Christians, by contrast, the earlier attitude of the Greek-speaking Jewish diaspora—that the scripture in Greek was simply the Word of God—lived on.

The notion, commonplace in our day, that if you have not read a work in the original, you have not read it was rare in the first centuries C.E. That notion became truly widespread only with the rise of printing and with the printing-generated concept of copyright. Before printing, there was little or no notion of authorship as ownership of a sort that did not entail physical control over the actual copies of a given work.[4] This separability of product from producer explains, in part, why so many ancient works are anonymous: Their authors lacked the motive that modern authors have for labeling their spiritual property. The same separability explains how in antiquity a translation could seem the equivalent of the original. For modernity, a work in translation stands at a perceptibly greater distance from its author than does the same work in the original. For antiquity, the original was already at so great a distance from its author that the translation could scarcely stand at any greater distance. Attribution, under these circumstances, was a property of the text rather than an indication that the text was the property of an author.

As just suggested, there is evidence that when recently exiled Aramaic- and Hebrew-speaking Jews encountered their own scriptures in the oppressor's Greek language, the result was a sharpened awareness of translation as such,[5] a new awareness whose long-term consequences have perhaps been too little recognized. For a majority of the long-established and acculturated Greek-speaking Jews of the Mediterranean diaspora, however, little or no such awareness clouded the use of translated scripture, and these were the Jews who, in essence, created the two-testament Christian Bible.

Christianity's new scriptures crystallized in time into something close to a canon. By 367 C.E., when Athanasius, the patriarch of Alexandria, used the word *canon* for a list of the twenty-seven books that still constitute the New Testament, the process was essentially complete. It is plausible, though not certain, that while the Christian canon was taking shape, Christian editors were taking a second look at the canon of Jewish scriptures in Greek and deciding to move the expectation-filled books of prophecy—Isaiah, Jeremiah, Ezekiel, and the twelve minor prophets—from the middle to the end of the collection. It may be, however, that this "Christian" order is actually a pre-Christian Jewish order favored in Alexandria over the Palestinian Torah-Prophets-Writings order that became standard in Rabbinic Judaism. In any event, reordered or not but seen stereoptically with the new Christian texts, the received Jewish texts became the Old Testament of the Christian Bible.[6]

The adjective *old* in the term Old Testament originally functioned, it should be noted, rather as *old* functions in the term Old World. The older covenantal relationship between God and the Jews, though sometimes disparaged, was often celebrated in the founding centuries of Christianity's new covenant and, in any case, was never simply repudiated. If it had been, the older scriptures would surely have been repudiated with it. This alternative was in fact proposed in the mid-second century, but, revealingly, it was rejected. A religious community whose ethnic majority was still Jewish found it morally impossible to regard the Jewish scriptures as other than the Word of God. It should be noted, in passing, that the referent of the word *testament* or *covenant* was not, in the first instance, a collection of texts but the relationship of a group of people to God. The old testament/covenant (in Latin, *testamentum* means what is meant in English by *covenant*) was the relationship of Israel to God; the new testament/covenant expanded that relationship to admit the rest of mankind.

Beyond canonization, one step toward scriptural unification remained to be taken. Greek-speaking Christianity, even after it began to group its scriptures into an Old Testament and a New Testament with fixed lists for the contents of each, still thought of them in the plural. The fusion of the many into one occurred only when the scriptures moved west of Italy, where Latin was, effectively, the only language in use. It was there that the Greek plural common noun *biblia,* meaning "books," began to be misconstrued in popular Latin usage as the Latin singular proper noun *Biblia* that was its homonym. This mistake was pregnant with cultural consequence, for Latin *Biblia,* thus construed, did not mean "books," it meant "The Bible" in, for the first time, our sense of the word. Western Christendom began to regard the many scriptures as effectively one. A grammatical misconception coincided with an epoch-making cultural reconception. Greek *biblia,* to repeat, was a common noun. Other books could be referred to by the same word. Latin *Biblia* would become a capitalized proper noun, a new and singular word for a new and singular thing.

Greek, which had a definite article, habitually used it when speaking of the Judeo-Christian scriptures; thus, the normal expression was *ta biblia,* "*the* books" or "*the* scriptures." Classical Latin lacked a definite article, but late Latin developed one and bequeathed it to the neo-Latin or Romance languages. When this happened, *Biblia* became, revealingly, *la Bible* in French, reflecting Christendom's attitude toward its scripture as not just singular but also definite. Language apart, the Bible became, everywhere in Christian Europe, a definite as well as a singular thing.[7]

Why it matters

That Greek was the language both of the new, rather rough-and-ready texts that charismatics like Paul were writing for the emergent Christianity and of the far longer and more formal texts that Greek-speaking Mediterranean Jewry had been reading for centuries, was of enormous literary consequence. Linguistic homogeneity between the old and the new facilitated an interaction between them that bears comparison with that between Greek tragedy and the whole of earlier Greek mythology. The onstage action of a tragedy like *Oedipus Rex* scarcely goes beyond Oedipus's discovery of the truth about his genealogy. Sophocles does not begin to review the whole of the mythology that the play presupposes. He takes it for granted that his audience in

Athens will bring a rich background in that mythology into the theater with them. Crucially, they will know that Oedipus has unwittingly slain his own father long before, onstage, Oedipus himself does. By drawing on this cultural common holding, the playwright can both simplify his exposition and immensely enhance its emotional impact. The Greek-speaking Jews who wrote the New Testament assume a comparable knowledge not just of the life of Christ but also of earlier Jewish written and oral tradition. Though they explain the occasional Aramaic word or latter-day Judean or Galilean custom for readers in cities like Antioch and Corinth, they assume rather than provide an acquaintance in translation with the Jewish sacred scriptures to which they so freely allude.

The Old Testament functioned, within the two-testament Christian Bible, as explicit or implicit harmony beneath the melody of the New Testament. All melodies have what musicians call implicit harmonies. When the Gounod melody of the Bach-Gounod "Ave Maria" is sung without the usual accompaniment of Bach's pristine arpeggiated chords, the Western ear "hears" those chords anyway. Once the Tanakh was turned into the Old Testament and bound with the New Testament between the covers of what was felt to be a single, composite work, Christian exegetes received a kind of standing invitation to hear the Old Testament within the New in a similar implicit and "harmonic" way even when they found no explicit reference to it.

Proceeding in this way, New Testament exegetes merely deferred to the intention of the New Testament writers themselves. Nothing could be clearer than that the founders of Christianity apprehended and expressed their own religious experience in inherited Jewish categories. The New Testament is new more by novel combination than by outright invention. The Old Testament provides virtually all the categories, images, diction, and narrative repertory or collective memory that the New Testament employs to convey its message. Sometimes the New Testament writers allude explicitly to the Old Testament. More often, the allusion is implicit but easily audible for those with ears to hear. In either case, the mechanism is both primitive and powerful. When I am speaking before a group and see heads nod at a reference, an almost physical bond springs up between me and those who thus acknowledge my story as theirs. The nod need not be a nod of agreement. What counts is that it is a nod of recognition. Paul and, after him, the authors of the Gospels employ Jewish scripture allusively so as to establish just this kind of intimacy with their Jewish readers and ultimately to persuade them of the continuity between the old revelation of God's covenant with Israel and the new revelation of the expansion of that covenant to include the entire human race.

The Old Testament provides the means, in other words, both to express and to authenticate the new religious vision. At the start of the Gospel of Luke, we read:

> Seeing that many others have undertaken to draw up accounts of the events *that have reached their fulfillment among us,* as these were handed down to us by those who from the outset were eyewitnesses and ministers of the Word, I in my turn, after carefully going over the whole story from the beginning, have decided to write an ordered account for you, Theophilus, so that your Excellency may learn *how well founded the teaching is* that you have received. (1:1–4, italics added)

What Luke promises Theophilus (an otherwise unknown early Christian) is not principally factual accuracy, though that notion is not altogether absent from this preamble. What he promises is a demonstration that the events he is about to report—events already known from reliable earlier reports—constitute a *fulfillment* of which he and Theophilus are a part. Luke will show this in good part by linking those events to the providential course of events as memorialized in the Old Testament. That the Christian teaching is well founded means, in practice, not that it is objective or empirically documented but that it links demonstrably with God's earlier work in the world. Scripture was not the only source of this knowledge, but for a literary undertaking it was the key source.

It is beyond doubt that the writers of the New Testament were subject to a set of powerful contemporary influences from the Greco-Roman culture that surrounded them. A historical assessment of their work properly requires allowing for these influences at every moment. A literary assessment, however, does not require this or, at the very least, does not require it to the same extent. Thus, for a historian, the cult of the murdered, divinized, world-saving young Christ, the leader of a semisecret society who created a rite for his followers in which flesh was symbolically eaten and blood was drunk, cries out for comparison with the mystery cults of the Roman empire. Yet for a literary critic, even one aware of this cultural context, this sort of comparison need not be pursued. The Jews who actually wrote Christianity's scriptures wrote them in such a way that they allude only to their own Jewish scriptures. Though a historian has every warrant to compare the cult of the divinized Jesus with, for example, the cult of the divinized Dionysus, a literary critic, finding no references to Dionysus in the text, has equally solid warrant to ignore him. Literary appreciation cultivates internal references, made for their aesthetic effect, by preference to external references, valuable for their historical information.

Allusion legitimizes an intrusion of one text upon another or of one portion of a text upon another portion. The "hypertextual" syncretism that results turns the reader who notices into a kind of writer. Moreover, a reader thus stimulated may continue in the same direction on his own, making linkages that the author himself may not have intended. Thus, hearing the New Testament over the "accompaniment" of the Old Testament, Christian exegetes over the centuries have done as the New Testament authors themselves did, but more so, employing other Old Testament texts than the original writers employed to produce effects that those writers might well appreciate but cannot have anticipated. It is ironic, perhaps, that university-based historical criticism of the Bible has imposed on itself a chaste respect for the intentions of a set of biblical authors who were by no means so chaste in interpreting one another. The biblical rule and, for that matter, the postbiblical rule, both Jewish and Christian, down to the threshold of modern times was not the rule of deference to original intent but the rule of creative reuse.

Appendix II

THE BIBLE AS ROSE WINDOW
(OR, HOW NOT TO SEE THROUGH THE BIBLE)

A work of literary art is like a stained-glass window: It exists essentially not to be seen through but to be looked at. This is just how literary criticism classically responds to a work of literature, even when its subject matter is historical. There was a historical Hamlet, but Shakespeare criticism spends little time talking about him, nor does it compensate for the inadequacy of information about him by attempting a historical reconstruction of the Denmark of his day.[1]

Why is New Testament criticism so very different? Rather than look at the rose window of the text, it labors endlessly to see through it. Overwhelmingly historical in its preoccupation, New Testament criticism pores over the text in the hope of finding a few passages, however brief, that may seem so devoid of ancient theological elaboration that through them the originating events themselves may be seen. Why does it do this? Why, if little independent historical information is to be had about Jesus, may such information not simply be dispensed with? Why may the Gospels not be read as the religiously motivated, artistically executed texts that an unforced reading would suggest them to be? Why take so narrowly instrumental an attitude toward a work of the imagination?

Why New Testament criticism strains to see through stained glass

There is about the historical criticism of the New Testament a Puritan heroism of renunciation that only religious commitment, buried as it often may be, can begin to explain. To appreciate how this ascetic attitude has come to the fore, we must return to the sixteenth century, when the Protestant Reformation, seeing, as it thought, the historical truth about Christ and Christianity in the New Testament, made that collection of ancient texts a criterion by which to reform the doctrine and the practice of the Roman Catholic church. Having assigned the New Testament this function, Protestantism acquired a motive to engage in the historical study of the New Testament with an accelerating intensity. At first this scrutiny, though it brought much to light that could be used to undermine the authority of Catholicism, brought little to light that could undermine the authority of the New Testament itself. But once the skeptical attitude of the eighteenth-century Enlightenment toward the miraculous was joined to the methodological skepticism of nineteenth-century critical history toward even the historically plausible, this situation changed radically. Critical lives of Jesus written in that century by David Friedrich Strauss in Germany and by Ernest Renan in France brought to the lay public in all of Europe a doubt about the historical reliability of the New Testament that had been building up among the learned for decades.

For Catholicism, it was a simple matter to reject Strauss and Renan: They were merely branches on a tree of rationalist history whose roots Rome had long since condemned. For Protestantism, the matter was much more complex, since Protestantism as a reform movement within Christianity had been built in part upon the historical reliability of the Bible. The emerging dilemma was exquisitely posed early in the twentieth century by Albert Schweitzer in an erudite but forcefully argued and indeed epoch-making work translated into English as *The Quest of the Historical Jesus.* Synthesizing a century and more of critical research, Schweitzer found one conclusion inescapable: Jesus of Nazareth had erroneously believed that the end of his earthly life and the end of the world were to be a single apocalyptic event. So inextricable was this idea from the rest of Jesus' preaching, Schweitzer thought, that no one could embrace the historical Jesus intellectually without accepting the mistake that, historically, Jesus had made. Poignantly, Schweitzer himself, who could not escape his own modernity, could not renounce Christianity either, though his commitment to it now became more mystical than intellectual. He resolved his dilemma not by any theological breakthrough but by a heroic act of Christian charity: his decision to become a medical doctor and move permanently to Africa—as if to say with the Paul of 1 Corinthians 13:13, "So faith, hope, love abide, these three; but the greatest of these is love."

Schweitzer believed that the historical Jesus not only could be but essentially had been recovered. When he wrote, "There is nothing more negative than the result of research into the life of Jesus," he did not mean to express any doubt that the quest for the historical Jesus had succeeded but only unflinching realism regarding the religious relevance of its success. "The mistake," he wrote,

> was to suppose that Jesus could come to mean more to our time by entering into it as a man like ourselves. That is not possible. First because such

a Jesus never existed. Second because, although historical knowledge can no doubt introduce greater clarity into an existing spiritual life, it can never call life into existence. History can destroy the present; it can reconcile the present with the past; can even to a certain extent transport the present into the past; but to contribute to the making of the present is not given unto it.[2]

During the century after Schweitzer, the response of intellectual Protestantism to the subversion of its trust in the historical reliability of the New Testament oscillated between two options. The first, beginning not long after World War I and fading toward the end of the century, was an attempt—much in the spirit of Schweitzer—to neutralize history rather than to use it. The second option, beginning in the mid-nineteenth century and climaxing at the beginning of the twenty-first, has been an attempt to create a religiously usable history by redoubled effort.

The first option is associated above all with the name of Rudolf Bultmann. Bultmann's strategy, a brilliant one, was to retreat from the Reformation motto *sola scriptura* ("by scripture alone") to the more basic motto *sola fide* ("by faith alone"). How important, he and his followers asked, should biographical information about Jesus be to the Christian of today if, quite clearly, such information was of little importance to Saint Paul? It is indeed the case that Paul, who was a contemporary of Jesus and who could presumably have provided much information about him to his many converts, never sees fit to do so in the letters that constitute so large a portion of the New Testament. Paul knows that Jesus died and rose and that he is the Savior of the world. There Paul is content to let the matter rest. There Martin Luther, whose preoccupations were theological rather than historical, had been content to let the matter rest. And there Bultmann was prepared to let the matter rest as well. What mattered was not how accurate or detailed one's historical knowledge of Jesus was. What mattered, rather, was whether, when Christ was preached, one could respond in faith. Thus, Paul became not just the archetypal believer but, by extrapolating from his attitude toward the facts of Jesus' life, the archetypal historical noncombatant. And thus Bultmann, tacitly conceding that sixteenth-century Protestant theology may have used the New Testament uncritically in challenging the Roman church, retreated to the position that interposing the authority of the historian between the repentant sinner and the Savior was little better than reintroducing the human authority of the Roman Catholic church in the same mediating role. Turning twentieth-century history against nineteenth-century historicism, Bultmann deployed his formidable learning to demonstrate that the Gospels were so fully subordinated to the needs of early Christian preaching and instruction that they could have no historical reliability whatsoever—but so be it: *What* happened, Bultmann maintained, was vastly less important than *that* it happened.[3]

The second option—in recent decades, the dominant option, though no single writer has assumed the importance of a Schweitzer or a Bultmann—was, first, to assert or imply a normative function for the New Testament not as a mere literary text but, rather, as the carrier of a "kernel of historical truth"; and, second, in pursuit of that historical kernel, to apply to the critique of the received text the same purgative fervor that sixteenth-century Protestantism brought to its critique of the received church. It was by this route that, during the latter decades of the twentieth century, the exposure of historical falsehood within the New Testament acquired the unmistakable mood of a religious mission. Yes, much of the canonical text had to be rejected as church invention, but something, it was clearly hoped, would remain that could function for all Christians—perhaps, some dared hope, even for non-Christians—as canonical scripture had functioned when Protestantism was young. Thus, reviewing a popularization of this historical criticism of the New Testament for *The New York Times,* one enthusiast exulted that it "does a better job than the canonical Gospels of presenting the root mythology of an expansive idea whose time, evidently, is still coming" and "accomplishes something the church itself would like to achieve: to wipe the slate clean of a shameful catalog of crimes and start over again with the original intention."[4] A brief reform movement in the Roman Catholic church, culminating in the Second Vatican Council (1962–65), resembled the Protestant Reformation in several regards, one of which was a readiness to invoke the Bible against church tradition and church authority. In this mood, a good many Catholic recruits were enrolled for this second of the two essentially Protestant options just mentioned.

What complicated historical criticism of the New Testament undertaken in this archetypally Protestant spirit was that the proportion of stained to clear glass was not what historical critics would have wished. A window that might at least have been partially clear was found, when examined pane by pane, to contain scarcely a single one unstained by art and religious ideology. Moreover, whenever one scholar labeled a pane clear, another scholar was likely to take a closer look and find it stained. By the turn of the century, almost all the panes were so labeled, and the end point of a learned adventure begun courageously in the spirit of *sola scriptura* had come to seem very nearly *sola ecclesia* ("by the church alone"). The church, which was to have been reformed using scripture as a norm, turned out to have created scripture for its own purposes.[5]

The secular alternatives: church history and literary appreciation

To the fully secular historian, of course, the New Testament would be of little interest *unless* a church of historic importance had grown up around the beliefs to which it gives expression. Indeed, genuinely secular New Testament scholars (and there certainly are some) understand themselves as, in effect, historians of the very early church. The Gospels of Matthew and John end with scenes in which Jesus commissions his disciples to spread his message around the world. The Gospel of Luke is half of a two-volume work, with the second volume devoted entirely to the foundation of the church. The Letters of Paul are all addressed to recently founded churches. New Testament scholars may easily enough rest the case for their research on the importance—large, even if not infinitely so—of the Christian church as a historical phenomenon.

As they do this, however, their study of the New Testament text undergoes—in principle, if not always in practice—a paradoxical change. This is so because passages in the text that, though not historical in themselves, have fostered the growth of the church acquire in the end greater historical importance than duller or more cryptic passages that may hint at what actually happened or what the historical Jesus was actually like. Thus, the line "Let him who is without sin cast the first stone" (John 8:7) is quite probably an invention of the early church, but that line captured the imagination of the world. It is, accordingly, quite properly described as a historic line. The New Testament contains a great many such brilliant adulterations of the historical record. Were it otherwise, no one would now remember cryptic but probably authentic lines like "Let the dead bury their dead" (Matt. 8:22).

Historical truth within the New Testament text has survived, in other words, only because it has been carried within imaginative invention that enjoyed historic success in the world at large. But to value the inventions over the preserved memories is an inversion of learned priorities that, for a great many historical critics, is almost literally inconceivable. It is to abandon the heroic program of creating what might be called Jesusianity and capitulating to the disappointing but irreversible fact that it is Christianity that became a world religion—capitulating to the fact that had Jesus not been so effectively transformed into Christ and then into God Incarnate, in a process that begins on the earliest pages of the New Testament itself, no one today would be interested in engaging in any historical quest for him.

The religious relevance of history is not self-evident or self-establishing. A further, constructive step must be taken to establish that relevance, and this step is itself confessionally religious rather than neutrally historical. The action by which religious importance is assigned to history cannot be presented as a discovery but only proposed as a commitment. Thus, when Robert W. Funk, a founder of the "Jesus Seminar," writes in the prologue to his *Honest to Jesus: Jesus for a New Millennium,* "I confess I am more interested in what Jesus of Nazareth thinks about God's domain than in what Peter the fisherman and Paul the tentmaker thought about Jesus,"[6] one perfectly legitimate reply is: "I *confess* that I am not." Near the end of the book, when Funk reveals his twenty-one theses for the reform of the faith, explicitly evoking the memory of Martin Luther, he expands on his confession:

5. *We can no longer rest our faith on the faith of Peter or the faith of Paul.* I do not want my faith to be a secondhand faith. I am therefore fundamentally dissatisfied with versions of the faith that trace their origins only so far as the first believers; true faith, fundamental faith, must be related in some way directly to Jesus of Nazareth.[7]

But what if another man thinks that a faith that confesses its origins in Peter and Paul as well as in Jesus is superior to one that would admit no source but Jesus? What reply can be made to such a man? Jesus, in one of his best-attested teachings (reported both in the Synoptic Gospels and by Paul at 1 Corinthians 7:10–15), opposed divorce under all circumstances; Paul allowed it in some circumstances. Funk prefers Jesus; someone else might prefer Paul. Many in the nineteenth century preferred, on religious grounds, the consciously cosmopolitan Paul to the more ethnocentric Jesus. No historical argument or concatenation of historical facts can settle a dispute that is, in the end, a matter of religious opinion and religious commitment. The very success of historical criticism in showing how pervasive was the influence of "Peter and Paul," taking them as stand-ins for the entire process by which memory was transformed into literature, has made this religious question—a perfectly legitimate question, of course—increasingly unavoidable.

As this question comes to the fore, interestingly, a more thoroughgoing secularization and academic normalization of New Testament studies may also come within reach. Erstwhile New Testament scholars whose interests are genuinely and secularly historical may begin—some have already begun—to define their field, as historians do, by a period rather than by a text, while those who continue to define their field by the text may begin to locate their chosen text, for interpretative purposes, in the Western literary canon rather than in the first and second centuries C.E. The truly secular historians may broaden their inquiry into very early church history to include relatively neglected topics like the history of Syriac and Egyptian Christianity (Syria and Egypt being, after Palestine, the regions first Christianized) and the surprisingly early emergence and influence of monasticism. As for the truly secular New Testament critics, they may begin to deal with their chosen text as a work of art rather than mining it as a historical source. Either change brings with it a new set of secondary colleagues and analytic categories, and neither prejudices the continued study of scripture as sacred—that is, as relevant pastorally and theologically to the life of the church.

So long as history, literature, and religion remain ingredients in a single stew, the metahistory of how ancient writers combined scraps of actual history and remembered speech with literary inventions from various sources may continue to function as a surrogate sacred history for scholars who find that process more meaningful, religiously, than its product. Indeed, the fact that this metahistory, this history of composition, must itself be largely imagined, the evidence for it being so fragmentary, only makes the enterprise more deeply engaging for some of the historical critics committed to it. One begins to hear, however, a certain creaking at the seams.

The churches of today, which have in no small measure financed the latter stages of this research and have expected somehow to be its beneficiary, have begun to find themselves not so much offended by as oddly indifferent to its findings. The compositional story of "the making of the New Testament" is, after all, a dreadfully bookish story. Even if you accept it, it is not a story to set minds and hearts on fire. The stripped-down, historically defensible, original sayings of Jesus, even if you believe that they are not, rather, the accretion to Jesus of general Hellenistic or Judeo-Hellenistic wisdom, are anticlimactic in their plainness. The reconstructed early-church backdrop of polemic and counterpolemic, by any measure the most plausible part of the reconstruction, is nonetheless unedifying and rather dreary. The historical criticism of the New Testament has, in sum, all the kick of nonalcoholic beer, and some who were once intoxicated by it have awakened with a sobriety hangover.

Some years ago, as it began to dawn on a few Protestant critics that the reconstruction of the events supposedly behind the text or, worse, the reconstruction of the falsification of those events was in this way being substituted for the text itself as a source of religious authority, a reaction called "canon criticism" sprang up. According to this school of thought, whatever is in the canon must count for the church whether or not it counts for the historian. An older designation that some had come to apply to those passages that held the proverbial kernel of historical truth within the husk of ecclesiastical invention was "the canon within the canon." Canon criticism sought to deny the validity of any such intracanonical distinction; for if the canon were to be whittled down, then, among many other consequences, the great commentaries of the founding fathers of Protestantism—those of Jean Calvin, above all—could no longer be used. Canon criticism arose from a deep and correct intuition that, first, the game of seeking historical fact behind the text of the New Testament was ultimately a game without an outcome, much less a winner, and that, second, staying within the text rather than going beyond it via historical research could somehow be the first rule of a new game. In practice, however, those who led this movement engaged, most of the time, in the same laborious winnowing of the historical from the unhistorical, the same painstaking speculation about authorship and original audience and so forth, that had always exercised historical criticism. Canon criticism never quite offered a new game. It simply played the historical game more gently, stopping short of drawing the practical conclusions from historical research that the more radical among the historical critics were prepared, not to say eager, to draw.

Meanwhile, all along, an alternative had lain open that was neither religious history (historical Jesus as norm for reformation) nor secular history (Christian church as historical phenomenon). As one participant in the canon-criticism debate put it:

> A really non-historical, literary study of the Bible on the basis of its shapes, styles, and motifs could be very interesting. It would be much more original than canon criticism, which is really still completely tied up in the inherited problems of theology. Instead of endlessly seeking to correct the older [historical] biblical scholarship, it could simply accept the latter as valid and go on its way in its own direction, taking or leaving as much of traditional scholarship as it needed.[8]

This third option—lying still in the indefinite future as late as 1982, when James Barr spoke these words—was neither the Jesus of history nor the Christ of faith but the Jesus Christ of literature. This was the option of looking at, rather than seeing through, the rose window.

The notion of reading the Bible as literature in serene indifference to all that religious commentary has made of it is, at one level, an idea as old as the Enlightenment.[9] Barr's suggestion differs from that combatively secular notion because it emerged in and is deeply colored by an academic context that continues to care intensely about the received tradition of religious commentary, a tradition of which, for fully two hundred years, the larger portion has consisted of historical commentary. Yet a far more searching and programmatic suggestion along these lines was virtually ignored by Bible scholarship nearly a decade earlier when the late Hans W. Frei published *The Eclipse of Biblical Narrative: A Study in Eighteenth and Nineteenth Century Hermeneutics.*[10] Frei grasped, as no other contemporary writer on the Bible then seemed able to do, the novelty—even the oddity—of the notion of historical correspondence as a validating criterion for scriptural authority. He understood where this notion had come from and dreamed, clearly, of an aesthetic response that would recover the literary power that historicism had so eroded. That literary power lay in the delight of *internal rather than external correspondences,* in gestures from one part of the text to another rather than in confirmations of the text from extratextual evidence.

The paradigm that had to break down if a vision like Frei's was to be accommodated was the paradigm by which historical and theological criticism so divided the hermeneutical terrain between them that there was no room for a kind of critique that was neither historical nor theological in intent. Historical criticism understood itself to be the only school of criticism that was both serious and secular. It took theological commentary to be serious but nonsecular by definition. It took literary commentary other than the kind that was ultimately in the service of historical criticism to be secular but trivial. Canon criticism, trying to break the stranglehold of this dichotomy, sought to write a theological critique of the Bible that was also historically impeccable. But to do that was to grasp only half the problem. The other half of the problem—or, rather, the germ of the whole problem—was the need for a secular rationale for the study, under any rubric, of the works of the canonical Bible and those only.

When secular historical criticism arose in the eighteenth century, its first order of business was to insist on treating the books of the Bible just like any other books. Logically, the implication of this leveling was that the biblical canon—which assigned a privileged status to a group of books not necessarily different from other books of the same sort from the same period—should be disregarded. What happened instead was that the books of this historically arbitrary canon continued to receive far more attention from historical critics than other, comparable ancient works did, notwithstanding the fact that, once the examination began, canonical status guaranteed ever less in the way of special treatment. It was only in the late twentieth century that historical criticism of the Bible became self-conscious enough to call this uncalled question about its own inner consistency in even a preliminary way. Historical critics tended to dismiss canon criticism as the recrudescence of theology, and they were half-right about that, but something larger was ultimately at stake. If the canonical books of the Bible were to continue to receive on some secular grounds the disproportionate attention that religion had originally dictated they should receive, what grounds, if any, were available? Ancient history provided none. Where else might one look?

Without a secular rationale for the canonicity of the biblical canon, there can be no secular literary critique of the Bible as a finished, ended work of art. This is the question that Frank Kermode broached—brilliantly, if indirectly and in an unexpected context—in *The Sense of an Ending: Studies in the Theory of Fiction*.[11] Twenty years later, he addressed the same question explicitly in an essay entitled "The Canon" in *The Literary Guide to the Bible*. In that essay, he argues that the canonical works of the Bible deserve disproportionate attention—more attention than other, comparable works surviving from antiquity—because they have disproportionately influenced the literature and the consciousness of the West during the intervening centuries. Moreover, he further argues, they deserve this attention *as* a canon because it is as a canon that they have exerted this influence.

Kermode—in this, an exception among critics of modern literatures—is at pains not to dismiss classic historical criticism of the Bible. All the same, en route to his nuanced defense of the Bible as an integral whole legitimately subject as such to literary criticism, he sees fit to quote with approval the philosopher Hans-Georg Gadamer:

As . . . Gadamer has put it, the historical critic is always seeking in the text something that is not the text, something the text of itself is not seeking to provide; "he will always go back behind [the texts] and the meaning they express [which he will decline to regard as their true meaning] to enquire

into the reality of which they are the involuntary expression." But it is
possible to take an interest in the text and its own meaning; *that is literary
criticism proper* [italics added], and Gadamer believes that it has for too long
(in these circles) been regarded as "an ancillary discipline to history."[12]

Philosophically as well as literarily, it seemed that there was something wrong
with always and only seeing *through* the Bible. One way of righting that
wrong might be to allow the ancillary discipline to assume, for a change, the
dominant position.

Learning how not to see through the Bible

To the premodern mind, the opposite of truth was not fiction but falsehood:
deception, fraud, the deliberate lie. The only meaningful external question
about scripture, then, was whether or not it was all a gigantic hoax. Once
that question was settled in scripture's favor (and it was, of course, a question
that after the first few Christian centuries scarcely arose), the mind was free
to explore the Bible from within as if it were a wondrous garden whose paths
and glades and ponds and grottoes all intersected in endlessly surprising and
delightful ways. Peter J. Thuesen, in a recent book entitled *In Discordance
With the Scriptures,* writes perceptively of Hans Frei's dream of re-creating
some form of this response.[13] Frei's method, Thuesen writes, "does not exclude truth-questions but brackets them in favor of exegesis that treats the
Bible as something like a realistic novel. For Frei, the biblical novel's individual stories are to be read not primarily for their external referents in 'real history' but for their internal relations as part of a larger narrative."

A realistic novel, as an enclosed, complete text, is like a garden in that
doubling back to an early chapter is an experience rather like strolling back
toward the garden gate to refresh one's memory of something already seen
and to fix the plot (both gardens and novels are plotted) more satisfyingly in
the mind. Kermode addressed the relevance of this question to biblical criticism in *The Genesis of Secrecy,* a work appearing five years after Frei's *The
Eclipse of Biblical Narrative:*

> It may be said that in principle any Old Testament text had a narrative
> potential that could be realized in the New Testament. One might well
> suppose such an arrangement to be without parallel; but it is not alto-
> gether unlike the relation obtaining between the early pages of a long
> novel and its later pages. The earlier ones contain virtualities or germs,
> not all of which grow; there is a mass of narrative detail, existing in its
> own right and, like the Old Testament, viable without later "fulfillment,"
> though it may be fulfilled. A special kind of novel, the classic detective
> story, actually depends on our ability to distinguish, like the witches in
> *Macbeth,* which seeds will grow and which will not, sometimes puzzling
> us by making one kind look like the other.

The novel, exploiting such intermittent fulfillments, is a form of narrative inconceivable as anything but a book in the modern sense; it requires, in principle, that we be able to turn back and forth in its pages. A novel written on a roll would be something else. So it is of interest that the Christians, from a very early date, preferred the codex to the roll.[14]

Whether the Bible is read seriously when it is read as a work whose pleasure and value are established by inner articulation rather than outer validation may depend on how seriously a given reader is capable of taking finished art of any kind: any poem in which the last word has been written, any painting in which the last brushstroke has been applied. When the closed canon of scripture is allowed to function as a finished product, whether or not any individual did the finishing, it excites a response different in kind from the one it excites when it is taken as a great historical problem toward whose solution there is always "much work still to be done." There is no work still to be done on Michelangelo's *David;* the chisel has touched it for the last time. When the Bible is taken, despite its raggedness, as a closed canon to which no scriptures will be added and from which none will be subtracted, it may induce an emotional response as intense as the idolatry that the *David* can induce in a postsophisticated viewer.

I use the word *idolatry* by design, because it so well calls the question of the place of art in religion. The Bible's own attitude toward art, to the extent that it may be said to have one at all, is an attitude of indifference rising on occasion to hostility, and this may have something to do with the resistance of religiously motivated biblical scholarship to the aesthetic. The most relevant passage, in my opinion, is Isaiah 44:13–17:

> The wood carver takes his measurements, outlines the image with chalk, executes it with the chisel, following the outline with a compass. He makes it look like a human being, with human standards of beauty, so that it can reside in a house. He has cut down cedars, has selected an oak and a terebinth that he has grown for himself among the trees in the forest and has planted a pine tree that the rain has nourished. Once it is suitable to burn, he takes some of it to warm himself; having kindled it, he bakes bread. But he also makes a god and worships it; he makes an idol from it and bows down before it. Half of it he burns on the fire; over this half he roasts meat, eats it, and is replete. At the same time he warms himself and says, "Ah, how warm I am watching the flames!" With the remainder he makes a god, his idol, bows down before it, worships and prays to it. "Save me," he says, "for you are my god."

This late prose addition to a book otherwise written as poetry quite probably reflects an era in which many in the Greco-Roman world, not just a few in the Jewish corner of it, were asking new questions about the place of sacred images in religious practice. In its day, its question was pathbreaking, but our own world has moved beyond that question to ask a comparable one about the place of sacred texts in our contemporary religious practice, a question that might be expressed in a parody of the biblical parody:

> The scribe takes up his scroll, scores it in sepia, and writes upon it with quill and black ink, spacing the letters with measured exactness. He writes realistically, by human standards of plausibility, so that his words will persuade in the hall. He has slain livestock, has selected a calf and a lamb that he has raised for himself among the animals of the herd, and has nurtured a kid that the grass has fed. Once an animal is suitable for slaughter, he takes some of it to feed himself; having slaughtered it, he roasts the meat. But he also makes parchment of its skin and worships the parchment; he writes a scroll upon it and bows down before the writing. Half of it he tans for tenting; under this half he shelters and is at ease. He lies under the canopy and says, "Ah, how cozy I am here in my pavilion!" With the remainder he makes a scroll, his scripture, enthrones it, dances around it, swears upon it, and proclaims, "This is the Word of the Lord."

The Bible does not see writing as the *art* of writing in the way that it sees sculpture as the *art* of sculpture. When considering sculpture, it insists on seeing the sculptor in every demystifying detail of his work. The product is demeaned by being thus intimately linked to its merely human producer. The Bible never insists on seeing the writer in any similarly demeaning, demystifying way. The production of the written product is never comparably linked to its merely human producer.

In the West, modern literary criticism has made this linkage by intensifying stages. A case can be made, I think, that the demystification of the text in the eighteenth century was followed by a counter-mystification of the author in the nineteenth and then, especially in the latter decades of the twentieth century, by a demystification of the author—text and author alike being seen as reflexes of larger, impersonal sociocultural forces. This last stage—the inside-outing of literature—came to a climax of sorts with the publication in 1967 of Jacques Derrida's *De la grammatologie,* and has now begun to subside.[15]

In biblical criticism, which sometimes anticipates and sometimes lags behind general literary criticism, the demystification of the text in the eighteenth century was followed, in the nineteenth and twentieth, by a mystification of the *postulated* author (or school or community): thus, "Dtr," the postulated Deuteronomistic Historian; the postulated "Johannine School"; the imagined "Q-community" of early Christians or "Jesus people"; and so forth. Biblical criticism will fall into step with general literary criticism if and when it begins to "de-authorize" the entities it has been "author-izing" for a century and more. The recent, still somewhat tentative move toward social history may or may not portend such a change.

Meanwhile, general literary criticism, weary of its own demystification of the author, has begun to place a new emphasis on the work as a work and on the value of cultivating an aesthetic response to it. It has begun to move, in a word, to a new emphasis on beauty. The historical criticism of the Bible—a process that I have compared to the examination of a rose window, pane by pane, for signs of the *absence* of stain—may yet prove a paradoxically good preparation for this old/new kind of criticism, for, obviously, if you have checked every pane hoping to find one without stain, you end up knowing something about every pane as well as a great deal about stain. Traditional Bible scholars, though their research has almost always been at least nominally in the service of history, have, de facto, studied the development of images and motifs, noted allusions, explicit and implicit, and performed a thousand other services crucial to the literary appreciation of the Bible—so much so, indeed, that some of what is offered as literary criticism by those who lack their training and have not combed through the text as meticulously as they have may quite understandably strike them as too simpleminded for serious comment. But rather than dismiss literary criticism as sciolist dilettantism, historically trained critics could become literary critics themselves and try to improve the neighborhood.

The largest change to be realized from such a paradigm shift might be the introduction of courses and degree programs in the Christian Bible. It is strange but true that advanced degrees are not offered in this subject, and even undergraduate courses are rare. Jews take advanced degrees in the Tanakh, or Jewish Bible, but Christians must choose a degree either in the Old Testament (usually listed as "Hebrew Bible") or in the New. Advanced degrees in the whole of Christian scripture are simply not available. After completing their degrees, Christian scholars trained in either Old or New Testament seldom teach or publish on the far side of the pedagogical divide. The institutionalization of this divide, which rightly surprises scholars of literature and religion outside the hypertrophied culture of biblical research, has survived even the impact of the Dead Sea Scrolls, a large and astonishing body of literature that falls, in every sense, between the Old Testament and the New. A pedagogical bifurcation of some sort may be defensible if the goal is to write historical criticism of the Bible or outright history using the Bible as one source among others. After all, a thousand years of cultural evolution do separate Saul ben Kish, the doomed king of First Samuel, from Saul of Tarsus, the Apostle to the Gentiles. We do not expect a historian of France to specialize in both Charlemagne and Charles de Gaulle; why should we expect any comparable feat from a historian of ancient Jewry? If, however, the goal is not historiography but literary appreciation—the focused, stereoptic perception of the Old Testament and the New as a single, synthetic work in which the two Sauls have indeed come to rest between one pair of book covers—then pedagogical bifurcation is indefensible.

If there were such a thing as an advanced degree in the entirety of the Christian Bible, those seeking it might arguably not need to learn Hebrew and Aramaic so long as they mastered the Greek of the Septuagint and read the scriptures in the language in which Matthew, Mark, Luke, John, and Paul knew them. (See Appendix I on the status of the Septuagint as a divinely inspired "original" text for Hellenistic Judaism long before the birth of Jesus.) Obviously, however, it would be better if students of the Christian Bible did know Hebrew, and indeed far more fruitful for them to have read the Tanakh in the original Hebrew than to have read fourth-century Gnostic codices in the original Coptic. One has the distinct impression at gatherings of New Testament scholars that mastery of Coptic is more nearly *de rigueur* for the consummate New Testament scholar than is mastery of Hebrew and that, as a result, allusions to the Old Testament in the New are undervalued and sometimes missed altogether. Even scholars who are determined to stress, above all else, the Jewishness of Jesus are more likely to do so by reconstructing the Judaism of his day than by hearing echoes of the Tanakh in the New Testament. The institutional segregation of advanced study of the Old Testament from advanced study of the New Testament can scarcely avoid having a variety of such untoward consequences. Reference works preserving a heritage of theologically motivated intertextual noticing do not obviate the need for a New Testament scholar to be imaginatively steeped in the Old Testament: No reference work can substitute for a habit of mind and a well-stocked memory.

In the study of the Bible, historicism is still very much in the saddle. Though Hans Frei was respectfully read by intellectual historians during his lifetime, his impact on biblical studies was minimal then, and even now remains modest, because historicism has made the appreciation of the Bible as art seem trivial by comparison with the elaboration and confirmation of the Bible as history or, paradoxically, even with its disconfirmation as such. A bit ruefully, Frei called the liberals and fundamentalists who once fought (and sometimes still fight) so fiercely over the historical reliability of the Bible "siblings under the skin."[16] In their particular opinions they differ, but in the importance they assign to history they are one. Much the same may be said of the kind of postmodern literary criticism of the Bible that sees itself as attacking classic historical-critical scholarship from the left but is itself best described as neohistoricist. Frei is no more a prophet for that kind of postmodernism than is Eric Auerbach, whose 1946 *Mimesis: The Representation of Reality in Western Literature* Frei admired.[17] Like Frei, Auerbach is a thinker whose ideas, ever focused on aesthetic appreciation, have been more admired than applied, perhaps because they rest on an acquaintance with literature so anachronistically broad and deep as to defy imitation.

Frei's impact would perhaps have been greater had he more energetically offered ad hoc or, better yet, ad hominem applications of his insight to contemporary historical-critical commentary on the Bible. The literary option had been foreclosed, he believed, because of a mistake made in the late eighteenth and early nineteenth centuries. It was then that the [literarily] realistic or history-like quality of biblical narratives, [though] acknowledged by all, instead of being examined for the bearing it had in its own right on meaning and interpretation was immediately transposed into the quite different issue of whether or not the realistic narrative was historical.

This simple transposition and logical confusion between two categories or contexts of meaning and interpretation constitutes a story that has remained unresolved in the history of biblical interpretation ever since. Were we to pursue our theme into the biblical hermeneutics of the twentieth century, I believe we would find that with regard to the recognition of the distinctiveness of realistic biblical narrative and its implications for interpretation, historical criticism, and theology, the story has remained much the same.[18]

It has indeed remained much the same. In his occasional mentions of influential contemporaries, especially German exegetes and theologians like Rudolf Bultmann, Karl Rahner, and Jürgen Moltmann, Frei provides a glimpse of what might, if pursued, have grown into a remarkable critique. But though Frei's ideas were intrinsically controversial, he himself seems to have been no controversialist.

Frei published his magnum opus in 1974, and as of that date the middle path that he saw as logically "the most natural thing"—the path that was neither, to use his terminology, "explication" (history) nor "application" (theology)—remained anything but the most natural thing to most who wrote about the Bible.[19] During the last quarter of the century, thanks in part to Frei and Kermode, later joined by Harold Bloom, Robert Alter, Gabriel Josipovici, and a few others, the neglected option began to be explored. Even now, however, as compared with historical criticism, it remains a marginal option.

The art of contradiction

If the appreciation of the Bible as art ever moves from the margins to the center of biblical studies, it will bring a distinct new problematic with it, for what can be stated concisely enough as doctrine cannot be evoked concisely in narrative or poetry any more easily than it can be painted simply on canvas. Neil MacGregor, director of the National Gallery in London, writes in a discussion of Jan Gossaert's sixteenth-century masterpiece *The Adoration of the Kings:*

Making an image of God who has become man is . . . a tricky business. Artists attempting it have to negotiate a series of specifically visual problems, unknown to authors. Paradox is easy to write, but hard to paint. The Gospel tells us quite straightforwardly that the helpless, swaddled infant is in reality God incarnate, but how do you *show* that it is God in nappies, that the purpose of this child is to redeem the world by his death? How can a painter make clear that the man brutally being put to death on a cross, to every human eye a man completely ordinary and like any other, is also totally divine; that limitless power has chosen absolute submission?

Like all great religious images, Gossaert's *Adoration* neither simply illustrates a religious story nor interprets it according to the painter's own caprice. It translates into a visual language a pictorial theology, a distillation of the Western Church's teachings on the dual nature of Christ, as at once God and man, taking into account centuries of pious poring over sacred texts to find hidden meanings and correspondences, and to wring from them every drop of possible meaning. Gossaert's picture does not show us the birth of Christ: it paints a meditation on the meaning of the birth of Christ and why it matters to us now.[20]

MacGregor eloquently states the challenge that Gossaert faced and met, but he understates the comparable challenge that the authors of the Gospels faced, not to speak of the difficulty posed to modern readers by the mixed means the Gospels employ to meet that challenge. The nature of the challenge itself can easily be seen in two contrasting incidents from the Gospel According to Mark.

In Mark 14:34–38, Jesus is only an hour away from his arrest, and he knows it:

> He began to feel terror and anguish. And he said to them, "My soul is sorrowful to the point of death. Wait here, and stay awake." And, going on a little further, he threw himself on the ground and prayed that, if it were possible, this hour might pass him by. "*Abba,* Father!" he said. "For you everything is possible. Take this cup away from me. But let it be as you, not I, would have it." He came back and found them sleeping, and he said to Peter, "Simon, are you asleep? Had you not the strength to stay awake one hour? Stay awake and pray not to be put to the test. The spirit is willing enough, but human nature is weak."

In this passage, Jesus seems to speak not as God but as a man speaking *to* God. He prays to be spared his ordeal, much as the Psalmist prays in Psalm 59:1–4:

> Rescue me from my enemies, my God,
>   be my stronghold from my assailants.
> Rescue me from evil-doers,
>   from men of violence save me.
> Look at them, lurking to ambush me!
>   Violent men are attacking me,
> for no fault, no sin of mine, O Lord.
>   For no cause, they race to besiege me.

And yet earlier, in Mark 6:45–52, Jesus exercises an effortless, godlike power that belies his later, anguished prayer. In the earlier passage, we read:

> Right away he made his followers get into a boat and go on ahead to the other side [of the Sea of Galilee], near Bethsaida, while he himself dismissed the crowd. Having seen them off, he headed up into the hills to pray. As night fell, the boat was well out on the sea, while he himself was still on the land. He watched them straining at the oars, the wind having turned against them, and then, just before dawn, he came toward them, walking on the sea. He would have walked past them, but they saw him walking there on the sea, thought he was a ghost, and cried out because the look of him terrified them. But then he spoke up and said to them, "Take heart. It is I. Don't be afraid." Then he got into the boat with them, and the wind dropped off. They were absolutely and totally dumbfounded.

In this passage, Jesus seems as un-human as in the earlier passage he seems un-divine. This is particularly so if we recall that in the Old Testament power over the sea is one of the signature powers of the Lord God. Thus, Psalm 107:23–30 (RSV), to choose one among many possible examples, reads:

> Doing business on the great waters,
>   they saw the deeds of the Lord,
>   his wondrous works in the deep.
> For he commanded, and raised the stormy wind,
>   which lifted up the waves of the sea.
> They mounted up to heaven, they went down to the depths;
>   their courage melted away in their evil plight;
> They reeled and staggered like drunken men,
>   and were at their wits' end.
> Then they cried to the Lord in their trouble,
>   and he delivered them from their distress;
> He made the storm be still,
>   and the waves of the sea were hushed.
> Then they were glad because they had quiet,
>   and he brought them to their desired haven.

Which of these two portrayals is correct? In the year 325, the Council of Nicaea, the first ecumenical council in church history, defined—by what may fairly be characterized as an act of premodern literary criticism—the dogma that both were true.[21] At that time, the emperor Constantine prevailed upon church leaders to paper over the textual inconsistencies of the now centuries-old New Testament, not to speak of their own political differences, by defining Christ as, once and for all, both human and divine. Historical criticism is capable of, in effect, repealing this dogma, rejecting those parts of the New Testament that attribute divinity to Christ as later inventions, and reconstructing upon the foundation of what appear to be the earliest verses alone an internally consistent, merely human historical Jesus. For decades there was a distinctly modernist, confrontational excitement about just that undertaking.

Yet times change. In our own day, postmodern criticism, though scarcely a tool of ecclesiastical orthodoxy, relishes contradiction and values sheer interest, even ironic interest, over progress, about which, at least as regards artistic creation, it tends to be dubious.[22] If the agreement to disagree that the emperor imposed at the Council of Nicaea proved stimulating for so many earlier centuries in art, architecture, poetry, and music, why may we not once again experience the same contradiction—the same inconsistency, if you wish—as stimulating in the New Testament text itself?

Modern historical criticism remains free, in other words, in the pursuit of its own still-legitimate purposes to resolve the contradiction between two passages like those quoted above from the Gospel According to Mark by tracing them to two originally separate, originally noncontradictory sources, one of which regarded Jesus as divine while the other did not. But postmodern literary criticism, at least when it is post- rather than neohistoricist, is equally free to stress that however these two contradictory passages may have found their way into the same Gospel, they produce in combination a unique effect upon a reader open to experiencing that effect. Centuries of premodern readers possessed the necessary openness as a deeply ingrained cultural habit. Postmodern readers can perhaps manage only a semblance of the same openness, but the rewards of doing so are significant, for the dramatic power of Christ as a character on the page is inseparable from this contradiction. The Incarnation is Christianity's breathtaking addition to Judaism's already long list of divine self-contradictions.

Passages that assert or strongly suggest the divinity of Christ are undeniably less frequent in the New Testament than those asserting or strongly suggesting his humanity. However, the divinity passages tint all the others the way a drop of dye tints a glass of clear water. If I have seen you drunk and brawling once, I can see you sober and peaceable any number of times and know that the full truth about you is not, just then, on display. There is something similarly scandalous, even monstrous, about divinity. Once glimpsed, it remains in the mind. There is, most especially, something monstrous about the Jewish deity. Yahweh Elohim is not the Jewish Zeus. The Greek gods all had genealogies and offspring. Human in form, they were reassuringly human in identity as well, because they existed in a population of others like themselves, interacting with them, competing with them, just as humans do with one another. Not so Yahweh Elohim: The God of the Jews is alone in the cosmos, sexless, fatherless, motherless, and, for long, also childless. After creating the human race in his image, God relates to his creature at first only as original to image, not as father to child. God must *adopt* fatherhood. He must *choose* it. It is not, so to speak, natural to him. In the monstrosity of *this* deity's assuming human form lies the elusive remoteness, the uncanniness, that radiates so unmistakably from the pages of the New Testament, most especially from the pages of the Gospels. What staggers the imagination and gives the Christian myth its power is not that some god or other should have become some man or other but that Yahweh should have become Jesus.

Gospel as a mixed genre

Reading the Gospels as literature means assigning them to a genre that combines history, fiction, and fairy tale. The poet W. H. Auden described the difference between fiction and fairy tale—with history as the understood background for both—in a brief, penetrating afterword to George MacDonald's modern fairy tale *The Golden Key.* "Every human being," Auden wrote,

> is interested in two kinds of worlds: the Primary, everyday, world which he knows through his senses, and a Secondary world or worlds which he not only can create in his imagination, but also cannot stop himself creating.
>
> A person incapable of imagining another world than that given him by his senses would be sub-human, and a person who identifies his imaginary world with the world of sensory fact has become insane.
>
> Stories about the Primary world may be called Feigned Histories; stories about a Secondary world, myths or fairy tales. A story about the Primary world, that is to say, may be fiction—the characters in it and the events may have been "made up" by the writer—but the story must affect the reader in the same way that an historical narrative does: the reader must be able to say to himself, "Yes, I have met people like that, and that is how, I know from experience, such people talk and act."
>
> . . . A Secondary world may be full of extraordinary beings . . . and extraordinary events . . . but, like the Primary world, it must, if it is to carry conviction, seem to be a world governed by laws, not by pure chance. Its creator, like the inventor of a game, is at liberty to decide what the laws shall be, but, once he has decided, his story must obey them. . . .
>
> History, actual or feigned, demands that the reader be at one and the same time inside the story, sharing in the feelings and events narrated, and outside it, checking these against his own experiences. A fairy tale . . . on the other hand, demands of the reader total surrender; so long as he is in its world, there must for him be no other.[23]

Following Auden, how should we respond to the story of Jesus praying to be spared his final agony? Conceding that the event is fictional (after all, the Gospel accounts say that the only possible witnesses to this event were asleep when it occurred), we may nonetheless be affected by it just as we would be by a strict report, for we can easily say to ourselves, "Yes, I have met people like that, and that is how, I know from experience, such people talk and act." Jesus in this moving instance of feigned history conducts himself as any man might whose friends have failed him in his moment of greatest need.

As for the way in which Jesus' anguished prayer may recall the words of Psalm 59, historians have good reason to find the fit suspiciously close and to suspect that the episode itself was constructed or modified to match the Psalm. The literary critic, by contrast, conceding that the episode may be partly or wholly an invention, will be content to prescind from that question and allow the allusions and quotations to produce their intended effect, unconcerned that real and feigned history may be mingling.

So much for the first episode. What of the second, Jesus' walking on the water and stilling the storm? Following Auden, we should respond to the miracle proper, the core of the episode, with "total surrender," asking only that it conform to its own rules of operation—which, in this case, entails our taking the point that Jesus is God Incarnate. It is to this idea that we must yield. But because the Gospel is a mixed form rather than pure fairy tale, our response to this episode in its entirety is more complex than simple surrender. There was a historical Jesus, after all, and he did have followers. Moreover, even in a story that has elements of fairy tale, there may occur elements of fiction as distinct from fairy tale. Of this episode, we may legitimately ask, for example, Why did Jesus wait all night before coming to his disciples' rescue? If he knew they were in trouble, why did he not rescue them sooner? These questions are proper to fiction rather than to either history or fairy tale.

It is neither possible nor advisable for a twenty-first-century man or woman to wave away two thousand years of intellectual history and attempt to respond to the fantastical or miraculous in the New Testament as readers or hearers may have done in the first century. A premodern response to the miraculous is virtually impossible for any contemporary adult. But Auden does not require this. He urges only that we allow ourselves to approach in a mood of serious play a text that rewards such an approach. The mood of serious play may take some cultivation, but it still lies within our reach. Without denying that the New Testament does sometimes report historical events, we can open ourselves to its power in a new way if we can respond to the fantastical and the fictive within it as equal in importance to the historical.

To this I would add only that engaging the New Testament by hearing the Old Testament within it engages what is most distinctive about the New Testament as a work of literary art. As Kermode has written,

> The literary relations of the Gospels to the Old Testament [the same can be said of the entire New Testament] are as close and intimate as any that one can imagine between two texts. In establishing this intimacy the evangelists not only authenticated their story but discovered its materials.

In constructing a realistic, history-like narrative in such an unusual way they created a distinctive genre; and in terms of that genre they produced unique works of art.[24]

Because quoting a historically remote Psalm when discussing a passage in Mark is the sort of thing that preachers have done to good effect for centuries, secular critics, and not historical critics alone, have seemed to feel that if they did the same, they would be joining the church. Kermode is right that for the evangelists themselves these echoes were not just harmony but religious authentication. But those in our day who decline to acknowledge the allusions as authentication can nonetheless enjoy them as harmony—and must do so if they are not to miss the haunting elegance and acrobatic virtuosity of the New Testament performance.

What the sea would say

For a significant and growing population of lay readers, the appeal of the Bible as art, good or bad, sacred or secular, has come to exceed its value as history, true or false. No doubt those for whom the Bible is only itself, only sacred, to the extent that it corresponds with some set of intrinsically sacred events, will resist this development. To them, the Bible as art will seem worthy of the library, perhaps, but unworthy of the sanctuary. I myself believe that the Bible, read as art, may remain sacred so long as a distinction can continue to be made between religious art and secular art.

Since the rise of modernism, this distinction has commonly been made, even if it has usually been made to the disparagement of religious art. Art produced in service to a received, collective religious vision has been thought inferior to art whose vision—the original, personal creation of the artist— emerges only in and through the making. Leaving aside that value judgment, I would insist for the moment only on the distinction itself, which in most instances is perfectly valid. Religious art does differ, and in just the way alleged, from secular art. Religious history differs from secular history in the same way. The Gospels are the despair of secular historians, for they were not written, as secular history must be written, for the sake of history itself but, rather, for the sake of the faith. The authors of the Gospels know the meaning of the events they narrate before they begin the narration; they knew it before they began whatever, for them, constituted research. By the same token, the medieval religious sculptor knew the point of his statue before he began to carve it. Framed in this way, the distinction between religious and secular art remains valid, breaking down only in the case of the neoreligious modern artist, the artist whose personal vision can be described not just as personally but also as pedagogically and interpersonally spiritual, though in the service of no group beyond the congregation of those whom the artist aspires to "convert" to the vision that shapes her work itself.

In a comment made while the National Gallery in London was still showing the exhibition "Seeing Salvation," Neil MacGregor said:

> One of the aims of this exhibition is to demonstrate that religious paintings can hold on to their spiritual dimension in the exhibition rooms of a museum. Every visitor is free to discover what interests him or her, but every religious painting has a specific aim, which is different from the aim of a secular painting: to transform the soul of the spectator.[25]

MacGregor makes two relevant points. First, even though a work of art may have been produced in service to a received, collective vision, a vision not personally that of the artist, its power need not disintegrate when the collectivity breaks up. An altarpiece without a church, at which no liturgy is any longer celebrated—an altarpiece moved to a museum—may lose much, but it does not lose everything. Second, there is a difference between artists whose ambition is "to transform the soul of the spectator" and those who have no such ambition. I would add that those who might say that any true artist *must* have such a vision have themselves unacknowledged ambitions on the souls of all artists, for to say such a thing is to deny artists the hard-won freedom of genuine secularity, secularity that is neither explicitly nor even implicitly religious.

Once the inherent artfulness of all writing has been acknowledged and a distinction between religious and secular art has been accepted, the two necessary conditions have been met for a latter-day sacralization of the Bible on the basis of its character as art rather than its reliability as a testimony to ancient events. If the sacredness of historical events does not inhere in the events themselves but must be conferred upon them by interpretation, then interpretation may also confer sacredness upon imagined events. Creation and interpretation are points on a mental continuum in both history and fiction. The act by which a historical report is created is interpretive vis-à-vis some event: Creation entails interpretation. Conversely, the act by which the same report is later interpreted is inevitably countercreative vis-à-vis the originating event: Interpretation entails re-creation. Similarly, the act by which a fictional story is invented is interpretive vis-à-vis the author's not-yet-verbalized experience, which must ultimately be the source of the story: The author's creation entails interpretation of his own experience. Similarly again, the act by which the same story is later criticized is inevitably re-creative or countercreative vis-à-vis the story as first told: Interpretation duplicates creation at least to some extent. Without erasing the line between the real and the imagined, one may insist on the close analogy that exists between the creation and appropriation of history, on the one hand, and of fiction, on the other. In both cases, creator and interpreter—the historian and the critic of history, the storyteller and the critic of fiction—may be either two people in dialogue or one person talking to himself. In both cases, when the motive is religious, the results are religious. In short, an event need not have happened for it to convey religious meaning, while the fact that an event did happen does not in and of itself make the event religiously meaningful.

The point may be illustrated by imagining that Jesus' parable of the Good Samaritan—a parable that Christian preaching has always read as a fictional but nonetheless paradigmatic expression of Christianity's reinterpretation of the Old Testament command (Lev. 19:18) to "love your neighbor"—appeared in the Gospel of Luke as an episode in which, instead of a Samaritan rescuing a Jew, Jesus himself rescued a Samaritan. A story now fruitful for preaching, though it is only a story, would then have crossed the line and become a kind of history. But what if we further imagine that the consensus of historical scholarship about this episode in the career of Jesus were that it never happened? Suppose historians were unanimous that the historical Jesus never actually rescued any such Samaritan? What would have been lost? The episode would be fiction by Luke instead of fiction by Jesus, but would its meaning not be the same, and could it not continue to function as revelation? (Many scholars believe, even now, that the story as told by Jesus in the Gospel of Luke is actually Luke's creation, though there is no real way to determine this.) Moreover, even if the scholarly consensus were that the historical Jesus did indeed rescue some such Samaritan, his deed would only have paradigmatic force if a subsequent, religiously motivated decision had granted it that force. Kindness may speak for itself, but what it says is never "I am a paradigm."

While insisting in this way on the legitimacy of a religious appropriation of the Bible as art, or, perhaps better, on an artistic appropriation of the Bible as religious, I would insist with equal force on the possibility and legitimacy of a fully secular appreciation of the art of the Bible. Never underestimate the human capacity for sympathy across ideological lines. One need not be a Nazi to appreciate the brilliance of Leni Riefenstahl's film *Triumph of the Will*. One need not love American materialism to be awestruck at the Manhattan skyline. There is, of course, a risk: One thing may lead to another. Someone may begin merely acknowledging that a certain power lingers in a Christian painting displayed at the National Gallery and end up at the baptismal font. But if one thing *may* lead to another, it *need* not. At this point in the history of the West, the secular option is open for good. We need only note, by way of balance, that so is the religious option. In our era, a detached but sympathetic openness to the art and literature of unbelief is no more difficult for believers than the reverse is for unbelievers.

The intellectual and emotional access that belief and unbelief, religious participation and religious abstention, have to one another in our era reminds me of a famous poem and a much less famous reply to it. Matthew Arnold wrote in "Dover Beach" (I quote only part of a longer poem):

> Listen! You hear the grating roar
> Of pebbles which the waves draw back, and fling,
> At their return, up the high strand,
> Begin, and cease, and then again begin,
> With tremulous cadence slow, and bring
> The eternal note of sadness in.
>
> Sophocles long ago
> Heard it on the Aegaean, and it brought
> Into his mind the turbid ebb and flow
> Of human misery; we
> Find also in the sound a thought,
> Hearing it by this distant northern sea.
>
> The Sea of Faith
> Was once, too, at the full, and round earth's shore
> Lay like the folds of a bright girdle furled.
> But now I only hear
> Its melancholy, long, withdrawing roar,
> Retreating, to the breath
> Of the night-wind, down the vast edges drear
> And naked shingles of the world.[26]

Half a century later, W. B. Yeats replied laconically in "The Nineteenth Century and After" (this is the whole poem):

> Though the great song return no more,
> There's keen delight in what we have:
> The rattle of pebbles on the shore,
> Under the receding wave.[27]

If the tide of religion will inevitably recede to the point that there is no sea at all, Yeats seems to say, we may still enjoy, for now, the sound of the pebbles under the receding wave. But then, too, he implies with the faintest of smiles, do we really fear, as the tide goes out, that the sea will not be there in the morning?

A half-century and more after Yeats, at the dawn of the twenty-first century, the Protestant/Catholic polemics of the sixteenth century are extremely remote even for most Protestants and Catholics. Rather more important, perhaps, the religious/secular polemics of the nineteenth and early-twentieth centuries—the cultural anxieties and furies that linked Arnold and Yeats—are almost equally remote. An immense population that thinks of itself as neither particularly religious nor particularly antireligious neither gloats if much of the Bible proves unhistorical nor feels any noteworthy quickening of interest if some of it proves historical after all. The fascination of the text—and clearly it does continue to fascinate—begins to lie elsewhere, in the work itself rather than in the events that the work may partially record or in the tangled history of how the work came to be written. Pebbles under a receding wave? Perhaps, but I prefer the analogy that I started with. What attracts viewers, believing or unbelieving, to the great rose window of the Bible is neither what can be seen through it nor how the glass for it was stained and assembled, but what the window looks like in and for itself and what all those jagged fragments of light and color, working together, make happen behind the eye of the beholder.

Acknowledgments

As Luke tells the story, Simon Peter had fished all night in the Sea of Galilee and caught nothing when Jesus told him to put out into the deep water and let down his nets one last time. "'Master,' Simon replied, 'we have worked all night long and caught nothing. But if you say so, I will let down the nets.' When they did, they caught so many fish that their nets were about to break. . . . But when Simon Peter saw it, he fell down at Jesus' knees, saying, 'Go away from me, Lord, for I am a sinful man!'" (Luke 5:5–8).

No one who lets his nets down into the sea of the New Testament can have escaped a moment of terror like Peter's—terror at the abundance and at one's own inadequacy to it. The list of those who have helped me keep my nets from breaking begins with Barry Munitz, president of the J. Paul Getty Trust, to whom my debt could scarcely be larger than it is. It is a pleasure to thank as well, and for the second time, Joel Conarroe, president of the John Simon Guggenheim Foundation, whose support in 1990 led to the book that led to this book. Jonathan Segal, who has edited both books for Alfred A. Knopf, is a consummate professional and a treasured friend, working for the best publisher in America. I honor the memory of the late Charles Ronsac of Éditions Robert Laffont, Paris, whose wit during a four-year, bilingual e-mail correspondence brightened many a dark day. For winning my work a welcome around the world, I am pleased to acknowledge the support and friendship of my literary agent, Georges Borchardt, as well as Anne Borchardt and the staff of the agency. For comments of varying length at various points during the gestation of this work, I am grateful to Frederick Borsch, Junko and Rafael Chodos, Nicholas Goodhue, Thomas Jenkins, George Leonard, Ross Miller, Philip Roth, Mark C. Taylor, and Peter J. Thuesen.

As regards my translations of quoted passages from the New Testament, I am reminded of how the late John Ciardi spoke of his predecessors in translating Dante. He acknowledged "a debt of borrowed courage to all other translators of Dante; without their failures I should never have attempted my own." In some similar sense, having never taken even an undergraduate course in the New Testament, I am both humbled by and remote from the mighty enterprise that is contemporary New Testament scholarship. Let me then acknowledge its greatness in the round but spare individual scholars from a paternity claim that might be most unwelcome.

Finally, I thank my wife, Jacqueline, and our daughter, Kathleen, for courage, endless patience, and the consolation, through ten years of time, that they and they alone could provide.

Notes

PROLOGUE

3   *"Someone dying in such a hideous way":* How strange it is that a scene of supreme ugliness should have become the supreme subject of Western art. Though there are many ways to make art of this subject, there is no way to make beauty of it; and its largest impact on Western art may consist of the space that it opened between the concept of art and the concept of beauty. Its inherent repugnance is ineradicable except perhaps by the aesthetic (or anaesthetic) expedient of displaying the cross without the crucified.

The reaction of a non-Christian Japanese to this icon is the correct reaction, then, yet it is worth recalling that the concepts of suicide and martyrdom, which diverged in the West after Augustine (see p. 166), have remained far less divergent in Japan. Though suicides in the eyes of the West, the kamikaze pilots of World War II were martyrs in the eyes of the Japanese; their deaths were understood to be not just heroic but also religiously sanctioned and supremely, artistically beautiful. Something very similar may be said of the Vietnamese Buddhist monks who immolated themselves during the Vietnam War; see Richard Jock Hearn, *The Soldier and the Monk* (Ann Arbor, Mich.: University Microfilms International, 1984).

4   *"Truth forever on the scaffold":* from James Russell Lowell, "The Present Crisis," in *American Poetry: The Nineteenth Century,* Volume One: Philip Freneau to Walt Whitman, selected and annotated by John Hollander (New York: The Library of America, 1993), p. 684.

5   *The guilt of God:* To speak of the guilt of God or, as elsewhere in this book, of a wound in God or a crisis that God faces or a change that must and does occur in God is to open oneself to the

charge of Gnosticism. But then Gnosticism—the ancient heresy in which, broadly, divinity and humanity save each other reciprocally—does not constitute a "charge" that can legitimately be brought against literary criticism. Theology may have a mandate to conform to the agreed-upon teaching of a church, even if not all who call themselves theologians accept that mandate. But there exists no church of literature in the first place, and therefore no true orthodoxy or heterodoxy in literary criticism.

5   *"The real reason":* Albert Camus, *The Fall,* translated by Justin O'Brien (New York: Vintage Books, 1956), p. 112. I have slightly modified the translation.

6   *"God on the cross":* The Anti-Christ, no. 51, quoted from *The Portable Nietzsche,* selected and translated, with an introduction, prefaces, and notes, by Walter Kaufmann (New York: Penguin Books, 1959), p. 634. The phrase that Kaufmann translates as "the horrible secret thoughts" is, in Nietzsche's German, "die furchtbare Hintergedanklichkeit." This is the phrase that I re-translate as "the frightening hidden premise" in the paragraph immediately following on this page. See *Der Antichrist,* no. 51, critical study edition edited by Giorgio Colli and Mazzino Montinari (Munich: Deutscher Taschenbuch Verlag, 1988), vol. 6, p. 232.

6   *stank in his nostrils:* The Anti-Christ, no. 46: ". . . one does well to put on gloves when reading the New Testament. The proximity of so much uncleanliness almost forces one to do this. We would no more choose the 'first Christians' to associate with than Polish Jews—not that one even required any objection to them: they both do not smell good." Ibid., p. 625. The first of these two sentences is often quoted; the last, never.

6   *"What is good?":* Ibid., p. 572.

8   *to give him just these verses:* The Ethiopian, a diaspora Jew, is reading the Jewish scriptures in Greek, for the verses quoted translate the Septuagint, the pre-Christian Greek edition of the Jewish scriptures. The Septuagint differs from the Masoretic, the surviving Hebrew text of the Tanakh, in a way suggesting that certain passages must have been translated from a variant Hebrew original. This passage from Isaiah may be one such. See Appendix I on the importance of the Septuagint in Christian exegesis and in the genesis of the Bible.

9   *eternal life—as atonement:* "Atonement" in Christian theology ordinarily refers to atonement by Christ to God for the sins of mankind. Atonement theology, though its roots are medieval, had a particularly long and active history in American Protestantism through the nineteenth and into the twentieth century. See Thomas E. Jenkins, *The Character of God: Recovering the Lost Liter-*

ary *Power of American Protestantism* (New York: Oxford University Press, 1997). A German Protestant theologian not afraid to speak of the suffering of God as God is Jürgen Moltmann, *The Crucified God: The Cross of Christ as the Foundation and Criticism of Christian Theology* (Minneapolis: Fortress Press, 1993). Yet this notion, though more generously accommodated in such contemporary theology than when it was dismissed as the "patripassionist" heresy, lives on even now principally in the informal, unregulated rest of the Christian tradition—which is to say in its literature, its music, and its art. For a striking confrontation of Christian art and Protestant atonement theology, see Thomas J. J. Altizer, "The Protestant Jesus: Milton and Blake," in *The Contemporary Jesus* (Albany, N.Y.: SUNY Press, 1997), pp. 115–37.

10   *"I haven't noticed":* Louis Begley, *Mistler's Exit* (New York: Alfred A. Knopf, 1998), p. 92.

10   *elevates the body . . . above an altar:* The fact that Masaccio portrays the Trinity above an altar and inside a chapel whose architecture is part of the painting may suggest that the painting was not, in fact, an altarpiece. However, the meaning of the work is the same in either case. Art historian John Shearman writes that the altar shown below the chapel in the painting

> is a part of its meaning, in that the antetype [of the chapel] in the Old Testament, the Tabernacle of the Covenant, had an altar outside it; but this is a fiction of an altar, and fictions cannot be consecrated. I think there is no good evidence of a real altar to which the fresco served as *dossale;* and a real altar seems rendered redundant by the fiction. For that reason the Trinity is not strictly an altarpiece. But because it is one virtually, it had a great effect upon the way artists thought about altarpieces, nowhere more than in Venice.

Only Connect: Art and the Spectator in the Italian Renaissance (Princeton, N.J.: Princeton University Press, 1988), p. 66.

10   *"awareness that, before we die":* Allen Wheelis, *The Listener: A Psychoanalyst Examines His Life* (New York: Norton, 1999), p. 210.

PART ONE

15   *Back then, it says:* Among the four canonical Gospels, the Gospel of John appears last, but its opening scene evokes the true opening scene of the life story of God the Son.

No one writing on Jesus is spared the task of making some expository sense of *Mamalujo,* to borrow James Joyce's coinage (in *Finnegans Wake*) for the fusion in the Western mind of Matthew,

Mark, Luke, and John. Historical criticism has coped with the knotty quadruplication of the Gospel story by separating *Mamalu*—the three "Synoptic" Gospels—from *Jo,* noting the enormous overlap among Matthew, Mark, and Luke and then usually assigning priority to Mark as a source for the other two. If Mark came first, then Mark, so the hypothesis goes, may lie closest to remembered truth about the historical Jesus. Then would come Matthew, then Luke, and last, as furthest from the historical truth, would come John.

For a discussion of Jesus as God Incarnate, however, a different strategy is in order, one that assigns priority to John and, after John, to Luke. The Gospel of Luke, though one of the three Synoptics, differs from the others in that it is the first half of a two-volume work with a clearly mythic structure. In the first volume, the Gospel proper, the Spirit of God descends invisibly upon the Virgin Mary to conceive God's human self in her womb. The Spirit descends again, this time visibly, to acclaim her child, now grown to manhood, at his baptism, when his redemptive work begins. In the second volume, the Acts of the Apostles, the Spirit descends once again to conceive the church—"the mystical body of Christ," as Paul will call it—in the hearts of Christ's followers.

In the New Testament as we now have it, an ancient editor has inserted the Gospel of John between Luke and Acts, perhaps because this arrangement provides a striking new setting for the climactic dialogue that comes at John 13–17 on the night when Jesus is arrested. In this dialogue, interpreted in this book as the last testament of God, Jesus explains to his followers that during his lifetime he has been their "Paraclete," an untranslatable Greek word combining the meanings of the English words *counselor, ally, advocate, comforter,* and even *inspiration* (as in "You have been an inspiration to me"). Facing death, he promises to send them "another Paraclete," his own Spirit in another form. After his death, he will keep this promise by visiting them after his resurrection and breathing his Spirit into them (John 20) and then, a second time, by sending his Spirit upon them in the form of tongues of flame (Acts 2). When Acts follows John, this second, confirming fulfillment of Jesus' promise—commemorated still in the Christian sacrament of confirmation—thus follows quickly upon the promise itself.

Scholars usually assume that John follows Luke because an ancient editor wanted all four Gospels grouped together and because it was somehow evident that John was written last. Against this hypothesis, it must be noted that John comes second rather than fourth in some ancient manuscripts. *Mamalu* and *Jo* were evidently not separated in the second century by the chasm that separates them in the twenty-first. In any event, by whatever editorial process the sequence Luke-John-Acts came into being, these three works taken together now constitute 37 percent of the total text of the New Testament; and in this sequence they strikingly highlight the activity of the Spirit of God. In other words, God is more noticeably the protagonist in Luke-John-Acts—whether as Jesus or as the Spirit of God determining the course of events before Jesus' birth and after his death—than he is in Matthew-Mark.

Broadly, the Gospel story told in this book follows the order of events as given in John but expands it by inserting in Part Two an "infancy narrative" and a Galilean ministry from the Synoptics, especially from Luke. Parts of Acts (as well as, *much* more briefly, certain later books of the New Testament) are then discussed in Part Four. This eclectic procedure undeniably neglects the literary specificity of each work thus touched on; but the intent of the procedure is not to discuss all or indeed any of the books of the New Testament as separate works, much less to reconstruct the historical truth about Jesus, but rather and only to discuss God Incarnate as a character found in all of them. By a further narrowing, the intent is not to discuss every passage involving Jesus but only to examine a selection of passages that foreground his identity as God Incarnate and highlight the revision that is accomplished through him of the identity of God as previously revealed in the Old Testament.

The Gospel of John gives powerful expression to an exalted understanding of Jesus' identity that arose well before curiosity about the historical details of his life. It was not by slow, piecemeal elaboration but by a bold and early stroke of genius that the memory of an enigmatic Galilean preacher, wrongly and wrongfully executed for sedition, was transformed into the myth of God Incarnate sacrificing himself to reconcile the human race and its creator. In the letters of Paul, which date from the fifties and sixties C.E., a generation before the writing of the four Gospels and only a generation after the death of Jesus, this myth is already substantially in place. The historical Jesus has already been transcended by the divine Christ, whose self-sacrifice is already memorialized in the central recurring ritual of emergent Christianity. The fact, then, that among the four Gospels it is John that most fully shares this early "high Christology" with Paul suggests that John lies quite near to that original tradition-transforming impulse.

The debate that dominated Christian theology for two centuries after the last works of the New Testament had been written and before the First Council of Nicaea introduced formal dogma into the life of the church was a debate not about *whether* Jesus was God Incarnate but only about *when* the Incarnation—taking that event to be both the humanization of God and the divinization of a man—actually occurred. Had God the Son existed as God from the beginning of time? Did his life as both God and man begin at Jesus' conception? Was divinity conferred when the Spirit descended upon him at his baptism? Was his divinization of a piece with the miracle of his resurrection? Or did he really become divine only when he ascended into heaven after his death? There are echoes of all the opinions implicit in these questions in different parts of the New Testament, but no New Testament text would prove more important to this debate than the Gospel of John. John is the stem from which blossomed the myth that defined Christendom, capturing the imagination of the Western world and holding it for a thousand years and more. It is perhaps for this reason that the name John in its many variations (like Ivo, João, Hans, Sean), diminutives (like Juanito and Gianni), and compounds (Jean-Paul, Gianfrancesco) is the most common masculine given name in the West.

I do not intend to justify the reading attempted here by claiming that, if we but formulate the question properly, John is more historical than Mark; much less that literary criticism is better at history than is standard historical criticism. John is not without value for those seeking to reconstruct the historical Jesus, but that is not the point. I concede that the reading offered here—a latter-day Gospel harmony—is literary and imaginative rather than historical, and therefore that it is inevitably subjective: the close reading of no more than a modest set of Gospel passages selected to bring a particular interpretive option into high relief. The apology I would make for such a reading is, first, that, as historical critics are always noting of one another, the most objective reading never entirely escapes subjectivity, particularly when the inner pluralism of the New Testament all but requires a degree of anterior selectivity in the interpreter; and, second, that this process of selectivity and recombination is not just inevitable but fruitful and rewarding.

15   *John says in his oracular way:* For convenience, I refer to the authors of the component works of the New Testament by the names that tradition has assigned them. Whether the author of the fourth Gospel is in fact John the son of Zebedee or "the beloved disciple" or indeed any single individual rather than several authors

rewriting one another over time is a question that historical criticism will continue to ponder, but the authorship question must not be allowed to obscure more immediately relevant literary questions.

Authorship and publication did not divide in antiquity, in any event, quite as they do in modernity. The variability of textual witnesses to the several works that constitute the New Testament—a far greater variability than obtains among extant textual witnesses to the Torah—suggests that the border between composition (authorship) and copying (publication) was particularly fluid for the literate but geographically decentralized and war-disrupted movement that brought these works into existence. Publication, which was manual copying, seems commonly to have begun before composition was complete. A copyist might function as an editor, making what seemed sensible corrections in works that were not, at the start, regarded as sacred scripture. Taking a step beyond correction, he might function as, in modern parlance, a "contributing editor" and add to the received account.

The result of this process should not be regarded as merely the frustration of any given author's intention, though that is surely among its effects. The result was, rather, the creation of a distinct aesthetic effect—the Gospel effect, we might call it—as different minds forged different links between Jewish tradition and the remembered life story of Jesus. A story modified by successive editors and contributors to the point that no one can truly claim to be its author acquires the special privilege and elusive power of true anonymity. When the Gospels are heard as anonymous, as stories we have "always known," they do indeed tend to blend together, but it is just then that they begin to function as myth and to produce their most powerful effect.

With this in mind, I refer to the authors of the Gospels as infrequently as possible in my own discussion. When I do mention them, without intending to disparage the historical criticism that has so ingeniously recovered their individuality, I eschew circumspect historical-critical locutions like "the author or authors of the fourth Gospel." So long as the focus is synthetic, on the effect of a text, rather than analytic, on the intent of an author or authors, such conscientiousness serves no purpose.

20 *Mal. 4:5–6; some editions, 3:23–24:* The Hebrew text of Malachi is divided into three chapters, while the ancient Greek translation of Malachi is divided into four. Verse by verse, the two texts are virtually identical; only the chapter division differs. Jewish editions of this book of the Bible follow the Hebrew text and have

twenty-four verses in chapter three. Most, but not all, Christian editions follow the Greek text and have eighteen verses in chapter three plus six in chapter four.

28 *God's great enemy, the Devil:* Most translators do not capitalize *devil* or attach as much importance as I do to the fact that the Greek definite article is used when the Devil is referred to in the story of the temptation of Jesus. My translation reflects my belief that the linked angelology and demonology of Hellenistic Judaism and early Christianity are ultimately Persian in origin.

The history of Israelite and Jewish belief about the sources of evil in the world has roughly an hourglass shape. At the start, in the upper end of the hourglass, there are three such sources. One: the gods of other nations, to whom a large measure of reality is conceded and who, when those nations oppose Yahweh, are seen as evil. The supreme example of a god at war with Yahweh is the divine Pharaoh, in his violent opposition to Yahweh's intention to confer miraculous fertility upon his people in Pharaoh's country. Two: Israel's disobedience. It is Israel, rather than any rival deity, whose endless duel with Yahweh gives the Tanakh (the Hebrew scriptures in the Jewish order) most of its forward momentum and epic definition. Israel's is the opposition that provokes Yahweh to grief and rage. Three: the mixed character of Yahweh himself, whose unpredictable power to do harm matches his power to do good. "I am Yahweh," he says,

> and there is no other.
> I light the light, I dark the dark.
> I cause prosperity, I wreak disaster.
> I, Yahweh, do all these things.
>
> (Isa. 45:6–7)

Let me offer just one illustration of this last and perhaps somewhat surprising source of evil. King David and a huge entourage have loaded the Ark of the Covenant onto an oxcart and are transporting it to Jerusalem, David's new capital:

> And when they came to the threshing floor of Nacon, Uzzah put out his hand to the ark of God and took hold of it, for the oxen stumbled. And the anger of the Lord was kindled against Uzzah; and God smote him there because he put forth his hand to the ark; and he died there beside the ark of God. And David was angry because the Lord had broken forth upon Uzzah.... And David was afraid of the Lord that day;

and he said, "How can the ark of the Lord come to me?" So David was not willing to take the ark of the Lord into the city of David; but David took it aside to the house of Obed-edom the Gittite. And the ark of the Lord remained in the house of Obed-edom the Gittite three months; and the Lord blessed Obed-edom and all his household.

And it was told King David, "The Lord has blessed the household of Obed-edom and all that belongs to him, because of the ark of God." So David went and brought up the ark of God from the house of Obed-edom to the City of David with rejoicing. (RSV; 2 Sam. 6:6–12)

Uzzah is destroyed by Yahweh, and Obed-edom blessed by him, for reasons that defy explanation. Obed-edom—a Philistine born in Gath, to judge from his designation as "the Gittite"—has done nothing to merit especially good treatment by Yahweh. Uzzah, an Israelite who understandably and (one would think) laudably sought to prevent Yahweh's ark from falling to the ground, has done nothing to merit capital punishment. David reacts to the execution of Uzzah just as the reader might: first with anger and then with fear. Later, when Obed-edom's prosperity suggests that Yahweh's anger has abated, David successfully brings the ark the rest of the way to Jerusalem and rejoices in the thought that his own household will now prosper just as the Philistine's did.

When the sole god or even the dominant god in a pantheon doles out weal and woe with unfathomable unpredictability, the question How could a good god permit . . . ? does not come up, and there is no logical need to postulate the existence of some evil god in order to explain human misfortune. One god, if the god is of a sufficiently mixed type, will suffice. How could a good god permit . . . ? certainly did become a burning question in the course of Israelite and, especially, of Jewish history, but it was not a burning question at the start, for good and evil alternated in the God of Israel almost as unpredictably as good and ill fortune alternate in human existence.

At the neck of the historical hourglass of ancient Israelite and proto-Jewish thinking on this question, two developments combined to pinch the cosmology just summarized to a new and painful narrowness. First, in a process well illustrated in the latter chapters of the Book of Isaiah, Israel began to view the deities of other nations as altogether illusory rather than merely inferior to Israel's deity. Second, Yahweh began to function as exclusively a principle of good rather than as, simultaneously, a principle of good and of evil. The consequences are obvious: As God became both a consistently good god and the only real god, the question How could a good god permit . . . ? suddenly became unavoidable and indeed is faced for the first time in chapters adjacent to those in which the reality of all other gods is denied.

Just at this point in its history, as it happened, Israel was massively exposed to a persuasive answer to the new question. The empire that succeeded the Babylonian in Israel was the Persian, and Persian Zoroastrianism recognized two competing deities: Ahura Mazdah, the personification of good, and Angra Mainyu, the personification of evil. These two were not the only supernatural beings in existence, but all others were organized around them. The process by which Persian religious thought penetrated Israelite thought is impossible to reconstruct, for the record of their interaction during the two centuries when Persia ruled Israel is extremely slender. It is undeniable, however, that after this period the long Israelite entanglement with Semitic polytheism seems to be over, while a dramatic growth in the importance of Satan, or the Devil (definite article, capital letter), is easy to document, not to mention a concomitant growth in the number and importance of angels serving God and of devils serving the "new" Satan. In this transformation, the broadening that occurs at the base of the historical hourglass, erstwhile national deities are replaced by nationally "assigned" angels and devils. One sees this change most easily in the extracanonical Jewish literature of the last pre-Christian centuries, but it is also evident in the canonical Book of Daniel, especially at 10:20–21, where God speaks to Daniel in a vision:

> "Do you know why I have come to you?" he asked. "Soon I must fight the prince of Persia again. When I leave, the prince of Greece will come. But let me tell you what is written in the Book of Truth: 'No one fights by my side against all these except Michael, your prince.'"

Michael is the prince of Israel, the angel or subaltern deity who has that special assignment. What we find after the Persian occupation of Israel is a mythology significantly different from the Canaanite-flavored mythology that preceded it. When God says "No one fights by my side . . . except Michael," he makes clear that he needs allies and that his enemies are by no means entirely under his control; unlike Babylon and Assyria as described in Isaiah, they are much more than mere tools in his hand.

In short, the Devil who tempts God in the Gospel According

to Luke is an enemy of cosmic proportions and, unlike God's erstwhile Canaanite rivals, is evil by definition. As the Gospel story
develops, its way of allowing Satan to subsume all historical opposition to God's people will become a way of indefinitely postponing divine military action—action like that which God once took
against Pharaoh. Indefinite postponement of itself turns historical
action into cosmic action inasmuch as the end of time is the end
of the cosmos as mankind has known it.

34   *In the life of God:* The Aramaic of Daniel 7:13 is the indefinite *bar
       'enaš,* yielding in the Greek *huios anthropou,* "a son of man" or "a
       human being," and suggesting, in context, a symbol rather than a
       personage. Daniel sees "a lion with eagle's wings," "a bear with
       three ribs in its mouth," and eventually "a human being." In the
       Gospels, however, where Jesus uses this phrase of himself dozens
       of times and nobody else does so even once, the standard wording
       is definite: *ho huios tou anthropou.* He turns Daniel's image into a
       personage and identifies himself as that personage.

39   *the Persians, who were the real power:* For more on the Jewish
       restoration under Cyrus and on the Second Temple of Zerubba-
       bel as a Persian project, see John L. Berquist, *Judaism in Persia's
       Shadow: A Social and Historical Approach* (Minneapolis: Fortress
       Press, 1995).

51   *The celibacy—more exactly, the asexuality—of the Lord God:* Jesus is a
       historical figure, but God the Son is not. The sexuality of God the
       Son cannot then be a proper subject for historical discussion. The
       emphasis here is, accordingly, on the words of God the Father in
       the Old Testament as evidence of what would be in character for
       him if and when he became a male human being as God the Son.
       There has, of course, been extensive speculation about the sexual-
       ity of the historical Jesus. Different scholars have offered different,
       more or less plausible reasons to believe that Jesus was celibate, or
       that he was not; that he never left his mother's home, or that he
       did; that he was married, or that he was not; that he had children,
       or that he did not; that he was homosexual, or that he was not;
       and so forth. For a good discussion of these and other psycholog-
       ical speculations about the historical Jesus, see John W. Miller,
       Jesus at Thirty: A Psychological and Historical Portrait (Minneapolis,
       Minn.: Fortress Press, 1997).

64   *the Judean exiles when they returned:* The word *Jewish,* referring to a
       large, internationally dispersed population retaining nonetheless a
       national identity and homeland, is an anachronism as applied to
       the group that returned from exile in 538 B.C.E. *Judean* or *Judahite*
       is preferable, though the point need not be insisted on.

PART TWO

90　　*already being hunted:* In departing from John's exposition to include
so much of Luke and, here, briefly departing from Luke to insert
something from Matthew, I obviously obscure the separate literary intentions of these authors. However, as historical criticism
has made clear, one cannot speak of their intentions as separate
without immediate qualification. Before the four canonical Gospels took the shape they now have, they underwent considerable,
even massive, mutual interpenetration, and that fact has always li-
censed commentators, consciously or unconsciously, to continue
in the same direction—that is, to continue mixing them.

In the introduction to his *The Honest Account of a Memorable
Life, An Apocryphal Gospel* (Rocky Mount: North Carolina Wesleyan College Press, 1994), p. vii, Reynolds Price writes:

> Such a shuffling of sources is frowned upon by many New
> Testament scholars as disruptive of what they take to be the
> mutually exclusive errands of the four evangelists. I dissent
> from their prohibition, as did most early Christian writers, for
> one large reason. The first three gospels may well have been
> built by just such a process of conflation and interleaving; and
> since the most inexplicable acts of Jesus are described with a
> flat-footed refusal to heighten their marvels, most of those
> events mix well with one another. From whichever gospel we
> draw them, they seem so starkly matter-of-fact that in general
> they lie together easily.

The early Christian writer most to Price's point is Tatian, who
produced his *Diatessaron,* a harmonization of the four (not just the
first three) canonical Gospels only a few decades after they were
written. If the process of canonization had proceeded a bit more
slowly, Tatian's text might well have become "the" Gospel, and
scholars in our day would have to factor out its four (or more)
sources in the way they have done for the Pentateuch. Since this
did not happen, the utility of separate exegesis of the four canonical Gospels is self-evident, but Price is nonetheless correct to
note the narrative compatibility and susceptibility to rearrangement of the contents of the three Synoptic Gospels. (See above,
pp. 295–96.)

To what he says, I would add that even the gap between the
Synoptics and the fourth Gospel shrinks when the focus is kept on
the character revealed through the stories as distinct from those
stories themselves. Under a heading like "Jesus Endangered" or
"Jesus Misunderstood" or "Jesus the Teacher," the Synoptics and

John adduce different evidence—that is, they tell different stories. But the character about whom they give testimony is recognizably the same character, and they approach him with much the same set of underlying preoccupations.

Read in the original, the four Gospels are much more quickly recognizable by their style than they are in any translation that I know of. Stylistically, Matthew and John differ much more in Greek than the Elohist and Yahwist sources of the Pentateuch differ in Hebrew. Despite this, if an episode from Matthew is inserted into John or vice versa, the effect is one of no more than mild surprise: An always unpredictable character is seen to have done something particularly unpredictable but not something utterly out of character. This may explain why, even when the Gospels were read in Greek by native Greek-speakers, the impulse toward harmonization was so strong, and why it remains alive today. The distinct and distinctly engaging aesthetic effect that the canonical Gospels produce as a quartet is an effect of interrupted editing. As the reader notices this, he feels himself not just invited but practically required to resume the editorial process. It is virtually impossible to finish a reading of the four without having already begun unconsciously to harmonize them. Since all professional writers are at least the editors of their own work, they may experience this "Gospel effect" with particular intensity and then manifest it by producing in writing—as Reynolds Price did—the written Gospel harmonies that ordinary readers produce only in their minds.

99   *a head-smashing kind of god:* If the distinction between friend and foe were to be abolished to such an extent that God could no longer be said to have enemies and his worshippers could no longer ask him for help in defeating their own enemies, then the Book of Psalms would have to be retired almost in its entirety, for there are very few Psalms that do not, at some point, allude to a fight in progress and ask God's assistance in winning it. This is true even of the most poetic and meditative of the Psalms. Psalm 139, for example, contains these beautiful quatrains:

> Whither shall I go from thy Spirit?
>   Or whither shall I flee from thy presence?
> If I ascend to heaven, thou art there!
>   If I make my bed in Sheol, thou art there!
> If I take the wings of morning
>   and dwell in the uttermost parts of the sea,
> even there thy hand shall lead me,
>   and thy right hand shall hold me.

If I say, "Let only darkness cover me,
        and the light about me become night,"
even the darkness is not dark to thee,
        the night is bright as the day,
        for darkness to thee is as light.

(139:7–12)

But the same Psalm, before it concludes, presents the Psalmist urging that God become the enemy of his enemies because he himself has so assiduously been the enemy of God's enemies:

Do I not hate them that hate thee, O Lord?
        And do I not loathe them that rise up against thee?
I hate them with perfect hatred;
        I count them my enemies.
Search me, O God, and know my heart!
        Try me and know my thoughts!
And see if there be any wicked way in me,
        and lead me on the path everlasting!

(139:22–24)

To the modern sensibility, hatred and contention come jarringly in after "the wings of morning," but such juxtapositions of delicate sentiment and virulent hatred were familiar and indeed almost conventional when the Psalms were written, or so we must infer from their extreme frequency. That modern readers have the reaction they do is one measure of the historic success of Jesus' radical "pacification" of the image of God. There are times, of course, when Jesus speaks in a more warlike way, not to mention innumerable times in the course of history when warlike Christians have embraced the bloodiest verses of the Old Testament precisely because they *were* bloody. Nonetheless, the incongruity between Jesus' inaugural sermon and a very long list of earlier biblical texts cannot be gainsaid even after all necessary lexical and anthropological qualifications have been made.

110   *Jewish population in the first century:* Estimates have been lowered somewhat in the past generation, but not in a way that would affect the claim that the Roman and the Nazi *shoahs* bear comparison. Salo W. Baron estimated the Jewish population within the borders of the Roman empire at just under 7 million, with slightly more than a million others living outside its borders, mostly to the east; the Jewish population of Palestine he placed at not higher than 2.5 million (*Encyclopaedia Judaica* [New York: Macmillan, 1972], vol. 13, p. 871). Paul Johnson writes: "Though it is impos-

sible to present accurate figures, it is clear that by the time of Christ the diaspora Jews greatly outnumbered the settled Jews of Palestine: perhaps by as many as 4.5 million to 1" (*A History of Christianity* [New York: Atheneum, 1976], p. 12). Subsequent estimates generally fall between these extremes. Thus, Wayne Meeks in *The First Urban Christians* (New Haven, Conn.: Yale University Press, 1983) estimates 1 million Jews in Palestine, 5 million to 6 million in the diaspora.

111 *The first-century historian Josephus:* Josephus, *The Wars of the Jews,* book 6, chapter 9, section 3.

not as implausible as they might otherwise seem: Cf. Salo W. Baron, above: "The figures transmitted by such distinguished historians as Josephus and Tacitus ranging between 600,000 fatalities and 1,197,000 dead and captured are not quite so out of line as they appear at first glance. Jerusalem's population had been swelled by countless numbers of pilgrims from all over the Dispersion and refugees from the provinces previously occupied by the Roman legions."

116 *"whether there is any likelihood":* Raymond E. Brown, *The Gospel According to John I–XII,* Anchor Bible Series, vol. 29 (New York: Doubleday, 1966), pp. 367–68.

117 *Rabbi Ovadia Yosef:* John F. Burns, "Israeli Rabbi Sets Off a Political Firestorm Over the Holocaust," *The New York Times,* August 8, 2000, sec. A, p. 10.

118 *"The SS hanged two Jewish men":* Elie Wiesel, *Night* (New York: Bantam Doubleday Dell, 1982), p. 79; originally published in 1958.

"To the martyrs": Abraham J. Heschel, *The Prophets, Volume II* (New York: Harper Torchbooks, 1975) ©1962. A more recent, psychologically shaped Jewish theology is found in David R. Blumenthal, *Facing the Abusing God: A Theology of Protest* (Louisville, Ky.: Westminster John Knox Press, 1993). Theological reflection on these passages seems almost inevitably, in our day, to yield a theology of protest. Literary reflection on them in the first century may have yielded at least a protest in pantomime.

128 *Historically, this genesis:* See Daniel Boyarin, *Dying for God: Martyrdom and the Making of Christianity and Judaism* (Stanford, Calif.: Stanford University Press, 1999); Arthur J. Droge and James Tabor, *Noble Death: Suicide and Martyrdom Among Christians and Jews in Antiquity* (San Francisco: Harper San Francisco, 1992); and Lacy Baldwin Smith, *Fools, Martyrs, Traitors: The Story of Martyrdom in the Western World* (New York: Alfred A. Knopf, 1997). Of exceptional interest for showing how the possibly suicidal death of Jesus was seen in a Hellenistic culture that tolerated and even ad-

mired suicide is Pierre-Emmanuel Dauzat, *Le Suicide du Christ,
Une Théologie* (Paris: Presses Universitaires de France, 1998).

133   *alternately* yehoshua' *or* yeshua' *in Hebrew:* Like so many Hebrew
names, this name is a sentence, in this case meaning "The Lord
(*yeho* or *ye*) is salvation (*shua*')." The Gospel of Matthew, which
often seems to presume a knowledge of Hebrew in its readers, has
an angel instruct Joseph: "You must name him Jesus because he is
the one who is to save his people from their sins" (1:21).

The form *yehoshua'* is standard in the Hebrew of the earlier
books of the Tanakh, notably the Book of Joshua itself; the form
yeshua' sometimes replaces it in the Hebrew of later books like
Ezra. In the Greek of the Septuagint (the pre-Christian Greek
translation of the Tanakh), *Iēsous* is the word that translates both
Hebrew forms of the name Joshua. In the Greek of the Gospels,
Iēsous is also the name of the Savior. How, then, does it happen
that the Savior's name has not come down to us as Joshua rather
than as Jesus?

Joshua would in fact have become the name by which the Savior was known in modern translations were it not for a confusion
that resulted in the fourth century when Jerome translated the
Bible into Latin from Hebrew and Aramaic (for the Old Testament) and from Greek (for the New Testament). Whenever
Jerome found *Iēsous* in the New Testament Greek, he translated it
as Latin *Jesus,* whether Jesus or Joshua was the man being named.
(There are, obviously, many references to Jesus in the New Testament and only a few—notably Acts 7:45 and Hebrews 4:8—to
Joshua.) Regrettably, when translating *yehoshua'* or *yeshua'* from
Old Testament Hebrew, he was not so consistent. He translated
late occurrences of either name interchangeably as either Latin
Jesus or Latin *Josue.* (Cf. Vulgate at Zechariah 6:11 [*Jesus* for
yehoshua'] and at Ezra 3:2 [*Josue* for *yeshua'*].) But in the all-
important Book of Joshua itself, he used only Latin *Josue.* The result was that most references to Joshua in the Latin Old Testament
became *Josue,* while all references to Jesus in the Latin New Testament became *Jesus.* The striking fact that the two historical figures
bore the same name was thus fatally obscured in what would be
Western Christendom's only Bible for a millennium.

Conceivably, the Reformation, as it began to set aside Jerome's
Latin in favor of new vernacular translations from the Hebrew and
Greek originals, might also have set aside Jerome's Joshua/Jesus
distinction as linguistically indefensible and might have thence-
forth called either Joshua Jesus or Jesus Joshua. Had the change
been made in either direction, God's historic mission as military
warrior for Israel (the mission discharged through the first Joshua)

might have more audibly and ironically intruded upon his historic mission as pacifist warrior for the world (the mission discharged through Jesus, the second Joshua). But the Reformers apparently found the thousand-year-old mistake too deeply rooted for correction.

136 *"During the night"*: Jesus' stilling the storm is a miracle that appears in all four Gospels and in several different forms, with or without the walking on water. I offer here a harmonized version in which vertical strokes separate the combined sections from one another.

141 *Caesarea Philippi*: "Philip's Caesarea," so called to distinguish it from another Caesarea on the Mediterranean coast, was ruled by Herod Philip, who—perhaps not surprisingly—seems to have surrendered his wife, Herodias, to his half-brother, Herod Antipas, without protest.

PART THREE

165 *"The theme of these pages"*: Pierre-Emmanuel Dauzat, *Le Suicide du Christ: Une théologie* (Paris: Presses Universitaires de France, 1998), p. 1, my translation.

165 *"Christ first bows his head"*: Ibid., pp. 52–3.

166 *a remarkable passage in Paul's Letter*: See A. J. Droge, *"Mori lucrum*: Paul and Ancient Theories of Suicide," *Novum Testamentum* 30 (1988):263–86.

167 *"Both the durability of the theme"*: *Le Suicide du Christ*, p. 1.

167 *"From the agnostic side"*: Ibid., p. 4.

170 *"une vie dont on ne meurt pas"*: Ibid., p. 182.

173 *they who are under the Devil's control*: The history of anti-Semitism, and the place within that history of the demonization of "the Jews" in the Gospel of John, is not the proper subject of this book; but lest silence on this subject seem to imply some degree of acquiescence, let me make a preemptive statement. Because anti-Semitism, like any other kind of ethnic prejudice, is evil in itself, any use of the Gospel text that fosters it is also evil. However, with apologies to the Shakespeare of *Julius Caesar,* the fault, dear Brutus, is not in our texts but in ourselves. The cure for Christian anti-Semitism cannot lie in the emendation or bowdlerization of Christian texts but only in the reform of Christian habits. Let the texts say what they say and, as necessary, use them as material to teach against anti-Semitism. No text is so evil that it cannot be put to good use, or so good that it cannot be put to evil use.

Both a literary and a historical disservice is done when it is suggested that because Jesus was a Jew, there can have been no hostility, even murderous hostility, between him and other Jews, up to and including the Jewish authorities of his day. In our own day, Yitzhak Rabin, the late prime minister of Israel, faced murderous, rabbinically endorsed hostility in the person of his assassin, Yigal Amir. (See Jacques Derogy and Hesi Carmel, *Ils ont tué Rabin* [Paris: Robert Laffont, 1996].) Rabin—whom some religious Israelis regarded as a *rodef*, a persecutor, or a *moser*, a traitor—was clearly not a victim of anti-Semitism, but there can be no doubt whatsoever that he was a victim of hatred. The point, of course, is that anti-Semitism is not the only form of hatred, and that Jews did not all get along in Jesus' day any more than they do now.

In John 8, Jesus and the Jews whom he is confronting, not to say baiting, in the Temple demonize *one another.* In a verbal joust of great subtlety, even brilliance, they compete with one another in demonization. I have chosen to linger over rather than to hurry past this mutual demonization. Other critics may attach less importance to it than I do, but to eliminate it altogether from this chapter would be to eviscerate the chapter as literature. The same must be said of the suggestion that passages suggesting Jewish complicity in the judicial murder of Jesus should be eliminated outright because these passages are historically dubious and have been made grounds for anti-Semitism. Implicit in that suggestion is the truly sinister notion that if the passages in question were historically reliable, then they could properly be grounds for anti-Semitism. This last is just the error that must be identified, quarantined, and repudiated. The Italians of the twenty-first century are not Christ-killers because first-century Italians drove the nails, any more than the Jews of the twenty-first century would be Christ-killers even if it should someday be proven—as someday it might be—that first-century Jews brought the charge.

187   *Only a few modern translations:* One that seems to is Everett Fox's in *The Five Books of Moses* (New York: Schocken Books, 1995; p. 27):

> If you intend good, bear-it-aloft,
> but if you do not intend good,
> at the entrance is sin, a crouching-demon,
> toward you his lust—
> but you can rule over him.

188   *What is it that has been hidden:* In *Things Hidden Since the Foundation of the World* (Stanford, Calif.: Stanford University Press, 1987), critic René Girard, in collaboration with Jean-Michel Oughourlian and Guy Lefort, explores the relevance of his seminal theory

of "mimetic desire" and "mimetic violence" for the interpretation of the Gospels.

For Girard, covetousness and envy are the most primitive forms of desire, all desire being learned. Covetousness and envy that cannot be contained as productive ambition and benign emulation may degenerate into malign and destructive rivalry. When such rivalry grows violent enough and spreads far enough to infect an entire society, it can climax with the identification of a scapegoat who is blamed for the violence and whose sacrifice temporarily restores peace. In Girard's view, the process by which mimetic desire leads to mimetic violence is more ancient than literature, more ancient perhaps than speech. Its most archaic surviving evidence is to be found in the violence of the oldest myths, and these provide most of the evidence for the theory.

Girard reads the Gospels not as one more myth among the many that his theory aims to explain but as, uniquely, the repudiation of the cruel logic that all the other myths have in common, the logic by which an innocent victim is gratuitously defined as guilty, singled out as the source of contagion in a community, and then wantonly sacrificed for the supposed health of the community. In the Gospels, as Girard reads them, the innocent Christ is seen as innocent even as he is sacrificed. It is this which makes the Gospel story exceptional. When his innocence is vindicated, the demonic guilt-transference process is exposed and, in principle, repudiated. That repudiation—in which, so to speak, scapegoating itself is scapegoated—is, for Girard, the essence of Christian revelation and the start of Christian redemption.

The point of contact between Girard's theory and the reading of the Gospels offered here is a broadly shared understanding of resentment. For both, resentment leads to war, and the transcendence of resentment to peace. Both see in Christ's preaching as well as in the Gospel story a vision of resentment transcended. The point of difference between the two lies in the view taken toward sacrifice and, above all, toward scapegoating. The deliberate, even suicidal, self-sacrifice of God is central to the interpretation offered here. Girard, by contrast, attending very little to God as a character in the Gospel story, has been reluctant to interpret the Crucifixion sacrificially, seeing sacrificial interpretations of the Gospel as entailing a pollution by pagan myth of the great Christian antimyth. As he once said in an interview, "I scapegoated [the Letter to the] Hebrews and I scapegoated the word 'sacrifice'" (*Religion & Literature,* 25, 2, Summer, 1993, p. 29). In the interpretation offered here, Hebrews is honored, and repentant self-sacrifice is distinguished from the victimization of the innocent

that, as Girard's theory correctly stresses, the Gospels were the first
to identify as such.

195   *The Greek word* hosanna: The Hebrew imperative at Psalm 118:25
is *hoši'ah,* followed by the particle of entreaty *na'.* Though Aramaic was the most widely spoken language of the country, a Hebrew word frozen into a cheer may well have been used even by
Aramaic-speaking Jews. If a crowd of Aramaic-speakers chose to
cry "Hosanna, Jesus!" in Aramaic, allowing the first word to have
its normal lexical force, the words would be *hoša'-na' yešu'ah,* a
rhyming pun deriving from the fact that the name *Jesus* and the
cry *Hosanna!* have a common root. But apart from the fact that
the text does not in fact read "Hosanna, Jesus," there is little of
this kind of Semitic punning in the Gospel of John, which is an
original composition in Greek. Though the Gospel plays many
word games, the games are semantic far more often than they are
morphological.

PART FOUR

199   *writings by Samuel Beckett: I Can't Go On, I'll Go On: A Selection
From Samuel Beckett's Work,* edited and introduced by Richard W.
Seaver (New York: Grove Press, 1977).

199   *tended to accrue by reattribution:* See Jack Miles, *God: A Biography*
(New York: Alfred A. Knopf, 1995), pp. 19–24.

210   *turn the Jordan Valley into a torrent of death:* Visions like this one—
indeed, far more extravagant visions than this one—fill the Book
of Revelation, a book whose inclusion in the Christian Bible
came only after a long debate. While that book undeniably represents a late explosion of apocalyptic imagery, its overall effect is an
ironic reversal of classic apocalyptic hope. In early Christian imagery, the lamb of the apocalypse was often represented holding a
war pennant crooked in his front foreleg over the caption, in
Greek, NIKA, "He conquers." The caption and pennant may seem
to be the negation of the lamb, but a more plausible reading,
given the whole course of the New Testament before the Book of
Revelation, is that the lamb negates the pennant and the caption.
And as for the derived icon, so also for the text itself.

224   *"in the case of the Gospel":* Jorge Luis Borges, *This Craft of Verse*
(Cambridge: Harvard University Press, 2000). I quote from an ex-
cerpt published in *The Atlantic Monthly,* September 2000, pp.
63–6.

EPILOGUE

247   *In an earlier book:* That earlier book was to have been this book.
More exactly, the two books were to have been just one book.

My initial intention, inspired by a recording of J. S. Bach's *St. Matthew Passion,* was to write a biography-shaped reading of the Bible that would show how the Lord of Hosts became the Lamb of God. Emotionally, this intention arose from the opening antiphonal chorus of the oratorio, which expresses a dismayed astonishment, a grief-stricken horror, that seemed to me to have vanished from contemporary aesthetic responses to the Gospel.

> See him!
> Whom?
> The Bridegroom!
> See him!
> How?
> As if a lamb!

The Bridegroom of Israel turned into a sacrificial animal! The two choirs sob out their agitation and incomprehension. Later in the chorale that, sung five times, holds the enormous oratorio together, their question receives a fuller formulation:

> Before your noble visage
> World powers would shrink and quail.
> Why are you spat upon so?
> Why are you deathly pale?
> Your eyes, they shone so brightly
> No light could equal them.
> Who turns that light to darkness,
> To judgment, and to shame?
>
> (my translation)

There was nowhere to look for an explanation of this enormous change in God, except in God's own past. But since my way of looking into God's past, as I began to develop it, envisioned a sequential reading of scripture, I had to choose whether to write about the Hebrew scriptures in the Jewish or in the Christian order, the order of the Tanakh or the order of the Old Testament. That Jews and Christians do not follow the same order in reading the same texts is a fact largely ignored by both groups, and my initial, uncritical expectation was that either order would work for the purpose I had in mind.

There seemed to be two key literary facts. First, God Incarnate moves the action forward in the Gospels just as God does in Genesis and Exodus. The Gospel According to John, deliberately echoing the Book of Genesis, begins "In the beginning." Whatever the metaphysical relationship between Yahweh and Jesus (father to son, speaker to word, priest to victim, and so forth), they are dramatically equivalent or at least suggestively similar on the page. Second, whether the Gospels are read after the Writings, which conclude the Tanakh, or after the twelve minor prophets, which conclude the Old Testament, the effect is that of a sudden burst of divine activity following a long lull.

I chose the Tanakh over the Old Testament because in it this slowing or ebbing is so much more pronounced. At the end of the Old Testament, the expectation that God may return to action is still alive despite God's failure to act. Crucially, though God is doing nothing, he is still speaking through his prophets. He is, so to speak, still keeping in touch. By the end of the Tanakh, however, God has not only ceased acting, he has also ceased speaking, and his silence weighs heavily. Though he has not disappeared, he is rarely addressed, and little indeed seems to be expected of him. An examination of his character as developed first in the Tanakh and then in the New Testament could therefore have, I supposed, the structure of a Classical symphony, minus the minuet (there is no minuet, no scherzo in the Bible). The first movement, the Allegro, would be God at the start of the Tanakh. The second movement, the Largo, would be God at the end of the Tanakh. The third movement, the Presto, would be God Incarnate in the New Testament.

What I discovered, instead, as I approached the end of a book-length discussion of the Tanakh, was the pervasive sense of an ending which that collection conveys through its closing books. My judgment—surely debatable, but I felt it quite powerfully—was that the collection in this order "wanted" to end where it did. Its structure was not Allegro, Largo, Presto but Allegro, Andante, Largo. I felt, as I might even more impressionistically put it, the encroaching presence of an ancient editor wrapping things up and shutting things down. Deferring to him, allowing my book to end where his ended, I let the pen fall from my own hand.

This, then, is how *God: A Biography,* which never discusses and only rarely even mentions the New Testament, came into existence. Instead of the one book I had set out to write, I concluded that there would have to be two books: one each on the West's two distinct and long-hallowed editions of sacred scripture, Judaism's Tanakh and Christianity's two-testament Bible. The second book would pursue the original idea. The first book, *God: A Biography,* would report what I had found on the alternate path that I had trod half by accident.

251   *in critic Harold Bloom's sense:* See *The Anxiety of Influence: A Theory of Poetry* (New York and Oxford: Oxford University Press, 1973).

As a poetic misprision of the Tanakh, the New Testament falls into Bloom's second category, "*Tessera,* which is completion and antithesis": "A poet antithetically 'completes' his precursor, by so reading the parent-poem as to retain its terms but to mean them in another sense, as though the precursor had failed to go far enough" (p. 14).

The most interesting Bible critic now writing in English on the subject of antithetical completion or supersessionism—the view that the Christian Bible has "superseded" the Jewish Tanakh and that Christianity has "superseded" Judaism—is Jon D. Levenson, Albert A. List Professor of Jewish Studies at Harvard University. In an essay entitled "Theological Consensus or Historicist Evasion? Jews and Christians in Biblical Studies" (quotations from Levenson, here and following pages, from Levenson, *The Hebrew Bible, the Old Testament, and Historical Criticism: Jews and Christians in Biblical Studies* [Louisville, Ky.: Westminster/John Knox Press, 1993], pp. 100–102), Levenson cites as a latter-day example of supersessionism the work of Walter Eichrodt, a German theologian who

> thought history would bear out his claim that the Hebrew bible stands in "*essential coherence*" with the New Testament. It is this notion that accounts for the anti-Judaism that pervades Eichrodt's *Theology [of the Old Testament,* published in German in 1933 and in English translation in 1961], as when he wrote of the "torso-like appearance of Judaism in separation from Christianity." Strange, is it not, that the Jews have never noticed that their tradition is only a torso—especially since Christians have been telling them this for nearly two millennia?

Levenson's charge, as suggested by the title of his essay, is that Eichrodt evaded what was properly a religious commitment by basing it on historicist argumentation that could not (and cannot) bear the weight. Levenson then asks whether literary argumentation can bear the same weight, contrasting two literary commentaries on the Bible, both published in 1981: Northrop Frye's *The Great Code* on the Christian Bible, and Robert Alter's *The Art of Biblical Narrative* on the Jewish Bible. Levenson notes that Alter concedes a certain continuity between the Tanakh and the New Testament,

> but he goes on to say that "the narratives of the latter were written in a different language, at a later time, and, by and large, according to different literary assumptions. It therefore

does not seem to me that these two bodies of ancient literature can be comfortably set in the same critical framework."
Here I am tempted to invert my remark about Eichrodt and to
ask why, if the two Testaments do not constitute a profound
unity, Christians for thousands of years (including Northrop
Frye in our time) have never noticed.

Though neither Frye nor Alter writes as a representative of
a religious tradition, and though both seem impatient with
theology, the truth is that the unit each chooses for his study is
dictated by his heritage, Christianity for Frye, Judaism for
Alter. I suppose each could come up with an *aesthetic* argument for the superiority of his own canon, but the chances of
winning the other over would be about as great as the chance
that Pablo Christiani or Nachmanides could have won over
his opponent [at a famous theological debate] in Barcelona in
1263.

Levenson detects a tone of sovereign indifference bordering on
condescension in both Frye and Alter and infers that, if they ever
did meet in debate, aesthetic superiority would surely have to be
the issue before them. At the same time, neither Frye nor Alter
denies the legitimacy of the other's enterprise, and one may imagine another similarly assorted pair of critics willing to concede
(and not just as a way of dismissing) the aesthetic distinctness of
each other's canons—distinctness, I stress, not superiority. A step
beyond that would come when each went on to write a book-
length aesthetic appreciation of the other's canon.

This step is not necessarily a large one. At any rate, it will not
seem large once it begins to be taken, for in our day the postmod-
ernist notion that art does not progress is becoming commonplace. In the first lecture of her popular televised history of
painting, Sister Wendy Beckett says, apropos of the cave paintings
at Lascaux, "Art changes, but it doesn't get better; and in the great
hall of the bulls, with these images of majesty and power, so
strong and so dignified, we understand that painting starts at the
top" (*Sister Wendy's Story of Painting,* British Broadcasting Company, 1996, cassette one). Painting starts at the top, in other words,
and goes neither up nor down but forward. I submit that scripture
too may be understood to start at the top and yet to go forward.

The art of the New Testament consists overwhelmingly in its
artful reuse of the Hebrew scriptures. This reuse is often (not always) intentionally supersessionist, but I would insist that to appreciate this supersessionism *artistically* is to reduce it to mere
succession—to reduce it, in other words, to a strong misreading.
Challenging the validity of this option, Levenson writes:

To say that the Hebrew Bible has complete integrity over against the New Testament is to cast grave doubt upon the unity of the Christian Bible. It is like saying one can read the first ten books of the *Aeneid* as if the last two did not exist, and this, in turn, is to say that the last two add nothing essential: the story can just as credibly end without Aeneas's slaying Turnus.

To this, I can only respond as someone who has attempted to do what Levenson says cannot be done. In *God: A Biography,* I observed, as a literary critic rather than a theologian or a historian, that the first ten books of the biblical *Aeneid* existed in two different arrangements, that of the Tanakh and that of the Old Testament. I then proceeded to read the Tanakh as if neither the Old Testament arrangement of its contents nor the New Testament epilogue to them—equivalently, the last two books of the *Aeneid*—existed. In *Christ: A Crisis in the Life of God,* I turn, equivalently, to a reading of all twelve books. I would note, in my defense, that the *Aeneid* does not exist in two distinct editions with authority and antiquity comparable to the Jewish and Christian editions of the scriptures that both Jews and Christians read. Yet I would concede that a crucial opening step is taken—a step much larger than it sometimes looks—when one confronts the Bible as a secular classic, as if, indeed, it were just the *Aeneid*. That step made, an infinity of aesthetic experiments becomes possible, and thereafter the proof of the pudding must be in the eating.

253   *others put [those words] into his mouth:* Many of the sayings of Jesus in the Gospels fall into the category of perennial Jewish or Judeo-Hellenistic wisdom. Their interest, such as it may be, owes little to the fact that they are spoken by the Messiah or the Son of God or God Incarnate. As spoken by any Jew or, for that matter, by any Gentile, they would be equally interesting. Such a saying is Matthew 18:15–17 (NJB):

> If your brother does something wrong, go and have it out with him alone, between your two selves. If he listens to you, you have won back your brother. If he does not listen, take one or two others along with you. . . . But if he refuses to listen to these, report it to the community; and if he refuses to listen to the community, treat him like a gentile or a tax collector.

This is the sort of thing that, nowadays, tends to be collected in a thin book with wide margins and large print and published as *The Management Principles of Jesus of Nazareth.*

Many other Gospel sayings, however, fall outside the borders of perennial Jewish or Judeo-Hellenistic wisdom, for they relate not to the human condition in general but uniquely to Jesus' own condition. And of these a great many refer, as does "No one is taking [my life] from me. / I lay it down of my own accord," to the exceptional circumstances of Jesus' death. That saying refers, in other words, uniquely to God Incarnate and uniquely to his crucifixion.

Sayings of this second type occur in all four Gospels but with particular frequency in John. When they occur, they interpret the plot in the way that stage directions interpret—that is, deliberately narrow and specify—the meaning of a dramatic action. A reading of the Gospel built around God Incarnate as its protagonist and around the Crucifixion as its central action inevitably highlights sayings of this second type.

As for the rest of Jesus' teachings, those that in some way illumine the central action receive more attention here than teachings or sayings that might have been spoken by anyone on any appropriate occasion. The latter, much attended to in recent commentary, may or may not be the surest path back to the Jesus of history. What is beyond argument is that the Jesus Christ of literature lives on principally in the Gospel plot and in the words, historical or not, that most directly enhance it.

APPENDIX I

1. Aramaic and its descendant Syriac remained in use from Palestine eastward until the Muslim conquests of the early seventh century C.E. Aramaic would be the language of the Gemara, the larger, latter portion of the Talmud, whose two editions were completed in Palestine and in Persian (Sassanian) Mesopotamia just before that conquest. One cannot speak of "world Jewry" without including this large and immensely influential eastern Jewry. It is still probable, however, that, worldwide, more Jews spoke Greek than spoke either Hebrew or Aramaic at the time when Hellenistic Jewry was at its peak and the Septuagint was produced.

2. For a full discussion of this phenomenon, see Mogens Müller, *The First Bible of the Church: A Plea for the Septuagint* (Sheffield, England,: Sheffield Academic Press, 1996), and Karen H. Jobes and Moisés Silva, *Invitation to the Septuagint* (Grand Rapids, Mich.: Baker Academic, 2000).

The literature of Hellenistic Jewry, it should be noted, included much more than just the Septuagint. Its most important thinker was the prolific and philosophically sophisticated Philo of Alexandria, an exact contemporary of Jesus; but it contained examples in various other genres. See, as an example of recent attention to this literature and the culture that produced it, John M. G. Barclay, *Jews in the Mediterranean Diaspora, From Alexander to Trajan (323 BCE–117 CE)* (Berkeley: University of California Press, 1996).

3. See "The Mission to the Jews: Why It Probably Succeeded" in Rodney Stark, *The Rise of Christianity: A Sociologist Reconsiders History* (Princeton, N.J.: Princeton University Press, 1996). Recent archaeological evidence cited by Stark suggests that a clear and final separation of the two religiously and ethnically related communities—Hellenistic Judaism and Greek-speaking, ethnically Jewish Christianity—was not complete until the fourth century in Palestine and even later in other locations. That starting around 100 C.E. an explosion of Christian writing in Greek, most of it the work of Christian Jews, coincided with a sudden decline in Greek literary production by Judaist Jews certainly suggests an explanation for that otherwise unexplained decline. See Shaye J. Cohen, "Judaism," in G. W. Bowersock, Peter Brown, and Oleg Grabar, editors, *Late Antiquity: A Guide to the Postclassical World* (Cambridge: Harvard University Press, 1999).

4. In *Authors and Owners: The Invention of Copyright* (Cambridge: Harvard University Press, 1993, p. 3), Michael Rose writes:

> Discussions of copyright not infrequently regard intellectual property as an "ancient and eternal idea" or "a natural need of the human mind." But copyright—the practice of securing marketable rights in texts that are treated as commodities—is a specifically modern institution, the creature of the printing press, the individualization of authorship in the late Middle Ages and early Renaissance, and the development of the advanced marketplace society in the seventeenth and eighteenth centuries.

5. Aquila, a second-century convert from paganism to Christianity and then from Christianity to Judaism, set out to retranslate the Jewish scriptures from Hebrew and Aramaic into a Greek that would follow the original word for word. The results, essentially unreadable by anyone who does not understand Hebrew (and have the Hebrew text at hand), were a conscious challenge to the legitimacy of the far more readable Septuagint. Aquila's translation, which deliberately sought to seem foreign, bespeaks a new and culturally fateful subordination of translation to original, a

new awareness that a translation is *only* a translation. Rabbinic Judaism effectively fostered the same awareness by instituting the bar
mitzvah requirement that every male member of the community,
on coming of age, demonstrate an ability to read the scripture
aloud in the original language. The very difficulty of this requirement in the diaspora, where no one spoke Hebrew in daily inter-
course, guaranteed that it would impart a vivid sense that the
original was not to be confused with any translation of it.

A comparable but far more restricted translation-awareness
began to develop within Christianity only two centuries later
when Jerome, a Christian monk translating the Bible into Latin,
moved to Palestine, apprenticed himself to rabbis, mastered Hebrew, and made the culturally significant decision to translate the
Old Testament from the Hebrew rather than from the Greek.
Jerome's deference to the original language, not to minimize its
importance, remained restricted, within Christianity, to a narrow
class of scholar-monks like himself. At the popular level, the older
attitude of diaspora Jewry toward the scripture in translation lived
on as the standard Christian attitude. It would remain standard
until the Reformation, and, to a considerable extent, it remains so
down to the present.

6. The rearrangement that Christianity was to impose upon the
canon of scripture that it had inherited from Judaism may be seen
at a glance by comparing the two canons as they have come down
to our time:

OLD TESTAMENT	TANAKH
(*Jewish scriptures in Greek as reordered by Christianity*)	(*Jewish scriptures in Hebrew*)
Genesis	Genesis
Exodus	Exodus
Leviticus	Leviticus
Numbers	Numbers
Deuteronomy	Deuteronomy
Joshua	Joshua
Judges	Judges
Ruth	
Samuel	Samuel
Kings	Kings
	Isaiah
	Jeremiah
	Ezekiel
	Twelve Minor Prophets
Chronicles	Psalms

OLD TESTAMENT	TANAKH
(Jewish scriptures in Greek as reordered by Christianity)	*(Jewish scriptures in Hebrew)*

Ezra	Proverbs
Nehemiah	Job
Tobit*	
Judith*	
Esther	Song of Songs
Maccabees*	Ruth
Job	Lamentations
Psalms	Ecclesiastes
Proverbs	Esther
Ecclesiastes	Daniel
Song of Songs	Ezra
Wisdom*	Nehemiah
Ecclesiasticus (Sirach)*	Chronicles
Isaiah	
Jeremiah	
Lamentations	
Baruch*	
Ezekiel	
Daniel	
Twelve Minor Prophets	

Within the group of about a dozen books, some quite short, that runs from Chronicles to Ecclesiasticus in the Christian canon and from Psalms to Chronicles in the Jewish canon, both the contents and the order were quite fluid in the Jewish canon during the years when the New Testament was being written and indeed for some time thereafter. In Latin-speaking Western Christendom, both the contents and the order of the canon were effectively fixed in the early fifth century when Jerome completed his semiofficial new translation from Hebrew, Aramaic, and Greek into Latin. Early in the following century, the monk Cassiodorus introduced the one-volume format in southern Italy, and a standard was set that would be maintained in the West for a millennium. The standard changed in the sixteenth century when Protestantism decanonized those books (asterisked above) of the traditional Christian Old Testament for which no Hebrew original was in hand at the time, while Eastern Orthodoxy and Roman Catholicism retained the older canon and made it official. (When translating, Protestantism also expanded the Book of Jeremiah and condensed the Books of Daniel and Esther so as to have its translations conform to the Hebrew text against the traditional Greek.)

When determining the order of the works it accepted as canonical, however, the Reformation did not follow the Hebrew text but instead retained the traditional Christian order, for the same apologetic reason that had dictated its adoption in the first place.

In our own day, although the traditional Christian canon has been largely replaced by the Protestant in Protestant-majority countries, the older canon remains the majority canon of world Christianity, a statistical fact that has not been without consequence. Thus, some recent critical translations of the Christian Bible into English even under other than Roman Catholic or Eastern Orthodox auspices have gone halfway back to the traditional canon by including an appendix of "apocryphal" or "deuterocanonical" works—namely, the books and book-portions of the traditional canon that Protestantism had grown accustomed to dropping. (The King James Version, interestingly enough, originally included such an appendix, but over time it became standard Protestant practice for printed editions of that version to dispense with the appendix.)

A few widely used contemporary translations, notably the Jerusalem Bible, have gone so far as to restore the deleted books and the deleted sections of retained books to their traditional position, and other even more searching innovations continue to occur. Thus, *La Bible, Traduction oecuménique, édition intégrale,* a brilliant French translation (Paris: Les Éditions du Cerf, 1995), has placed Isaiah, Jeremiah, Ezekiel, and the twelve minor prophets in the position they occupy in the Jewish canon while including but segregating the apocryphal/deuterocanonical texts. So long as the Bible remains in active use, further such adjustments of the canon, or canons, are not just possible but likely. Their significance must not be exaggerated, but neither should it be ignored.

7. As that singular definite thing, the Bible is a Christian invention, and the expression *the Bible*—including both the article and the capital letter—may be said to refer, properly, to the two-testament Christian Bible. Judaism retains to this day a far stronger working awareness of the inner plurality of scripture than Christianity does, beginning with the fact that it sees an almost metaphysical difference between Torah (the first five books of the Tanakh) and the rest of the canon. Some Jews, sensitive to the somewhat un-Jewish implications of using *the Bible* to refer to their scriptures, avoid the expression, but others use it freely. In this, as in all linguistic (and, for that matter, religious) matters, usage controls.

The development of the Bible into the definite, singular thing it became in Christendom may owe something to a technological breakthrough as well. The codex—the book as we know it, consisting of cut pages bound on one side—may conceivably have been a Christian invention. This cannot be known, but it is suggested by the fact that virtually all the earliest surviving codices contain Christian texts. What is clear, however, is that Christianity led the way in replacing the scroll with the codex and in developing the technology that produced ever larger and more capacious codices.

The technical advantages of the codex over the scroll are, essentially, economy and convenience. Because one writes on only the inner side of a scroll but on both sides of the pages of a codex, the codex is more efficient in its use of writing space. Because one may enter a codex in the middle but must enter a scroll at the beginning and unroll to the middle, the codex is more convenient. Once codices large enough to contain many scrolls had developed, the codex would seem almost inevitably to have had a unitizing effect on the once physically separate works it contained, not to speak of a literally binding effect on the order in which they would appear. In this way, Christianity's unitization of the scriptures it inherited from Judaism may well have been fostered by technology. At the same time, it must be stressed that the technology need not necessarily have had this effect. Judaism, which now routinely uses the codex except during its liturgy, retains nonetheless a strong sense of the inner plurality of scripture. By the same token, some sense of the unity of scripture had to precede Christianity's adoption of the codex for Bible copying, or large codices of Christian scripture would not exist at all.

We must remember, finally, that a large codex was a costly object in antiquity, and a very large codex—one large enough to contain both the Old Testament and the New—even more costly. A very large *parchment* codex would also have been both extremely costly—requiring, quite literally, the slaughter of hundreds of animals, an extraordinary expense in an era when livestock were a major form of wealth—and extremely cumbersome to house. The fact that so many ancient codices contain only the Gospels or only the Gospels and Psalms may thus bespeak considerations of economy and convenience more than any larger conceptual considerations. It is for this reason that, though the first one-volume codex containing both Old and New Testaments was produced in Italy as early as the sixth century, such codices did not come into relatively common use until the ninth.

APPENDIX II

1. I would distinguish commentary that aims to supplement the historical information in a work of historical art, the usual case in New Testament criticism, from criticism that aims to illumine the artfulness of a work of historical art by creating a rival work from the same information. John Updike has illumined the artfulness of Shakespeare's *Hamlet* by drawing on Shakespeare's twelfth- and fifteenth-century sources to write his novel *Gertrude and Claudius* (New York: Alfred A. Knopf, 2000). Another novelist, Reynolds Price, has done something comparable for the Gospels by writing his own apocryphal gospel, *The Honest Account of a Memorable Life* (Rocky Mount: North Carolina Wesleyan College Press, 1994). These works of art are simultaneously works of criticism, but neither intends to be a work of history.

Shakespeare scholarship, of course, attends a great deal to the historical Shakespeare and to Elizabethan England as the cultural matrix of his work; but Shakespeare scholarship is distinguished, on the one hand, from the history of Elizabethan England and, on the other, from Shakespeare criticism, whose concerns are character, diction, and other more or less extra-historical aesthetic issues. The contrast with New Testament studies in this regard is clear. On the one hand, New Testament scholarship is less and less distinguishable from the history of the founding era of Christianity. On the other, New Testament criticism as distinct from either New Testament scholarship or early church history—a New Testament criticism concerned with character, diction, and some set of extra-historical aesthetic issues—has, until recently, scarcely existed at all. New Testament scholars have tended to think of New Testament criticism, what little of it was written, as a species of popular theology if not simply as impressionistic or "fanciful" scholarship. By referring to New Testament scholars in this appendix as "historical critics" of the New Testament, I seek quite deliberately to reverse this tactic—seeing scholarship as peculiar criticism rather than criticism as peculiar scholarship.

2. Albert Schweitzer, *The Quest of the Historical Jesus,* first complete edition, edited by John Bowden, translated by W. Montgomery, J. R. Coates, Susan Cupitt, and John Bowden from the German (London: SCM Press, 2000, p. 479; originally published as *Geschichte der Leben-Jesu-Forschung* [Tübingen: J.C.B. Mohr, 1913]). Schweitzer's reading of historical research down to his own day as a religiously irrelevant intellectual triumph depends, in effect, on his transformation of its findings into a psychohistorical reconstruction of the consciousness of Jesus. This reconstruction

has its fullest development in his slightly earlier *The Mystery of the Kingdom of God: The Secret of Jesus' Messiahship and Passion.* Hans Frei in *The Eclipse of Biblical Narrative* rightly sees the specter of suicide haunting Schweitzer's vision of Jesus. Schweitzer's Jesus, a self-conscious agent of God's apocalyptic, final intervention in human history—an intervention that never came about—might be described as suicidally confident in the power of his own martyrdom. For an era no longer open to self-martyrdom as a religiously meaningful action, Schweitzer believed that the historical Jesus, thus finally and correctly understood, would be religiously irrelevant except, as noted, through a mystical willingness to live in, as it were, suicidal disregard of social norms—to live, that is, as if this world were about to pass away. Historical research could neither create nor destroy that kind of Christianity.

3. *"Das entscheidende ist schlechthin das Dass"* ("What is decisive is simply the 'that'"). This revealing remark, made near the end of Bultmann's career, came in a lecture for the Heidelberg Academy of Sciences in 1960. I cite it as quoted in an essay by the Dutch scholar Marinus de Jonge, "Theological Considerations in the Search for the Historical Jesus," in *Jesus, the Servant-Messiah* (New Haven, Conn.: Yale University Press, 1991), p. 23. I see this stance as much in the spirit of the Schweitzer who, having declared historical Jesus research religiously irrelevant, cited 2 Corinthians 5:16, where Paul seems to allude to, and in the same breath dismiss as religiously irrelevant, the possibility that he had known his Nazarene contemporary personally:

> Our experience is like Paul's. Just as we come nearer to the historical Jesus than anyone has ever come and our hands reach out to draw him into our own time, we are forced to give up the effort and admit our failure in that paradoxical dictum *If we knew Christ according to the flesh, yet starting now we know him no longer.* Moreover, we must come to terms with the fact that historical knowledge of the personality and life of Jesus will not be a help but perhaps even an offense to religion. (*Von Reimarus zu Wrede: Eine Geschichte der Leben-Jesu-Forschung* [Tübingen: Mohr, 1906], p. 399; my translation)

In the first edition of his great work, Schweitzer risked a quasi-Nietzschean sarcasm in certain lines and passages that he excised from later editions. The passage just quoted is one such.

The deepest question in this discussion, deeper than the question of history as a criterion for truth in religion, is What, *if anything,* can function as such a criterion? Can scripture, read historically or allegorically or in any other way, play that role? In the earliest Reformation debates, Catholics cogently objected that without some outside authentication, no one would be able to distinguish what was scripture from what was not. Scripture, therefore, could not in and of itself be the needed criterion. Then could tradition as interpreted by church authority be the needed criterion? Protestants cogently counterobjected that without some outside authentication, no one would be able to distinguish who was pope from who was not. Tradition, therefore, could not be the needed criterion either. Intellectually, as Richard H. Popkin shows in "The Intellectual Crisis of the Reformation" (chapter one in *The History of Scepticism From Erasmus to Spinoza* [Berkeley: University of California Press, 1979, revised edition]), the two sides fought each other to an intellectual draw as completely as, in the Thirty Years War, they would fight themselves to a military draw. Yet their debate was anything but inconsequential. As Popkin shows, the writings of Sextus Empiricus and therewith the core of the classical tradition of skepticism became available just as the Reformation debate was being joined. The result was that the intellectual crisis of the Reformation became a rehearsal for the intellectual crisis of the Enlightenment. That is, the question of whether scripture could serve as a criterion for religious truth became a rehearsal for the broader question of whether anything could serve as a criterion for truth in general— the question that received a provisional but surprisingly durable answer when Descartes, to quote a contemporary French cleric, "taught his age the art of making Skepticism give birth to philosophical Certainty" (cited in Popkin, p. 172). Though Popkin's subject is skepticism rather than biblical interpretation, his work well illustrates the dictum that to understand the history of biblical interpretation in the West is to understand the history of Western thought itself.

For much of the twentieth century, it was a commonplace of New Testament studies to oppose "the Jesus of history" to "the Christ of faith." Discussion of the Jesus of history was invariably linked to the name of Albert Schweitzer. Discussion of the Christ of faith was much less frequently linked than it should have been to the name of Martin Kähler, the author—in 1892, years before Schweitzer's 1906 sensation—of *The So-Called Historical Jesus and the Historic, Biblical Christ* (Philadelphia: Fortress Press, 1964). Where Schweitzer thought the quest of the historical Jesus an intellectual success but a religious irrelevancy, Kähler thought it an intellectual failure as well as a religious irrelevancy. Bultmann, especially as linked to the "neo-orthodox" theology of Karl Barth, might seem the descendant of Kähler rather than of Schweitzer. I link him to Schweitzer because, like Schweitzer, he so energetically and impressively mastered what he had determined, in advance, to be irrelevant.

4. Paul William Roberts, reviewing Thomas Cahill, *Desire of the Everlasting Hills: The World Before and After Jesus,* in *The New York Times,* April 23, 2000. The reviewer may exaggerate the religious aspirations of historical criticism, but not by much.

5. For a lively but serious review of this research, paying particular attention to American scholarship, see Charlotte Allen, *The Human Christ: The Search for the Historical Jesus* (New York: The Free Press, 1998). A penetrating analysis of the methodology of "the quest for the historical Jesus" is to be found as an appendix to Donald Harman Akenson's *Surpassing Wonder: The Invention of the Bible and the Talmuds* (New York: Harcourt Brace, 1998); Akenson develops his critique further, noting that the Christ of Paul appeared a generation before the Jesus of any of the Gospels, in *Saint Saul: A Skeleton Key to the Historical Jesus* (Oxford and New York: Oxford University Press, 2000). A more neutral, international, and academic survey may be found in Gerd Theissen and Annette Merz, *The Historical Jesus: A Comprehensive Guide,* translated by John Bowden (Minneapolis: Fortress Press, 1998; originally published as *Der historische Jesus: Ein Lehrbuch* [Göttingen: Vandenhoeck und Ruprecht, 1996]). The case for and against the success and/or relevance of historical-Jesus research is argued in *The Jesus Controversy: Perspectives in Conflict* (Harrisburg, Pa.: Trinity Press, 1999) by two American scholars, John Dominic Crossan (for) and Luke Timothy Johnson (against), with the tie-breaking vote (for, with qualifications) cast by a German scholar teaching in the United States, Werner H. Kelber.

6. Ibid., p. 10.

7. Ibid., p. 298.

8. James Barr, *Holy Scripture: Canon, Authority, Criticism* (Philadelphia: The Westminster Press, 1983), p. 159.

9. An American example in this vein, published just before Enlightenment thinking went into hibernation in American cultural and political life, is Thomas Smith Grimké, *Oration on the Advantages, to Be Derived from the Introduction of the Bible, and of Sacred Literature, as Essential Parts of All Education, in a Literary point of View Merely, from the Primary School, to the University. Delivered Before the Connecticut Alpha of the ΦΒΚ Society, on Tuesday, September 7, 1830* (New Haven, Conn.: printed by Hezekiah Howe, 1830).

10. Frei, *The Eclipse of Biblical Narrative* (New Haven, Conn.: Yale University Press, 1974). See also Frei's *Types of Christian Theology,*

edited by George Hunsinger and William C. Placher (New Haven, Conn.: Yale University Press, 1992), and his *Theology and Narrative: Selected Essays,* edited by George Hunsinger and William C. Placher (New York: Oxford University Press, 1993).

11. Kermode, *The Sense of an Ending* (London: Oxford University Press, 1967).

12. Robert Alter and Frank Kermode, editors, *The Literary Guide to the Bible* (Cambridge: Belknap Press/Harvard University Press, 1987), p. 607. See also Kermode's summary, concluding statement on p. 609:

> It is an empirical fact that each book has its own history; it is also true that the association of many books in a canon was the result of a long historical process and owed much to chance and much to the needs and the thinking of people we know little or nothing about. But it is also a fact that works transmitted inside a canon are understood differently from those without, so that, if only in that sense, the canon, however assembled, forms an integral whole, the internal and external relations of which are both proper subjects of disinterested inquiry. Nor need we suppose that we have altogether eliminated from our study of canonical works every scrap of the old organicist assumptions, every concession to a magical view of these worlds and their profound, obscure correspondences. When we have achieved *that* degree of disinterest we shall have little use for the canon or for its constituents, and we shall have little use either for poetry.

The phenomenal history *of* the Bible as an anthology of uniquely wide diffusion is commonly but illogically invoked as a justification for the study of historical phenomena *in* the Bible. That is, the influence of this text in so many places over so many centuries is invoked as a reason to pay particular attention to the events and circumstances that are recounted in the text or that formed the cultural matrix for its original composition. But to this claim one might well reply, "Non sequitur," objecting that if it is the influence that is important, then it is the influence that most deserves study. Don't study sunspots and sun storms if it is sunburn that concerns you.

The Bible has not usually wielded its influence in conjunction with any independently acquired knowledge of the ancient world from which it emerged. The extent to which it does so even now is debatable, though surely the assumption by so many scholars, enacted in so many school curricula, is that this is how the Bible *should* wield its influence. The deeper trouble is that historical criticism, by dissecting the Bible and considering its component parts separately, offers for contemplation a text that has had—in just that dissected, anatomized form—no influence before modern times. There is room, then—and to claim this is surely not to claim too much—for a form of Bible study that would stress the effect that the collection produces as a whole rather than the effects produced separately by its separable parts.

13. Peter J. Thuesen, *In Discordance With the Scriptures: American Protestant Battles Over Translating the Bible* (New York: Oxford University Press, 1999), p. 154.

14. Frank Kermode, *The Genesis of Secrecy: On the Interpretation of Narrative* (Cambridge: Harvard University Press, 1979), p. 88. It would be interesting to hear Kermode's views on the experience of listening to a novel on audiotape.

Cf. Kermode (*The Literary Guide to the Bible,* p. 454) on the literary technique of John the Evangelist:

> The method by which [John] arranges . . . inconspicuous repetitions of word, idea, or incident—the literary devices which add up to what E. M. Forster called "rhythms"—may well owe something to Jewish liturgical practice. In the Passover readings the bread of the ceremony is said to replace the forbidden fruit of Genesis 2 and to foretell the manna which will again descend at the coming of Messiah. It has sometimes occurred to me that the subtleties of construction, the more or less occult relationship of parts, that we admire in favored novels owes a largely unconscious debt to ancient liturgical practice. This is a part of one's justification for calling John a protonovelist.

15. Jacques Derrida, *De la grammatologie* (Paris: Éditions de Minuit, 1967). See, especially, the subchapter "Le Dehors et Le Dedans," pp. 46ff.

16. Cited in Thuesen, *In Discordance With the Scriptures,* p. 3.

17. Eric Auerbach, *Mimesis: The Representation of Reality in Western Literature,* translated from the German by Willard Trask (New York: Anchor Books, 1957). *Mimesis* appeared in German in 1946 and was first published in English by Princeton University Press in 1953.

18. Hans Frei, *The Eclipse of Biblical Narrative* (New Haven: Yale University Press, 1974), p. 16.

19. "Hermeneutically, it may well be the most natural thing to say that what these accounts are about is the story of Jesus the Messiah, even if there was no such person; or, if there was, he was not in fact the Messiah; and quite regardless of whether or not he (if

he did exist) thought of himself as such; and regardless finally of the possible applicative significance of such a story and of the messianic concept to a modern context. Many elements may enter into the way a story makes sense, but its sheer narrative shape is an important and distinctive one which should not be confused with others—especially that of estimating its abiding religious meaning and that of assessing the narrative's cultural context or the reliability of the "facts" told in the story." (Ibid., pp. 133–4)

20. Neil MacGregor with Erika Langmuir, *Seeing Salvation: Images of Christ in Art* (London: BBC Worldwide Limited, 2000), p. 13. The dean of a California seminary commented to me in 1999 that many of her students do not recognize a painting of the Madonna and Child as other than a painting of an unidentified woman with a baby. Yet I suspect that however lost the iconographic language of European religious art may be, it may be through the recovery of that language that a more fully lost language—the language of medieval biblical commentary as set forth in Henri de Lubac's four-volume *Exégèse médiévale* (Paris: Aubier, 1964)—may come to seem worth recovering. The language of intense and intensely playful internal reference continued to be spoken in painting well after it had become a dead language in written exegesis.

21. For an excellent popular account of this decisive event in Christian history, see Richard E. Rubenstein, *When Jesus Became God: The Epic Fight over Christ's Divinity in the Last Days of Rome* (New York: Harcourt Brace, 1999).

22. Defined differently by everyone who invokes it, postmodernism is, for me, not a period that succeeds modernism but, rather, an attitude that rejects periodization as such. Modernism felt a great Hegelian confidence that history had a direction, even a destination. Thus, the recovery of the historical Jesus seemed the destined outcome of the history of New Testament criticism. Postmodernism, by contrast, has no such confidence and therefore feels none of the obligation that modernism felt to go where history is headed. History is going nowhere, it thinks, and so what's the rush? Its mood is Kierkegaardian and ironic.

As regards literature, postmodernism recognizes no large, collective enterprise with a clear direction that all legitimate participants must respect. Though the history of interpretation is not cyclical, there is no reason why what has been done already in interpretation may not be done again if we find it rewarding. *God: A Biography* was indebted to the character criticism of A. C. Bradley, whose major work, *Shakespearean Tragedy,* appeared in 1904. The more innovation comes to seem mere variation, the more easily the old and neglected can become new again. There exists no historical imperative to be obeyed or disobeyed. Nothing must be done. Anything might be done. When the results are interesting, they are not interesting because they constitute "progress." Evidence coerces. Art merely seduces.

Postmodern literary criticism has been faulted for arrogance toward the author and the author's claims. Michel Foucault famously remarked that "the author is the dead man in the game of writing." Though I do not regard this view to be the wave of "the" future (there is no "the" future), neither do I regard it as a fad that is now happily behind us. It is here to stay, along with all that preceded it. However, I must say that if the great fault of postmodern criticism has been that, in effect, it treats all books as if they were anonymously written, then this school of criticism may suit the Bible particularly well, because so much of the Bible is irretrievably anonymous and the authorship even of those portions of the Bible that bear some kind of attribution is quite often in dispute.

Modern historical criticism has labored diligently to bring the Bible to the "normal" condition of clearly identified authors with consistent agendas and clearly identified audiences. Postmodern criticism can and should acknowledge the value, even the grandeur, of this enterprise of rationalization and yet not surrender its right to observe that historical criticism almost inevitably aborts certain highly stimulating and fruitful kinds of literary engagement. For me, both kinds of criticism are interesting and legitimate. And certainly for the modest purposes of this book, the matter need not be pushed much past the recognition that an unintended effect is a real effect, which may be welcomed without prejudice to intended effects. Or, to use the nomenclature of historical criticism, one may ignore questions of authorship and dating in a given discussion while conceding their relevance to many other discussions. One may also concede that what "causes" an unintended effect may be someone's first experiencing it and then talking about it.

At such a moment, facing such an unintended effect and sensing the presence of an intrusive subjectivity, modernist historical criticism, like virtually all modernist criticism, catches itself in time, and muffles its inclination to join in the discussion as one might muffle one's inclination to join in a laugh at a funeral. The critic may find the joke funny, but to laugh at it would interrupt the ceremony—or, in this instance, retard the collective enterprise. Postmodern criticism—going nowhere, we might say—feels no such inhibition. More important, it has time to linger over distractions and chance arrangements that, like a sunset, are intended by nobody but may lift the spirits of anybody willing to be led outdoors for a look.

23. George MacDonald, *The Golden Key,* with pictures by Maurice Sendak, afterword by W. H. Auden (New York: Farrar, Straus and Giroux, 1967), pp. 81–4.

24. Kermode, *The Literary Guide to the Bible,* pp. 382–3.

25. Interview in *The Art Newspaper,* No. 100, February 2000.

26. *The New Oxford Book of English Verse 1250–1950,* chosen and edited by Helen Gardner (New York and Oxford: Oxford University Press, 1972), p. 703.

27. *The Collected Works of W. B. Yeats,* volume I, *The Poems,* revised, edited by Richard J. Finneran (New York: Macmillan, 1989), p. 240.

Index of Scripture Citations

Numbers in *italics* are the text pages where the given citations appear.

General Index

Abel, 187, 188, 189
Abraham (Abram), 67, 103, 171, 172, 200, 215
    aborted sacrifice of Isaac, 220
    God commands him to go to Canaan, 33, 75–6
Acts of the Apostles, 239
    lamb as symbol in, 7–8
Adam, 53, 85, 139, 187, 189
    original sin and, 24–6
    sexuality of, 61
    see also Eden, Garden of
Adoration of the Kings, The, 279
adultery, 58, 62, 176, 177
    under Jewish law, 152
    as offense against God, 152, 179
    refusal of Jesus to condemn an adulteress, 152–60, 177, 179
Ahab, king of Israel, 102, 133
Akenson, Donald Harman, 327n
Akiba, Rabbi, 175
Allen, Charlotte, 327n
allusion, New Testament to Old, 63, 65, 261–2, 278
Alter, Robert, 279, 315n
    and Frank Kermode, 327n
Altizer, Thomas J. J., 295n
Amalekites, vengeance against, 101–2
angels, 61, 90, 249
    immortality of, 61
Annas, 225
Anti-Christ (Nietzsche), 6

apocalypticism, 176, 206–7
    literature of, 206, 207
apostasy, 152, 154
apostles, 140
    selection of, 93
Aquila, 319
Aramaic, 33–4
    alphabet, and written Hebrew, 257
    as world language, 318
    use of, for Jewish scripture, 257
Arnold, Matthew, 288
art, Christian
    the Crucifixion in, 10, 11
    guilt of God reflected in, 5
art, sacred vs. secular, 285–6
ascension of Jesus to heaven, 239–40
asexuality of God, 51–2, 54, 56, 200
Assyria, 64, 77–8, 79, 114, 117, 158, 196, 201, 205, 244
Athanasius, 259
atonement for sins, commensurate, 26
"atonement" theology, 167
Auden, W. H., 283–4
Auerbach, Eric, 278
Augustine of Hippo, 166

Babylonia, 105, 117, 158, 194, 196, 201, 244